THE CRITICAL
WALTZ

THE CRITICAL WALTZ

Essays on the Work of Dorothy Parker

Edited by
Rhonda S. Pettit

Madison • Teaneck
Fairleigh Dickinson University Press

Associated University Presses
2010 Eastpark Boulevard
Cranbury, NJ 08512

The paper used in this publication meets the requirements of the American National Standard for Permanence of Paper for Printed Library Materials Z39.48-1984.

Library of Congress Cataloging-in-Publication Data

The critical waltz : essays on the work of Dorothy Parker / edited by Rhonda S. Pettit.
    p. cm.
    Includes bibliographical references and index.
    ISBN 0-8386-3968-2 (alk. paper)
    1. Parker, Dorothy, 1893–1967—Criticism and interpretation.   2. Women and literature—United States—History—20th century.   I. Pettit, Rhonda S., 1955–
PS3531.A5855Z624   2005
818'.5209—dc22

2004019978

To
Michael L. Horn, with love and gratitude

And to the memory of
Nancy A. Walker
(1942–2000)

Contents

Preface

Regina Barreca

WHEN I GREW UP, I TOLD MYSELF, I WANTED TO BE DOROTHY PARKER.
I cut my preconceived notions of life on the shards of her brilliant and ruthless prose in an otherwise fuzzy anthology of modern fiction I read in high school. I felt myself to be her blood-sister, an apprentice cynic, a Parkerette kept only briefly (I thought) in the domestic cage of regulation family life and merely disguised as a teenager.

It wasn't until college that I learned I was only one of many Parkerettes. There we were, lined up in a dark-suited row, all equally cynical and slyly witty (we thought), quipping Parker's lines in unison the way the Rockettes (a rival group, usually found at Radio City in rather different uniforms) kicked up their heels. We didn't kick up our heels, but instead we talked about every one of the heels who walked into our lives: the wicked, evasive, gorgeously self-centered men who had left us hanging by the telephone, hanging by our fingernails, and hanging onto frayed copies of Parker's *Enough Rope.*

We knew nearly every line to "A Telephone Call" and "Just a Little One." Certainly there was the expectation that even remote acquaintances would know that the phrase "And I am Marie of Romania" implied a certain measure of doubt concerning the validity of true romance ("Oh life is a glorious cycle of song / A medley of extemporania / And love is a thing that can never go wrong / And I am Marie of Romania"). And, looking back on it now, I think Parker would have had strong feelings about our little group.

I think she would have hated us.

Oh, maybe not hated us exactly, but been more than impatient with the idea that her words were being used by yet another generation of women to map their own desperately absurd emotional, social, and even cultural experiences. Parker provided an answer, although she didn't know it, for such criticism when she wrote that one of her characters "had drawn a new set of rules for it, had narrowed it, pointed it, made it stricter. Like all games, it was the more absorbing for being more difficult."

Parker is so good at what she does, she tricks us: she makes it seem easy. Yet no writer has been able to cut quite as deeply with as much finesse as she; no later version or updated imitator of Parker's style has been able to wear her heart on her sleeve with such style. Her brilliance with language, so effective and subtle that it is sometimes overshadowed by her deft portrayal of emotional complications, is what these essays explore. They will help to ensure that yet more readers understand, appreciate, and applaud the singular work of this remarkable writer.

Acknowledgments

Rhonda S. Pettit

For we think back through our mothers if we are women.
—Virginia Woolf

FROM THE END OF THE GREAT DEPRESSION TO SHORTLY AFTER WORLD War II, when she met and married my father, Opal Katherine Anderson was a single workingwoman: a corporate secretary in Cincinnati, Ohio. She loved music and books, and while living at home with her parents in northern Kentucky, she could afford both, buying a white Acrosonic piano and monthly selections from the Book of the Month Club and the Literary Guild. When I was a child I often perused the bookcase she must have bought to house her colorful, jacketed hardbacks. Most of the books were by men. I noticed this. Of the few books by women, only one woman—Dorothy Parker—was represented twice. I noticed this also. *Here Lies* and *Not So Deep as a Well* always sat side by side. And I was struck by the name—*Dorothy Parker*—it seemed so plain, so ordinary. It didn't have the grandiose syllables that, in my mind, should name those people intelligent enough to write and publish *a* book, never mind *two*. I began to believe that anyone could be a writer, and not long after that, I started to write poems and stories. More importantly for this collection, I never forgot that I wanted to know more about this Dorothy Parker. She became the topic of my first bibliography project in graduate school, and the focus of my research after that. I would like to acknowledge, by way of this minimemoir, my mother's role in this collection: she bought, read, and *saved* her books, and instilled in me a love of reading.

This book has been several years in the making, requiring the patience and support of many people. While my authors' publication acknowledgments are listed below, I would like also to thank Arthur F. Kinney for his additional efforts to obtain, and then grant, permission to reprint the Parker-Woollcott letters, and Regina Barreca for offering at an early stage in this project to write the preface.

13

Special thanks go to Debbie Thomayer, of the University of Cincinnati Raymond Walters College, who had to retype many of the essays while fulfilling other duties for two departments and approximately sixty-five full- and part-time faculty. Her speed and accuracy were indeed impressive under such conditions. As a coworker on this project she offered, to quote Parker quoting Hemingway, "grace under pressure."

My gratitude extends to my family for their understanding and support, and to those who expressed confidence in this volume: longtime friends and influences (in particular Ann Merritt), and colleagues at the University of Cincinnati, particularly those in the Women's Studies Program, and at Raymond Walters College. Librarians and staff in the Raymond Walters College Library provided valuable assistance in tracking down some of the articles and sources.

I also want to offer a general note of thanks to all those granting the necessary permissions, and to the people at Fairleigh Dickinson University Press and Associated University Presses for all their work and guidance.

The author wishes to thank the National Association for the Advancement of Colored People for authorizing the use of Dorothy Parker's works.

From THE PORTABLE DOROTHY PARKER by Dorothy Parker, edited by Brendan Gill, copyright 1928, renewed © 1956 by Dorothy Parker. Used by permission of Viking Penguin, a division of Penguin Group (USA) Inc.

From LADIES OF THE CORRIDOR by Dorothy Parker and Arnaud d'Usseau, copyright 1954 by Dorothy Parker and Arnaud d'Usseau. Used by permission of Viking Penguin, a division of Penguin Group (USA) Inc.

From DOROTHY PARKER: COMPLETE STORIES by Dorothy Parker, copyright 1924–29, 1931–34, 1937–39, 1941, 1943, 1955, 1958, 1995, by The National Association for the Advancement of Colored People. Used by permission of Viking Penguin, a division of Penguin Group (USA) Inc.

From DOROTHY PARKER: COMPLETE POEMS by Dorothy Parker, copyright © 1999 by The National Association for the Advancement of Colored People. Used by permission of Viking Penguin, a division of Penguin Group (USA) Inc.

Various excerpts of poems and other writings by Dorothy Parker are published throughout the United Kingdom British Commonwealth by permission of Gerald Duckworth & Co. Ltd.

Various excerpts from *Gentlemen Prefer Blondes* by Anita Loos are published in the U. S. by permission of Liveright Publishers, and in the United Kingdom by permission of the Anita Loos Trust and Mrs. Ray Corsini.

Ruthmarie H. Mitsch's "Parker's 'Iseult of Brittany'" originally appeared in *Explicator* 4:22 (Winter 1986), 37–40. Reprinted with permission of the Helen Dwight Reid Educational Foundation. Published by Heldref Publications, 1319 Eighteenth Street, NW, Washington, DC 20036–1802. Copyright 1986.

Nina Miller's "Making Love Modern: Dorothy Parker and Her Reading Public" originally appeared in *American Literature* 64:4 (December 1992): 763–84. Copyright 1992, Duke University Press. Reprinted with permission. A revised version of the article became a chapter in *Making Love Modern,* by Nina Miller, copyright 1999 by Oxford University Press.

Ken Johnson's "Dorothy Parker's Perpetual Motion" originally appeared in *American Women Short Story Writers,* edited by Julie Brown, p. 251–65, copyright 1995. Reproduced by permission of Routledge/Taylor & Francis Books, Inc.

An earlier version of Rhonda S. Pettit's "Material Girls in the Jazz Age: Dorothy Parker's 'Big Blonde' as an Answer to Anita Loos's *Gentlemen Prefer Blondes*" was voted Best of Section at the 24th Annual Conference of the Kentucky Philological Association, and later appeared in *Kentucky Philological Review* 12 (1997): 48–54. Reprinted with permission of the editor.

Emily Toth's "Dorothy Parker, Erica Jong, and New Feminist Humor" originally appeared in *Regionalism and the Female Imagination* 3 (1977/1978): 70–85. Reprinted with permission of the author.

Suzanne Bunkers's "'I Am Outraged Womanhood': Dorothy Parker as Feminist and Social Critic" originally appeared in *Regionalism and the Female Imagination* 4.2 (1978): 24–34. Reprinted with permission of the author.

Paula A. Treichler's "Verbal Subversions in Dorothy Parker: 'Trapped Like a Trap in a Trap'" originally appeared in *Language and Style* 13 (1980): 46–61. Reprinted with permission of the author.

Amelia Simpson's "Black on Blonde: The Africanist Presence in Dorothy Parker's 'Big Blonde'" originally appeared in *College Literature* 23:3 (October 1996). Reprinted with permission of the editor.

Ellen Pollak's "Premium Swift: Dorothy Parker's Iron Mask of Femininity" originally appeared in *Pope, Swift, and Women Writers,* edited by Donald C. Mell, published by University of Delaware Press. Copyright 1996 by Associated University Presses. Reprinted with permission of Associated University Presses.

Nancy A. Walker's "The Remarkably Constant Reader: Dorothy Parker as Book Reviewer" originally appeared in *Studies in American Humor,* New Series 3:4 (1997): 1–14. Reprinted with permission of *Studies in American Humor.*

Andrea Ivanov-Craig's "Being and Dying as a Woman in the Short Fiction of Dorothy Parker" originally appeared in *Performing Gender and Comedy: Theories, Texts, and Contexts,* edited by Shannon Hengen, 95–110. Copyright 1998 by Gordon and Breach Publishers. Reprinted with permission of Taylor and Francis Group (Gordon and Breach).

Ellen Lansky's "Female Trouble: Dorothy Parker, Katherine Anne Porter, and Alcoholism" originally appeared in *Literature and Medicine* 17:2 (Fall 1998): 212–30. Copyright 1998 by Johns Hopkins University Press. Reprinted with permission of Johns Hopkins University Press.

Phillip Arrington's "Reading, Responding, Composing: A Revisionary Approach" originally appeared in *JAC* 5 (1984): 37–49. Reprinted with permission of *JAC.*

Arthur F. Kinney's "Dorothy Parker's Letters to Alexander Woollcott" originally appeared in *Massachusetts Review* 30:3 (Autumn 1989): 487–515. Copyright 1989 *Massachusetts Review,* assigned to Arthur F. Kinney 2003. Reprinted with permission of the author.

Marion Capron's interview with Dorothy Parker originally appeared in *The Paris Review* 13, Summer 1956. Reprinted by the permission of Regal Literary as agent for *The Paris Review.* Copyright 1956 by *The Paris Review.*

Introduction
"Two Stumbles, Slip, and a Twenty-Yard Dash": Dorothy Parker and the Waltz of Literary Criticism

Rhonda S. Pettit

WHY A COLLECTION OF ESSAYS ON THE WORK OF DOROTHY PARKER? Perhaps a more pertinent question would be, why hasn't a collection appeared before now? Like her more extensively studied modernist contemporaries—Ezra Pound, T. S. Eliot, William Carlos Williams, and Marianne Moore—a significant portion of Parker's poetry, fiction, and essays have remained in print throughout the twentieth century. Yet unlike them, and more like another contemporary, Edna St. Vincent Millay, Parker's literary reputation suffered from both neglect and the short-sightedness that accompanied many New Critical readings of women writers, poets in particular, at the mid-century.

Parker once compared herself negatively with Millay, telling Marion Capron in an interview contained in this collection that she "was following in the exquisite footsteps of Miss Millay unhappily in my own horrible sneakers." Nevertheless, the careers of Millay and Parker have much in common. Although Parker did not give public readings of her work as did Millay, both can be considered Celebrity Poets of the Jazz Age, their work immensely popular, selling very well, and receiving, for the most part, positive critical reviews by their contemporaries in the 1920s and early 1930s.[1] Both poets wrote of women's experience and sensibility using primarily conventional forms rather than free verse, and worked in other genres besides poetry. Both devoted part of their lives and work to political and social issues beyond those related to gender, attacking militarism, fascism, racism, and class politics. And despite the modernist outlook, concision, irony, and imagery that permeated their so-called conservative forms, their accessibility would contribute to their later nonavailability in the classroom. Recent scholars of Millay

17

have discussed her treatment at the hands of Cleanth Brooks, Allen Tate, and John Crowe Ransom, New Critical defenders of the modernist realm who found Millay's work too closely associated with feeling rather than intellect.[2]

Parker's work would face a similar charge. As I have argued elsewhere, several reviewers, later critics, and biographers accused Parker of sentimentality with regard to her personal life, politics, and writing, a position that led, in many cases, to simplistic readings of her work, and to questionable assignments of writing technique to gender.[3] Two of the later critics are worth mentioning here because of their position relative to New Critical reading and canon formation, and the influential venues in which they published. In 1934, Mark Van Doren examined Parker's poetry and fiction in an essay published in the *English Journal*. Although he praises her poem "Recurrence," Van Doren claims that Parker's poetry is popular because it is "sentimental." He finds "the bulk" of Parker's poetry "thin and voiceless" when compared to the work of Matthew Prior; he prefers her fiction but adds, "She is not a master even here, since she does not deal with any very great or significant area of life." A later critique, this one by Herbert Marshall McLuhan against "The New York Wits" published in the *Kenyon Review* (1945), (m)aligns Parker with Millay. McLuhan writes that Millay is a mere "purveyor of cliché sentiment" and "an exhibitionist with no discoverable sensibility of her own," while Parker "exhibits a mechanism of sensibility which is about as complicated as a village pump, though it masquerades as daring *avant garde* naughtiness and revolt."[4]

These critical sentiments—and I use that word deliberately—are part of an intellectual movement that will define modernism against a form of sentimentality perceived by these critics as feminine and female-generated. They will be followed by widely read articles, memoirs, and biographies published from the 1950s through the seventies that will cast a nostalgic light on the Roaring Twenties and emphasize, at least as far as Parker is concerned, the life over the work. Known for caustic wit and sentiment in both areas (what could have been, but wasn't until recently, appreciated as a useful tension), Parker, like Millay, would remain in print but out of the canonical picture in terms of literary modernism. In effect, her well-known life in consort with the New Critical factory reproduced her as a minor character in a well-known literary period, in effect reducing the author to an anecdote. Van Doren admits it is difficult to separate the writer's life from the life of the writing, but that is as close as he comes to recognizing the limits of his own reading.

In the mid-1970s, Parker's work received new consideration as the second wave of feminism began to challenge entrenched categories of thinking at all levels of society, and other theoretical approaches to literary study came into vogue. Yet even in this welcomed transitional period, old arguments reappeared. Ross Labrie, in a 1976 article published in the *Canadian Review of American Studies*, offers a case in point. In "Dorothy Parker Revisited," Labrie provides a generally positive overview of Parker's fiction, suggesting that her work is influenced by Ernest Hemingway, Ring Lardner, and Sinclair Lewis. He praises her stories as "models of precision," but later adds that Parker's "slope toward sentimentality" weakens some of her work. Is this balanced criticism, or an inability to read sentimental texts prior to Jane Tompkins's groundbreaking study, *Sensational Designs* (1985)?[5] As the essays in this collection suggest, no easy consensus exists now about Parker's work, but the nature and terms of the debate have evolved in such a way to suggest that it stands up to closer and more complex scrutiny.

For purposes of this collection, the late-1970s is primarily where *The Critical Waltz*—a title that appropriates one of its key terms from Parker's much anthologized short story, "The Waltz"—begins. Whether read as an allegorical critique of heterosexual marriage or a humorous view of social custom, "The Waltz" presents two voices that offer contrasting views about the narrator's attitude toward, among other things, her dancing partner and experience. The narrator's external voice is polite and submissive to her apparently inept dancing partner while an internal voice—characterized, as Paula A. Treichler points out in an essay included in this collection, by a range of language styles—criticizes the partner and curses fate. Given this conflict, what the narrator truly desires is a matter of interpretation, a dance of language between writer and reader. Parker's waltz offers a metaphor for the kind of interpretive work, ongoing since the late 1970s and offering at times contrasting views, about Parker's poetry, fiction, plays, and essays. This "new critical" work of another order produces an exchange of ideas that deepens our understanding of Parker's texts and her place in literary history, rather than a premature dismissal based on New Critical standards alone.

The contradiction evident in "The Waltz" and embedded in much of Parker's work seems to have been a factor in her life as well, though that does not mean her work is a simple transcription of her experience. Alexander Woollcott, recalling a selection of her famous bon mots, affectionately referred to her as "so odd a blend of Little Nell and Lady MacBeth"—an electric Kool-Aid of innocence and vitriol that may have reflected the times she lived in as much as her personality.[6] She was a fin de siècle baby, born to J. Henry and Eliza A. (Marston) Rothschild in 1893, losing her mother four years later, and unable to bond with her stepmother. Her father, a clothing manufacturer, died by the time she was twenty. Her formal education had ended when she was fourteen but she, like many in her generation, was in many ways self-taught through her voluminous reading. During the midteens of the twentieth century she began her writing career and married Edwin Pond Parker II, whose drug and alcohol addiction following his service in World War I took its toll on their marriage. Her own alcohol consumption and her advancing literary career contributed to their problems. By then she had become part of the Algonquin Round Table, a group of mostly male, Manhattan literati that included Robert Benchley, Franklin Pierce Adams, and Alexander Woollcott, and was establishing her reputation as the witty and wicked Mrs. Parker. Her life seemed to conform to the Jazz Age stereotype with its series of love affairs, parties, and speakeasy soirees. It had its downside, though: heartbreak, unwanted pregnancy, abortion, and suicide attempts. She divorced Edwin in 1928 following a four-year separation, but kept his name, even after she married Alan Campbell, an actor and writer from Virginia, in 1934 (they divorced in 1947 and remarried in 1950). They launched a joint career writing Hollywood screenplays, and wanted children, but two pregnancies ended in miscarriage. Parker would outlive both of her husbands and most of her Round Table friends, dying alone in a New York hotel in 1967. At her request she was cremated, but no one claimed her ashes. For more than twenty years, they remained in the office of her lawyer.

That Parker's remains were treated this way is an irony she might have anticipated given the tension between her famous lifestyle and her serious pursuits. Amid the surface glamour and melodrama of Parker's life were her social and political concerns; these need to be kept in mind if her harsh and witty criticism of the human condition is to be seen as anything other than misanthropic. Though she often associated with the wealthy as her reputation grew, Parker had a penchant for the underdog, often acting on behalf of others. She supported striking waiters and actors in New York City, marched in protest of the Sacco and Vanzetti executions in Boston, traveled to Spain and helped to raise money on behalf of the Loyalists during the Spanish Civil War, and helped to organize the Screen Writers Guild and the Anti-Fascist League while living in California. Her communist sympathies led her to be blacklisted in Hollywood and put under scrutiny by the House Un-American Activities Committee. She left her estate to Dr. Martin Luther King, Jr., a man she admired but never met, and to the National Association for the Advancement of Colored People in the event of his death. In 1988, following what Randall Calhoun has called "a reverent but joyous ceremony," Parker's ashes were interred in the garden of the NAACP headquarters in Baltimore at the suggestion of Dr. Benjamin Hooks.[7]

As useful as biographical elements can be, the facts of Parker's *writing* life are far more pertinent to this collection of essays. She was not merely a personality, a victim, or a Jazz Age relic. Dorothy Parker was a writer of poetry, short stories and sketches, plays, screenplays, theater reviews, book reviews, general essays, journalism, and song lyrics. Her poetry, using conventional forms and strategies associated with the light (and not so light) verse tradition, is thoroughly modern in its content—urban, ironic, antiromantic, angry, and at times re-visionary. The sparse narrative in her dialogues (e.g., "Here We Are," "The Mantle of Whistler," "The Last Tea") and the stream-of-consciousness narrative, psychological penetration, and irony of her interior monologues (e.g., "The Waltz," "The Garter," "A Telephone Call") demonstrate her contribution to the modernist short story. She uses another modernist technique—the self-deprecating persona—in her book reviews and some of her poems and essays. Parker did not consider her work worthy enough to be called satire (as a critic she was no less hard on herself than on others), but her editors, readers, and reviewers knew otherwise. Yet, as important as satire and other humorous elements are to her work, they remain a means to an end. She offers clear if disturbing portraits of human behavior and social codes that both predate and transcend the glitzy Jazz Age in which her work originated.

Throughout the late teens, twenties, and early thirties of the twentieth century, Parker's work appeared in magazines that helped define the age—*Vogue, Vanity Fair, New Yorker, Smart Set, Saturday Evening Post,* and the old *Life* (then a magazine of humor). When she gathered her work into collections they became best sellers that went into multiple printings. Her poetry volumes include *Enough Rope* (1926), *Sunset Gun* (1928), *Death and Taxes* (1931), and *Not So Deep as a Well* (1936, collected poems). Her fiction volumes include *Laments for the Living* (1930), *After Such Pleasures* (1933), *Here Lies* (1939, collected stories), and *Collected Stories* (1942). The anthology that kept her work in print, however, was *The Portable Dorothy Parker,* selected by Parker in 1944, and later revised and expanded with an introduction by Brendan Gill in 1973. This Viking anthology provides a hefty selection of Parker's poetry, short stories, play reviews, book reviews, and other essays, but it is far from complete. It lacks her early poetry, a number of stories and reviews, and her three published plays: *Close Harmony* (1924, written with Elmer Rice), *The Coast of Illyria* (1949, written with Ross Evans and now available in a separate volume edited by Arthur F. Kinney), and *The Ladies of the Corridor* (1953, written with Arnaud d'Usseau).[8] More recent volumes edited by Colleen Breese (*Complete Stories* [1995] and *Complete Poems* [1999]) and Stuart Y. Silverstein (*Not Much Fun: The Lost Poems of Dorothy Parker* [1996]) include most of the earlier poetry and fiction.[9]

What is the significance of this body of work? This is the question *The Critical Waltz: Essays on the Work of Dorothy Parker* begins to answer by offering the first collection of criticism about Parker's writing. Five new essays, as well as two student essays, join thirteen essays published in journals and books since 1977. Organized into four parts—Modernist Contexts, Feminist Issues, Classroom Encounters, and Conversations—the arrangement of this volume reflects broad categories that, not surprisingly, have emerged in the critical discussion of Parker's work since the late 1970s, followed by Parker's conversations about her career and life. The essays within each category are arranged chronologically by year of publication to document the critical conversation about Parker's work—poetry, fiction, book reviews, and a play—that has occurred among scholars, and to give the reader a sense of how that conversation has evolved over time. Some of these scholars respond to each other, while others move in different directions. A variety of approaches exists, ranging from close textual readings and comparisons of Parker's work with her contemporaries, to applications of theoretical concepts developed by Mikhail Bakhtin, Roland Barthes, Michel Foucault, Judith Butler, Joan Riviere, Jan Montefiore, and Gabriel M. Della-Piana, to inventive, highly contextualized commentary. Viewed collectively, these essays demonstrate an observation made herein by Ann M. Fox: that criticism defining Parker's scope and range as narrow seems dated in light of the alternative critical approaches available today. Furthermore, our critical focus should be directed on the work Parker has given us rather than on the assumption that her "masterpiece" novel never materialized.

Readers of Parker's work may be surprised to find that humor is not a category for discussion, since it is a prevailing characteristic of her work, and since she has been included in more than one anthology seeking to define American humor. As a strategy for exploring ideas, humor in its various guises—irony, satire, wit, hyperbole, parody, sarcasm—has served Parker well. As a label used to define a career, however, "humorist" can blind us to other elements of a particular work. For example, when viewed primarily through the lens of humor, Parker's modernist irony, appearing as it did in periodicals targeting mass culture, may have been read—and written off—as comedic entertainment. Humor's absence as a category in this collection also forces what has been, for me, a compelling question: who is Dorothy Parker, and what can her work mean to us, if she is not conveniently labeled as a humorist? Humor, rather than an imposing category, is an important thread running through all the categories used to organize this book. Additionally, the categories themselves are somewhat fluid; feminist issues at times intersect with modernist themes, and both of these areas appear or intersect in the essays generated from teaching Parker's work. Authors throughout the collection refer at times to each other's work, and/or draw on Parker's interview with Marion Capron.

Part I. Modernist Contexts

Part I of this collection, Modernist Contexts, examines Parker's work and reputation in light of our evolving sense of literary modernism. The process of redefining modernism during the latter part of the twentieth century is by now well known.[10] Dated anywhere between 1890 and 1940, modernism was for some time granted period status by virtue of aesthetic definition—a narrow one at that, valuing experimental and abstract responses to the alienating aspects of early-twentieth-century culture, coupled with a rejection of the immediate past. When scholars began to read the noncanonical writers of this period, they discovered that the canon based on an experimental aesthetic left out most of the women (Gertrude Stein, H. D., and Virginia Woolf come immediately to mind) who had helped develop it. They also discovered not only a broader range of forms and responses, but a broader range of issues to which writers felt compelled to respond: racism, sexism, economic inequities, social justice, war, domestic relations, and competing notions of artistic purpose and aesthetic value. It thus became clear, given the number of writers who used the experimental aesthetic but remained invisible, and given the rejection of those like Millay, Parker, and many minority writers who offered what is arguably a more complex response combining the traditional with the modern, that the canon had been drawn up along gender, color, and class lines. What was once understood as a radical, experimental aesthetic began to look reactionary; adjectives like "conventional" and "traditional" are now used to describe it in light of its missing texts.

Whether we reject "modernism" as a period-defining term altogether, or think in terms of *modernisms*—that is, a multiplicity of

strategies and themes converging in early-twentieth-century literature, of which experimentalism is just one strategy, alienation just
one theme—we learn more about the complexities of early-twentieth-century literature by considering Parker's work within both its
historical context and the arguments that attempt to define that
context. The essays in part I locate in Parker's work both ties to and
tensions against modernism as it was originally defined. Ruthmarie
H. Mitsch provides an appropriately concise and convincing presentation of how Parker applies modernist concision to the complex
legend of Tristan and Iseult in her poem, "Iseult of Brittany." In
"Making Love Modern: Dorothy Parker and Her Public," Nina
Miller draws on Roland Barthes's *A Lover's Discourse* and Jan Montefiore's discussion of the "I-Thou dyad" to demonstrate how Parker's love poetry incorporates the constraints of an old era with the
relative freedoms of a new one to mock the romantic convention
without losing her conventional readership. Ken Johnson focuses on
Parker's strategy of repetition in "Dorothy Parker's Perpetual Motion," comparing her fiction with that of three male modernists—
Ernest Hemingway, Ring Lardner, and William Faulkner—as well as
with Edgar Allan Poe. I also consider Parker's fiction with regard to
one of her contemporaries, but one who, like Parker (and to some
extent Ring Lardner), was excluded from the canon. A story and a
serialized novel are approached within the context of modern sexual economics in "Material Girls in the Jazz Age: Dorothy Parker's
'Big Blonde' as an Answer to Anita Loos's *Gentlemen Prefer Blondes*."
In a new essay, Robert D. Arner considers the effect of publication
venue on readers of one of Parker's frequently anthologized stories
in "Textual Transmission and the Transformation of Texts: On the
Dialogic Margins of Dorothy Parker's 'The Waltz.'" Drawing on
Mikhail Bakhtin's essay "Discourse in the Novel," Arner examines
"The Waltz" as it appears in three publications: *New Yorker* magazine, *Scholastic* magazine, and her collection *After Such Pleasures*, arguing that the story has been subjected to, and as a parody is the
means of, a process of recontextualization that affects our response
to the story.

Finally, Parker's career as a modern writer is radically recontextu-
alized in the two new essays that close part I, making issues of identity the focus. When an author of fiction becomes a character of
fiction, what kinds of questions are raised about the relationship between life and art? This is a charged question in light of the tendency among some scholars, at times justifiable as in Parker's "But
the One on the Right," to read Parker as a character in her own
fictional and poetic narratives. Arthur F. Kinney, who has written ex-

tensively about Parker's life and work, writes here about "The Other Dorothy Parkers," fictional renditions of Parker appearing in three twentieth-century novels: Gertrude Atherton's *Black Oxen* (1923), Edwin Corley's *Shadows* (1975), and George Baxt's *The Dorothy Parker Murder Case* (1984). Another fictional speaker and contemporary of Parker's, brought to life by Lynn Z. Bloom, provides a fitting segue into part II. In "Here Lies by Mehitabel," Bloom considers Parker's life and career through the eyes of Mehitabel, the famous kitty side-kick of Archy the cockroach, popular characters created by humorist Don Marquis in his newspaper columns of the 1920s and 1930s. (In reality, Archy typed these columns at night after Don left the office, without the benefit of capital letters because he couldn't use the shift key. Mehitabel, in what must be close to the last of her nine lives, has no doubt usurped Bloom's computer—so like her to remain current—and done likewise!) What results is a cat's-eye overview of Parker's work, concluding that her women characters and speakers, particularly those in her play *The Ladies of the Corridor*, are, "according to feminist standards, politically incorrect." Parker's feminism is one of the issues addressed generally in part II, and in part III Ann M. Fox will offer a counterpoint to Bloom's—*I mean, Mehitabel's*—reading of Parker's play.

Part II. Feminist Issues

Like modernism, feminism, particularly since the second wave, is a concept that has been altered by redefinition and theorizing over time, moving from essentialist assumptions about female experience to a plurality of approaches and theories, some of which incorporate other identity issues in addition to sex, such as race, class, sexual orientation, cultural location, language, or nationality.[11] While it is true that performing a feminist analysis of Parker's work now is a much different project than it was on the heels of earlier activist and recovery feminism, it must be remembered that much of her work has yet to be given the attention that "Big Blonde" and "The Waltz" have received. Part II of this collection, Feminist Issues, addresses the extent to which Parker and her work can be considered feminist in its intent and execution. Here as with the issue of modernism, contextual issues remain important. Most of Parker's poetry and fiction was written from the late teens through the early 1930s, a period marked by both the mass marketing of modern femininity, and a range of feminist activism regarding women's equality *with* and uniqueness *from* men, in addition to the better known suffrage movement.[12] Parker, noted for her stylish feminine attire and her verbal jousting with "the boys in the back," seems to embody the double-edged feminism of her day. In 1926 she wrote to Alexander Woollcott from Antibes, documenting her struggle to write a novel there with, "Dear God, please make me stop writing like a woman." What she means by "writing like a woman" might be inferred by her dismissal, thirty years later, of Edna Ferber (another Algonquinite), Kathleen Norris, Clare Booth Luce, and other of her popular female contemporaries, followed by her claim, "I'm a feminist . . ." We can put this apparent contradiction into perspective in light of possible differences in literary taste or even professional jealousy, but we should also consider Colleen Breese's observation that Parker lived in a time when serious literature was still considered male territory. She had little to gain by identifying her writing with her gender, particularly when critics tended to compare her with male, rather than female, authors. Breese concludes, however, that Parker's feminism is "undeniable."[13] Some of the scholars in this collection agree with Breese; others question this reading.

As mentioned earlier, a new focus on Parker's work began with the literary retrieval projects stemming from the second wave of feminism. The essays in this section by Emily Toth ("Dorothy Parker, Erica Jong, and New Feminist Humor") and Suzanne L. Bunkers ("'I Am Outraged Womanhood': Dorothy Parker as Feminist and Social Critic") provide two early examples of this important work, and draw different conclusions. Both acknowledge Parker's use of satire, but Toth reads Parker's point of view as "female, . . . not feminist," while Bunkers clearly aligns Parker with a feminist perspective. In another early essay, Paula A. Treichler, like Toth, also questions the extent to which we can read Parker's satire as a feminist analysis. Applying concepts from Robin Lakoff's *Language and Woman's Place*, Treichler closely examines Parker's "The Waltz" ("Verbal Subversions in Dorothy Parker: 'Trapped Like a Trap in a Trap'"), arguing that the story's language reveals its complicity with patriarchal culture. Several authors in this collection draw on Treichler's rich analysis of Parker's language, and two in particular—Robert D. Arner and Andrea Ivanov Craig—offer, among other assertions, alternative readings of "The Waltz," seeing parody rather than satire at work. Gender serves as a point of departure in Amelia Simpson's essay, "Black on Blonde: The Africanist Presence in Dorothy Parker's 'Big Blonde'," which examines the issue of race in Parker's "Big Blonde." Concepts from Toni Morrison's *Playing in the Dark: Whiteness and Literary Imagination* (1992) are applied in Simpson's focus on characters typically overlooked in the story: Nettie (the maid), George (the elevator operator), and a "dark girl" (observed with the doctor).

Parker's book reviews receive attention in the next two essays of part II. Like Emily Toth, Ellen Pollak asserts that Parker was influenced by Jonathan Swift, making this the focus of her analysis of Parker's "The Professor Goes in for Sweetness and Light," a review of *Happiness* by William Lyon Phelps. In "Premium Swift: Dorothy Parker's Iron Mask of Femininity," Pollak establishes an "intertextual relationship" between Swift's *The Battle of the Books* and *A Tale of a Tub* (both 1704), revealing both affinities and differences. This close examination of a single review is followed by an analysis of Parker's reviewer personae across a range of reviews, in an essay that also refers to, among others, her review of *Happiness*. Nancy A. Walker, who elsewhere has identified Parker as a key figure in the tradition of American women's humor, examines Parker's self-deprecating and idiosyncratic reviewer personalities as a strategy for claiming authority in "The Remarkably Constant Reader: Dorothy Parker as Book Reviewer." These strategies, argues Walker, also make Parker's reviews distinctive from others published in the *New Yorker*, or later in *Esquire*. Just as Walker, Treichler, Bunkers, and Toth to some extent focus on Parker's humor and its role in feminist discourse, so too does Andrea Ivanov Craig in "Being and Dying as a Woman in the Short Fiction of Dorothy Parker." Drawing on Judith Butler's concept of gender performance, and Joan Riviere's discussion of the female masquerade, Craig examines Parker's gender parody and the strategy of death-as-escape in "A Telephone Call," "The Waltz," and "Big Blonde." Ellen Lansky also applies theory to a reading of Parker's "Big Blonde" in "Female Trouble: Dorothy Parker, Katherine Anne Porter, and Alcoholism." Michel Foucault's concept of "panopticism" becomes the lens through which Lansky examines the cultural stigma against the female alcoholic in Parker's story and Porter's novel, *Ship of Fools*.

PART III. CLASSROOM ENCOUNTERS

Many of the essays in part I and part II may have derived from the authors' experiences with teaching Parker; mine was to some extent, and the coda to Suzanne Bunkers's essay describes her classroom encounters, via Emily Toth in one case, with Parker. The essays in part 3, Classroom Encounters, most certainly did, and demonstrate the value of teaching Parker not only in American literature and women's studies courses, but in composition and political science

classrooms, as well as in seminars and courses using a multidiscipli-
nary approach. Thus, Parker's work has implications for the evolving
field of teaching pedagogy. In the first essay, "Reading, Responding,
Composing: A Revisionary Approach," Phillip Arrington's concern
is not primarily with Parker as a literary figure per se, but with Parker's work as a tool for teaching advanced composition in light of
recent theories of rhetoric.[14] Arrington discusses his use of Parker's
story "But the One on the Right" in an advanced composition class
to test Gabriel M. Della-Piana's revisionist model of composing. He
describes his sequence of assignments based on that single text, as
well as the process through which students respond to and revise
both their writing and their understanding of the story.

In a similar vein, Parker's "Big Blonde" helps Sophia Mihic's political science students more deeply engage with the abstract works
of philosophers such as Jean-Jacques Rousseau and Mary Wollstonecraft. As described in her new essay "Mrs. Parker and the History of
Political Thought," Mihic uses John Schaar's "The Uses of Literature for the Study of Politics" as a basis for bringing Parker into the
political science classroom; she then reveals the ways in which Parker's story elucidates key concepts of the political theories she
teaches. In another new essay, Ann M. Fox's "The Hall Monitor
Who Broke the Rules: Teaching Dorothy Parker's *The Ladies of the
Corridor* as Feminist Drama," the topics of modernism, feminism,
pedagogy, and canon construction converge. Fox analyzes Parker's
play in the context of other modern dramatists, illustrates the teaching value of the play, and argues that construction of a feminist
canon of drama should include realistic drama such as Parker's.

The last two essays, written by students, are included to show prospective teachers of Parker's work what kind of student writing is
possible. Both essays show evidence of synthesizing material across
disciplines, close textual analysis, and critical thinking skills. Timothy P. McMackin's essay, "'They Can See Me If I Cry': Feminine Language and Reader Identification in Dorothy Parker's 'Sentiment,'"
stems from first reading Parker's work in an American Humor
course, and then reading feminist criticism in a senior seminar. His
essay applies the concept of female self-reflexive behavior described
in John Berger's "Ways of Seeing" to a reading of Parker's story
"Sentiment," and is a revised version of his senior thesis for Xavier
University (Cincinnati). Donna Stamm, a student at the University
of Cincinnati, also draws on two undergraduate courses, a women's
literature course in which Parker's work was assigned, and a psychology course covering Freudian psychology, to produce "Behavior at
Its Worst: Freudian Concepts in the Writing of Dorothy Parker."

Stamm analyzes several stories and poems to demonstrate Parker's knowledge of defense mechanisms, the phallic personality, and the death wish.

PART IV. CONVERSATIONS

The last part of this volume allows Dorothy Parker to speak for herself, first in a series of letters, then in an interview. While both pieces focus largely on Parker's life, they also contain comments about her writing, and reveal as well the wit exhibited in much of her work. They are arranged by date of content rather than by publication date to provide a sense of continuity. In "Dorothy Parker's Letters to Alexander Woollcott," Arthur F. Kinney guides us through Parker's correspondence to a close friend from her Algonquin days, beginning in 1926 and lasting into the World War II period. Parker's half of the exchange, which ended when Woollcott died in 1943, is highly personal and frank, and describes her difficulties writing in Europe and Hollywood, among other issues and observations that can be linked to her work. This is followed by Marion Capron's famous interview with Parker for the *Paris Review* in the late 1950s, referred to by several scholars in this volume. Both the letters and the interview are valuable source documents, but they cannot provide the final word on Parker's career.

Overall *The Critical Waltz* offers a nod toward the future, defining the debates about Parker's work to this point, and suggesting what is possible in terms of Parker studies and approaches to teaching her work. A reader of this collection in its early form commented that it would be nice to see more articles addressing works other than "Big Blonde." While I shared that reader's concern, I could not include what had not yet been written. Now that this collection exists and demonstrates, by virtue of what *has* been written about Parker's work, what *might* be written, I am convinced that the waltz of Parker criticism will continue—and continue to evolve. If I am correct, future scholars will grant that reader's wish.

NOTES

1. Part of Parker's reputation was achieved through her fiction and reviews, whereas Millay was primarily known—and continues to be known—as a poet. Both writers achieved notoriety through their Jazz Age lifestyles. See the biographies of Parker listed in the bibliography, and Nancy Milford, *Savage Beauty: The Life of Edna St. Vincent Millay* (New York: Random House, 2001), and Daniel Mark Epstein, *What*

Lips My Lips Have Kissed: The Loves and Love Poems of Edna St. Vincent Millay (New York: Henry Holt, 2001).

2. See Suzanne Clark, *Sentimental Modernism: Women Writers and the Revolution of the Word* (Bloomington: Indiana University Press, 1991), and Diane P. Freedman, ed., *Millay at 100: A Cultural Reappraisal* (Carbondale: Southern Illinois University Press, 1995).

3. In *A Gendered Collision: Sentimentalism and Modernism in Dorothy Parker's Poetry and Fiction* (Madison and Teaneck, NJ: Fairleigh Dickinson University Press, 2000), I also argue that Parker's work reveals a collision of competing aesthetic values—nineteenth-century sentimentalism and twentieth-century modernism—and that this collision more accurately defines modernism as a literary period than does the experimental aesthetic alone.

4. Mark Van Doren, "Dorothy Parker," *English Journal* 23:7 (September 1934): 535–43; Herbert Marshall McLuhan, "The New York Wits," *Kenyon Review* 7 (1945): 12–28. Compare Van Doren's essay with a more recent one, John Hollander's review of *Not Much Fun: The Lost Poems of Dorothy Parker*, ed. Stuart Y. Silverstein, in *Yale Review* 85:1 (1997), and also available on the Dorothy Parker Web page of the Modern American Poetry Web site, www.english.uiuc.edu/maps.

5. Ross Labrie, "Dorothy Parker Revisited," *Canadian Review of American Literature* 7:1 (Spring 1976): 48–56; Jane Tompkins, *Sensational Designs* (New York and Oxford: Oxford University Press, 1985).

6. Alexander Woollcott, "Our Mrs. Parker" in *When Rome Burns* (New York: Viking, 1934), 142–52. Ann Douglas also observes that several Jazz Age figures possessed this double-sided personality in *Terrible Honesty: Mongrel Manhattan in the 1920s* (New York: Noonday Press, 1995).

7. Randall Calhoun, *Dorothy Parker: A Bio-Bibliography* (Westport, CT: Greenwood Press, 1993), 31.

8. The unpublished, unproduced playscript, *The Ice Age* (1953), also written with d'Usseau, is at Columbia University.

9. "Who Might Be Interested," by Parker, missing in the *Portable* and Penguin collections, can be found in John Miller, ed., *Voices Against Tyranny: Writing of the Spanish Civil War* (New York: Scribner Signature Edition, 1986), 192–97. Other prose by Parker is yet to be collected.

10. A few of the studies devoted to this area that I have found useful include Astradur Eysteinsson, *The Concept of Modernism* (Ithaca: Cornell University Press, 1990); Sandra Gilbert and Susan Gubar, *No Man's Land: The War of the Words* (New Haven: Yale University Press, 1987); Andreas Huyssen, *After the Great Divide* (Bloomington: Indiana University Press, 1986); Michael Levenson, *A Genealogy of Modernism* (New York: Cambridge University Press, 1984).

11. See for example, Robyn R. Warhol and Denise Price Hendl, *Feminisms: An Anthology of Literary Theory and Criticism*, 2nd ed. (New Brunswick, NJ: Rutgers University Press, 1997); or Sandra Kemp and Judith Squires, eds., *Feminisms* (Oxford and New York: Oxford University Press, 1997).

12. Nancy F. Cott, *The Grounding of Modern Feminism* (New Haven: Yale University Press, 1987).

13. See the first letter in Arthur F. Kinney, "Dorothy Parker's Letters to Alexander Woollcott," *Massachusetts Review* 30:3 (Autumn 1989): 487–515, and included in this volume; "Dorothy Parker," interview with Marion Capron in Malcolm Cowley, ed., *Writers at Work: The "Paris Review" Interviews* (New York: Viking, 1958), 69–82, also included in this volume; Colleen Breese, introduction to Dorothy Parker, *Complete Poems* (New York: Penguin, 1999), xxvi.

14. See also Barbara Hill Hudson's use of passages by Parker to introduce students to a variety of social dialects in "Sociolinguistic Analysis of Dialogues and First-Person Narratives in Fiction" in Virginia P. Clark, Paul A. Eschholz, and Alfred F. Rosa, eds., *Language: Readings in Language and Culture*, 6th ed. (Boston and New York: Bedford/St. Martin's, 1998), 740–48.

THE CRITICAL
WALTZ

Part I
Modernist Contexts

Parkers's "Iseult of Brittany"

Ruthmarie H. Mitsch

So delicate my hands, and long
　　They might have been my pride.
And there were those to make them song
　　Who for their touch had died.

Too frail to cup a heart within,
　　Too soft to hold the free—
How long these lovely hands have been
　　A bitterness to me!

　　　　　　　　—Dorothy Parker, "Iseult of Brittany"

THE LEGEND OF TRISTAN AND ISEULT IS ONE THAT HAS ENDURED throughout the centuries. But most, and especially modern, treatments of the myth have tended to be complicated by ponderous psychological scrutiny of the tale's tormented characters; thus, most renditions are lengthy and oppressively heavy in tone. Dorothy Parker, however, in her inimitable way, unexpectedly seizes the essence of the Tristan myth in two quatrains despite (or perhaps by) a shift in point of view to a minor character.

"Iseult of Brittany" appears in *Death and Taxes and Other Poems* (1931), which can be found in *The Collected Poetry of Dorothy Parker* (1959) or in *The Portable Dorothy Parker* (rev. 1973). This little lyrical gem is in standard Parker format, that is, the common meter with its usual *abab* pattern, alternating four iambs with three. The verse is spoken by the wife of Tristan, who shares her name with Queen Iseult, her husband's mistress. Like Queen Iseult, this woman is beautiful. We know from the poet Thomas that Tristan wed her for her beauty and for her name.[1] The reader is kept at a distance from this beauty, because Parker's intentional omission of names creates a frosty, impersonal ambiance. At the same time, this avoidance of naming the real contributes to the strong aura of pathos in which the reader senses the "bitterness" felt by the speaker.

Most general readers know that Tristan and Iseult unwittingly drank a potion intended for Iseult and Tristan's uncle, King Mark of Cornwall, which was to have bound them in their married love. United, then, in passionate love, but not in marriage, the lives of Tristan and Iseult are reduced to numerous adulterous adventures. The profundity of the myth is that equation of complete surrender to passion with death; their love achieves oneness only in death. The actual mechanics of their death involve jealousy and spite on the part of the "uninitiated"—sometimes Mark, sometimes a would-be suitor, but very often Iseult aux Blanches Mains of Brittany.

This Iseult "of the White Hands" enters the story after Tristan ruefully acknowledges his duty to his uncle and to Queen Iseult's honor and leaves the king's court. Through chivalrous exploits and because of his attraction to her beauty and the name of Iseult of Brittany, he weds Iseult of Brittany. But on his wedding night, as he spies the ring given to him by his mistress as a symbol of their total devotion to each other in a state of confusion, he lyingly tells his new wife that a vow to the Virgin prevents him from consummating his marriage for one year, presenting a case of what the French call *un mariage blanc.* Briefly, the unhappy young wife learns of the deception only by overhearing a wounded, dying Tristan ask his brother-in-law to summon the queen, who alone can cure him. In a fit of jealousy, Iseult of Brittany causes the death of her husband by announcing black sails instead of the white she sees that signal the arrival of the queen. Queen Iseult then dies of grief at Tristan's side, and Iseult of Brittany is generally left to sulk away from the dirty deed.

Dorothy Parker is not the first to focus on the young bride of Brittany. Edwin Arlington Robinson, Charles Algernon Swinburne, and Matthew Arnold are among modern writers who have attempted interesting interpretations of the maiden. But the beauty and significance of Parker's poem is its grasp of the legend in eight short lines. Gertrude Schoepperle had studied the problem of two heroines with the same or similar names in her classic study, *Tristan and Isolt: A Study of the Sources of the Romance,* showing how early romantic tradition allowed heroes to pass from one exploit and its reward (a lady) to another exploit and its reward (another lady) without much thought, but how as psychological romances developed, heroes began to develop scruples about two ladies, posing interesting work for the poet.[2] The monologues of the Tristan of Thomas are the pith of that work, full or ratiocination, elegant but frequently monotonous.

White hands are a fairly standard attribute among medieval heroines, certainly an indication of noble status. Some have gone on to speculate that her "white" hands symbolize the innocence of Iseult of Brittany.[3] Yet, in that case, one would have to acknowledge the great irony of the epithet, for it is "White Hands" who is guilty of the dirty work in so many renditions of the tale because of her *mariage blanc* ("white marriage," i.e., unconsummated marriage).

Now, all this is but background to the bare-bones treatment accorded by Parker. Iseult of Brittany's hands here are on center stage, described as "delicate," suggesting her physical frailty, her weakness, and, ironically, her inability to muster the strength to master her situation. Among those who might have celebrated her beauty in song is Tristan, known throughout medieval literature as a master musician. Numerous episodes include his appearance at court as a harpist. Ironically, too, it was Tristan's hands (that is, the ring he wore) that prompted his deception of his wife. The devotion and worship—to the point of death—that she longed for were experienced painfully, only at second hand.

Again emphasizing her frailty, she refers to the cup, the magical, mystical chalice that held the "love drink" that united her husband with another woman. That potion united their hearts (physically, say some poets) taking away all free will, so that Tristan in essence is not "free" to love his wife. Parker's choice of "bitterness" as the final noun, which determines the tone of the lyrics, alludes to one of the famous wordplays in the legend: *la mer* is where the union of the two fated lovers first took place; *l'amer* (*l'amour*) is the essence of the legend; *l'amer* is the bitterness that infected the adulterous union. This particular play on words is developed by Gottried von Strassburg; "initiates" of the tale automatically bring the other two elements of the triad to this reading.[4] It is precisely the bitterness of the situation that we sense in this bittersweet lament of the young woman who has all the right attributes for the best of heroes (her delicacy, fragility, beauty, passivity) but who is cheated of her rights by Fate.

This bitterness that eats away at Iseult of Brittany will soon devour her conscience, pushing her to a definitive vengeance, whose threat we sense behind the lilt of the poem. The "second" Iseult is insulted at occupying second place; the delicate hands that might have been her pride, whose touch is incapable of curing the man she loves of his love disease, are now a symbol of her wounded pride. As in most of Parker's works, there is here a pessimism with bite just beneath the polite surface.

That Parker can draw so much of the legend of Tristan into her two quatrains and capture so many tones of so many layers of the myth is true poetry.

NOTES

1. "Sneyd," 1, ll. 197–98 in Bartina H. Wind, *Les Fragments du Roman de Tristan* (Geneva: Droz, 1960).

2. Gertrude Schoepperle, *Tristan and Isolt: A Study of the Sources of the Romance* (1913; repr., New York: B. Franklin, 1960).

3. Terrence Scully, "The Two Yseults," *Mediaevalia* 3 (1977): 25–36.

4. Gottfried von Strassburg, *Tristan*, trans. A. T. Hatto (Baltimore: Penguin, 1960).

Making Love Modern:
Dorothy Parker and Her Public

Nina Miller

In 1916, AFTER REPEATED ATTEMPTS TO BE PUBLISHED IN THE PRESTIGIOUS New York journal *Vanity Fair,* the as-yet unknown Dorothy Parker finally hit on a theme that impressed editor Frank Crowninshield. Her poem, "Women: A Hate Song," maliciously dissected a series of female types—so maliciously that Crowninshield advised her to publish pseudonymously.[1] He needn't have worried. The poem was so successful it demanded a sequel, this time a caustic attack on the men, for which Parker took full credit.[2] Crowninshield subsequently commissioned a series of "Hate Songs,"[3] now freely capitalizing on the quintessentially "sophisticated" lashings of a "sharp" female tongue.

Sophistication—that highly prized commodity that was to define the Jazz Age—meant cynicism and a barbed wit, and women like Parker were perfectly situated to dominate this discourse. In the twenties, as a wisecracking member of the celebrated Algonquin Round Table, Parker would be at the cutting edge of a mannered and satirical wittiness, one that determined the shape of her poetry in important ways. By the time of her first best-selling collection in 1926, she had made a national career for herself as the most luckless and sardonic woman lover on literary record.[4] And yet, bound up with her persona as a loser-in-love was an alternative—and highly enabling—model of self-other relations. From within Round Table sophistication and the popular discourse of "Modern Love," Parker forged a poetics that significantly transformed the roles and relations presented her by the literary tradition of lyric love poetry.

⋙

Modern Love was to be found as early as the midteens in newspapers and fashionable magazines, the substance of short fiction, humorous dialogues, satirical sketches, cartoons, and the occasional novel.[5] Both the discourse and the media through which it was propagated

41

were functions of a newly self-conscious urbanity centered in New York. Though that city had come into a sense of itself as the national guardian of high culture in the "genteel" 1880s and 1890s, the development of a distinctively urbane New York sensibility arose with a more general commodification of style in the consumerist 1910s and 1920s.[6] *Vanity Fair* itself, founded in 1914, had a vanguard function in this history with its focus on wit, urban society, and—as an organizing framework for both—Modern Love. Crossing many genres and widely diffused throughout public speech about sex and gender, Modern Love was somewhat amorphous but nevertheless had certain distinctive features. Principal among them was a focus on the social identities of its lovers to the virtual exclusion of any notion of private self or of attributes such as individuality, introspection, and intimacy. Rather, Modern Lovers took their definition and "character" from a set of common sociological types: the Debutante, the College Man, the Gold Digger, the Don Juan, the Newlyweds, and so forth.

Foundational to the ideology of Modern Love was the assumption that gender relations were permanently and intrinsically flawed. Situated in a mundane world structured by class and class pretensions, the fictional players of Modern Love were identifiably upper-, middle-, or (occasionally) working-class people to whom the world of modern gender relations had happened: the intellectual man and woman who find each other while seeking "elemental" love among the working classes, the businessman who finds himself working for his newly professional wife, the woman who finds the promise of modern marital bliss unattainable because both of her husbands irritatingly leave the cap off the toothpaste.[7] For their part, the readers of Modern Love discourse were left to conclude that heterosexuality was imperfect at best, taking comfort in the fact that the whole project was too comical and inevitable to bear much analysis or even emotional investment. As a popular discourse, Modern Love rendered a vision of heterosexuality toward which one could only assume a stance of cynical detachment; in a word, Modern Love flatteringly inscribed its readers as sophisticates.

Indeed, its purveyors understood Modern Love as a sophisticated response to a heterosexuality newly problematized by the growing presence of women in the previously male public of campus, office, and street—a heterosexuality newly organized around a heterosocial landscape.[8] Cultural observers—male and female—seemed to take up Modern Love whenever they engaged that other highly charged subject, the New Woman (or her trivialized sister, the Flapper).[9] At first making a show of their perplexity and surprise at her values and behavior, they inevitably discovered, by article's end, the eternal feminine just below the modern surface or the innocuous nature of the changes she represented. The typical title was redolent with sophisticated irony: "Prue Enlightening the World: A Disadvantage of the New Freedom for Women," or "The Doom of the Home: And What About Children? and Rubber Plants?"[10]

One of the primary organs of Modern Love, *Vanity Fair* was not coincidentally also the central vehicle of the larger discourse of sophistication. Structurally, this glossy magazine embodied modern heterosociality through its designated readership, which was expressly identified as both male and female.[11] Even more pointed was the editorial policy expressed through a page-long feature in each issue. Presumably for the sake of variety and disarming the reader, this editorial took various forms—essay, play, or diary entry—but each negotiated a terrain defined by sophistication and gender relations, with the strong implication that the two were inexorably intertwined.

"A Word About Debutantes," from the January 1915 issue, was in the form of a letter from "George" to "Harry." "My Dear Harry," it begins, "You ask me for the hottest news from New York—for items sizzling on the griddle of Fifth Avenue life." Harry is apparently laid up at a remote sanitorium and wants to be kept abreast of events in Society. George's response is to tell him about the New Women, specifically the new debutantes. True to the form of such discussions, George begins by sounding alarmed at their aggressions. Then, as the mark of his own sophistication (as compared to the secluded Harry), he declares them exciting—though he makes his ambivalence sardonically evident:

> The chief change in the world of fashion during this winter and last— has been directly due to the debutantes. They now run everything. Their energy, ability and knowledge of the world are simply appalling. . . . You left here in 1912, and already the social fabric has taken on—solely because of these youngsters—a new pattern, a pattern which you, in your ignorance, might think a devilish loud plaid. . . . But once you become used to them—to their intelligence, ability and energy, and to their remarkable knowledge of life—one finds it hard to leave them and go back to the old 1912 models. No, my boy, this year's lot are as quick as hawks, as strong as lions, and as keen as game-cocks.

But these fabulous monsters inspire real terror when it comes time for George to make his entrance at a dance in an all-women's club:

> Entrance to the Colony is made, for modest men like ourselves, a little less conspicuous and galling by the presence of a gentleman's entrance.

This corresponds to what, in our more select liquor saloons, is usually designated the "family" entrance. . . . As I entered that little door my heart stood still. (The clash of sex is a terrible thing!) To be, perhaps, the only man in a feminine club, behind closed doors, with two hundred or more ladies and debutantes—all of them strong and active, and most of them protected by mysterious club minutes and by-laws—was a thing almost too perturbing to contemplate.

He goes on to compare himself to Dante entering Hell and Achilles going among the women; but, as it turns out, his fears are all for naught:

Any one expecting to find fluted frills in the Colony Club, and French musk, and *punto a rilievo lace*, and ice cream soda, and Pomeranians, and a colored maid, and a booth for the sale of bon-bons, and all such pleasing secondary sexual characteristics, will be greatly disappointed, for I found it to be nothing more than a very sensible and well-regulated club. It was, indeed, quite like a man's club, save that the dinner was cooked with more art, and served with a hanged sight more alacrity. I also found the manicuring of the waiters to be more unexceptionable, and the decorations more vivid and cheering.

Having entertained the range of horrors female power suggests to him—from ravishment to captivity in a garish boudoir—George discovers that the new women are in fact very much like men with certain improving touches, for which he very gallantly gives them due credit. How have they achieved this transformation? "I asked them what they read and they all assured me that they never read anything but Vanity Fair. . . . It appears that it is solely due to Vanity Fair—and the rage for it here—that the debutantes have ceased being simpering little idiots and have developed into able and intelligent human beings."[12]

The scene of George's adventures among the women is important, for both his anxiety and its resolution are centered on society (in both senses of the word) and its ability to sustain itself and its members in the face of disruption. Here we are assured that the style of presentation and interaction known as sophistication—acquired through studious attention to *Vanity Fair*—will make the requisite new "equality" and proximity between the sexes not only possible but painless.

Painless, in the first instance, for the men involved: as the story of George and the debutantes illustrates, the struggle for sophistication was primarily a male drama enacted over the female terrain of society. Women—specifically, New Women—already had sophistication by virtue of their femininity, whereas for men it was most often something they needed to achieve. Indeed, for commentators on the New Woman the ultimate tone of patronizing celebration, the humorous enactment of her upset to convention, and the rhetorical dismissal of the threat she posed all functioned as testimony to this achievement. For the New Woman herself, the deployment and meanings of sophistication had to take account of the larger cultural identification between her and modernity.

As one of a handful of national exemplars, the Dorothy Parker persona was desirable to the extent that she was indeed modern and reassuring to the extent that she left certain basic feminities intact. Parker's rhetorical modernness lay in her daring sexuality (for which she paid by having her heart routinely broken) and in her sophisticated tone (which was feminine bitchiness revealed). And yet she successfully projected beauty and style, a near-total preoccupation with love and men, and a ladylike suppression of hostility (expressed only in "confidence" to her audience). The discursive space that she was able to create for herself depended partly on the gendered character of sophistication, and partly on the distinction between mass femininity—as represented by the *Vanity Fair* debutantes—and individual women. While the one was the very embodiment of female threat, the other concentrated the characteristics of "new womanhood" in iconic self-presentation, without any suggestion of alliance with the feminine horde—and indeed, with the strong suggestion of abhorrence of such alliance. In particular, the Dorothy Parker "personality" held out the promise that the New Woman's aggression would be titillatingly invested in the new heterosociality.

The success with which Parker maintained the tension between old and New made her an extremely appealing figure to a public ambivalent about women's sexual freedom and the modernity it stood for. For Parker herself, the public context in which she was to maintain this tension supplied its own ambivalences: it provided an alternative to conventional heterosexuality and yet left her inescapably embodied as a woman. But Parker's writing engaged the totality of her situation, and her literary strategies derive as much from her "constraints" as from her "freedoms." Her response to publicity was to exploit it for its utopian possibilities, to treat it as the enabling matrix that it arguably was.

⤳

Through what conjunction of publicity, contemporaneous love discourse, and traditional lyric conventions, then, does Parker generate her poetic praxis? What dialogue with her discursive milieu allows her to make love modern and herself a modern lover? Parker's career in the twenties, like that of her immediate circle, the Algonquin Round Table, was significantly structured and even constituted by publicity. For a woman writer attempting to form and sustain a highly public identity, particularly one that would project an appropriately sophisticated image, lyric love poetry—and more generally the traditional role of woman lover—were inherently problematic, founded as they were on feminine self-effacement. Parker solved the problem in large part through figurations and rhetorical modes that incorporated the public into her poetics, thereby providing her speaker the possibility of self-definition outside of the heterosexual dyad.

Within the legacy of romanticism, love has been conventionally premised on the uniqueness of the lover for the Other, and the context for mutual recognition of uniqueness has been the dyadic intersubjective relationship.[13] Roland Barthes's *A Lover's Discourse* captures the critical interdependence of love and individual identity for the amorous modern subject, expressed below in the characteristically cumulative, collage style of Barthes's text:

"Ah, whatever I know, anyone may know—[but] I alone have my heart."

I divine that the true site of originality and strength is neither the other nor myself, but our relation itself.

Once, speaking to me of ourselves, the other said: "a relation of quality"; this phrase was repugnant to me: it came suddenly from outside, flattening the specialty of the rapport by a conformist formula.

The other whom I love and who fascinates me is *atopos*. I cannot classify the other, for the other is, precisely, Unique, the singular Image which has miraculously come to correspond to the specialty of my desire. The other is the figure of my truth and cannot be imprisoned in any stereotype (which is the truth of others).[14]

Within the ideology Barthes describes, lovers are not answerable to common moral or aesthetic standards—"the world and I are not interested in the same thing" (52)—but perceive themselves as inhabiting an intersubjective space with its own private ethos.[15] The romantic relationship, then, is perceived as irreducible to objective cultural criteria of worth and compatibility. Most important, it is inaccessible to outsiders.

But within such a hermetic universe, differential positions become crucially important. Feminist critic Jan Montefiore has called the traditional literary expression of heterosexual romance the "I-Thou dyad." Focusing on the love sonnet in particular, Montefiore argues for the historically entrenched and psychoanalytically over-determined nature of the gender polarity these poems employ:

> The love poem as it appears in the Western tradition of poetry represented by Petrarch and Sidney is characteristically spoken by a male poet celebrating the beauty and virtue of an unattainable woman who is at once the object of his desire, the cause of his poetry and the mirror which defines his identity. . . . Problems arise [for the woman poet] from the complex processes of self-definition at work in the classic love poems. In the great tradition of Petrarch and Shakespeare, the lover-poet is principally concerned with defining his own self through his desire either for the image of his beloved or for his own image mediated through her response to him.[16]

The male speaker, then, is the subjective "I" to the female address-ee's objectified "Thou," a dyad in which the woman is reduced to a function of her lover's narcissism. Montefiore notes, moreover, "the obvious difficulty of speaking in a form which defines one as muse, not maker."

At the broadest level, Parker undercuts her own ascension to "muse" or loved object through her irony, a stance built into her Round Table imperative to perform as a humorist. But more important, in sacrificing the high seriousness of romantic love to humor, she breaks up the loving dyad of male and female through the implied intervention of her audience, for whom the joke is staged. Thus "triangulated," the lovers lose the psychodynamic logic supporting their lopsided interrelation; humor about love—not the dramatic irony attending the spectacle of bunglers but the acerbic wit of a sophisticated lover-narrator—has the power to rupture the magic circle of intersubjectivity by constructing its audience as a complicitous third party to the ridicule of one lover (the man) by the other (the woman).

In "Plea," humor constitutes the female speaker's first level of resistance to her lover's attempt to impose upon her a tyranny of privacy:

> Secrets, you said, would hold us two apart;
>   You'd have me know of you your least transgression
> And so the intimate places of your heart,
>   Kneeling, you bared to me, as in confession.

> Softly, you told of loves that went before—
>   Of clinging arms, of kisses gladly given;
> Luxuriously clean of heart once more,
>   You rose up, then, and stood before me, shriven.

In this first stanza, the speaker mockingly renders her lover's self-indulgence in the terms of his own self-justification, terms which the contemporaneous audience must recognize as a species of "enlightened" free love: the couple are to have no "secrets" to keep them "apart," anything that would sustain their separateness being self-evidently a bad thing. But as the poem so clearly demonstrates, this relation is not one of equality, and modern mutual honesty appears to be neither actively mutual nor, strictly speaking, honest. Rather, we see the male lover, under the guise of intimacy, attempt to reduce the woman to a function of his own psychic economy, an ego ideal to whom he can confess himself a sexual adventurer and thus emerge "luxuriously clean of heart."

Fully conscious of her lover's instrumental use of her, the speaker's protest goes beyond her mocking tone and the joke she has with her audience at his expense. The poem continues,

> When this, my day of happiness, is through,
>   And love, that bloomed so fair, turns brown and brittle,
> There is a thing that I shall ask of you—
>   I, who have given so much, and asked so little.
> Some day, when there's another in my stead;
>   Again you'll feel the need of absolution,
> And you will go to her, and bow your head,
>   And offer her your past, as contribution.
>
> When with your list of loves you overcome her,
> For heaven's sake, keep this one from her![17]

Here, Parker's response to the romantic love tradition extends to rejection of the very form of hermetic intersubjectivity itself. For underlying the depiction of gross inequality in "Plea" is an almost palpable disgust with the sort of relationship this modern love affair implies, even in its ideal (that is, genuinely mutual) form. It is not merely the self-serving use to which it is put in this instance, but the very idea of "the intimate places of [the lover's] heart" that is held at a critical distance; the speaker's distaste is clearly and extensively drawn around the idea of intimacy as such. Her repugnance is plainly evident from the first word: "Secrets," deliberately set off by a comma, signals the lover's self-infatuated exhibition to come.

When, later, the speaker situates herself within her own, more dignified model of love, it stands as a reproof to what preceded it.

Stanza two of "Plea" highlights the stark difference in the speaker's assumptions about the status of this affair in her life. The male
lover uses the ostensible telos of unbounded and unending mutuality to justify his lurid self-revelations, a pretext that is mocked by the
very nature of the confessions themselves. The female speaker, on
the other hand, augments the dignified distance she puts between
herself and him by assuming, with lyrical calm, the unlamented fini-
tude of their affair. She makes no pretense of being absorbed with
him in particular, but explicitly derives her pleasure from the experience of love itself. Their affair at its height is *her* "day of happiness,"
and the love that blooms and then wilts, as the metaphor suggests,
has its own objective existence and its own immanent course to run
independent of either of them. The assertion that she has "given so
much, and asked so little" functions to emphasize—even ironically
to flaunt—her restraint and self-sufficiency. Her protest to him, "For
Heaven's Sake," to keep their affair secret is ostensibly a plea for her
own future privacy, but the force behind the expletive, the force that
has been building steadily throughout the previous stanzas, derives
from her disgust with the absence of privacy in their present interactions.

Intersubjective love, what one Parker poem refers to as the "mist
of a mutual dream," places its practitioners in an unbounded relation to each other while sequestering them away from the emotional
reach of the ordinary world. But one might also see this as isolation
from one's community and its values, as Parker seems to do. For the
lovers' isolation is unequal: the woman, as "thou" to her male lover's "I," suffers the effacement that accompanies the role of psychic
mirror; defined by her sexuality, the woman-in-love has only effacement to identify her.

Parker's writing works actively toward transforming this private experience of love into a social identity within an arena of public discursive exchange. Within the given categories of gender and
relationship, Parker contrives a viable sexual-literary praxis through
her characteristic bitterness and the theme of an endless series of
doomed relationships. Surrounded by the apparatus of love and
men, the Parker persona remains legitimately within the sphere of
women's concerns, and she addresses her audience unquestionably
as a woman. But by virtue of her amorous "failures," she is free from
the all-consuming rapture that would bar her access to the world
(though granting her the "success" of submersion in a single
adored man).

The profoundly jaundiced notion of love structuring Modern Love discourse gave Parker license to displace the heterosexual relationship as the necessary center of her poems and instead make the poems' audience the site of her primary psychological investment. Foregrounding the listening audience, which lyric poetry conventionally suppresses, she transforms the solitary musings of a speaker addressing only herself or the figure of her lover into essentially public space and speech. The public Parker imagined for herself drew variously on family relations and New York urban culture, but whatever its particular dimensions, it represented the form of *cultural consensus*. Specifically, it stood for the authoritative and objectively verifiable values that ideally define a culture and in relation to which a woman love poet could define herself, as against the definition imposed on her in the "private" world of love. Moreover, it gave her the opportunity to appeal the injustice of her lot as lover to the higher court of cultural authority. Implicit in this schema was a fantasy of escape from sexualized embodiment, underwritten by an emotional and aesthetic investment in community for its own sake: relations between the Parker persona and the communities she evoked often carried the affective charge that would otherwise have been confined to the male lover.

The poem "Folk Tune" explicitly asserts the worth of consensual culture over a privatized ethos. Typically for Parker's work, it is structured as a single extended "setup" for a final punch line. For two stanzas the speaker lays out objective criteria by which her addressee must be judged unworthy as a lover. We are to recognize this as a rational argument with no ultimate force in what we know to be a "matter of the heart"; consequently, we are fully prepared for a conclusion based on what is ostensibly the radically different ground of feelings:

> Other lads, their ways are daring:
>   Other lads, they're not afraid;
> Other lads, they show they're caring;
>   Other lads—they know a maid.
> Wiser Jock than ever you were,
>   Will's with gayer spirit blest,
> Robin's kindlier and truer,—
>   Why should I love you the best?
>
> Other lads, their eyes are bolder.
>   Young they are, and strong and slim
> Ned is straight and broad of shoulder,
>   Donald has a way with him.

> David stands a head above you,
>   Dick's as brave as Lancelot—
> Why, ah why, then should I love you?
>   Naturally, I do not.

(68)

The movement of this poem—the force that leads us to expect a conclusion that flies in the face of all reason—depends on the conventional assumption that object choice in love is inexplicable or at least highly idiosyncratic. This expectation is, of course, subverted to humorous effect, and it is easy enough to see the reversal in "Naturally, I do not" as a surprise about the character of the speaker: she turns out to be not a "genuine" lover at all but a coldhearted cynic. And such a reading would be consistent with the Parker persona.

The alternative reading I would propose takes the concluding line and—rather than deflecting its import onto a revelation about the speaker—turns it back on her utterance in order to overturn the model of love it invokes. Love choice, the poem suggest, *does* in fact proceed out of a kind of rational deliberation; more accurately, it follows from culturally agreed upon standards. Here is where the title "Folk Tune" reveals its aptness to the poem beyond a certain quaintness of diction. If we take the final line to be continuous with what precedes it (rather than an ironic reversal of it), the poem presents a logic for love based on common consensual wisdom. Love alliance is forged according to the standards and blessings of the "folk," not as a private expression of individual taste. In addressing herself to the potential lover—seemingly appealing to what would be their shared arena of private values—the speaker's ultimate rejection of him on grounds of his objectively verifiable shortcomings must be seen as the rejection of the intersubjective ethos itself. The distinction between a consensual culture of "folk" as opposed to a modern notion of impersonal society suggests the speaker's positive motivation for rejecting her would-be lover. More than just the expression of hardened modern femininity (and the fulfillment of Parker's public image as such), the poem's eschewal of the privatized world of this love relationship gains the speaker access to a broader community, one based on cultural common ground as well as affective investment.

Still a lover, yet allied with this broader community, the Parker persona could deploy its terms within the romantic context to her own advantage, even circumventing her own gendered fate. A stark example is "Finis":

Now it's over, and now it's done;
　　Why does everything look the same?
Just as bright, the unheeding sun,—
　　Can't it see that the parting came?
People hurry and work and swear,
　　Laugh and grumble and die and wed,
Ponder what they will eat and wear,—

Don't they know that our love is dead?
　　Just as busy, the crowded street;
Cars and wagons go rolling on,
　　Children chuckle, and lovers meet,—
Don't they know that our love is gone?
　　No one pauses to pay a tear;
None walks slow, for the love that's through,—
　　I might mention, my recent dear,
I've reverted to normal, too.

　　　　　　　　　　　　　　　　　　　(82)

The speaker lures her lover into contemplating the opposition between the everyday social world and their private universe—more
specifically, into a vision of her own lonely vigil in the closed space
that they no longer share. But having spent two stanzas reestablish-
ing their mutuality, she effectively abandons the lover to uphold it
himself—the fate that was to have been "rightfully" hers as the
woman in the dyad. Simultaneously, she reveals that she has all
along been speaking from the other side of the dichotomy invoked
by her words: she is among the free social beings who profane their
lost love. Conventionally, the love poem is the "unconscious" display of private values for a public audience of worldly values. The
ultimate betrayal is the breach of this divide; by figuring her audience within the poem (as the "people"), Parker provides her
speaker the structure within which to commit this treason. Her betrayal is worse than the lover's betrayal of infidelity; it is the non-
lover's betrayal of being "normal."

　　Rejecting privatized intimacy and its dangers for her as a woman,
Parker adopts an antiromantic model of love governed by decorum
and propriety. The psychodynamic effect of such love is to infuse a
certain construction of the social field with the erotic investment
that would otherwise be fixed in a single defined locus, the heterosexual (male) Other. Formally, this model of love is consistent with
the drawing room aesthetic dominant in the culture of sophistication generally and of the Round Table in particular. "They Part"
uses an arch and mannered voice to directly counterpose decorum
with the emotional excesses of romantic love:

And if, my friend, you'd have it end,
   There's naught to hear or tell.
But need you try to black my eye
   In wishing me farewell?

Though I admit an edged wit
   In woe is warranted,
May I be frank? . . . Such words as "_____"
   Are better left unsaid.

There's rosemary for you and me;
   But is it usual, dear,
To hire a man, and fill a van
   By way of souvenir?

(59)

The lover's behavior in "They Part" appears at first a mere lapse in decorum without the justification of any social code, however misguided. In the world of this poem, the only protocol for love seems to be that set forth by the speaker. The poem is structured so that each of the three stanzas begins with a detail of amorous etiquette whose subtlety (the second half of the stanza reveals) is completely lost on the lover-addressee. The values that structure normative love in "They Part" are restraint, both thematized and enacted by the speaker, and tradition, as evidenced by the folkloric symbol of rosemary for remembrance.

The behavior of the lover, however, though seemingly shown merely for its vulgarity, does in fact derive from an opposing model—that of romantic love—in which passion drives the lover to the behavioral excesses that are the testament to its authenticity. The quality of the lover's feeling is conventionally gauged precisely by the degree to which it impedes his ability to adhere to social codes of behavior; social propriety and love, then, are seen to be mutually contradictory. In the speaker's conception, clearly the reverse is true. Love is to be enacted within the matrix of society; protocol and the tropes of consensual culture are of paramount importance.

"They Part" thus reverses the notion of "falling in love" as an escape into hermetic intersubjectivity. Building a notion of love around decorum and propriety means turning it into a publicly known and shared field of behaviors and roles into which "lovers" can then—freely and independently—interpolate themselves. Even in those poems in which the female speaker is depicted as acting foolishly, ostensibly the victim of her own lack of emotional control,

her "weakness" is figured in terms of a rigidly mannered context for
love. In "Pattern," a woman repeatedly resists, then finally capitu-
lates to the advances of a younger man.

> Leave me to my lonely pillow.
>   Go, and take your silly posies;
> Who has vowed to wear the willow
>   Looks a fool, tricked out in roses.
>
> Who are you, my lad, to ease me?
>   Leave your pretty words unspoken.
> Tinkling echoes little please me,
>   Now my heart is freshly broken.
>
> Over young are you to guide me,
>   And your blood is slow and sleeping.
> If you must, then sit beside me. . . .
>   Tell me, why have I been weeping?

(57)

At the most immediate level, we are perhaps to see the woman's invocation of conventional tropes of unrequited love as a function of
her self-ironization. Her vow "to wear the willow," which has apparently dissolved completely in the space of the ellipsis at the poem's
end, might lead us to see it not only as self-deluded but as artificially
imposed on the "true" emotional reality.

Certainly our romantic prejudices would support such a reading,
but it is in fact undermined at several points in the text. First of all,
the speaker's traditional posture of mourning is explicitly opposed
to an alternative, equally stereotyped behavior of "courting" on the
part of the young man. Given that nothing mitigates its integrity,
the framework of propriety stands; more specifically, the speaker's
ostensible dissolution into unmediated emotion is in fact the abandonment of one role for another. Finally, the title "Pattern" imposes a formal stereotyped character on the narrative as a whole; far
from describing love as an emotional arena in which the attempt at
personal self-control is rendered futile, the poem rescues even the
"older woman"—paradigm of the woman degraded by love—to the
dignity of protocol.

In a similar fashion, Parker's "Threnody" foregrounds the social
character of love in order to overturn the tragedy of the bereft
woman. A lament, the poem is constructed of tropes of romantic
suffering, but deployed in such a way as to dispel the profound isolation in which these tropes conventionally fix the mourning female
lover:

Lilacs blossom just as sweet
Now my heart is shattered.
If I bowled it down the street,
Who's to say it mattered?
If there's one that rode away
What would I be missing?
Lips that taste of tears, they say,
Are the best for kissing.

Eyes that watch the morning star
Seem a little brighter;
Arms held out to darkness are
Usually whiter.
Shall I bar the strolling guest,
Bind my brow with willow,
When, they say, the empty breast
Is the softer pillow?

That a heart falls tinkling down,
Never think it ceases.
Every likely lad in town
Gathers up the pieces.
If there's one gone whistling by
Would I let it grieve me?
Let him wonder if I lie;
Let him half believe me.

(11)

After invoking the full weight of pitiable romantic tragedy in a suc-
cinctly conventional opening, the speaker takes up her own sacred
lover's heart and commits a double outrage upon it: first literalizing
the metaphoric heart to mere object and then refusing its precious-
ness by cavalierly "bowl[ing] it down the street." The deflation complete, she is ready to assess her more readily visible attributes.

What is traditionally repressed in the lyric, the specularization of
the grieving woman as an erotic object, is here foregrounded and
put to practical good use. The intrinsic value of romantic suffering,
the poem suggests, is nil, but there is significant sexual capital in
inhabiting the image. Adherence to the role of tragic woman in all
its proper particulars—white arms, bright eyes, and so on—assures
her the ultimate benefits of the social contract it supports. In the
same way, the metaphor of the tragic heart provides its own solution.
The bereft and brittle unitary heart shatters into a liberating multiplicity; the speaker's erotic investment is freed from the doomed
dyad of self and (absent) other and goes out to multiple sites of de-

sire, to "every likely lad in town." Again, the public practice of
poetry provides Parker with the utopian relation of self to a ca-
thected social body and a field of conventional tropes through
which to construct and manipulate this relation.

Yet many of Parker's poems express significant anxiety over the
management of such complex publicity. "Braggart" contrasts two
models of inhabiting a public persona and public space in order to
suggest both the supreme value of community for Parker and what
she sees as its attendant dangers:

> The days will rally, wreathing
> Their crazy tarantelle;
> And you must go on breathing,
> But I'll be safe in hell.
>
> Like January weather,
> The years will bite and smart,
> And pull your bones together
> To wrap your chattering heart.
>
> The pretty stuff you're made of
> Will crack and crease and dry.
> The thing you are afraid of
> Will look from every eye.
>
> You will go faltering after
> The bright, imperious line,
> And split your throat on laughter,
> And burn your eyes with brine.
>
> You will be frail and musty
> With peering, furtive head,
> Whilst I am young and lusty
> Among the roaring dead.

(26)

The speaker taunts her (ambiguously gendered) addressee with the
dismal details of her/his future life, gloating over her own escape
into a quite different fate. The contrast of their respective worlds
carries with it certain expectations. We are prepared for "hell" to be
the atemporal antithesis of the relentlessly time-driven "life"; more
specifically, we are prepared for hell to be like that truly abstracted
alter-world, heaven. Knowing that the salient point of her association with hell is that she is "bad" rather than "good," we are likely
to overlook its other implications.

But while this "braggart's" reversal of values is shocking and icon-oclastic in typical Parker fashion, it introduces complications be-yond those suggested by a mere inversion, conditions that actually break down the dichotomy that ostensibly structures the poem. The addressee will suffer the physical ravages of old age, and yet the speaker, presumably dead, has not herself been released from her body. She is in hell, a place whose whole purpose depends on the continued embodiment (as capacity for suffering) of its subjects. Yet from the three lines of description the poem offers, we learn that hell provides the speaker with safety, youth, lustiness, and—most im-portant—company. Having surprised us first with embodied alterna-tive to life, the poem goes on to surprise us with the physical comforts of hell.

But the underplayed embodiment of the dead speaker is purpose-fully overshadowed by that of the live addressee, whose body is a source of pure agony. In the first two stanzas of this extended predic-tion (or curse), the addressee undergoes the disorientation and pain of aging, substantial enough in itself. But stanza 3 marks of a crucial shift away from the subjective to an even more horrifying di-mension of the process: as the surface of the body "crack[s] and crease[s] and dr[ies]," it becomes an increasingly opaque boundary dividing the person within the once "pretty stuff" from the "every eye" without. By the final stanza, the addressee has been reduced to a "peering, furtive" relation to the world, embodiment having finally—and paradoxically—given way to invisibility. The still-young speaker, meanwhile, belongs unproblematically to a powerful com-munity.

In this poem, then, both alienation and community are founded on embodiment; if the body has the power to isolate tragically, it is also the only means to connectedness. Which it will be is a matter of control, specifically, management of one's public persona. The woman who holds to a conventional image of femininity finds her-self at the mercy of publicity's "crazy tarantelle." Acceptable while she is able to conform, she must be put out of sight as soon as she shows signs of losing the hypostasized youth that is the essence of her appeal.

The alternative represented by the poem's speaker is to refuse the embodiment of feminine perfection and instead go to hell—and by her own volition. Going to hell occurs at two levels for the speaker; she positions herself as a "bad girl," and she constructs a commu-nity and a relation to that community that is not in any way subject to living time. Typical for Parker's use of the bad girl persona, the "lusty" speaker of "Braggart" functions to elicit from her audience the protectiveness and safety that the "roaring dead" provide within the poem. The community that grants her the kind of seemingly unmediated connectedness suggested here is precisely the one that this essay has attempted to describe: an imaginary relation of self and other (persona and audience) staged across the public space of a poem. Yet, though this relationship often seems to transcend embodiment, the presenting problem of the "braggart" is the effect of aging on her public identity, and her solution is to "die" into permanent youth. While she may be able to negotiate a femininity that circumvents the imperative for youthful perfection, her identification with her audience as she has imagined it depends on her own personification of the New York culture of sophistication, a culture defined by modernity and youth. The loss of either quality creates an irreconcilable rift. From this perspective, the relationship Parker has fashioned as an alternative to the heterosexual dyad presents her, ironically, with the same criterion for acceptance.

For Parker as a writerly persona, embodiment proves to be an inescapable and peculiarly feminine component of public identity, just as love itself proves to be her only means of entry into public speech. "A Well Worn Story" stands as a kind of allegory of ambivalence for both these moments in Parker's literary practice:

> In April, in April,
> My one love came along,
> And I ran the slope of my high hill
> To follow a thread of song.
>
> His eyes were hard as porphyry
> With looking on cruel lands:
> His voice went slipping over me
> Like terrible silver hands.
>
> Together we trod the secret lane
> And walked the muttering town.
> I wore my heart like a wet, red stain
> On the breast of a velvet gown.
>
> In April, in April
> My love went whistling by,
> And I stumbled here to my high hill
> Along the way of a lie.
>
> Now what should I do in this place
> But sit and count the chimes,

And splash cold water on my face
And spoil a page with rhymes?

(16)

The intersection of love and publicity structuring this narrative has an implicitly feudal cast in the proprietary stance the lover takes toward the speaker—his "silver-handed" "possession" of her like his visual possession of "cruel lands." This context accounts for the nature of their peculiarly joyless love affair. The single stanza describing it is concerned exclusively with the relationship between the lovers and their public, the town. The lane which they "trod" was secret—apparently the more oppressive for that; the town they walked was "muttering."

But if the public and even the male lover have the luxury of maintaining privacy within their ritual communication, the female speaker is bound by her position to total self-revelation. Where she had had freedom and privacy on her "high hill," in the town she must provide visible proof of her worthiness: a "wet, red stain" of hymenal blood testifying to her virginity, to her possession by this man, or even to her repentance, à la Hester Prynne. Typically for Parker, the image bypasses sex itself for a shockingly antiromantic physicality. Wearing one's heart on one's sleeve, thus violently literalized, even equates love with death by gruesome slaying. But beyond these narratively motivated stains, the singular obligation to bear a "wet, red" brand suggests the extranarrative expression of femininity per se, menstrual blood. Where the town and the male lover mutter, sing, and chime, the woman's expressions are all graphic. In the same way that, as a lover, she wears a stain on her gown, she later "spoils a page with rhymes" after being spurned. The equation renders her love poetry as involuntary feminine revelation before a public; at the same time, the poem's feudal resonances suggest that such revelation is obligatory if a royal—or celebrity—woman is to find acceptance among her followers.

Of Parker's various responses to public embodiment, the most spectacular are undoubtedly her many death poems—poems of gleeful suicide, live burial, rotting corpses, and grotesque visitations. Many of her books are titled with an eye toward cultivating this association with the macabre: *Enough Rope* (1926), *Sunset Gun* (1928), *Death and Taxes* (1931), and *Here Lies* (1939). Biographers have attributed this element in Parker's writing to a morbid personal obsession related directly to her several real-life attempts to die by her own hand.[18] Yet just as important, I would suggest, is the way in which the trope of the dead body becomes a carnivalesque flouting of the *sexualized* body that public visibility (in the press or in the street) would impose on a woman. For Parker didn't just write the occasional morbid lyric; she let it be known that she subscribed to mortuary science trade journals and wore tuberose perfume, the scent favored by morticians in their grisly ministerings.[19] As in her unrelenting focus on love, Parker took the womanly constraint of embodiment for granted—and used it directly to forge a literary identity.

To varying degrees of success, Parker's work managed a central contradiction: that of speaking to a public and *appearing* as a woman. Widespread commodification of femininity and love in the period of Parker's greatest prominence put her at increased risk of becoming a public spectacle in her own person; yet it also offered her greater capacity for manipulating the form and meaning of her persona as a love poet. Her writing as a whole worked actively to transform the conventionally private experience of love and its privatizing effects on the female lover into a social identity within an arena of public discursive exchange. More than simply releasing her from heterosexual claustrophobia, Parker's "public love" offered her female citizenship as a horizon of possibility rather than a contradiction in terms.

NOTES

1. "Women" was published under the name Henriette Rousseau in *Vanity Fair*, August 1916, 61.

2. *Vanity Fair*, February 1917, 65. Note that Parker was then writing under her maiden name, Dorothy Rothschild.

3. Arthur F. Kinney, *Dorothy Parker* (Boston: Twayne, 1978), 89.

4. For the biographical account of Parker's rocky love life, see Marion Meade, *Dorothy Parker: What Fresh Hell Is This?* (New York: Villard, 1988). My specific focus in the present essay is the genre of love poetry as a form of speech that produces both public and private valences; hence, in the interest of space, I will not be concerned with biographical events as the material of Parker's work.

5. See, for example, Franklin Pearce Adam's (F.P.A.) syndicated columns to the *New York Tribune* and the *World* collected in F.P.A., *So There!* (New York: Doubleday, Doran, 1923) and *Something Else Again* (Garden City, NY: Doubleday, Doran, 1920), among others; Anita Loos, *Gentlemen Prefer Blondes: The Illuminating Diary of a Professional Lady* (New York: Boni & Liveright, 1925) and *But Gentlemen Marry Brunettes* (New York: Boni & Liveright, 1928); Nancy Boyd (Edna St. Vincent Millay), *Distressing Dialogues* (New York: Harper & Brothers, 1924).

6. See Thomas Bender, *New York Intellect: A History of Intellectual Life in New York City, from 1750s to the Beginning of Our Own Time* (New York: Knopf, 1987), 221–28; James R. Gaines, *Wit's End: Days and Nights of the Algonquin Round Table* (New York: Harcourt Brace Jovanovich, 1977).

7. Frank Wright Tuttle, "Bumping the Bumps: A Depraved Midsummer Dialogue a propos of Cerebral Love," *Vanity Fair*, August 1920, 53, 94; Geoffrey Kerr, "Tired Men and Business Women" (1930), in *Vanity Fair: A Cavalcade of the 1920s and 1930s,* ed. Cleveland Amory and Frederic Bradlee (New York: Viking, 1960), 184, 85; Boyd [Millay], "No Bigger Than A Man's Hand," in *Distressing Dialogues,* 73, 81. Humorist Ring Lardner, called "the epic recorder of the Great American Bicker" (quoted in George McMichael, ed., *Anthology of American Literature,* 2 vols., 3rd ed. [New York: Macmillan, 1985], 2:1091), was unusual in focusing primarily on working-class characters. See for example, "Some Like Them Cold," in *How To Write Short Stories (with Samples)* (New York: Scribner, 1925), 45–78; and *Say It with Oil: A Few Remarks About Wives* (New York: George II, Doran, 1923).

8. Nancy Cott, *The Grounding of Modern Feminism* (New Haven: Yale University Press, 1987); Paula Fass, *The Damned and the Beautiful: American Youth in the 1920s* (New York: Oxford University Press, 1977); Lary May, *Screening Out the Past: The Birth of Mass Culture and the Motion Picture Industry* (New York: Oxford University Press, 1980; Mary P. Ryan, "The Projection of New Womanhood," in *Our American Sisters: Women in American Life and Thought,* 2nd ed., Jean E. Friedman and William G. Slade (Boston: Allyn & Bacon, 1976).

9. The seminal discussion of the New Woman is Carroll Smith-Rosenberg, "The New Woman as Androgyne: Social Disorder and Gender Crisis, 1870–1936," in *Disorderly Conduct: Visions of Gender in Victorian America* (New York: Oxford University Press, 1985); Fass discusses the flapper as a locus of cultural anxiety (*The Damned and the Beautiful,* 22–25).

10. *Vanity Fair,* January 1915, 39 and April 1915, 49. Both articles are by Anne O'Hagan, who wrote a regular feature for *Vanity Fair* seemingly for the precise purpose of feminist containment.

11. The inaugural editorial statement was, in fact, quite self-congratulatory (not to mention patronizing) on this point: "For women we intend to do something in a noble and missionary spirit, something which, so far as we can observe, has never before been done for them by an American magazine. We mean to make frequent appeals to their intellects. We dare to believe that they are, in their best moments, creatures of some cerebral activity; we even make bold to believe that it is they who are contributing what is most original, stimulating, and highly magnetized to the literature of our day, and we hereby announce ourselves as determined and bigoted feminists" (Frank Crowninshield, "In Vanity Fair," *Vanity Fair,* March 1914, 13).

12. "A Word About Debutantes," *Vanity Fair,* January 1915, 15.

13. Theorists such as Niklas Luhmann ("Romantic Love," in *Love as Passion: The Codification of Intimacy,* trans. Jeremy Gaines and Doris L. Jones [Cambridge, MA: Harvard University Press, 1986], 134–44) and John Brenkman ("Aesthetics of Male Fantasy," in *Culture and Domination* [Ithaca: Cornell University Press, 1987], 184–227) have argued that modern individuality itself is dependent on romantic love.

14. Roland Barthes, *A Lover's Discourse: Fragments,* trans. Richard Howard (New York: Farrar, Straus and Giroux, 1978), 52, 35, 26, 34. In the first passage, Barthes is quoting Goethe's *The Sorrows of Young Werther.*

15. Luhmann, *Love as Passion,* 138, 142.

16. Jan Montefiore, *Feminism and Poetry* (London: Pandora, 1987), 98.

17. Parker, *Enough Rope* (New York: Boni & Liveright, 1926), 56. Subsequent quotations from this volume will be cited parenthetically in the text.

18. See Meade, *Dorothy Parker,* and John Keats, *You Might as Well Live: The Life and Times of Dorothy Parker* (New York: Paragon House, 1970).

19. Meade, *Dorothy Parker,* 56.

Dorothy Parker's Perpetual Motion

Ken Johnson

Somehow it has always been rather easy to dismiss Dorothy Parker and her writing from the collective literary consciousness. After all, she never produced a "big" work such as a novel, and her few plays did not achieve long runs. In addition, she shares the ironic fate of most writers who become identified primarily as humorists working with shorter literary forms: they are not considered "serious." Parker's many celebrated, flip wisecracks (e.g., "One more drink and I'll be under the host") brought her the kind of notoriety that rarely carves a secure niche for itself in the Westminster Abbey of literary history. And worst of all, for those readers and critics who like to detonate a writer's achievement with unfortunate circumstances from her personal life, Dorothy Parker provides a perfect case of literary self-combustion. Her lack of self-discipline was notorious; her unsuccessful marriages, divorces, abortion, suicide attempts, and alcoholism invite snickering disapproval; and her dwindling output as years passed can reinforce a preconceived idea of marginality.

Yet Dorothy Parker produced a substantial body of work in a range of literary modes, including three volumes of poetry, three plays, several screenplays, a significant number of book and play reviews, and three volumes of short stories, as well as other uncollected stories, poems, and articles. Her career spanned more than four decades, from late in the second decade of the twentieth century to the early 1960s, and from the beginning of her popularity until the time of her death, her name carried celebrity status—in other words, once she established herself as a writer and gained an appreciative audience, she never completely faded from the public memory, regardless of her progressively dwindling output. More importantly, in terms of American literary history she was one of the formative voices of the influential *New Yorker* magazine, as well as one of the few women writers of short stories in America during the 1920s and 1930s who put out popularly best-selling collections of stories (*Laments for the Living*, 1930; *After Such Pleasures*, 1933; *Here Lies*, 1939) that remained in print into the 1990s (in their reincarnation as *The Portable Dorothy Parker* from Viking Press, and *Complete Stories* from Penguin). In contrast, other women fiction writers contemporary to Parker, such as Ruth Suckow, Ellen Glasgow, and Zora Neale Hurston, often saw their works pass out of print, for various reasons, during their lifetimes.

Also, Parker's stories were admired not just by the purchasing reading masses, but by other short-story writers acclaimed in their own right both then and now. In 1929, F. Scott Fitzgerald encouraged Maxwell Perkins at Scribner's to publish Parker, and in 1938 he commended his daughter for reading (and "liking") Parker's stories.[1] Parker's short stories, the most substantial portion of her output, display many of the same structural techniques hailed as groundbreaking experiments in the stories of Ring Lardner, William Faulkner, and Ernest Hemingway: the dramatic monologue, the "dialogue" story, and the juxtaposition of internal and external realities. One of Parker's fortes, the soliloquy story, has no exact precedent in the history of American short stories. Considering all these factors that would suggest the need for a closer study of Parker's work, it is curious indeed that sustained critical attention has rarely been given to her writing.

Four of her stories ("A Telephone Call," "Here We Are," "The Waltz," and "From the Diary of a New York Lady") demonstrate Parker's unique handling of the short-story form, and the technical sophistication of stories such as these should secure her a stable position within the canon. What Parker generally brings to the short-story form, and to these four in particular, is a unique use of repetition, creating a kind of eternal *perpetuum mobile* that consigns the stories' characters to an endless experiencing of their own superficiality and emptiness. Whether the structural handling of such stories prefigures or even imitates the technical approaches of Hemingway, Lardner, or Faulkner is less important for this essay than how Parker's stories expand on the possibilities of the form in her own way. Before examining Parker's use of repetition, however, a brief consideration of critical responses to her oeuvre is necessary in order to appreciate the ironic paradox that the most significant structural and thematic aspect of her fiction—repetition—is also the aspect that has probably contributed most to the frequent dismissal of her work as shallow, usually by male critics. On the other hand, feminist critics have been slow to reevaluate Parker's work for reasons that are not altogether clear.

The typical posthumous critical appraisal of Parker's overall achievement has been neatly, and nattily, summarized by Brendan

Gill in his introduction to *The Portable Dorothy Parker*. "The span of her work is narrow, and what it embraces is often slight." Gill's introduction is a study in supreme condescension, which is especially unfortunate since *The Portable Dorothy Parker* was for decades the only collection of Parker's works in print. Gill writes approvingly of other writers from the 1920s and early 1930s, such as Fitzgerald, Lardner, Hemingway, and "the other boys in the back room," and then as a sop to the reputation of their erstwhile female companion, he states that it is not "surprising that there should pop up among them, glass in hand, hat askew, her well-bred voice full of soft apologies, the droll, tiny figure of Mrs. Parker."[2]

Gill's backhanded dismissal of Parker and her writing differs from other critical judgments only in its extended explicitness. Mordecai Richler, while defending the selections for his anthology *The Best of Modern Humor*, pauses briefly to explain why Parker was not included: in 1980 her style seems, to him, too "brittle." Academic critics have also tended to avoid Parker: she rates only a few references in passing throughout the first two volumes of *No Man's Land*, Sandra Gilbert and Susan Gubar's monumental study of twentieth-century American women writers, and no attention at all is given to her in a large-scale reference work such as *American Women Writers: Bibliographical Essays*.[3] While noting the resurrection by feminist scholars of so many previously forgotten American women writers, one might wonder why Dorothy Parker's works have not been likewise resuscitated during the past two decades. For one thing, the reanimation of literary reputations seems to occur more frequently with nineteenth-century women writers—for example, Elizabeth Drew Stoddard, Rebecca Harding Davis, or Margaret Fuller—in order to demonstrate a number of points: that women were indeed producing substantial writing in an otherwise male-dominated writers' marketplace, that women writers were frequently depicting the unique experiences of female characters from distinctly feminist viewpoints, and that such women writers and their works have been silenced through the hegemony of patriarchal criticism.

Of these concerns, only the last one really applies to Parker's case. Early in her career she cracked the publishing market: *Vanity Fair* began publishing her poetry in 1914, and her first published story appeared in H. L. Mencken and George Nathan's *The Smart Set* in 1922. Once established, Parker was sought after on the basis of her ability and popularity, and she has never been completely swept into the dustbin of literary amnesia, as was the case for many nineteenth- and early-twentieth-century women writers. While Parker's fiction is filled with female characters, many of whom dominate the center of their respective stories, her work is generally devoid of the approaches to women's experiences that often appeal first to academic feminist critics: the kind of overt feminist agenda associated with the fiction of numerous later twentieth-century women writers such as Toni Morrison or Alice Walker, or the depiction of a successful (or doomed) awakening of a female protagonist, or a celebration of a community of independent, self-sustaining women. Nonetheless, in her interview for the *Paris Review* in the 1950s, Parker labeled herself a feminist who had been active in the women's movement since the time when New York City "was scarcely safe from buffaloes."[4] But in the same passage she criticizes the lack of artistry in the works of women writers such as Edna Ferber and Kathleen Norris and condemns their proliferation as a result of the very struggle for equality in which she claims to have been a participant. During most of her career she seemed indifferent, even adverse, to placing herself within a tradition of women's writing: in 1929, while working on a novel she would never complete, she wrote in a letter to Alexander Woollcott, "Dear God, please make me stop writing like a woman. For Jesus Christ's sake, amen."[5] Finally, Parker has probably missed out on a warm embrace from feminist critics in part because, after all, she has been dead only since 1967, and while her reputation has languished, the fact that it has never been firmly established or dismissed places her in a weird nebula where she seems to need neither reevaluation nor rescue—when actually she needs both.

Parker's work has regularly been dismissed, moreover, on the basis of triviality, in content, style, and technique, usually with the implication underlying such a critique that the content, style, and technique of her contemporary male short-story writers are hallmarks of substance and depth. Apparently bullfights, African safaris, washed-up expatriate writers in France, and ill-starred southern gentry and field hands serve as more suitable subjects for fiction than the lives of middle-and upper-class white urbanites, usually women. Certainly Parker's subject matter does not encompass a wide range of social classes or situations, but the same could be said of Faulkner's subject matter, or Fitzgerald's or just about any writer's, depending on the slant from which it is described. Instead of merely cataloguing the number of different topics an author chooses to deal with, a better way to consider an author's subject matter might be to study the methods in which it is presented. Parker's female characters rarely lead lives beyond the role defined by patriarchy (mother, wife, mistress, housekeeper, secretary), and their abiding concerns often revolve around the status of a relationship with a man. These women are frequently the victims of the roles created for them by society, but Parker's stories do not deal solely with the oppression of women: Parker's male characters are no less victims of their own circumstances. More importantly, all of Parker's characters, male or female, usually create their predicaments in the same degree to which other forces contribute to those predicaments.

However, Parker usually portrays her characters within only a brief time frame (the consequences of which will be discussed shortly), frequently avoids giving them distinguishing idiosyncratic characteristics, and often uses the speaking passages of a central character to reveal characterization. Indeed, Parker develops many of her typical female characters through their speech rather than through narrative exposition—reflecting Rosalind Coward's assertion that in the twentieth century "above all, the female protagonist has become the speaking sex"—and in all of Parker's stories mentioned earlier (except "Here We Are"), the speech or writing of the female protagonist *is* the story.[6] Parker clearly intends to work with surfaces, an intention that is neither accidental nor a botched attempt to analyze the motivation of her characters. Paula Treichler has observed that a "language-centered analysis" of Parker's stories is crucial due to their stylistic intricacy.[7] Unfortunately, a result of Parker's constant stylistic repetition of action and language, coupled with the naturally repetitive cadences of a character's pervasive speaking voice, has often been the critical charge of shallowness. The point of so many Parker stories, however, is to portray *shallowness itself* as it occurs in the lives of her characters. In fact, Parker's technique of repeating action and repeating language creates an innovative fictional effect of perpetual motion in many of her stories that would seem to extend the lives of her characters beyond the beginning and ending boundary of each story.

Much of this sense of perpetual shallowness is achieved through the time frame established in Parker's stories. Arthur F. Kinney has described her fiction as "radically condensed," and it is especially in her more original short stories (such as those mentioned earlier) that the shortened time frame contributes to the thematic effect of superficiality.[8] Indeed, Jean Pickering has suggested that all the elements of a short story, including "structure, theme, characterization, language . . . are influenced by [their] particular relation to time."[9] The dancer in "The Waltz" thinks her poisonous thoughts only throughout the duration of a single waltz; the voice of the soliloquizer in "A Telephone Call" speaks as long as it takes to mull through six pages of stream-of-consciousness thinking; and the newlyweds in "Here We Are" converse for about half an hour while their train approaches New York City. "From the Diary of a New York

Lady" follows, obviously, an altogether different structure with its use of daily entries and therefore a different kind of time frame, yet the tone of each entry gives the sense of hasty composition, in part through the capsule references to repeated and similar activities. In each case the time frame of action is severely limited, and consequently all aspects of the respective stories are affected, the most significant being characterization. None of the characters in these stories achieves the kind of full development that critics, and readers, often seek. As a matter of fact, none of the characters in these four particular stories is even given a name.

But Parker is not attempting to dissect the psyches of these characters; her intent seems closer to that of Edgar Allan Poe with his nameless, deranged characters in their dramatic monologues, such as "The Tell-Tale Heart" or "The Cask of Amontillado," in which the speakers relate their involvement in gruesome murders, often detailing physical action with sordid precision, but rarely pausing to examine the motivation behind their actions or their confession. The tales horrify as much because of their gruesome content as because of the superficially conceived tone of the narrators' voices. Parker's stories do not rely on Gothic horror to draw out the psychological shallowness of her characters, but her characters in these four stories do share with Poe's characters that anonymity, in both name and personality, which heightens what is surely one of the author's thematic concerns about the horror of shallow self-understanding.

The short time frame in each of Parker's stories does not allow for complex psychological development of the characters. Even though, in the case of three of these stories, the central character does all the speaking, how much depth can a character believably reveal within one fifteen-minute speech, especially when the speech is permeated with a single, obsessive concern?

Valerie Shaw has warned about the problem of character free will, and consequently of characterization itself, inherent to the "tightly controlled quality" of the short-story form:

> [it reduces] the possibility of showing characters making free, let alone complicated choices. Willpower often seems to have become the privilege of the author alone: paradoxically, [her] desire to give a story inevitability may have the effect of depriving [her] characters of any self-determining power, making them appear to be locked in a structure which has been specially designed to fate them to passivity and sameness.[10]

For authors who intend to portray highly developed, individual characters (and for the readers who expect to read about them), Shaw's caveat certainly carries weight, but a conception of the importance of this kind of character development excludes the uses (the necessity, even) of other types of characterization. In fact, Shaw's statement implies that an author has some sort of responsibility for creating characters with absolute free will. (Here, one might remember that when questioned whether his characters take on independent realities of their own during the process of creation, Vladimir Nabokov snorted in negation and referred to his characters as "galley slaves."[11]) What about an author who wants to make a deterministic point about "passivity and sameness"?

While Parker's characters are not necessarily at the mercy of overwhelmingly deterministic forces and consequently do not come across as helpless pawns in some inscrutable chess game, her characters do often seem limited in their choices. But such limitations come about through an inability to rise above or see beyond obsession and pettiness. The soliloquizer in "A Telephone Call" could attempt to move on with her life by simply moving beyond the range of her telephone. The dancer in "The Waltz" could decline another dance. The newlyweds in "Here We Are" could go to bed and get past the initial trauma of sexuality. The socialite in "From the Diary of a New York Lady" could surely look beyond the color of her fingernail polish.

Of course, it is Parker herself who does not allow these characters to make such substantial changes in their actions and personalities: superficiality is the aim of these Parker stories, but superficiality for a purpose. Not only are the characters illustrative targets of a satiric ideal of shallowness, but they also give the impression of eternal sameness, and in this way, Parker's stories are often every bit as horrifying as Poe's stories because they imply an everlasting repetition of superficiality and emptiness; in a Poe story the gory action has already occurred in the past and is being remembered, or even confessed, for unexplained reasons by one of the nameless participants, whereas Parker's stories imply ongoing action (indeed, the events of "The Waltz" and "A Telephone Call" unfold in the present tense while the first-person narrators speak) that will continue forever. In other words, these four Parker stories resist closure. Of course, open-ended fiction is hardly a revolutionary construction, but the open-endedness of Parker's stories results not so much from a range of ambivalent interpretations—Parker's satiric intentions are not so subtle as to be inscrutable; rather, the open-endedness of her stories comes about through the implication of continuing, repetitive action.

Parker achieves this implication through both the content of the stories and the stylistic device of repetition. In "Here We Are," the greatest portion of Parker's satire is given over to the unstated anticipation of the sexual consummation of the honeymoon night, with the husband barely concealing his squirming expectation with the verbal tic "I mean—I mean" whenever his statements veer too closely to references about the approaching night. Parker also takes aim at petty marital discord—in this case, taken to the extreme since the couple has been married for only a few hours. Their entire conversation is a study in vacuity: they discuss how the bridesmaids looked, they discuss the wife's new hat, they discuss the millions of marriages that must have occurred concurrently with theirs, they discuss how quickly the day has passed. And they quarrel. The wife accuses the husband of disliking her family, disliking her new hat, making eyes at one of the bridesmaids; the husband accuses the wife of wanting to marry an old boyfriend, misunderstanding him. Does this unlikable couple suffer merely from a case of honeymoon jitters? Hardly, since readers discover from the wife seven pages into the bickering, after the husband exclaims, "Hell, honey lamb, this is our honeymoon. What's the matter?" that "[they] used to squabble a lot when [they] were going together and then engaged and everything, but [she] thought everything would be so different as soon as [they] were married."[12] Clearly this couple has been quarreling since they met; Parker shows them at a brief, key point in time in their relationship—during the honeymoon, the official beginning of the new life together—still quarreling. At the end of the story, the husband's mind is still focused on the approaching sexual activity, and Parker concludes with a final repetition of the husband's verbal tic as well as another more subtle repetition in the closing words of both characters:

> "Pretty soon we'll be regular old married people. I mean, I mean, in a few minutes we'll be getting in to New York, and then we'll be going to the hotel, and then everything will be all right. I mean—well, look at us! Here we are married! Here we are!"
> "Yes, here we are," she said. "Aren't we?" (134)

The final line of the story would seem to freeze the action of these two characters as well as of the entire story, in part because it is the final line, but also because the words refer to a specific juncture in time and space, both literal and figurative: end of train journey/ beginning of wedded life; train compartment/temple of marriage. Yet Parker's construction of the story, with its repetition of content and speaking style in this couple's dialogue, implies continued and continuing motion, so that the final printed statements of the husband and wife, spoken by each ("Here we are"), are really just another step in the series of actions and speeches that Parker has constructed for this pair to send them into their fictional eternity—especially since the concluding statements also serve as the very first words that Parker allows these characters to speak in the opening of the story.

Parker's characters never become aware that they are doomed to a fictional infinity of superficiality; the newlyweds in "Here We Are" might delude themselves momentarily into expecting a peaceful future, but readers know better from Parker's depiction of them. The socialite whose diary is reproduced in "From the Diary of a New York Lady" has no power of self-criticism whatsoever, and it is especially in this highly stylized story that Parker uses repetition of content to underscore both a projection into eternity for this character and a damnation of her shallowness. This story shares a structural similarity with Charlotte Perkins Gilman's *The Yellow Wallpaper* in its use of diary entries of a nameless female protagonist who has lost control of her life. Gilman's protagonist is fully aware of her powerlessness while consigned by her doctor-husband to a "rest" therapy in the country; the grim irony of the story asserts itself at the end when the diarist, confident that she has regained control of her sanity, has actually lost it.[13]

In contrast, Parker's protagonist never seems aware that she lacks control of her life: the emptiness of her daily life is a secret shared by Parker and her readers. During five consecutive nights she cannot decide which dress to wear to the opening night of five new plays with titles like *Never Say Good Morning, Everybody Up,* and *Run Like a Rabbit* (even these titles imply continuing movement), and then flits off to parties (always escorted by some flunky named Ollie Martin, after failing to land one of her "new cute numbers") at which the same Hungarian musicians in green coats perform, and where the same cutup named Stewie Hunter always vies for attention by leading the band with a lamp or a fork or some other outrageous pseudobaton. Each morning she recovers from a hangover, sends messages to unreceptive "new numbers," and worries about the condition of her fingernails. The story has no conclusion in any traditional sense: the entries merely stop after the fifth day, having presented a sequence of actions that is a representative slice of a much longer sequence of the same actions. The interest in such a story lies not in finding out what ultimately happens to the diarist because there is never any sense of "ultimateness" or climax, as in the more traditionally plotted *The Yellow Wallpaper,* where a climax occurs when the diarist finally disintegrates psychologically. Rather, the interest in Parker's story lies in discerning the pattern of the diarist's life and realizing that the pattern never changes in substance or direction, only in detail and sequence (e.g., What new calamity will befall the diarist's fingernails? When will the diarist again damn Miss Rose, her manicurist?). Parker has set this woman into a literal perpetual motion, like a top, consigned night after night to spinning through the emptiest of lives with the most vacuous of companions.

Parker's masterful use of repetition and variation distinguishes a story like "From the Diary of a New York Lady," but it also serves to propel the perpetually repeating superficiality beyond the final line of the story. Parker uses the same technique in her best soliloquy, "A Telephone Call," in which a female speaker agonizes while waiting for a male acquaintance to call. She begins countless sentences with the word "maybe," as she runs through every conceivable possibility for why he has not called. She carries on a one-sided dialogue with God, asking, begging, pleading, threatening—working through every rhetorical device available in order to arrive at an understanding about the man's apparent rejection of her. And she counts. In the second paragraph of the story she decides that the phone might ring by the time she has counted to five hundred by fives; she makes it to fifty before reverting to her stream-of-consciousness meanderings. Nearly halfway through the story she decides to count again to prove that a supplication to God will bring about results by the time she reaches five hundred by fives; she makes it to fifty-five. At the very end of the story she decides to count a third time, and the soliloquizer is last heard at the number thirty-five followed by an ellipsis. That she would reach five hundred is doubtful considering her previous attempts, and the ellipsis is certainly Parker's way of dooming this anonymous, speaking neurotic to endless repetitions of the same cycle.

Because of its content (as indicated by the title), "The Waltz" best illustrates Parker's use of structural repetition in conjunction with a story's content to fling a character into everlasting motion. In "The Waltz" a female character traps herself into dancing with a man: she warmly accepts the dance invitation (the words of which Parker represents in italics) and then launches into an interior diatribe against her partner and his dancing ability. This woman has the opportunity, in the first place, to decline the dance invitation, but she only exacerbates her unhappiness when she coyly blames herself (in the words she speaks to her partner) after he stomps on her feet, inwardly cursing him. To herself she claims the dance has lasted "thirty-five years" and envisions being trapped with her partner "throughout eternity" (50). Yet she agrees to dance throughout the band's encore, and in the story's final paragraph, Parker leaves the woman speaking to her partner:

> Oh, they've stopped, the mean things. They're not going to play any more. Oh, darn. Oh, do you think they would? Do you really think so, if you gave them twenty dollars? Oh, that would be lovely. And look, do tell them to play this same thing. I'd simply adore to go on waltzing. (51)

Despite nearly five pages of inward griping, the speaker has consigned herself to another waltz, one of which has already dissolved the boundary of her perception of time. When she falsely declares that she would "simply adore to go on waltzing" it is clear that Parker has granted that wish in terms of the structure of the story: as the story concludes, the speaker will be seen whirling off into her fictional eternity on a dance floor with a klutz, sharing the fate of perpetual, superficial motion that Parker visits upon her other characters.

Each of these stories exhibits Parker's skillful ability to use the structural device of repetition in a unique way, producing stories that embody endless motion through an overall structuring uncommon to most American short stories. While this aspect of her stories represents one contribution to the short-story form, it also indicates a useful approach to her work for feminist scholars: despite Parker's own prayer that she not "write like a woman," the lack of climax in many of her stories, her abiding use of stylistic repetition, and the open-ended nature of the action of her stories all point to what some critics view as a distinctive women's way of writing. This assessment complements the arguments of Kathryn Allen Rabuzzi, who maintains that the repetitive nature of the traditional domestic existence of women has influenced the way women writers structure their work: the progressiveness of the Aristotelian plot is replaced by a structure favoring stasis and cyclicity.[14] With the structural spin that she initiates for most of her characters, Parker may have been writing "like a woman" whether she wanted to or not.

In any case, Parker rarely seems to have much sympathy for her characters, male or female; certainly they do not seem to realize that their personalities have trapped them in an eternal spin. Of course, it is Parker herself who orchestrates the action of each story and creates the participating personalities, and it is she who does not allow her characters to realize what has happened to them. The fate that Parker devises for her characters might be expressed in the same words that clergyman and theologian Jonathan Edwards used to warn his congregation of everlasting damnation: ". . . there will be no End to this exquisite horrible Misery: when you look forward, you shall see a long Forever, a boundless Duration before you, which will swallow up your Thoughts, and amaze your Soul; and you will absolutely despair of ever having any Deliverance, any End, any Mitigation, any Rest at all . . ."[15] Unlike Edwards's God, however, Parker gives her characters no warning, no chance for repentance and redemption. Instead, she has created the particular situations with her own distinctive fictional technique of repetition, demonstrating Nancy Walker's assertion that American female humorists create "forms suited to their own lives and needs" to satirize superficiality in a number of its manifestations, and to condemn such superficiality to eternal, repeating perpetual motion.[16]

NOTES

1. F. Scott Fitzgerald, *The Letters of F. Scott Fitzgerald,* ed. Andrew Turnbull (New York: Scribner, 1963), 25, 215.

2. Brendan Gill, introduction to *The Portable Dorothy Parker,* by Dorothy Parker (New York: Viking, 1973), xxvii, xxii, xxii.

3. Mordecai Richler, introduction to *The Best of Modern Humor,* ed. Mordecai Richler (New York: Knopf, 1983); Sandra Gilbert and Susan Gubar *No Man's Land: The Place of the Woman Writer in the Twentieth Century, Vol: 1, The War of the Words* (New Haven and London: Yale University Press, 1988), and *vol. 2, Sexchanges* (New Haven and London: Yale University Press, 1989); Maurice Duke, Jackson R. Bryer, and M. Thomas Inge, eds., *American Women Writers: Bibliographical Essays* (Westport, CT: Greenwood Press, 1983).

4. Dorothy Parker, interview by Marion Capron in *Writers at Work: The "Paris Review" Interviews,* ed. Malcolm Cowley (New York: Viking, 1958), 77.

5. Marion Meade, *Dorothy Parker: What Fresh Hell Is This?* (New York: Penguin, 1989), 203.

6. Rosalind Coward, "The True Story of How I Became My Own Person," in *The Feminist Reader: Essays in Gender & the Politics of Literary Criticism,* ed. Catherine Belsey and Jane Moore (Cambridge, MA: Blackwell, 1989), 35–47.

7. Paula A. Treichler, "Verbal Subversions in Dorothy Parker: 'Trapped Like a Trap in a Trap.'" *Language and Style* 13.4 (Fall 1980): 46–61.

8. Arthur F. Kinney, *Dorothy Parker* (Boston: Twayne, 1978), 143.

9. Jean Pickering, "Time and the Short Story" in *Rereading the Short Story,* ed. Clare Hanson (New York: St. Martin's, 1989), 45–54.

10. Valerie Shaw, *The Short Story: A Critical Introduction* (London: Longman, 1983), 208.

11. Vladimir Nabokov, *Strong Opinions* (New York: Vintage International, 1990), 95.

12. Dorothy Parker, *The Portable Dorothy Parker* (New York: Viking, 1973), 131; subsequent references will be cited by page number parenthetically in the text.

13. Charlotte Perkins Gilman, *The Yellow Wallpaper* (1899; repr., New York: Feminist Press, 1973).

14. Kathryn Allen Rabuzzi, *The Sacred and the Feminine: Toward a Theology of Housework* (New York: Seabury, 1982), 163–67.

15. Jonathan Edwards, "Sinners in the Hands of an Angry God," in *American Sermons: The Pilgrims to Martin Luther King, Jr.*, ed. Michael Warner (New York: Library of America, 1999), 361.

16. Nancy A. Walker, *A Very Serious Thing: Women's Humor and American Culture* (Minneapolis: University of Minnesota Press, 1988), 12.

Material Girls in the Jazz Age:
Dorothy Parker's "Big Blonde" as an Answer to Anita Loos's *Gentlemen Prefer Blondes*

Rhonda S. Pettit

BOTH ANITA LOOS AND DOROTHY PARKER ADVANCED THEIR WRITING CA-
reers in the 1920s, a decade that saw the rise of a consumer society
and the loosening of sexual mores. Historian T. J. Jackson Lears has
documented how the modernist forms of advertising sold an image
instead of a product and, particularly where women were concerned, "promised fake liberation through consumption." At the
same time, a sexual paradigm shift away from the procreation emphasis of Victorian morality was occurring. A demand for sexual satisfaction led to an increase in sexual experimentation outside of
marriage. To paraphrase Steven Seidman, romantic love was becoming eroticized.[1] No image suggests this combination of conspicuous
consumption and sexuality more than the flapper. Shorter, looser
garments replaced corsets and crinoline; bobbed hair replaced
buns; cigarettes and gin flasks replaced the parasol; cosmetics rede-
fined the natural face. Her slender, youthful image, captured first by
F. Scott Fitzgerald and then by artist John Held, Jr., illustrated articles and advertisements in the *New Yorker, Life, Vanity Fair, Vogue*, and
Harper's Bazaar, among others.

Loos and Parker, both born in 1893 and in their thirties during
the 1920s, were too old to be members of the flapper generation per
se, but they had plenty to say about it. Two years after the publication of Fitzgerald's 1920 volume *Flappers and Philosophers*, Parker preserves the flapper's disruptive reputation in her sequence of poems,
"Figures in Popular Literature," a portion of which reads: "Her girlish ways may make a stir, / Her manners cause a scene, / But there
is no more harm in her / Than in a submarine." A year later, Parker
considers them a passing fad; "Where did the flappers disappear?"
forms the refrain and envoi in "Ballade of a Not Insupportable
Loss."[2] Loos, on the other hand, takes a different approach in *Gentlemen Prefer Blondes*, a 1925 novel whose intended satire not only

backfires but, as I will argue, prompts a fictional response from Parker in her 1929 short story, "Big Blonde."[3]

Loos's novel is written in the form of a diary penned by Lorelei Lee, the prototype of the gold-digging, "dizzy" or "dumb blonde" stereotype that has remained in currency for most of this century. Lorelei describes the events leading up to her marriage, many of them involving a friend who, significantly, is characterized as a brunette named Dorothy.[4] Although she has bobbed hair, Lorelei does not consider herself a flapper; she is instead "an old-fashioned girl," one who doesn't say exactly what she thinks, as does Dorothy (106). But Lorelei does think of herself and her life in economic terms. Recalling the attacks on her character by Mr. Bartlett, the district attorney who unsuccessfully prosecuted her for shooting Mr. Jennings, Lorelei notes, "A gentleman never pays for those things but a girl always pays" (54). As a single woman living in a time when being financially independent meant working in low-paying labor or clerical jobs, Lorelei's quest is to make the gentleman—any gentleman—pay.[5] She uses flirtation, tears, and sexual blackmail to manipulate a series of men into providing her the best in jewels, travel, and champagne.

Loos's introduction to a 1963 edition of *Gentlemen Prefer Blondes* reveals the novel's origins as well as her urban, elitist attitudes and intention regarding the narrative. She based her fiction on observed fact: H. L. Mencken, a close friend of hers, at times paid more attention to uneducated but attractive blondes than he did to Loos, an educated, attractive brunette. Loos set out to satirize the "witless blonde," and drawing on Mencken's bias against provincial America, used Arkansas as her protagonist's place of origin because she "wanted Lorelei to be a symbol of the lowest possible mentality of our nation" (13). Lorelei's rise from poverty and her ignorance regarding history, culture, politics, and current events become the focus of Loos's ridicule. Therefore, Lorelei assumes sophistication as she reveals a number of "half-brow" preferences and assumptions: she prefers shopping to reading Benvenuto Cellini, Coty and Cartiers to Place Vendome; she thinks books by Joseph Conrad are about ocean travel, and that "bird life is the highest form of civilization" (29).[6] Her diary is a catalog of misused diction, improper grammar, wrong or missing punctuation, and misspelled words.[7] But significantly, Lorelei knows how to spell "chandelier" (24), "champagne" (27), "emerald bracelet" (22), "pearls" (39), "diamond tiara" (59–60), "the Ritz" (79), and other words associated with upper-class acquisition, as well as the names of the men who buy her such gifts.

Given the cultural context in which Lorelei must survive—a culture that values money and the acquisition of material goods without providing women the opportunity to achieve them on their own—she is highly intelligent. Lorelei wants material comforts without the confines of a marriage that would deter her continued acquisition and her ultimate goal of becoming a film star. This process leads her to invert one of capitalism's primary tenets. Men, rather than the material goods they provide, embody an accelerated, built-in obsolescence. Most of these men, much older than Lorelei, are content to have her as a showpiece, to parade her in the jewels and clothing they have bought for her. By using an unmarried protagonist, Loos (perhaps unwittingly) modernizes a turn-of-the-century figure found in the novels of Edith Wharton: that of the married, leisure-class woman whose primary function is to display the wealth of her husband.[8] Unlike her married predecessors, however, Lorelei is aware of her commodity status, and she uses this knowledge to continue the acquisition of her own commodities. Falling in love, she declares, is dangerous for a woman, particularly if the lover in question cannot serve her financially: "When a girl really enjoys being with a gentleman, it puts her to a disadvantage and no real good can come of it" (63).

Another example of Lorelei's intelligence can be found in the ironic subtext of her refrain, "Fate keeps on happening," for Lorelei leaves nothing to fate. She plans and executes a number of escapades, including assault, blackmail, espionage, theft, and pseudo-adultery before she finally marries Henry Spoffard, a rich, self-righteous man who agrees to launch her film career but who will more or less leave her alone. The novel thus deromanticizes love, and at the same time offers the classic romantic ending: poor girl marries rich man. "Failure" is not a word in Lorelei's vocabulary; neither is "age." Outside of flashbacks, the diary covers less than a year in Lorelei's life; the novel's vision of her aligns success with perpetual youth and beauty.

Unlike its protagonist, *Gentlemen Prefer Blondes* as a satiric novel has its moment of failure. Once the acquisitive economy that is both the subtext and context of the novel is recognized, the character of Lorelei turns out to be far more intelligent than the real-life blondes Loos set out to satirize. Loos fails to create in her protagonist an object of ridicule; Lorelei is far too successful to warrant our sympathy or derision. Instead, her supposed ignorance becomes the mechanism through which a number of cultural pillars and practices are ridiculed; here is where the novel triumphs as satire.

We have already seen how Lorelei makes a mockery of marriage as a romantic convention; in fact, none of the novel's marriages contain romantic love. The value and forms of education also draw fire. Readers may define Lorelei's adventure as a quest for marriage, or money, or happiness, but Lorelei defines it as a quest for education. The diary opens with Gus Eisman the Button King who, as Lorelei tells us, "is the gentleman who is interested in educating me, so of course he is always coming down to New York to see how my brains have improved since the last time" (20). Gus convinces her to keep a diary, read books he sends her, and travel, all under the guise of "educating a girl," when in fact he is trying to keep her occupied while he is out of town (20). Lorelei keeps her diary, but she avoids the books that bore her, and finds it "much more educational" to shop or talk with a small-time bootlegger than to visit the art museums of Munich (51, 114). She equates education with monetary rather than mental assets, as her critique of Dorothy makes clear: "But Dorothy really does not care about her mind and I always scold her because she does nothing but waste her time by going around with gentlemen who do not have anything, when Eddie Goldmark of the Goldmark Films is really quite wealthy and can make a girl delightful presents" (43). Later in the novel, education and intelligence, insofar as they are represented by one of the great minds of the twentieth century, as well as psychoanalysis are deflated when Lorelei meets Freud and disproves his theories. By the time Lorelei closes her diary with a chapter titled, "Brains Are Really Everything," a life of luxury is at hand, aligning education with the acquisition of wealth.

Loos also takes aim at male vulnerability to female beauty. Older men, such as Sir Francis Beekman, rich men such as Gus Eisman and Henry Spoffard, and powerful men in the form of judges, prosecutors, and police officers find themselves seduced by Lorelei's powers. Even a Parisian pair of con men are outconned by Lorelei as they try to retrieve the $7,500 diamond tiara given to Lorelei, after her careful planning and manipulation, by Sir Francis Beekman. The tiara, with its crownlike appearance, provides a fitting symbol for Lorelei's power over men. In addition to male vulnerability, several institutions are embodied in this ridicule—British aristocracy and royalty, capitalism, the American judicial system, and the American legal system.

Feminism and families fare no better. As suggested by the diamond tiara, equality with men would be, for Lorelei, a step down. She pities Gerry Lamson, who felt pressured to marry a suffragette he doesn't love—"she was a suffragette and asked him to marry her, so what could he do?" (29). And Lorelei's future sister-in-law, having found a certain amount of autonomy during World War I, is now an anomaly at home:

> So it seems that Henry's sister has never been the same since the war, because she never had on a man's collar and a necktie until she drove an ambulants in the war, and now they cannot get her to take them off. Because ever since the armistice Henry's sister seems to have the idea that regular womens clothes are effiminate. So Henry's sister seems to think of nothing but either horses or automobiles. . . . Henry's sister does not go to church because Henry's sister always likes to spend every Sunday in the garage taking their Ford farm truck apart and putting it back together again. Henry says that what the war did to a girl like his sister is really worse than the war itself. ([*sic*]; 144–45)

This portrait of Henry's sister, of course, is not one of a political being, but is merely a caricature, a popular image of a feminist. At the same time, she seems odd in light of the conventional standards of feminine appearance and behavior that Lorelei uses to her advantage. By placing these two figures together, Loos unwittingly underscores an important point: In a market economy focused on consumers of youth and beauty, feminism is a hard sell. Significantly, Henry's sister disappears both literally and figuratively from the novel; neither feminist nor conventionally feminine, her lack of identity symbolizes the waning of feminist political activity after the passage of the nineteenth amendment.

Other members of the family prove to be hypocrites. Beneath the twining veils of religious piety and old money, Henry's mother is a closet lush, his father a closet letch. Henry, a self-proclaimed moral censor, anxiously spends "all his time looking at things that spoil people's morals" (106). Lorelei concludes: "Life was really to [*sic*] short to spend it in being proud of your family, even if they did have a great deal of money" (145). The family, for Lorelei, is a kind of bank employing clerks and tellers no one else would hire.

Finally, even the diary form itself, which in this case involves an actual author and a fictional author, is ridiculed. The novel forces the question: Which author is in control? While *Gentlemen Prefer Blondes* contains more wisdom than perhaps Loos intended, it withholds information and draws attention to its gaps, instead of providing intimate disclosures we have come to associate with diary writing. Although Lorelei claims "to believe in the old addage, Say it in writing," her diary is significantly vague about whether she is sexually active or merely sexually promising ([*sic*]; 126). In her account of her trial, Lorelei tells us Mr. Bartlett "called me names that I would not even put in my diary" (48). She refuses to provide the details of

the government secrets she later learns from Bartlett, not out of regard for her country's security, but ·because they are "to [*sic*] long
to put in my diary" (48). Regarding her conversations with Gerry
Lamson and Freud, Lorelei also admits to saying "things I would not
even put in my diary" (29, 126). Lorelei appears morally tainted by
implication, by what is *not* said, a strategy Loos possibly felt was necessary to get her work published in 1924, although Edna St. Vincent
Millay, for example, was publishing sexually frank poems at that
time. These omissions also can be read as Lorelei's attempt to protect herself, to maintain the stance of innocence that is so useful in
her acquisition strategies—the very strategies that undercut Loos's
intended satire. If so, we are left to believe that the fictional author
wrote this diary self-consciously, with an eye toward publication and
payment. Even the rules regarding signification and meaning are
questioned. Lorelei's sentence-level errors provide one challenge to
writing norms; her rhetoric, characterized by a lack of transitional
phrases, provides another. Most of Lorelei's sentences start with "I
mean" and "So," implying that Lorelei is unable to connect her
thoughts logically, or to render complex relationships among events
and concepts. Yet these limitations do not prevent Lorelei from telling her story clearly, thereby seducing a reading public. On one
level, the economy-conscious, fictional author of *Gentlemen Prefer
Blondes* employs strategies that outwit the actual author.

If the application of an economic context and subtext to *Gentlemen Prefer Blondes* seems like a deliberate misreading, we should remember that this novel has a history of inviting misreadings. *Harper's
Bazaar* published the novel serially in 1924. When *Gentlemen Prefer
Blondes* came out in book form in 1925, single women were reading
it as a serious how-to manual, and the book went through forty-five
editions and thirteen translations; it would later inspire two stage
productions and two films. In her 1963 introduction, Loos acknowledges the economic success of her novel, but dismisses any economic readings of her novel as "strip[ping] *Gentlemen Prefer Blondes*
of all its fun" (13). However, the economic context embedded in
her story cannot be denied. Loos's ridicule became a recipe for survival because in a time of limited economic opportunities for
women, Lorelei always won, and those she vanquished continued to
love her. Youth, beauty, and money never fade into age or poverty.

It is highly likely that Dorothy Parker, whose circle of Algonquin
Round Table friends included Loos's husband John Emerson
(though not Loos), would have read *Gentlemen Prefer Blondes*, if not
as a novel, then in its magazine form. She was an avid reader and,
located among the New York literati, she was constantly exposed to

the cultural trends and celebrities of the period. At times Parker could assume a cultural elitism similar to that of Loos; "Poem in the American Manner," for example, mocks provincial narrow-mindedness using a rural dialect, and the narrator of her short story "The Waltz" refers to her inept dance partner as someone "who grew up in hill country, and never had no larnin'." Yet Parker spent most of her time satirizing the nouveau rich and urban sophisticates she associated with, and always had a soft heart for the underdog.[9] As a child, she sympathized with the workers in her father's garment factory. She sided with striking waiters and actors in the teens, marched in protest of the Sacco-Vanzetti execution in the twenties, and organized the Screen Writers Guild and Anti-Fascist League in the thirties. Stories like "Arrangement in Black and White" and "Clothe the Naked" address racism and economic issues; "Soldiers of the Republic" and "Who Might Be Interested" sympathize with the republicans during the Spanish Civil War. In a 1939 article for *New Masses*, Parker passionately declared that poetry should move away from the personal lyric and address social issues: "Now the poet speaks not just for himself but for all of us."[10] Given this history of compassion, it seems likely that Parker, separated from her first husband and at times struggling to make financial ends meet, would cringe at the ease with which Lorelei Lee made her way in the world.

"Big Blonde," with its blend of sex and economics, first appeared in the *Bookman* in February 1929, eight months before the stock market crash in October of that year. The story shares several characteristics with *Gentlemen Prefer Blondes* before taking them in new directions. It seems to have an autobiographical component—Hazel Morse, the blond protagonist, attempts suicide, as did Parker on more than one occasion. Unfortunately, this incident, combined with Hazel's drinking and her sentimental love for animals, has led biographers to put too much emphasis on the autobiographical elements of the story.[11] Yet Hazel's physical features (blond, full-figured), the types of men she associates with (middle-class, traveling businessmen, not writers and sophisticates), and her lack of an occupation after marriage and divorce remain significantly outside the realm of Parker's life. While these could be considered masking devices, the story reflects not so much Parker's life as the life of a woman located on the underside of Roaring Twenties' glamour. The serious nature of the suicide attempt in "Big Blonde" provides a crucial point of departure from Loos's novel.

Hazel exhibits the same kind of "good time" behavior with a number of men as does Lorelei, and is initially successful:

Men liked you because you were fun, and when they liked you they took
you out, and there you were. So, and successfully, she was fun. She was a
good sport. Men liked a good sport. (187)

Hazel never questions these male-derived values or the possible consequences of her actions. Like Loos, Parker associates this behavior
with a particular *type* of woman, though not necessarily a flapper:
"[Hazel's] ideas, or, better, her acceptances, ran right along with
those of the other substantially built blondes in whom she found her
friends" (187). The generalized types in both narratives seem to
reify an offensive stereotype—the dumb blonde—while at the same
time using it to critique the culture that gave rise to it. Parker might
stand accused of "borrowing" a successful formula from Loos, but
since "Big Blonde" is not a satire, it seems more likely that she was
creating a textual marker that would tie her narrative to Loos's
novel.

Parties, drinking, and marriage enter into both narratives, but the
progression of these elements differs. Rather than end with a marriage, "Big Blonde" begins with one. Hazel is a full-figured dress
model in her early thirties when she meets and marries Herbie
Morse. Clothing, however, is not a symbol of material acquisition for
Hazel as it is for Lorelei. As a model, she is wearing the clothes of
others, not her own possessions. Furthermore, Hazel forces her feet
into "snub-nosed, high-heeled slippers of the shortest bearable
size," symbolic of the ill-fitting role of "good sport" (187). Married
life for Hazel constitutes a reprieve from the rigors of single life: "It
was a delight, a new game, a holiday, to give up being a good
sport. . . . To her who had laughed so much, crying was delicious"
(189). Tears had been a useful tool of manipulation for Lorelei, but
Hazel's tears for "kidnapped babies, deserted wives, unemployed
men, strayed cats," in short, for "all the sadness there is in the
world," repulsed Herbie (189). Hazel's tears are not just the weep-
ing of a sentimental figure, but a sign of dissatisfaction; as such, they
have to be controlled, and they ultimately lead to her manipulation.
Herbie eventually leaves her because she ceases to be a "good sport"
and Hazel becomes the kept woman of a series of men who insist
that she drink and remain cheerful.

As with some of Lorelei's men, Hazel's men exhibit a certain
pride of ownership. The nature of that ownership, however, differs
greatly. When Ed, the first of Hazel's men after Herbie, "had a good
year," he gave Hazel a sealskin coat, but such gifts were rare from
middle-class men with wives and children (199). The typical "gift"
was rent, food, drink, and other necessities. Where Lorelei modeled

the wealth of her admirers by wearing the jewels they gave her, Hazel the ex-model and kept woman was herself the sign of her keepers' success; she was the jewel worn, though closer to the paste Lorelei cleverly avoided than to diamonds. Hazel appealed at best to the middle-class sense of worldliness her men could afford. Ed admired Hazel's "romantic uselessness"—she refused to do any housekeep-ing—"and felt doubly a man of the world in abetting it" by hiring a maid to clean Hazel's flat (197). In exchange for this support, Hazel provides not only sexual companionship, but the more difficult of-fering of constant gaiety. "What you got to do," Ed tells her when she's depressed, "you got to be a sport and forget it" (199). All of Hazel's men agree, keeping her in a haze of alcohol and denial. The circular narration of Parker's much anthologized short story "The Waltz," with its signature phrase, "There was I, trapped. Trapped like a trap in a trap" (47), comes to mind here. The "romantic use-lessness" valued by Hazel's men becomes a trap: it contributes to Hazel's economic survival as it perpetuates the cycle of inertia that keeps her from changing her life. Other Parker characters—Camilla in "Horsie" and Mrs. Lanier in "The Custard Heart," for example— also exhibit "romantic uselessness," but without its devastating ef-fects because of their secure, high-income status.

Both Lorelei and Hazel are dependent on men for economic sur-vival, and neither of them possess deep feelings for these men. How-ever, no diamond tiara sits in Hazel's closet; Lorelei controls her men, while Hazel remains controlled by hers. Hazel's men are not Lorelei's millionaires, but traveling businessmen; Hazel's drinking is not Lorelei's champagne enhancement, but scotch whiskey's es-cape. "Alcohol kept her fat," the narrator says of Hazel (197). As pointed out earlier, Lorelei never ages in her novel, but Hazel's story adds years to her character. Older and overweight by the end of the story, Hazel takes an overdose of sleeping pills and alcohol, but does not die. Nor does her second chance at life offer new opportunities; she continues drinking. Her botched attempt at suicide and the bleak future to follow offers the harshest contrast to Lorelei's ongo-ing success.

Taken together, these two works suggest that if, indeed, gentle-men prefer blondes, they prefer them perpetually young, thin, at-tractive, and cheerful; here is where their thematic similarities end. In her attempt to ridicule her female rivals, Loos both creates a fig-ure who thrives in a capitalist economy, and ends up ridiculing many of the cultural and economic practices she means to protect from the likes of Lorelei. At the same time, the novel poses no real threat to these practices because its point of view is that of an uneducated rube who succeeds, who pulls herself up by her T-straps. Lorelei is not a "symbol of the lowest possible mentality of our nation," but a cover girl for the American Dream. Parker, long before her declaration of communist sympathies in the late 1930s, may have appreciated the novel's humor, but must have recognized as well the danger of its false depiction of female success within patriarchal capitalism. Both Lorelei and Hazel play the commodities game with their male counterparts, but Hazel, through her physical, mental, and emotional decline, portrays the high price such a game exacts on the vast majority of women who play it. "Big Blonde" answers Lorelei's well-executed but glib success by offering a much harsher critique of the commodification of women.

Not surprisingly, "Big Blonde" received more critical acclaim than commercial attention; it won the O. Henry Prize, and there was talk of a film that never materialized. Its topic was likely too real, too depressing for a Depression-era audience that took refuge in films about the Three Stooges, Spanky and Our Gang, and the triumphs of Shirley Temple. Four years later, in 1933, Parker would publish another short story, "From the Diary of a New York Lady," in which she uses the diary form and a distinctive narrative voice to ridicule the vacuous concerns of the upper class to which Lorelei Lee has ascended. The narrator is "too nervous" or "too exhausted" to read, and is focused on gossip, clothes, and the color of her fingernails. The language of her lame comment about her gossipy manicurist—"I really think that a lot of times people like that are a lot more intelligent than a lot of people" (328)—recalls Lorelei's assertion that "brains are really everything." One wonders if Parker was not continuing her critique of Lorelei, or at least of the type of success and cultural climate Lorelei ultimately represented. By then, both Parker and Loos would be in Hollywood commanding large salaries for screenplays, a decade of speakeasy living and flappers behind them.

Notes

1. T. J. Jackson Lears, "From Salvation to Self-Realization: Advertising and the Therapeutic Roots of the Consumer Culture, 1880–1930," in *The Culture of Consumption: Critical Essays in American History, 1880–1990,* ed. Richard Wightman Fox (New York: Pantheon Books, 1983), 27; Steve Seidman, *Romantic Longings: Love in America, 1830–1990* (New York: Routledge, 1991), 65–66.
2. Dorothy Parker, *Not Much Fun: The Lost Poems of Dorothy Parker,* comp. Stuart Y. Silverstein (New York: Scribner, 1996), 105, 122, 157.
3. All page references to Loos's novel and Parker's story refer to the following

texts: Anita Loos, *Gentlemen Prefer Blondes* (1925; repr., New York: Penguin Books, 1992). This edition includes Loos's introduction, but contains some minor discrepancies from the 1925 edition. Dorothy Parker, "Big Blonde," in *The Portable Dorothy Parker* (New York: Viking, 1973), 187–210.

4. Gary Carey, in *Anita Loos: A Biography* (New York: Alfred A. Knopf, 1988), claims that Dorothy is a composite of Loos and Connie Talmadge (100), but the name "Dorothy" as well as the hair color and wit she exhibits suggest Parker as well.

5. For an overview of the employment status of early-twentieth-century women, see Lois W. Banner, *Women in Modern America: A Brief History* (New York: Harcourt Brace Jovanovich, 1974), 155–60.

6. Apparently a "direct transcription" of actress Lillian Gish. See Carey, 101.

7. A *few* examples include the following: misused diction, "So when he introduced us to each other I dropped her a courtesy" (123); improper grammar, "all of we real friends of his . . ." (23); wrong or missing punctuation, "womens clubs" (35), "others ways" (111); misspelled words, "authrodox" (22), "riskay" (31), "anteek" (63), "Eyefull Tower" (79).

8. See Elizabeth Ammons, "Edith Wharton's Hard-Working Lily: *The House of Mirth* and the Marriage Market," in *The House of Mirth*, ed. Elizabeth Ammons (1905; repr., New York: Norton Critical Edition, 1990), 345–57; she refers to Thorstein Veblen's 1899 study, *The Theory of the Leisure Class: An Economic Study of Institutions*.

9. *Not Much Fun*, 122; *Portable*, 49. Parker ridicules the vacuous lifestyles of rich and pseudo-rich women in "Song of the Shirt" (*Portable*, 65–73); "Horsie" (*Portable*, 260–75); "The Custard Heart" (*Portable*, 319–27); "From the Diary of a New York Lady" (*Portable*, 328–32); "Clothe the Naked" (*Portable*, 360–69); "A Certain Lady" (Colleen Breese, ed., *Dorothy Parker Complete Stories* [New York: Penguin, 1995] 33–35); "Mrs. Carrington and Mrs. Crane" (Breese, 200–203).

10. For an account of Parker's sympathy with garment workers, see Marion Meade, *Dorothy Parker: What Fresh Hell Is This?* (New York: Villard Books, 1988), 180; for Parker's Parker's sympathy with striking actors, see her two pieces, "The New Plays—If Any," *Vanity Fair*, October 1919, 41, 112, and "The Union Forever!" *Vanity Fair*, November 1919, 37, 84; for Parker's protest against Sacco-Vanzetti executions, see Meade, 180–86; for Parker's Screen Writers Guild and Anti-Fascist League organizing, see Meade, 178–86 and 269–78. "Arrangement in Black and White," "Clothe the Naked," and "Soldiers of the Republic" are included in *The Portable*; "Who Might Be Interested" is in John Miller, ed., *Voices Against Tyranny: Writings of the Spanish Civil War* (New York: Charles Scribner & Sons, 1986), 192–97. Parker's comments about poetry are found in "Sophisticated Poetry and the Hell with It" under "Review and Comment by Dorothy Parker and Sylvia Townsend Warner," *New Masses*, 27 June 1939, 21.

11. See Arthur F. Kinney, *Dorothy Parker* (Boston: Twayne, 1978), 50; Meade, 96–97, 106–7, 110–60, 195–96, 303; and, to a lesser extent, John Keats, *You Might as Well Live: The Life and Times of Dorothy Parker* (New York: Paragon House, 1970), 146.

Textual Transmission and the Transformation of Texts: On the Dialogic Margins of Dorothy Parker's "The Waltz"

Robert D. Arner

[The waltz is] the only dance which teaches girls to think.
—George Gordon, Lord Byron, *Don Juan,* 11: lxviii

In *THE DIALOGIC IMAGINATION,* MIKHAIL BAKHTIN COMMENTS AT CONSIDerable length on the transformations in implication, inflection, and "content" that inevitably occur when any part of a text is transported from one verbal site to another contextual locale. "The speech of another," he writes in "Discourse in the Novel," perhaps the most important of the four essays that comprise his best-known and most frequently cited contribution to contemporary literary theory and critical practice, "once enclosed in context, is—no matter how accurately transmitted—always subject to certain semantic changes."

> The context embracing another's word is responsible for its dialogizing background, whose influence can be very great. . . . [O]ne may bring about fundamental changes even in another's utterance accurately quoted . . . [I]t is, for instance, very easy to make the most serious utterance comical. Another's discourse, when introduced into a speech context, enters the speech that frames it not in a mechanical bond but in a chemical union (on the semantic and emotionally expressive level); the degree of dialogized influence, one on the other, can be enormous. For this reason, we cannot, when studying the various forms for transmitting another's speech, treat any of these forms in isolation from the means for its contextualized (dialogizing) framing—the one is indissolubly linked with the other. The formulation of another's speech as well as its framing . . . both express the unitary act of dialogic interaction with that speech, a relation determining the entire nature of its transmission and all the changes in meaning and accent that take place in it during transmission.[1]

Although these remarks are meant to refer principally to limited literary quotation, to the conventional or creative introduction of language originally uttered in one context into another, often totally different milieu or to portions of texts inserted into a new literary environment—what we ordinarily mean when we speak of allusion or parody, among other literary devices—I see no reason why Bakhtin's perceptions may not be usefully extended to illuminate, along with the more familiar sorts of literary business, the whole vexed and vexing process of textual transmission. The authority and authenticity of the text have been, of course, the traditional concerns of bibliographers rather than critical theorists or interpretive critics, textual scholars who struggle to establish the "ideal" form of a given literary text but often pay little or no attention (at least until recently) to the extratextual dimensions of reading and meaning, and specifically to the influence that graphic, paratextual, and other contextual discourses might (and, indeed, must) have on the act of interpretation for many readers. The range of effects made possible by recontextualization, that is to say, relates not only to the past, to the text as received historically as the legacy of a particular author or as an example of a particular genre, but also to the immediate moment of re-presentation and the reception of the text by the reader. The false sense of modernity generated by our careful contemporary versions of John Milton's poems, for example, alters the experience of encountering this seventeenth-century author, transforming *Paradise Lost* by the addition of scholarly paraphernalia, clear, clean, and essentially invisible typefaces, illustrative covers, and pure white acid-free paper into a vastly different book from the work in its original printing. This transformation, in turn, possesses interpretive implications. It is easy to argue (and to believe) that modern textual presentations of established literary works, whatever their indisputable value to certain entirely legitimate critical pursuits and lines of inquiry, help to inspire and, indeed, may be taken to authorize the imposition of anachronistic critical methodologies on compositions that belong to the sensibility of another and quite different century and that were written out of a different set of assumptions about the purposes and functions of literature. More complexly, even the brief histories of textual reproduction that typically accompany modernized editions, by demonstrating that literary works are unstable even as material objects, can be construed both as legitimizing the most radically new and theoretically biased of critical approaches and as encouraging only those readings that acknowledge all texts as rooted in their own time and place and embedded within a specialized, historically determined and defined critical and generic discourse. As a result of its preservation and survival in and through time, the text achieves an inevitable multivocality that is different from and often just as important as a guide to understanding as any referential or ideological ambiguity we may think we have detected in the language considered in and of itself.

The relevance of these reflections to Dorothy Parker's "The Waltz," a text possessing far less literary prestige than my example of *Paradise Lost*, may at first seem remote but was suggested to me by the discovery that the second appearance of that story in a periodical publication, following its initial printing in the *New Yorker* (2 September 1933) and its subsequent inclusion (with ten other stories) in the anthology *After Such Pleasures* (1933), was in *Scholastic* magazine (23 March 1935), a publication subtitled "The American High School Weekly" and designed, as the masthead went on to declare, to introduce contemporary writing and social issues "for Supplementary Study in High School Classes in English, History, and Other Subjects." How, I began to wonder, might Parker's story have been received by such readers? How might it have been "transformed" (a word that implies a textual stability I do not at all concede) both editorially and, even more to the point, interpretively by readers who could be expected to bring to it an entirely different background of reading experiences, including texts in the same and other issues of the *Scholastic,* and a wholly different understanding of the world of dance and dating and of the nature of romantic relationships between supposedly mature men and women from those of the typical consumer of print at whom the *New Yorker* was aimed? How would the context of this "comprehensive quotation" (for want of a better term) of Parker's (to our eyes) cynical story have altered its implications, or, to be more precise, how would it have enabled the exposure of the circumstantial contingency involved in all interpretive acts? These questions are, of course, beyond any definitive answers, reading remaining a private affair between the person and the page, but because author, editor, and publisher all make an effort to be understood in a particular way to the exclusion of all other possible interpretations, because these efforts inevitably leave their traces in and around the text, and because the different styles and sorts of signs may contradict or even operate at cross purposes to each other, indulging in speculative readings inward from the margins as well as outward from the center of any literary text seems an unavoidable task confronting anyone who seeks more than a cursory understanding of a work of the creative imagination.

I mean by these rather elementary questions and observations about readers and textual reception neither to raise an entirely different (but related) critical issue—to venture unbidden and unprepared into the forbidding terrain of reader response—nor to patronize or attempt to construct profiles of the typical American high school student or teacher of the 1930s, but rather to suggest that the very different framing of "The Waltz" in the *Scholastic,* the *New Yorker,* and the short-story collection *After Such Pleasures,* frames that include both content and format (typography and graphic design) as well as other distinctive and distinguishing features of these several publications, indicates that, if anything, Bakhtin understates the subtlety, nature, importance, and range of the interpretive problems posed by the vulnerability and basic indeterminacy of all sorts of texts, whether printed, pictorial, or spoken. Most of Bakhtin's commentary seems, in fact, to regard the reader of a selected literary text as rather passive, uniformly perceptive, and constant throughout time and to emphasize re-contextualization as an authorial act, an intent to parody, quote, or allude to other texts or genres regardless of the reader's qualifications to detect what is going on in the text. I want to suggest, on the contrary, that recontextualization has its principal effect on the reader rather than on the text (though it may, of course, destabilize the text also), that parody and irony, like the infamous tree that falls in the forest, may indeed make no noise if there is no one attuned to the sound but that other forms of textual or extratextual disturbance may nevertheless come through to ears (or eyes) not otherwise accustomed to close listening (or viewing). To suggest but one of several alternate readings foregrounded by the story's appearance in *Scholastic,* for example, a reading at odds with the critical emphasis currently favored for "The Waltz" as an example of "the rhetoric of rage" (the memorable phrase is Sondra Melzer's)[2] we might contend that, rather than clarifying for readers the social and sexual oppression of the female as certain modern critics have argued, the story might have had almost the opposite effect on young males, convincing them that their culturally constructed notions of women as unpredictable, ungrateful, secretively vindictive, and impossible to please were in fact endorsed by the narrative. The story's selection as the weekly example of short fiction in *Scholastic* could only have contributed to this conviction by putting upon it, or so it must have seemed, an editorial and pedagogical seal of approval. For adolescent female readers, by contrast, the story might well have served to intensify their anxieties—not to say their terrors—about becoming a wallflower, an uncompanioned woman, or, worst of all, an old maid, a fear that, as a matter of fact, seems also to motivate the speaker of "The Waltz" to a degree that perhaps she herself may not fully understand (though Parker surely does). To these young women, the apparent reversal of the speaker's sentiments at the story's end might have come as no surprise or disappointment, though it strikes many modern readers that way, but may simply have signified what they had been told all along, that a boorish, clumsy dancing (or life) partner was better than none at all and that it was much preferable to have come late to one's senses than not to have come to them at all. For them, the story's "moral" might have seemed adequately glossed by any one of dozens of texts they might have read (or been force fed) on the subject, including the words of Lucile Marsh, a popular dance instructor of the era, who wrote in "No Girl Needs to Be a Wallflower" in *Parents* magazine,

> I have seen attractive girls develop into loud, racy adolescents in a desperate effort to escape the wallflower class. Other girls who do not succeed in getting the boys' attention, save their pride by pretending they dislike boys. One very charming girl, a college undergraduate, ran off with the first man who made love to her although she didn't care a thing about him. But . . . she had been a wallflower, and she was afraid he would be her only chance.[3]

A typical *Scholastic* in the 1930s consisted of thirty-two pages wrapped by a cover illustration and an advertisement. The masthead and contents on the first page were followed by an editorial, often illustrated with a photograph of some recent work of art, and then by the English and Social Studies Sections (about ten pages each) and a shorter Student Section of four to six pages; this began with "Sportchatter," several columns of "School News," a student-authored film review, a "Round Table," and, in the "Student Forum," the "Laughs of the Week." All commercial advertisements also appeared in this section. The English Section started with the weekly story—in 1935 "The Waltz" shared this distinction with Louis Untermeyer's "A Dog of Pompeii," Margery Kinnan Rawling's "Benny the Bird Dog," and one of G. K. Chesterton's Father Brown mysteries, "The Queer Feet," among other notable (and some not so notable) contributors and contributions—accompanied by a photograph and brief biographical treatment of the author. There was also an essay on some literary topic—in the same number as "The Waltz," the subject was travelers' views of America from the colonial to the modern period—a page about recent poetry, and a list of recommended readings by May Lamberton Becker, one of *Scholastic*'s editors. The Social Studies section featured articles on contemporary issues such as "How Shall We Insure Against Joblessness" (23 March) plus several regular features, always presented in order: "The Course of National Affairs," "The March of Events Around the World," "Who's Who in the News," and "Social Studies Signposts"; these last two categories tended to be anecdotal in nature, more focused on personalities than on newsworthy items. The overall structure, in other words, followed closely that of the standard day of school, with inspirational messages at the outset (the editorial as compared with the Pledge of Allegiance, the Lord's Prayer, and the reading of scripture with which each school day began in the 1930s), then "serious" study of items noticeably trailing off in importance or at least in immediate relevance, however, in both the Social Studies and the Student Sections (and, arguably, in the English Section as well), and finally the time reserved at the end of the day for student activities: sports, movie-going, or just hanging out and horsing around, telling jokes (we may well imagine, though, that despite this structure many students turned first to the page of jokes when they received their weekly *Scholastic*).

In spite of its emphasis on keeping students up to date with the world of current affairs, *Scholastic* was in many ways a throwback to an earlier time, when publishers and editors regularly used editorials to educate readers to a proper view of the world and refused to contaminate "serious" matter with notices from the world of business, thereby disguising its own commercial nature. Such a deep contradiction between form and substance was bound to be reflected in other ways in the magazine. The overall message of the structure, for example, contradicted the claim that the magazine was published for students, for it in fact placed student interests last and minimized them, presenting instead an implicitly coherent view of the world in which things that adults considered important were arranged in descending order and in which the role of the primary reader was dutifully to absorb the information and advice so thoughtfully presented to her or him each week. Student readers were, in effect, being trained to be consumers of information, not necessarily contributors to it, and in their responsibility to become knowledgeable consumers of culture as well, future subscribers to all or at least some of the appropriate middle-class magazines. Replicating in its essential format the dominant design, the managerial style, and the practical emphasis valued in society at large, *Scholastic* both is and is not a strange venue for Dorothy Parker's "The Waltz," a story that is more iconoclastic than it is generally given credit for being, and the collisions between her text and the content and ideological presuppositions of the magazine, though subtle and perhaps accessible only to the kind of reader adolescents were automatically assumed not to be, enrich both the story and its framing format in ways that are greatly instructive for an understanding of the semiotic and semantic transformations that may arise, whether intentionally or not, in any act of recontextualization.

It is typical, of course, of any commercial magazine, however rationalized its structure may seem to be on the surface, that one piece leads into another with little or no regard for its effect on, or its relationship to, the piece it "introduces," at least in the sense of being contiguous to the ensuing text. This effect of incoherence is, as we shall see, even more pronounced in a highly commercialized magazine such as the *New Yorker*, in which advertisements and cartoons on the same page regularly compete with essays and fiction for the reader's attention, but it is also in evidence even in the relatively more sedate and carefully managed pages of *Scholastic*. I have already noted, for example, that every issue of *Scholastic* began with a one-page editorial, always on some subject that reestablished the pedagogical tone of the publication with each new weekly number. One such essay admonished readers to "Be Your Age!" (4 May 1935), and the number in which Parker's story appeared began with "On Learning to Be Alone," in which a business executive who grew up in the late 1880s lamented the hectic pace of contemporary life—"the noisy contrivances of the newer age" that invited young people to "waste" their "inward forces . . . upon petty excitements'" (3)—and a college president deplored the fact that "theatres, movies, dancing, radio, and parties, parties, parties" have led to a loss among contemporary youth of the "'capacity for solitude'" (3). The nostalgia for a more stable past revealed in this passage is, of course, incompatible with *Scholastic*'s stated goal of emphasizing current literature, world news, and current events, but the editor does not comment on this small discrepancy or help readers to understand the contradiction. The specific reason for citing this passage, however, is that the sentiments expressed in the editorial leach ambiguously into Dorothy Parker's story, perhaps complicating a narrative in which a lack of clarity is already a problem. "If social life is cheap and tawdry," the editor, Maurice R. Robinson, asserts, young people have only themselves to blame, "unless . . . they learn, before it is too late, to cultivate their minds, to read books, to look at paintings, to listen to music . . . to be alone" (3). Such sentiments, I would argue, with their condemnation of frivolous behavior and their valorization of a stable, inviolable inner world of thought and feeling possess the potential to affect the reader's response to Dorothy Parker's speaker in complex ways. The speaker's words (though not her actions) make it clear that she would indeed prefer solitude to companionship—"I ask so little—just to be left alone in my quiet corner of the table to do my evening brooding over all my sorrows" (4)—but her melancholy and self-reflexively ironic tone are not in tune with the rewards of solitude promised in the editorial. Parker's speaker seems to share the executive's and the editor's contempt for the unexamined life as a particular problem of Americans—"It's this constant rush, rush, rush, that's the curse of American life" (4)—but, of course, given the verbal dynamics of the story, we cannot take this sentiment with entire seriousness; it seems, rather, merely a repetition and, therefore, a parody of similar ideas expressed by journalists and other pundits who, like George Jean Nathan (explicitly mentioned in Parker's story), have made part of their reputation and at least some of their living by publishing dire indictments of the pace of American social life.[4] The speaker recognizes as clearly as anyone can, it would seem, that her social life is indeed cheap and tawdry, as well as insincere, but she still finds herself drawn into social situations, and specifically to the dance, by powerful cultural imperatives she may not entirely understand and can articulate only indirectly, by appropriating the clichés of male experience and the empty conventions of female speech and transforming them into a language that, as one critic has argued, is so devoid of substance as to be, finally, virtually meaningless.[5] That may indeed be the first impression produced by Parker's assemblage of clichés and other catch phrases—it certainly strikes Arthur F. Kinney in the same way, for example[6]—but I think a more sympathetic and accurate perception, as I want to argue later in this paper, is that Parker's words communicate most precisely when they may appear most like secondhand, memorized speech indistinguishable from the "meaningless" patter one is likely to overhear at any fashionable cocktail party in New York.

Once we begin to consider more closely the issue of *Scholastic* in which "The Waltz" appeared, other possible sources of confusion or interference with the reader's ability to interpret Parker's story become apparent. The cover illustration, for example, shows a young woman artist in her studio: what might that suggest about the proper way a woman might be spending her time, rather than attending a dance from which she takes no delight? By contrast, the final full-page advertisement in the same issue is for a radio program known as "Kellogg's College Prom," sponsored by Kellogg's Pep Bran Flakes—specially formulated to *"keep [you] going with PEP!"*—and promoting not the intellectual atmosphere of the college campus but "the excitement of whirlwind athletics," the "beautiful songs" of Ruth Etting, and the sounds of Red Nichols and his Pennies "playing syncopation for a collegiate dance" (32). Such an ad-vertisement certainly seems to endorse, without equivocation, the values that the speaker of "The Waltz" seems most to be satirizing, including the world of competitive sports, source of some of the most striking and amusing images in Parker's story, and would un-doubtedly have made it more difficult for readers to perceive the various levels of ironic treatment that social dancing receives at Par-ker's hands. Even the material immediately surrounding Parker's story, moreover, would not have sent a clear message, for readers were informed in the biographical sketch of Parker that she is a "deadly wit" and "Mistress of the bon mot, which in this instance is French for 'dirty crack'" (5), a claim that not only seems to disap-prove of Parker's attitude but also appears to advise readers not to distinguish between the author and the speaker of "The Waltz." Yet the illustration accompanying the story, featuring a young woman whose back is turned toward the reader as she embraces her dancing partner—an interesting faceless inversion of the story itself, in which it is only the girl's or woman's voice and thoughts that we hear—and a tall, goofy-looking male dancer seems to promise a story in the lighthearted vein of the *Saturday Evening Post*, whose style of illustrat-ing a line in the story this drawing manifestly copies (the illustration, however, also suggests that everything the speaker has to say about her dancing partner is literally true, which again oversimplifies the story). Finally, the story's title is presented in *Scholastic* in large let-ters with a scripted, elegant flourish, as if the tale were really going to be about the typical romantic situation depicted in so much pop-ular fiction in which the young woman or, less frequently, the young man at last meets and dances with the partner of her or his dreams. The graphic material surrounding the story, in other words, unin-tentionally replicates the multivocality of the text, sending mixed messages to the reader that could not have helped to stabilize the multiple ironies of the text.

One special problem raised by the recontextualization on "The Waltz" in *Scholastic* is that the editors of that magazine did not faith-fully reproduce the text of the story. Instead, they silently altered Parker's language, in obedience, we must surmise, not only to their own notions of what was appropriate fare for an adolescent reader and to their editorial understanding of the "ideal" level of that read-er's linguistic competence, but also to their own ideas of what Parker probably intended her story to "mean," or at least what pedagogical purposes it could be made to serve (not the same things, of course). Editorial excisions, in other words, work subtly to guide the reading of the text into acceptable channels, the more persuasively (and perniciously) so when they are not identified or acknowledged by the editors. This is, indeed, the kind of textual consideration customarily of concern to bibliographers, who often, however, fail to speculate about how the presumed needs and desires of an imagined audience within a particular venue of recontextualization have been editorially balanced against the demands of textual integrity. So readers of "The Waltz" in *Scholastic* will miss possibly the most important figure of speech in the story as it appears in *After Such Pleasures*, the speaker's despairing sense that she has been "trapped like a trap in a trap,"[7] which becomes instead the entirely conventional "trapped like a rat in a trap" (4). Perhaps the editors of *Scholastic* imagined that Parker herself had made a mistake, one which they took it upon themselves to correct, or perhaps they thought that Parker's unusual phrasing would prove too much of a distraction from the "plot" of the story or be too difficult to explain when the subject of similes and other figures of speech came up for discussion in English class: how can you logically compare something to itself? Whatever their motives, however, what the editors of *Scholastic* also accomplished was to add an unauthorized stroke to the portrait of the speaker as a woman paradoxically more trapped by the conventions of language, less able to manipulate them for her own purposes, than she is in the original version. The change assumes an expectation of the obvious and guides readers toward a preference for the conventional over the unconventional, whether in verbal or other forms of social behavior, and thus implicitly weighs in on the side of "good" manners at any cost, no matter what personal anguish the speaker of the story avers that being mannerly engenders.

A second alteration in *Scholastic* from the original text appears near the end of the story, in the speaker's brief catalogue of catastrophes that have previously befallen her but that now seem insignificant compared with her present travails. In the *New Yorker* and in *After Such Pleasures*, that catalogue included "the night the drunken lady threw a bronze ash-tray at her own true love and got me instead," but this memory, a distinctly adult one, has been cut out of the story.[8] If this was primarily a moral decision, an adult rejection of anyone's drunken behavior or an attempt to protect youthful readers from seeing drinking treated more or less casually, the deletion also removes a bit of evidence about the age of the speaker and suggests that she is some years younger than most subsequent critics, attracted by what they take to be the autobiographical elements of the story, have thought her to be. An additional price paid for such editorial vigilance (or fussy overfastidiousness) is the loss of Parker's culminating image of love gone bad, her reductio ad absurdum of the romantic mystique encapsulated in the ironic phrase "her own true love," which borrows from the language of sentimental balladry in order to signal its ironic intent. This is no small loss to the story, for, as I want to argue elsewhere in this paper, "The Waltz" constitutes a sustained attack on romantic clichés associated with the dance as part of the ritual of courtship in Western society. Whether or not the expurgated remark records an episode from Parker's own biography, an event in which she was the thrower rather than the accidental target of the throwee, may be left to others to determine (although that reading seems very likely), but that "The Waltz" as it appears in the *Scholastic* is imaginatively diminished by editorial intervention to nearly the same degree that it is ambiguously framed in that same publication seems beyond argument or question.

II

Just as the appearance of "The Waltz" in the pages of the *Scholastic* reveals or releases nuances and inflections not immediately apparent to readers who encounter the work in a standard anthology of American literature, so the first publication of Parker's story in the *New Yorker* and then its subsequent inclusion in the collection of eleven pieces entitled *After Such Pleasures* complicate and extend the possibilities of interpretation. At the outset, for example, we might acknowledge that the story's appearance in the collected volume was a significant step toward transforming "The Waltz" from a transient *New Yorker* casual, a piece not much different, at least by implication, from the journalistic essays, the film and theater reviews, and even the advertisements that surround it, into a work of continuing literary interest. Like the material that surrounds it in the magazine, "The Waltz" appears initially as a commodity to be consumed, a disposable entertainment meant for the pleasure and (perhaps) the edification of those who were affluent enough (especially in 1933 when the story first appeared) to be able to afford the luxury of purchasing a magazine meant merely for amusement as well as the leisure required for casual reading. It was, like most if not all of the other content, a decorative part of the landscape of the reader's life—a reader who, on turning the pages, found herself or himself in new and equally entertaining, momentarily engaging "cultural" environments, whether those environments were experienced as short fiction about the follies and foibles of middle-class urban existence or as advertisements for Brooks Brothers or Bonwit-Teller. The experience of reading the *New Yorker* from cover to cover in its early halcyon days (did anyone really undertake so sustained an endeavor?) might be compared to overhearing conversation at one of those innumerable cocktail parties that seem so often to provide the backdrop for the *New Yorker*'s stories, essays, and cartoons, consisting of light talk conducted on a clever, thoroughly worldly plane on which one could eavesdrop for a while undetected and uncommitted before moving on to another circle of current gossip or events. Even if the subject matter seemed occasionally unpleasant, as was sometimes the case with Parker's more socially conscious short fictions, the reader could be reassured by reflecting that *New Yorker* stories were never to be taken too seriously, a fact underlined by Harold Ross's insistence on calling them "casuals"—descriptive not only of style and content (and, as James Thurber argued, entirely deceptive with regard to the amount of work that went into writing them successfully) but also of an ideal calculated impression on the reader; they are meant to evoke at most a wry smile, a knowing nod about the follies and foibles of all human beings (except, perhaps, the nodder's own self), an amused and tolerant and withal superior and sophisticated detachment.

In an odd way, the *New Yorker*, although apparently far more diffuse and wide-ranging in its subject matter and content than *Scholastic*, is in reality a more coherent magazine, retailing a cluster of recurrent images as the sometimes glitzy, sometimes elegant world of leisure—going shopping, going to a concert, the movies, or the theater, going out to dine, and so on must be done well and by the latest rules of taste and fashion—as well as the gendered politics of power and money and the commodification of sexuality in a continuous narrative consisting of articles, fiction, weekly columns, topical cartoons, and advertisements running from cover to cover. Into this milieu, "The Waltz" fits unobtrusively, a commodity within a commodity (another implication of Parker's "trap within a trap") that might easily be mistaken for a comment on or extension of the recurring advertisements for Arthur Murray's Dance Studio—"Give Arthur Murray 10 days—and he'll make you a marvelous dancing partner!"—or the wonders of Madame Nina's Geranium Cream: "Don't be a wallflower . . . Men like them young," among the many other items always for sale.[9] Since everything speaks the language of money in the *New Yorker*, the ending of Parker's story, with its suggestion that the orchestra will indeed play the same waltz again for an additional fifty dollars, rings profoundly true, and what Paula Treichler, has described as the commercialization of language and has seen as a fault in the story is in fact an indication of Parker's brilliant success at finding for her fiction the exact inflection of the magazine in which her writing most frequently and famously appeared.

The paradox of experiencing a trivial social moment such as a waltz or an awkward conversation as extending toward a meaninglessly repetitive but otherwise ill-defined eternity—"I'd love to go on waltzing with you"—belongs precisely to the scale of values promoted by the *New Yorker*, in one way exactly inverting and in another way exactly replicating the deepest messages emanating from the commercial clutter that surrounds "The Waltz" in the *New Yorker*. Where everything is seasonal or newly designed, from furniture to automobiles to hats and other apparel, from the most recent smash hit in the theatre to the latest rage in cuisine, each experience is merely the gateway to an as-yet-unspecified future—next year, next season, next week—and another set of events designed to stimulate rather than satisfy, another round of experiences to be consumed in the desperate pursuit for some permanence in pleasure. Similarly, where emphasis falls so markedly on obsolescence and a radical impermanence, being out of style or fashion, the idea of impermanence enters human consciousness, as in "The Waltz," as an obsession with the fleeting passage of time, the speaker's description of herself as "a woman of my age," for example, or as frustration with anything new (such as innovative dance steps) or with culturally mandated social performances. Matched with an almost unthinking acquiescence in dancing and in other demands of the social whirl, the speaker's awareness of how shallow is the culture in which she is nonetheless and apparently willingly immersed culminates logically and psychologically in the self-disgust registered in Parker's story in the several "dance of death" references. In this as in many of Parker's other stories, culture itself becomes poisonous, a seemingly endless series of empty and repetitive but always fashionable gestures as recorded in her sketch "From the Diary of a New York Lady," and lead to a focus on bodily violence, self-disgust and self-destruction, and the almost continuous contemplation of suicide.[10]

"The Waltz" is framed in its immediate context in the *New Yorker* by two cartoons, the second a half-page panel showing a man and woman who have obviously fallen on hard (but not too hard) times in this fourth year of the Great Depression who are inspecting a small apartment and trying to imagine life without room for a piano. The other cartoon, which faces Parker's story, is a full-page depiction by Peter Arno of two men at a nudists' gathering, one of whom comments dejectedly to the other as nine naked women parade around and before them, "A bit boring this weekend. Just the same old faces."[11] In context, Arno's cartoon may be taken as an ironic introduction to, reflection of, and commentary upon the same hopeless ennui that also impels Parker's story (the absence of any clear setting combined with the nudity makes Arno's cartoon seem like a scene in Hell), specifically on the institution of stag lines and the boring but mandatory dance and display of sex, as well as an excellent illustration of that curious mixture of voyeuristic lust paired with sexual disinterest (if not actual impotence) that seems to afflict *New Yorker* males in general. As a contribution to the *New Yorker*, Arno's cartoon seems both more dramatic and more significant than Parker's story, which is signed at the end in the unobtrusive type reserved for authorial bylines in the *New Yorker*, in contrast to the flamboyant, highly stylized signature in the upper left-hand corner of Arno's art (indeed, Parker's identity as author of "The Waltz" is even less dramatically presented than that of the author of a signed and specifically illustrated advertisement for Heinz consommé in the same issue of the *New Yorker*). Parker's verbal sketch is, moreover, disrupted by being fragmented over two pages in four discrete columns and is forced to compete for space and attention with another cartoon (briefly described above), concluding, in fact, in two additional three-inch columns wedged like mere footnotes into the page below that cartoon. While Parker's characteristically caustic wit is much in evidence in this story, it is less immediately accessible than Arno's joke, nor does it seem in context to rise much above or to leave a more lasting impression than the witty banter and often mean-spirited character assassination frequently indulged in by members of the Round Table, who would certainly have been numbered among the most appreciative audiences of this particular piece. In no quantifiable way does "The Waltz" seem significantly different from the prose piece that follows it, Clifford Orr's "Savage Homecoming," which focuses on a situation almost as stereotypical as the dance, the return of an urchin from summer camp with a new and generally unintelligible vocabulary and a newly fashionable, falsely natural outlook on life.[12] Even to the most sympathetic eye, in short, Parker's story in its first appearance in the *New Yorker* would seem to be a most unlikely candidate for the kind of canonization that has subsequently befallen it by reason of its inclusion in several current and much-employed anthologies of American literature.

The case is quite different with regard to the story's publication in *After Such Pleasures*, where "The Waltz" appears as the fifth of eleven pieces in the collection and is introduced by one sketch, "From the Diary of a New York Lady," which might lead us to emphasize by extension the shallowness of the young lady in "The Waltz," who can do nothing but criticize the ineptness of her dancing partner and who seems thereby to be projecting her own self-loathing (a destructive emotion that may well be in large part cultur-ally determined) onto her male companion. In the same way, the New York lady disguises from herself and her diary the emptiness of her life and the shallow stupidity of the crowd whose company she frequents for entertainment. That such a person, who possesses no inner life to record, should even keep a diary is a comment on her sense of self-importance, her successful self-deception, and her over-mastering desire to comply with all the accepted female fashions, in which she is similar to the narrator of "The Waltz." The woman in "The Waltz," on the other hand, seems more tragic, both desiring (as a cultural and perhaps even personal imperative) and despising the company of men, whom she inevitably discovers to be both boor-ish and boring but whose romantic absence from her life, though romantic only in appearance, would expose her to social ridicule as well as to the loneliness she is convinced she would feel without a life partner.

Perhaps the most important transformation in status and implica-tion that Parker's inclusion of "The Waltz" in a collection of short stories effected by the editorial act of recontextualizing the piece in *After Such Pleasures* is that it compelled the reader to see the story as part of a comprehensive, thematically, and intonationally organized unit rather than as an isolated fragment of readerly experience over-whelmed by its immediate surroundings, as it was in the *New Yorker*. The stories in *After Such Pleasures*, in fact, as the comments above on the relationship between "From the Diary of a New York Lady" and "The Waltz" may have indicated, are intricately related one to an-other by verbal echoes, similar vocabulary, shared stylistic devices, and the like—a dimension of Parker's achievement that has not yet been fully appreciated by critics and that would never be noticed unless the pieces were arranged contiguously, as in this collection. One text now penetrates, amplifies, and interprets another in the best approved (and thoroughly fashionable) model of, say, Ander-son's *Winesburg, Ohio,* or Hemingway's *In Our Time*. Thus, for exam-ple, one might be tempted to describe "The Waltz" in the way that Paula Treichler does, as a story about "the delicate line that women walk obsessively between what can be said and what is forbidden," detecting only the struggle of the female speaker in the discrepancy between the inner voice that bitterly assails the male dancing part-ner and the italicized voice that speaks in polite, ladylike phrases reflecting a learned submission to second-class status and a wish to conform to the image of femininity imposed by the dominant male culture.[13] A comparison of the verbal strategies employed by a male character in another story in the same collection, however, the character of Jerry Cruger in "Horsie," who indulges in similarly internalized flights of fancy directed against a woman he regards as his social inferior while withholding any actual expression of his anger and contempt, confounds any simplistic understanding of Parker's portrayal of the relationships between and among language, self-expression, gendered power, sex, and self-definition. Moreover, once we realize that Jerry's attitude toward this woman, a hired nurse whom he nicknames Horsie in the privacy of his own disdain for her, and his very different, worshipful attitude toward his wife, Camilla, arise from the same "Angel in the House" mythology and that he, too, is therefore a victim of his unthinking acceptance of the traditional images of femininity that his own gender has created, we may attain a perspective on the social criticism in both stories that places each piece beyond the effective reach of any narrowly ideological reading. Though *After Such Pleasures* lacks a central unifying character or characters, then, and in this way differs from Anderson's or Hemingway's or Faulkner's short-story sagas, it possesses a unifying voice, a unifying emphasis on social situations that are both more shallow and more highly charged with stifled emotion and subliminal cultural meaning than appears on the surface, and a unifying tone that enriches each story and compels comparison with male modernist authors whom Parker admired but whose literary prestige perhaps unjustly overshadows her own.

Parker's chief strategy for enlarging the context and thus the implications of the stories she collected is the line from John Donne's "Farewell to Love" that she settled upon only after wisely discarding *The Infernal Grove* and offering it to John O'Hara. It is a brilliantly evocative title, far better than the one it replaces (although *The Infernal Grove* does have the virtue of indicating that Parker was thinking of the locale of *The Waste Land*), in large measure because it invokes not only literary but also recent social history. Published in the wake of the riotous excesses of the Roaring Twenties, it captures at once the mood of regret for ever having indulged in "such pleasures" and the self-disgust for ever having imagined that such delusions were real while at the same time implying a continuing longing or nostalgia for those same lost pleasures that must now, by the dictates of circumstance, be reluctantly abjured (somewhat similar to the delicate evocation of a Janus-faced mood achieved by F. Scott Fitzgerald in "Babylon Revisited"). The word "after" carries both implications nicely, suggesting at once that such pleasures are over, a thing of the past, and that we are still "after" them, that is, still pursuing them, in that endless American round of frenetic activity supposed eventually to lead to happiness but more often, in the depressed atmosphere of Parker's 1930s, compelling confrontations with frustration, loneliness, and despair.

In appropriating John Donne's "Farewell to Love" as a comment on her own moods and attitudes, Parker identifies her stories and the cast of her imagination with far larger and more serious literary aspirations than any reader who had come across "The Waltz" (or any of Parker's other contributions to the *New Yorker, Cosmopolitan, Harper's Bazaar,* or even the *New Masses,* for that matter) might have been inclined to suspect. At one stroke, she aligns herself with T. S. Eliot, whose famous essay on the metaphysical poets had appeared as the introduction to Herbert J. C. Grierson's edition of *Metaphysical Lyrics and Poems of the Seventeenth Century* in 1929, and she puts into practice the modernist technique of employing an apparently straightforward allusion to one specific passage of another literary text as a way of invoking the entire context of all of that absent author's relevant writing and inviting—indeed, compelling—the reader to encounter all eleven stories in her collection through the lens of Donne's disillusionment with earthly pleasures and his simultaneously deep delight in bawdy contemplation and sexual performance. The full text of "Farewell to Love" in particular can be seen as a searching and scathing critique of the lack of love in modern life as exhibited in the stories in *After Such Pleasures,* of the sterile misuse and abuse of language by means of which men and women isolate themselves from each other and from their own true feelings, and of the failure, finally, of physical love or sexual passion or anything else to fill the void of lives lived in the shadow of the waste land. Donne's disparaging attitude toward women, especially toward women's intelligence, and his alternating resistance and surrender to desire, are also inscribed into Parker's texts, sometimes as self-loathing, sometimes as critiques of the shallowness of society women, as intimately as though she had planned to make them a part of her stories from the beginning—a conclusion belied, of course, by her late decision to settle on this title. The unhealthy fascination with "things which had endamaged me" that Donne expresses in "Farewell to Love," the lure of destructive pleasures, together with Donne's often complex, sardonic, and subtle phallic puns and other mocking references to sexual performances provide a stylistic and thematic model for many of the stories in *After Such Pleasures* and become inextricably integrated into Parker's own commentary on a world of lost pleasures found too late to be illusory and vain, comprised of an almost endless round of unsatisfying emotional and physical experiences that leave in their wake only "a kind of sorrowing dulness to the mind."[14] Parker's choice of title insure that Donne's sentiments will serve as provocative glosses on the impossible psychological and social predicaments of many characters in her stories, including the masochistic behavior of the narrator of "The Waltz," who, though both physically and psychologically damaged by her encounter with this "leering, bestial" dancing partner and disappointed generally in her quest for love, yet finds herself at the end paying the orchestra to play the same old music once again. She hopes, of course, even as she knows better than to hope, that this time the tune will be harmonious, unlike all the other times before, and the waltz will at last perform its promised magic by bringing kindred souls together.

III

Thus far I have been considering only some of the ways in which recontextualization might affect textual reception and interpretation once an author relinquishes control of her text to editors and publishers, and then some of the ways in which she might regain at least a measure of control over the reader by careful intra- and intertextual strategies, such as through a judicious selection of thematically and tonally related narratives and through the choice of a title that predisposes readers to "discover" and emphasize those themes during reading. Now I want to return to the more familiar sort of recontextualization or multivocality that arises from an author's mostly deliberate insertion and redeployment of recognized conventional discourses within a secondary textual system for which the convention was not originally intended and which causes us, therefore, to reexamine both the convention and the context of assumptions that normally endorse and authorize its social acceptance. I refer to this as "mostly deliberate" because, of course, cultural paradigms, not necessarily fully attended to by an author, continue to exert their considerable presence in the creative processes, language being the common property of all who speak it in one dialect or another. Here again the insights of Mikhail Bakhtin can be of service. "In all areas of life and ideological activity," Bakhtin writes, "our speech is filled to overflowing with other people's words which are transmitted with highly varied degrees of accuracy and impartiality."[15] The creator of what we normally call parodic literature not only acknowledges but actively embraces this proposition, fashioning what is often a dizzying labyrinth of language that looks just enough like the original it is meant to impersonate to fool the naive reader but that is just enough unlike the real thing, just abundant enough in sharps and flats and other strained, false notes of style, to alert the initiated reader and give away the game. Such use of language also and inevitably calls into question the authenticity or "reality" of the "real thing" itself, reminding us, like Rene Magritte's famous painting *This Is Not a Pipe*, that fictive worlds depend for their reality and "serious" content on the merest wink of a word. If the publication of "The Waltz" in *Scholastic* offers no other food for speculation, it at least functions to remind us that the story is indeed embedded in preexisting fictive worlds, in forms and genres and modes of speech that the custodians of culture more or less take for granted as the desirable common property of those readers whose tastes they would shape for the future. Parker's text not only depends upon but also, as parody, sets out to undermine and redefine these conventions; we will understand it only as we understand all daily discourse, by acknowledging the other, similar languages Parker might have used and locating meaning in difference as well as in the similarity: what these words and phrases were most commonly intended to mean in their initial context and how her recontextualization changes that meaning and indeed the words themselves. What other kind of text or story might "The Waltz" have become in the hands of a different author, and how do those rejected narratives remain within the text, determining the direction of the story at crucial linguistic moments and contributing their otherwise rejected meanings to the new narrative that has been fashioned out of their fragments?

It is because of insufficient attention—or no attention at all—to "The Waltz" as a parody which recontextualizes and, in recontextualizing, redefines motifs and language that Parker's previous critics, who have complained about the "thin, attenuated style" of the story or about the "commercialized" quality of a language that renders words unable to convey any fundamental social or moral truths, have seriously misread or under-read the text.[16] Treichler in particular has built her reading around the apparent but ultimately only illusory differences between the public and the private voices of the speaker without taking into account what I believe to be a far more basic dichotomy of utterance crucial to our understanding of the accomplishment of the story, the ability it possesses, like all significant works of literature, to produce the sense that there remains something very important still unsaid by any critical discourse and that can be ascribed only to the untranslatable and unstable interplay between and among the text, the "theme," the form, and the language. This elusive multivocality of the artifact, a sense of the story's own sense that it means something beyond the surfaces of its words, implications arising from a contemplation of the complex whole both within its immediate context as well as of the literary antecedents which it uneasily recontextualizes within itself, is in some measure explained by Bakhtin's hypothesis that there coexist within any "artistic image of a language" at least two linguistic consciousnesses, "the one being represented and the one doing the representing, with each belonging to a different system of language."[17] This important perception of the obligatory double-voicedness of any literary text, but especially on one that we can recognize as parodic, can serve as a starting point for a fresh examination of the multidimensional language of the story.

The archetypal story of ballrooms, beautiful people, and miraculous transformations of identity and revelations of true character is, of course, the story of Cinderella, at least as collected and retooled for bourgeois consumption by the Brothers Grimm in the early nineteenth century. For sheer hyperventilated prose on the subjects of waltzes and falling in love, however, it is hard to surpass *The Sorrows of Young Werther*: "Never have I moved so lightly. I was no longer a mortal being. To hold that loveliest creature in my arms and to whirl around with her like the wind so that the surroundings disappeared."[18] In Russia a few decades later, Leo Tolstoy elevated young Werther's transient moment of ecstasy toward epic significance in his account of Natásha Rostova's first night at the ball, much of it spent in the arms and under the watchful gaze of Prince André Bolkonsky in book 6, chapter 9 of *War and Peace*. The scene recalls Cinderella (though Natásha was never an *Aschenpüttel*) through special attention to Natásha's delicate feet "in their white satin dancing shoes" (504) and to the irrepressible feeling of euphoria and personal triumph that the evening engenders within her: "She was at the height of bliss when one becomes completely kind and good and does not believe in the possibility of evil, unhappiness, or sorrow."[19] Parker's readers might have been more immediately moved by the magical glitter of the waltz from reading their contemporary, F. Scott Fitzgerald, for whom the dance and the dancers retains much of the social and symbolic richness that it held for nineteenth-century Western authors, but similar stories of love lost or discovered at a memorable, transformative dance were so numerous and so nearly ubiquitous in all forms of popular culture—"Dancing with Tears in My Eyes," "Dancing in the Dark," and "The Waltz You Saved for Me" were all hit songs of the early 1930s, for example—that no one would have needed to know any novels to understand that something was meant in the way of parody by Parker's amusing but caustically antisentimental short story.

With the backgrounded tradition of Western romance brought into view, we can begin to appreciate "The Waltz" for the brilliant example of parody that it is. The ironic presence of Cinderella, for instance, which at some deep, even subliminal level structures the story, may be inferred from a chain of images that includes soiled slippers, torn gowns, mutilated feet, and, instead of a handsome Prince Charming, a "hulking peasant" who has to be thrown on his back in order "to get shoes on him"[20]—an ironic gender inversion of Cinderella herself. As for young Werther's "loveliest creature," she becomes, in Parker's formulation, "something out of 'The Fall of the House of Usher'" (211). That "something," of course, would be the Lady Madeline Usher, a gauzy, filmy figure at best who flits into view just long enough to become the obsessive object of her brother's incestuous desires and to bear the blame for his hypochondrosis—a familiar paradigm of the fate of the female in patriarchal society at large, where women need do nothing at all to function as the fixated focus of desire, reinvented to fill the psychological needs of the male voyeur. Inverting Werther's language still further by changing the gender, "that loveliest creature in my arms" transforms into "this creature I'm chained to" (211), a man of "degenerate cunning" with a "leering, bestial face" (211), while all of Werther's images of flight and transcendence of the physical are relentlessly recycled into images of entrapment and physical pain. In place of Natásha Rostova's worried, wistful gaze as she wonders whether anyone will ask her to dance, Parker gives us the following: "Just think, not a quarter of an hour ago, here I was sitting, feeling so sorry for the poor girl he was dancing with. And now *I'm* going to be the poor girl" (209), thus sardonically inverting the mythicized moment of self-discovery, the revelation of a new romantic self and a new social identity that supposedly follows when the ripe and expectant maiden embraces for the first time and to the strains of a dreamy waltz the "right man" with whom she has been unknowingly fated to spend the rest of her life. Parker's speaker's description of the young man's "com[ing] into my life" ironically preserves the theme that a chance encounter at a dance may be decisive in a woman's destiny, a turning point in her personal history, without at all endorsing the attitude that such moments of life's transformation in the arms of an absolute stranger are to be eagerly awaited and welcomed or, indeed, that they are even true or that they ever come to pass. Except as parody, finally, there seems no way to explain Parker's speaker's sudden and surprising protestations of love for her dancing partner, an aspect of the story's language usually skirted or ignored by feminist readings: "Why, I'm getting positively drawn to the Triple Threat here. He's my hero. He has the heart of a lion, and the sinews of a buffalo. . . . I love him. I love him better than anybody in the whole world" (211). This becomes funny because it is what is *supposed* to happen according to the cultural script, and to show it happening here in a most incongruous manner and for no intrinsic reason at all allows Parker not only to underscore the depth of her speaker's entrapment by traditional romantic platitudes and linguistic postures but also the inherent emptiness of the language in which such attitudes are expressed and out of which they are born and sustained.

Point by parodic point, in short, "The Waltz" reduces the romantic paradigm to rubble. Other inverted images of romance, this time derived from predominantly male narratives of battle, the hunt, and competitive games, also figure into the verbal dynamics of the story, offering ironic insights into the Western construction of masculine identity through the creation and subjugation of an alien female Other, taking us all the way back into dim prehistory when, so anthropologists tell us, today's social dances began to take shape as rhythmic rituals designed to insure success to the nation's warrior or hunters. Patriarchal hegemony is preserved in the waltz as in all ballroom protocol by the female's need to await the male's invitation to dance and follow his lead on the floor, a situation that proves nearly disastrous to the speaker of Parker's "The Waltz"—"[I]t was just a bit tricky at first, but now I think I've got it. Two stumbles, slip, and a twenty-yard dash" (211)—and through the male spectatorial emphasis on the elegant, delicate, almost unworldly figure of the waltzing female form. Here is a key link between the waltz and romantic ballet as epitomized in *Les Sylphidés* and *Swan Lake*, among others, which simultaneously exalts and impossibly constrains the athletic female body, denaturing and dominating its disturbing sexual power by means of the metaphor of art.[21] Parker's response to such self-serving male disavowals of sexual interest in the sexualized female form is to emphasize the woman's body as both the site and object of male control and the source of pain rather than pleasure for the dominated waltzing woman.

Additional male narratives of conquest and control appear in Parker's story as a pattern of complex and latently metaphoric allusions and images, commencing with the many references to football and other athletic competitions. The "two stumbles, slip, and twenty-yard dash" in the passage above, for example, might also serve as a figure of the inept, uninitiated male's fumbling attempts at sexual intercourse—two stumbles and a slip—and, in the twenty-yard dash, of the characteristic "wham-bam, thank you, ma'm" style of masculine sex, while the shattered shinbone resulting from this encounter—"My poor, poor shin, that I've had ever since I was a little girl!" (210)—seems an obvious if somewhat grotesquely parodic version of the broken and much-prized female hymen that plays so large a part in the male's own myth of masculine conquest and in his sense of his own honor (a point previously made by Treichler and others); a special psychological twist is that, through the strategy of inversion, the broken bone symbolizes as well the speaker's deep dwelling desire to see the source of all phallic aggression, the male "bone" itself, similarly shattered. Another of Parker's allusions blends games and warfare in the manner of modern sports commentators (or battlefield generals themselves, for that matter), bringing together the football scrimmage—"Come on, Butch, right through them!"—with a reference to perhaps the most famous phrase to come out of America's involvement in World War I, Gunnery Sergeant Dan Daly's "Come on, you sonsabitches! Do you want to live forever," uttered during the battle for Belleau Wood on 6 June 1918. This classic exhortation, which contemporary readers would have recognized in Parker's "Who wants to live forever?" (211) more readily than we do because of its historical proximity, had long since entered the lore of the Marine Corps and popular consciousness as America's answer to élan vital, the ultimate heroic defiance in the face of overwhelming odds and obstacles, and may be taken here, in its mock heroic applications, as a small contribution to the growing literature of disillusionment over the true results of the war to make the world safe for democracy. In its full context in Parker's story, moreover, introduced by other examples of inflated heroic diction—"And shall it be said that I hung back? No, a thousand times no" (211)—the phrase further debunks the masculine ideal of military heroism and takes on an overtone of desperate hedonism, as well as contributing to the pattern of images of wounds, death, and disease that is the distinguishing stylistic feature of this story. Images of the masculine hunt, meanwhile, survive in Parker's story in the speaker's ironic allusion to big-game hunter Frank Buck's boast (and book), *Bring 'Em Back Alive* (1930)—"I suppose I'll be lucky if he brings me back alive," she reflects (211)—involving a conflation of male and female narratives that makes explicit the role of the woman as the male's prey and allows us to recognize the mythic resonances of the dance as a predatory "hunt" for a sexual partner.

"Comedic forms," observes Kathleen K. Rowe in "Women, Comedy, and the Carnivalesque," "contain the potential of representing

radical inversions of women's relationship to power by not only un-
masking the myths and heroes of patriarchal culture, but by opening up space for transgression, parody and exposure of the 'masks'
of 'femininity.' "[22] Misapprehending the complexity of Parker's allusive and parodic language in "The Waltz," the only "comedic form"
that is open to an author as opposed to a comic performer, Parker's
critics have heretofore tended to argue that all of the italicized
speech in this story represents a false language of a different sort
from that which I have been examining in the previous paragraphs,
a version not of what a woman so abusively beset by a clumsy dancing
partner would actually say but of what she would be expected to
utter. The above examples establish, I think, that the male diction
that Parker's speaker confides only to the recesses of her own mind
(and to the eavesdropping reader) is equally false, or constitutive
only of an aggressive male code of behavior that is consistently
mocked throughout the story. This speech reveals Parker's awareness of an ideology falsely constructed along lines of gender both to
mask and to justify the male's demand for ownership of the female
body within the conventions of Western romanticism, a literature
comprised of equally false and arbitrary "male" narratives of adventure and "female" narratives of domesticity and devotion. False diction, therefore, is by no means relegated to the italicized passages,
as Treichler contends, nor is all the language within those passages
identically inflected.[23] The speaker's use of the word "adore" as in
"I'd adore to" is a case in point, for it is excessive even by the formal
standards of dance etiquette and seems intended to satirize the
speaker as much as it does the social conventions that leave her
hopelessly "trapped like a trap in a trap" when she is asked to dance
(the buried social imperative for a woman to suffer in silence, to
"shut your trap," that lurks in the pun is perhaps the operative
ironic locution of the narrative; recall also the designation of the
female as a "tender trap," or, more aggressively, a "man trap,"
phrases about which Treichler has already meditated, but, in my
view, incompletely).[24] Dance etiquette, after all, would have allowed
her to say, "No thank you, I'm not dancing this one," but she does
not. What we have here, I think, is another one of Parker's problematic women, someone whose sense of desperation at possibly being
abandoned without any partner at all arises from an unexamined
cultural bias that sees in the heterosexual pairing of the dance an
emblem of the only sort of social relationship it endorses and from
her fear of the social stigma of being labeled a wallflower. At the
same time, she is also her own worst enemy, at least to the degree
that she has internalized and even intensified the false social values

that prescribe courting rituals and behavior and that identify marriage as the only legitimate destiny for a woman to pursue.

Another purpose of Parker's linguistic irony, easy to detect once the element of parody is recognized in her story, is to expose courtly and romantic diction, and by extension the literature of manners. Her speaker's description of the young man who comes into her life "all smiles and city manners, to sue me for the favor of one memorable mazurka" (209) resonates on all sorts of "absent texts" having to do with courtship and prescribed social behavior between the sexes, the innocent and compliant country girl confronted by the smart, predatory, urban man on the make, for example, with the whole tradition collapsing on the concluding self-conscious alliteration and final word, "mazurka," posited here by Parker as a word if not a dance, perhaps the polar opposite of the elegant imagery associated with the waltz. Elsewhere, when the music momentarily concludes, the speaker hears "a silence like the sound of angels' wings," perhaps a specific allusion (I have not been able to track it down, however) and certainly an example of the kind of overblown and self-consciously precious Victorian similes suitable for only the most sentimental literature of love and romance—the sort of diction remorselessly exploited and deflated in Parker's own "love" poetry. Parker's speaker's use of the phrase performs the additional function of revealing her susceptibility to exactly those same conventions of language, conduct and courtship that she is otherwise engaged in undermining and exposing. Another instance of ironic and multiple manipulation of "absent texts" may be found in the speaker's play on the medievalism "wot" in "little does he wot. I don't wot his name, either . . ." (209). Here the archaic diction, appropriate once again to a "male" narrative of suspense and adventure, is echoed by and blends imperceptibly into the slangy contemporary (and generally contemptuous) "What's-His-Name" that lurks just beyond the edge of the speaker's "I don't wot his name." The disorienting Joycean pun that results brings the historical past into the present, realigning sound and sense in the same syntagmatic space and producing a kind of cubist effect in the prose (the same thing that happens, I have already contended, in "trapped like a trap in a trap").

To some extent what we are witnessing in Parker's appropriation and parodic redeployment of the language of late-Victorian sentimentality is but another version of modernism's assault on what modernist artists took to be the empty conventions of the complacent generations that had immediately preceded their own, a dismissal of a worldview and the forms and images that expressed it that had become entirely untenable after the deaths of untold numbers of soldiers and civilians in the Great War. The waltz itself is of course a prime illustration of a similar romantic and Victorian ethe-realizing of bodily reality that cries out for realistic rather than ro-mantic treatment, rooted as it is in bawdy folk culture,[25] but having been so completely transformed in the bourgeois and even the aris-tocratic imagination into a symbol of imperial elegance and class, of patriarchal cultural hegemony, as represented most familiarly by classical nineteenth-century ballet or by the conspicuous display of wealth and power that was the Viennese ballroom at the turn of the century. Toned down somewhat and made functionally middle-class in the America of the 1920s and 30s, mastery of the waltz still prom-ised popularity and, by extension, economic power, as evidenced, for example, in the advertisement for Arthur Murray dance studios we have already encountered in the *New Yorker*: "Give Arthur Murray 10 days—and he'll make you a marvelous dancing partner!" The ac-cent, of course, falls on the word "marvellous," promising a Cinder-ella-like transformation from a dull, everyday drudge into "an interesting, popular, sought-after dancer . . . imbue[d] with poise and ease of manner in meeting people."[26] This romantic attitude persists elsewhere in other contemporary sentimental literature as well, as in the following description of the waltz as "a strain of poetry that we cannot forget [,] . . . a bit of our best selves that does not desert us no matter how futile or unworthy our behavior may be,"[27] an assertion that invites exactly the sort of ironic demolition with which Parker rewards it in "The Waltz."

This reading of "The Waltz," together with these remarks con-cerning textual transmission and, as I have argued, transformation, though specific to Parker's story, are not of course restricted to a single literary text. Many of the classic works of American literature first found their way into print in the pages of magazines, from the *Broadway Journal, Harper's,* and *Godey's Lady's Book* to *Scribner's* and the *Saturday Evening Post,* and many have subsequently also found their way into collections and anthologies representing the suppos-edly "best" work of a particular author. In such cases, however, tradi-tional scholarship and criticism have been concerned almost exclusively with substantive changes within the text, and not with the influence that the full contextual and paratextual presentation might exert on the reception and interpretation of the text, or even on the reader's sense of the text's stability and status as a "classic" or "minor" literary work. These marginal matters, I hope I also have shown in this paper, are not truly marginal; they affect not merely the framing and first impressions that readers may receive of a text but also the themes and thoughts that readers may find there, foregrounding or causing to recede invisibly into the background issues that enrich the text, perhaps beyond the bounds and borders of an author's full attention. In the case of "The Waltz," these multiple transformations offer perspectives that challenge the received reading of the story as a quasi-autobiographical discourse reflecting the division in Parker's own mind between being smart and cute, the two alternative attitudes toward life that she later remarked, in a famous interview in the *Paris Review,* were the only, inadequate, and mutually contradictory choices available to her as a woman in the early twentieth century.[28] Approaching the story by acknowledging the transformative power of contextualization, that is, by paying attention not only to the story's appearance in a particular magazine at a particular time but also to its initial publication at a definable moment in literary history, we may come to have a deeper appreciation of the complex parodic dimensions of the language of "The Waltz," of the full ironic function of what Bakhtin would call the "social dialects" of the story.[29] In so doing, we will come also to a more complex understanding and appreciation of Dorothy Parker's artistry, an awareness of how in this story at least, and presumably in other stories as well, she both altered and incorporated the textual environment of the early 1930s, simultaneously accepting and resisting the language of popular literature to produce a work that, even under the closest scrutiny, deserves its status as one of the finest examples of early-twentieth-century short fiction.

NOTES

1. Mikhail Bakhtin, *The Dialogic Imagination: Four Essays,* ed. Vadim Liapunov, trans. Michael Holquist and Caryl Emerson (1981; rpt. Austin: University of Texas Press, 1990), 340.

2. Sondra Melzer, *The Rhetoric of Rage: Women in Dorothy Parker* (New York: Peter Lang, 1997).

3. Lucile Marsh, "No Girl Needs to Be a Wallflower," *Parents,* January 1932, 18.

4. The page numbers following quotations to "The Waltz" here refer to its location in *Scholastic,* 23 March 1935.

5. Paula A. Treichler, "Verbal Subversions in Dorothy Parker: 'Trapped like a Trap in a Trap,'" *Language and Style* 13:4 (1980): 58.

6. Arthur F. Kinney, *Dorothy Parker* (Boston: Twayne, 1977), 165.

7. Dorothy Parker, "The Waltz," in *After Such Pleasures* (New York: Simon and Schuster, 1933), 209.

8. *After Such Pleasures,* 212.

9. *New Yorker,* 5 March 1932, 63, 58.

10. *After Such Pleasures,* 85–96.

11. *New Yorker,* 5 March 1932, 10.

12. Ibid., 13–14.

13. Treichler, 47.

14. John Donne, "Farewell to Love," in *Poems of John Donne*, vol. 1, ed. E. K. Chambers (London: Lawrence & Bullen, 1896), 76–77.

15. Bakhtin, 337.

16. Kinney, 165; Treichler, 58.

17. Bakhtin, 359.

18. Johann Wolfgang von Goethe, *The Sorrows of Young Werther*, trans. W. H. Auden (1971; repr., New York: Random House, 1990), 27.

19. Leo Tolstoi, *War and Peace*, trans. Constance Garnett (New York: Modern Library, 2002), 504, 506.

20. *After Such Pleasures*, 211, 210. Subsequent references by page number in the text refer to this edition.

21. These remarks represent an extreme condensation of points made about romantic ballet by Lyn Garafola in her introduction to *Rethinking the Sylph: New Perspectives on the Romantic Ballet* (Hanover, NH: University Press of New England, 1997), 1–10. Among other ideas that helped to stimulate my own thoughts about the relevance and importance of at least a generalized historical balletic background to an understanding of the language of "The Waltz" is Garafola's emphasis on the ballerina as "a creature apart, an embodiment of beauty, desire, and otherness" (2).

22. Quoted in Henry Jenkins, *What Made Pistachio Nuts? Early Sound Comedy and the Vaudeville Aesthetic* (New York: Columbia University Press, 1992), 266.

23. Treichler, 51–53.

24. Ibid., 56.

25. Curt Sachs briefly discusses the folk origins of the waltz, in which female dancers frequently lifted their skirts, and the difficult time the dance had in receiving genteel approval in some nations, including Britain, in "The Age of the Waltz, 1750–1900," in *World History of the Dance* (New York: W. W. Norton, 1937), 430–31.

26. *New Yorker*, 2 March 1932, 63.

27. L. H. Chalif, "Long Skirts and the Waltz," *The Outlook and Independent* 154 (1 January 1930): 9–11.

28. Dorothy Parker, interview with Marion Capron in Malcolm Cowley, ed., *Writers at Work: The "Paris Review" Interviews* (New York: Viking, 1958).

29. Bakhtin, 262.

The Other Dorothy Parkers

Arthur F. Kinney

"AFTER SLITTING HER WRISTS, DOROTHY PARKER SAT IN THE BATHROOM patiently waiting to be rescued.

Her delicate hands were submerged in the washbasin, which was filled almost to the brim with warm water. Her previous attempts at slitting her wrists had been messy and painful, and a kindly nurse at St. Luke's had suggested the submersion in warm water for future reference. She recognized suicide in Mrs. Parker as a chronic condition. The nurse had confided to a trainee impressed by Mrs. Parker's growing celebrity: 'They're all alike, these halfway suicides. Just looking for sympathy. A kind word. Or just blackmailing the poor son of a bitch what threw them over. The idea is to fill the bastard with guilt once he gets wind of the news she tried to pass over with a straight-edge razor. This one didn't really cut deep enough. It's all superficial. If she'd really meant to go, she'd have jumped off the roof.'" Dorothy Parker, we are told, heard the nurse: "'I'm afraid of heights,' said Mrs. Parker to the nurse, who blushed."[1]

All the records extant of Parker—holograph, textual, reportorial, memorial, conventional—point to the probability of just such a scene, but in fact it opens a novel by George Baxt entitled *The Dorothy Parker Murder Case*. Baxt's fiction draws with insight and ingenuity on the public and private lives of Parker and the legendary Round Table at the Algonquin Hotel. A little later on, she returns to this failed attempt without the wisecracks.

> The bathroom was stifling. Mrs. Parker thought, who but a damned fool like me would attempt suicide on one of the hottest days in August? Her brow was damp, and her eyes were moist as she thought of MacArthur and Lardner and her unrequited love for Bob Benchley. She thought of Edwin Parker and faced the truth that she had never been in love with him, that she married him because she was tired of being Miss Rothschild. She wanted to be Mrs. Anybody and prove to her despised stepmother that she was perfectly capable of attracting and winning a man of her own.[2]

114

There are a few slippages here—she would have thought "Mr. Benchley," not "Bob Benchley," and "Eddie Parker," not "Edwin," and she likely married Parker not only for his Gentile name but for his money and social standing as the scion of a Hartford insurance family. But those affairs, and others acknowledged later in the novel, have been verified, and her natural habits of thought, which not only connected her to, but saw her identity as largely constitutive of, the Round Table, is right on the mark.

Baxt is recalling "Big Blonde," Parker's most famous story, which won the O. Henry Award for Fiction in 1929 and was collected in a volume of her stories, *Laments for the Living*, in 1930. "Big Blonde" is the tragic story of Hazel Morse, a panoramic but sharply condensed biography of a despairing woman who turns to lifelong alcoholism and repeated failed attempts at suicide because of her failed marriage and casual affairs. For her, life is as fragile as her faltering self-respect. She is haunted by a sense of unrealized possibilities and self-pity and she turns, before slashing her wrists, to Veronal, a barbital sedative which was popular under the counter but, when the story was written, was available in New York State only by prescription. There is every reason to think—as many of her readers who knew her at the time did think—that the power and penetrating insight of the story came from Parker's own autobiography, her own increasing bouts of alcoholism, her increasing despair, and her loss of her first husband who had divorced her and moved back to Hartford. We now know that Hazel Morse's despair was actually depression and what she suffered, in her wild swings from party girl to solitary drinker, was manic depression. Parker herself was a manic-depressive; and by the early 1920s she had, like Hazel Morse, become fascinated with the possibility of suicide. She studied various means of taking her own life, and searched the daily newspaper obituaries hoping to find useful details, afraid to discuss her anxieties and obsession with others, including Benchley. In mid-January 1923, she awoke late—not unusual for her—and although she was due to go to the theater that evening, she instead ordered a meal from the nearby Swiss Alps restaurant. She also began drinking. When she went to the bathroom, she discovered an old discarded razor that Eddie Parker had left behind. In "Big Blonde," Parker writes of Hazel that alcohol "could still soothe her for most of the time, but there were sudden, inexplicable moments when the cloud fell treacherously away from her." Parker cut veins in both her wrists and was found (as she knew she would be) fallen to the bathroom floor when the restaurant delivered her meal. While Baxt thought of himself as Parker's friend and admirer and while her role in the novel is major and positive, the allusion to suicide that opens it suggests that he, like so many of her friends, did not recognize her true psychological and physical condition.

Baxt was not, however, the first person to put the Round Table, and Parker with it, into fiction. Her fictional debut was by an occasional member of the Round Table, Gertrude Atherton, in her novel *Black Oxen,* published by Parker's publisher of the near-contemporary volume of poems, *Enough Rope,* Boni and Liveright, in 1923. Here members of the Round Table are called the Sophisticates. The socialite Anne Goodrich asks the protagonist Clavering to introduce her to them: "I want really to know people whose minds are constantly at work, who are doing the things we get the benefit of when we are intelligent enough to appreciate them."[3] While agreeing with Anne, Clavering turns her very popular judgment into satire.

> "They are workers, engaged in doing the things they think most worthwhile—which are worthwhile because they furnish what the intelligent public is demanding just now, and upon which the current market places a high value. And you are merely an intellectual young woman of leisure. They might think it a pity you didn't have to work, but secretly, no matter what their regard, they'd consider you negligible because you belong to a class that is content to be, not to do. I assure you they consider themselves the most important group in New York—in America—at present: the life-giving group of suns round which far-off planets humbly revolve." (151)

The description is derisive, but Anne Goodrich, her friends, and Clavering, do not see it that way. For them, the Sophisticates are a means for socializing and an index to their own social success. The evolving satire concludes a few pages later when the true sophisticate of the novel—or so it first appears—the European-bred Madame Zattiany, seeks to meet them before becoming disgusted with the Sophisticates' self-congratulatory appeal to the trivial and commercial.

> "Tell me, what do they do at these parties besides talk—dance?"
> "Not always. They have charades, spelling matches, pick a word out of a hat and make impromptu speeches—"
> "But *Mon dieu!*" She stopped short and pushed back her scarf. Whatever expression she may have wished to conceal there was nothing now in her face but dismay. "But you did not tell me this or I should not have accepted. I never bore myself. I understand these were your intellectuals. Charades! Spelling matches! Words in the hat! It sounds like a small town moved to New York." (153)

In time Madame Zattiany will turn out to be other than what is expected herself: the elderly expatriate Mary Ogden made to look youthful again by pioneering European treatment that satirizes the American woman's dream. She herself is less than the reputation she fosters and, with another twist, we learn that from her perspective,

> It was certainly the "distinguished party" he had promised. There were some eight or ten of the best-known novelists and story-writers in the country, two dramatists, several of the younger publishers, most of the young editors, critics, columnists, and illustrators, famous in New York, at least; a few poets, artists; the more serious contributors to the magazines and reviews; an architect, an essayist, a sculptress, a famous girl librarian of a great private library, three correspondents of foreign newspapers, and two visiting British authors. The men wore evening dress. The women, if not all patrons of the ranking "houses" and dressmakers, were correct. Even the artistic gowns stopped short of delirium. And if many of the women wore their hair short, so did all of the men. Everybody in the room was reasonably young or had managed to preserve the appearance and spirit of youth . . . (155)

as, we discover in time, has the disguised Mary Ogden. Madame Zattiany as voyeur makes us voyeuristic, too, but it is difficult here—deliberately so, I think—to measure Atherton's purpose and tone. The fact that the party of Sophisticates includes the literary leaders and that they in turn command editors, foreign critics, and authors from overseas suggests that this is the literary as well as the fashion center of America. Either Madame Zattiany's judgments about wordplay miss the mark of verbal imagination and good times—not trivial at all but mirroring a deeper capacity for language—or literary fashion in New York remains self-satisfied and potentially or actually shallow. Like Atherton herself, who slipped in and out of daily gatherings of the Round Table at the Algonquin Hotel, this portrait of the Sophisticates equivocates.

The same is true, too, of the character who seems most like Dorothy Parker, although she is not named Parker as in Baxt, but rather Gora Dwight.

> Gora Dwight was a very ambitious woman and reveled in the authority that fame and success had brought her. She was also as disillusioned in regard to men as any unmarried woman could be; although quite aware that if she had lacked a gift to entice her emotions to her brain, she no doubt would even now be looking about for some man to fall in love with. But her pride was spared a succession of humiliating anticlimaxes,

and she had learned, younger than most women, or even men, that power, after sex has ceased from troubling, is the dominant passion in human nature. (336)

The description is revealing, for Parker never thought of herself as ambitious, but rather as indolent, doing just enough to get by, writing just enough to keep bringing home her paycheck. Nor if she was aware of the necessity of controlling her emotions with the brittle insights of her mind was she as enabled as Gora Dwight. Atherton's portrait, then, is only half-right, perhaps in an attempt to sidestep accusations that Parker was the source for her character.

But the wisecracks Atherton gives her character give her away. Such remarks as "your description of that prizefight last night . . . was about as thrilling as an account of a flower show" are transparently Parker, combining as they do both an adolescent cleverness and a stiletto-sharp critical judgment. (70) In the course of the novel, though, the Sophisticates have a minor if significant role: they support the courtship of Clavering for Madame Zattiany and allow it to ripen into the defeat it would in due course produce. Along the way, Gora, like Parker, shows sympathy in her counsel to Clavering. Yet by the time she appears in the novel, she is past her youth; she is an intellectual, perceptive, but contented spinster of middle age who no longer has any emotional entanglements of her own, again diverging from Parker as a model. It is as if Atherton, in writing *Black Oxen*, wanted to describe the Sophisticates and Parker because they are an unavoidable part of the New York literary scene where the novel is set, but at the same time she is unwilling either to admire or condemn them. Consequently, the part they play in the novel is limited and, to a degree, ineffective.

The competition, though, would be stiff, and in just another decade. George Oppenheimer based the character of Mary Hilliard on her in *Here Today* and Philip Barry used Parker as a model for Lily Malone in *Hotel Universe* (both 1932). Oppenheimer subtitled *Here Today* "A Comedy of Bad Manners." The play was directed by George S. Kaufman, another member of the Algonquin Round Table, who cast Ruth Gordon as Mary Hilliard. Parker was caricatured in both stage mannerisms and dialogue, but the satire, clear enough about its target, was superficial. That was not the case with *Merrily We Roll Along* which Kaufman wrote with Moss Hart (1934). Parker is portrayed in Julia Glenn, an alcoholic who likes to sleep with men younger than herself (a habit Parker, now putting on weight with her drinking, also had) and covers over her escapades with wisecracks. This was a much more humiliating portrayal than

Here Today. A decade later, in 1944, Ruth Gordon based the character of Paula Wharton on Parker in *Over Twenty-one*, but the resemblance is more generalized. Paula is a famous screenwriter and novelist whose husband is in Officer Candidate School at the age of thirty-nine, just as Parker's second husband, Alan Campbell, had insisted on signing up for officer's duty in World War II against Parker's wishes. Gordon's play was later made into a film with Irene Dunne playing Paula Wharton. Parker was treated with more restraint as a minor character in novels of this period, too: she appears as Mrs. Roger Barbee in *The Crazy Fool* by Donald Ogden Stewart (1925) and as Daisy Lester in *Entirely Surrounded* by Charles Brackett (1934), both romans à clef.

Dorothy Parker first appears as herself in fiction, and in a major role, in Edwin Corley's Hollywood novel *Shadows*.[4] Published eight years after Parker's death, *Shadows* also includes, as other major characters, Clark Gable, Carole Lombard (then his wife), Errol Flynn, Scott Fitzgerald, Humphrey Bogart, Vivien Leigh (anxious to win Gable for herself), William Randolph Hearst, Marion Davies (his wife who was ten years his junior and then a fading starlet), John Barrymore, and David O. Selznick. The central characters are Mitch Gardner, a scriptwriter of distinction who wishes to direct his first film, *The Donner Party*, with either Marion Davies or Vivien Leigh in the leading woman's role (causing considerable conflict), and his father Charlie, a famous Broadway actor as the male lead. In the novel, the film is underwritten by Hearst (in a contract with Warners) in another of his many attempts to advance Davies' career. The Gardners are fictitious, but the others are not. Nor are the background events in the novel, which opens with *Gone With the Wind* sweeping the Academy Awards, which are announced (as they were) by Bob Hope in the Ambassador Hotel in 1940, and ends when Hearst destroys the film to protect his sense of Davies' reputation. The film puts her in a serious role, which Hearst thought only embarrassed her. Davies' reputation depended on light roles as comedienne, and Corley's novel is rich in its firsthand knowledge of the ways of Hollywood. The novel, fast-paced, entertaining, and everywhere seemingly authentic in its many references, is grounded in the tension between the real lives of famous people, his inside information on producing Hollywood films in their heyday, and the fact that what they produce is at best fiction; as Tallulah Bankhead says to Mitch at one point (which also becomes the novel's epigraph), "What are motion pictures, really? Nothing but shadows on the wall, mummified memories of a performance someone gave long ago." Thus Atherton's apparent strategy—to reveal and withdraw the authenticity of her society romance—becomes Corley's basic theme. In this novel, Mitch's "great good friend Dorothy Parker" has the respect, as scriptwriter, of Ben Hecht, Charlie MacArthur, S. N. Behrman, and Sidney Howard, her reputation able to withstand the indiscretions of someone like George S. Kaufman (12, 64). Throughout her half-dozen or so appearances in the novel, Parker is both insightful and sympathetic and worn by sentiment. At one point she describes to Mitch Gardner the tragedy of Fitzgerald:

> "You might not have noticed, Mitch, because you never had a sensitive bone in your body. But when Scott was over at MGM with the rest of us—Anita Loos and Perelman and Ogden Nash—he'd come tippytoeing past our offices like a little mouse, and sometimes he'd tap on the door, but when he opened it, he wouldn't come in. I'd say, 'Park her there, pal,' and Scott would shake his head and mumble, 'No, you're just being nice. You don't really want to talk with me,' and nothing you'd say would get it out of his head that he was intruding. This, from the same Scotty who used to throw his hat over the transom into an editor's office and barge in like he owned the joint." The tiny writer shook her head. "Hollywood took the guts out of him."
> She fumbled in her purse and took out a silver flask.
> "Want a nip?" (81)

She is most distraught when Fitzgerald dies—in actuality, she was one of a handful at his funeral—and it followed (as was historically the case) with the car accident that killed Nathaniel West and his wife Eileen, other friends of Parker's. But in *Shadows*, Parker also received from Fitzgerald a poem, and this is pure fiction.

> "He knew he was dying, Mitch. Listen to this. He sent it to me only last week. It's a kind of poem." She smoothed a sheet of paper, and read:
> Your books were in your desk
>   I guess and some unfinished
> Chaos in your head
> Was dumped to nothing by the great janitress
>   Of destinies.
> She folded it carefully and put it back in her purse. "That's the lousy part, Mitch. He died thinking he'd failed. But that's not true. We all know that." (172)

As with so much of Corley's novel, the historic event is itself a shadow of larger matters—wasted talent, exploited people, art as merchandise—and thus reflects its own shadows on both Parker and Mitch. It is also prophetic: as it speaks analogously to Parker's floundering career in film writing, so it looks forward to Hearst's anger and revenge and to Davies' loss of a serious role in her attempt for stardom. The historic Donner party, the lost party of emigrants who resorted to cannibalism to stay alive, is used as a symbol of the cannibalism of Hollywood as a business. More subtly, where life slips into art, where art mirrors or exaggerates or even destroys life, and may therefore threaten art, is the chief concern of *Shadows*, and Parker's role as Mitch's confidante who always sees these potential dangers makes her credible and likeable, although it does not dismiss her own shortcomings. Corley's novel, which critics and reviewers found enjoyable, delightful, or fantastic in its treatment of the renowned golden days of Hollywood, is also a tragedy, too sympathetic ever to become satiric. At first swift and entertaining, it is by the end brooding and troubling. William Randolph Hearst, speaking to Mitch Gardner, provides the epigraph for chapter 1 of the novel: "Do not look back, young man. There is nothing there. It ceases to exist the moment you pass it by."

In transferring Parker from a supporting character to the title role, Baxt is just as precise and accurate. The plot of *The Dorothy Parker Murder Case* pits Parker and Alexander Woollcott as sleuths who, with the aid of police detective Jacob Singer, attempt to identify the murderer of a prostitute found dead in the bed of George Kaufman's hideaway in uptown Manhattan. Parker is portrayed as bright, clever, self-deprecating, courageous—and vulnerable. Her character is rounded and full-bodied, seasoned by a certain edge of self-consciousness. She identifies herself in a woman's room at one point when interrogating the suspect prostitute of Texas Guinan's, the fictional Lily Robson.

> "Listen, lady, I don't hardly know you."
> "My name is Dorothy Parker. I write short stories, poems, articles and poison-pen letters. I am frequently quoted, though most of the time incorrectly. All sorts of supposedly witty bitcheries are attributed to me, but I can assure you, most of them are apocryphal." The girl seemed perplexed by "apocryphal." Mrs. Parker couldn't resist what followed.
> "Surely you've heard of the four horsemen of the apocryphal."
> "Oh, yeah, I saw the movie."
> "You can trust me."[5]

Throughout her investigation, she is ingenious, inventive, cautious. Before anyone suspects that the initial murder will lead Parker and others into an international crime and drug syndicate that is highly dangerous, she volunteers her services to protect Kaufman: "these people are more accessible to people like Alec and myself. We intend to investigate, you know, like ambassadors without portfolio. Of course everything we learn we'll turn over to you," she tells Singer, in exchange for his keeping the location of the prostitute's death secret. (25) Singer comes to admire her skills of investigation and deduction. "You're making a lot of sense, Mrs. Parker," he tells her later, and adds, "I'm beginning to understand you when you go quiet all of a sudden. I used to have an aunt who would do that at times. It used to drive my uncle nuts. Then she'd come up with one hell of a recipe" (91). But her theories grow out of her sense of human nature, and of art. "She wanted to be alone to sort out her thoughts, because she had an idea who Lacey Van Weber really was. It had been nagging at her mind for most of the day, a solution she kept piecing together from little droplets of information that escaped from him indirectly, and the reports from the Los Angeles police. She didn't want to discuss it with either Singer or Woollcott until it made complete sense in her own mind, the way she wouldn't submit a poem or a short story until she was certain that every word was where it belonged, precise and crisp" (229).

Yet Baxt's Dorothy Parker seems always authentic in his portrayal because her rational precision is countered by her emotional vulnerability—that caused the fake suicide at the novel's opening. The man she comes to suspect is at first bedazzling, and the phrasing (as with the pharaohs) much like Parker's own.

> She looked up and suppressed a gasp of sexual excitement. He was almost six feet tall with the physique of an athlete. His eyes were a cobalt blue, and she knew they hid the secrets of the pharaohs. She would later describe his nose to Woollcott as "excruciatingly perfect." She could tell he had been poured into his Palm Beach suit. There wasn't a crease or wrinkle in evidence. He held his Panama hat lightly in his right hand. His smile filled her with fairy-tale enchantment. His teeth were of a Steinway grand quality, and the texture of his skin was enough to make a six-month infant scream with envy. He was too perfect and destroying her metabolism.
>
> "I do hope I'm Mrs. Parker," she said softly and girlishly, one hand at her chest because she was finding breathing difficult. He sat down next to her, his smile widening and more dazzling, and she wondered if this was how you felt when you're about to suffer a stroke. (42)

It becomes clear to the reader, long before it does to any of the characters, however, that Van Weber's situation and behavior are closely patterned on Fitzgerald's Gatsby and that, like Daisy, Parker's infatuation has no hope of success however likely it might first seem to be. The curious strategy of developing one fictional character from another may be Baxt's way of suggesting, as Corley did, that in a genre like faction—fiction based on fact—the borderline between reality and art, life and illusion, is always porous and indeterminate. Fictional Ilona Mercury is strangled the day Valentino dies.

Both Parker's intellectual inventiveness and emotional weakness are exposed, most frequently against the backdrop of gatherings of the Round Table, or in conversation with Woollcott, Neysa McMein (who lives across the corridor from Parker and keeps a watchful eye on her), and Robert Benchley. Benchley's counsel to "stop falling in love with the wrong men" and Parker's ingenuity at putting the word testosterone into a sentence—"At lunch, the waiter tossed salads for Lily and Elsie, but Tess tossed 'er own"—is interrupted by the discovery of newspapers of the dead body of Ilona Mercury in a vacant lot in the Canarsie section of Brooklyn (66–68); Parker abruptly leaves a noisy party at McMein's with freshly made bathtub gin to question Cora Gallagher, who barely survived an attempt to push her to her death by an unknown assailant for knowledge she has until now kept secret (227–32). Round Table repartees sag beneath the weight of multiplying murder(148, 156, 165, 216–17, 229). Here wordplay is not simply the characteristic of the Round Table, as it is in Atherton, but a deliberate way of offsetting the tawdriness of reality—of the strangled corpse in Kaufman's hideaway, the seediness of George Raft, the furnishings of the madam Texas Guinan:

> Texas Guinan's apartment in Greenwich Village was a monument to bad taste. Instead of doors, there were beaded drapes, which an old beau had suggested were probably inspired by her beady eyes. The furniture was frayed old plush, with oranges, reds and browns predominating. Strewn around the room was a variegated collection of Kewpie dolls and teddy bears. The grand piano groaned under the weight of numerous framed photographs of celebrities and relatives (she adored her brother, Tommy Guinan, a small-time hood in Larry Fay's employ), some autographed, some bogus, such as one of President Calvin Coolidge wearing an Indian headdress. The windows were draped with velvet green materials artfully run up for her by two reformed prostitutes she had financed with sewing machines (actually conned out of a scion of the Singer family who owed her a favor). The carpet covering the living room floor was interwoven with fauns and satyrs, uninhibited, and Texas was now reclining on a chaise lounge wishing George Raft would stop wearing a path in her favorite floor covering. (203)

Such vulgarity meant to be the most attractive fashion inverts Van Weber's mansion on Long Island.

> Half an hour later, Mrs. Parker was still being given the grand tour. She had been led to impeccably designed tiered gardens and had appropriately admired the oversized swimming pool. His private dock boasted a cabin cruiser as well as a motorboat moored nearby. A short distance ahead stood an impressive lighthouse, constructed on a spit of land that overlooked and protected the entrance to the estate's private bay. . . . Of course the interior was palatially furnished and decorated with immaculate taste . . . (167)

with Tintorettos, Van Goghs, and Van Dycks. But the huge estate with its servants, perfect trout luncheon, and tryst in the main bedroom, is also menacing, as Guinan's apartment ultimately is:

> He made a right turn, and they soon entered what looked like a compound within the compound, a huge stone structure topped by a slate chimney from which smoke poured forth. Two men came running out of the structure toward the car.
> "It's all right, boys. It's me. I took a wrong turning!"
> The men watched as Van Weber backed the vehicle out of the compound. Mrs. Parker suppressed a shudder. One man had an ugly scar on his right cheek running from his ear to his mouth. The other was missing part of his right ear. (171–72)

At the same time Parker risks her life in a solo flight with Van Weber, Woollcott is nearly run down in the street in an attempt to murder him.

More than mere turns and twists of plot, such inconsistencies and juxtapositions renew the need for rational thought and the escape in wordplay. Just as Parker's ability to sympathize with others leads her to understand their possible behavior and motives, so this same openness to feelings as well as thoughts brings her into dangerous situations, especially through her infatuation for Van Weber. This puts the activities of the Algonquin Round Table into a light that enlarges the need and deceptive safety of wit, as well as the willed ignorance of how such wit needs to be bought and sold (as with Benchley's need to move to Hollywood simply to support his family (66). Reality keeps intruding on art, inspiring it, encouraging it, defeating it. All of this is best embodied in the characterization of Parker herself. The first person, in the end, to penetrate Van Weber's disguise and involvement, she solves a multiple murder case because of and at the expense of her own infatuation. Benchley predicts this in an obtuse and clumsy way—"I wish you'd stop falling in love with the wrong men"—but it is Woollcott who measures its final effect at the end (66).

> Now Woollcott stared at himself in the mirror as he knotted his tie. His words to Mrs. Adler had come back to haunt him. Straightedge razor. Peculiar hunger.
>
> "Hell fire and damnation!" shouted Woollcott as he grabbed his jacket off the back of a chair and went hurrying out of his room.
>
> Mrs. Parker sat in the bathroom, the razor poised over one of her wrists, her eyes and soul damp with tears. She pressed the razor against the outline of the previous slashing.
>
> She would wait to be rescued. (284)

Such opening and closing scenes also allude, of course, to Parker's poem "Résumé."

> Razors pain you;
> Rivers are damp;
> Acids stain you;
> And drugs cause cramp.
> Guns aren't lawful;
> Nooses give;
> Gas smells awful;
> You might as well live.[6]

Yet in capturing the high cost of mordant wit, the powers of mind and the temptations of life at cross purposes, both Corley and Baxt measure the cost of Parker's personality and art. And by placing their other Dorothy Parkers in works of fiction, they suggest how good art can be serious even when it pretends only to entertain, while the facts of our lives are the very stuff such art is made of. The line between the best art and the most energetic lives can become, under scrutiny, invisible.

NOTES

1. George Baxt, *The Dorothy Parker Murder Case* (New York: St. Martin's Press, 1984), 1.

2. Ibid., 4.

3. Gertrude Atherton, *Black Oxen* (New York: Boni & Liveright, 1923), 150. Subsequent references by page number in the text refer to this edition.

4. Edwin Corley, *Shadows* (New York: Stein and Day, 1975; repr., New York: First

Day Books, 1978); subsequent references by page number in the text are to the reprint edition.

5. Baxt, *The Dorothy Parker Murder Case*, 128; subsequent references are given by page number in the text.

6. Dorothy Parker, *Enough Rope* (New York: Boni and Liverright, 1926), 61.

Here Lies
by
Mehitabel

Lynn Z. Bloom

CALL ME MEHITABEL. THAT'S WHAT i SAID, KID, MEHITABEL, AN ALLEY CAT and proud of it, the life of lower Manhattan's moveable feast, "never / anything vulgar always free footed," and "a good mixer too."[1] If this reminiscence—how I do love those high-class words—of my life with Dorothy Parker reveals that both of us, and Dorothy's heroines too, may have "seen better days," "whats the use of kicking kid its / all in the game." Our motto, a suitable creed for Hazel, Dorothy's "Big Blonde," and her hapless ilk, is "toujours gai kid toujours gai" (30).

In fact, everybody and their brother waxes eloquent on the gay life and the longest liquid lunch of the Roaring Twenties, at the Algonquin Round Table, where a bunch of the swell gents—Robert Benchley, Alexander Woollcott, Heywood Broun, and Harold Ross, yes the one who founded the *New Yorker*—was whooping it up with Dorothy Parker, their mascot with barbed tongue. Dorothy she was to me, too, too smart to be called Dot, too unmarried for Mrs. Parker, really *did* say when challenged by Franklin P. Adams to use *horticulture* in a sentence, "You can lead a horticulture but you can't make her think." A line on par, I thought, for I pricked up my ears at that one, with "Men seldom make passes / At girls who wear glasses." Yes, I heard both of these with my own ears, bon mots that don't cut the mustard nowadays with feminist critics but wotthehell.

I was there under that Round Table every lunch; Dorothy fed me on the sly with her own generous hand—raw oysters, which she hated, steak-and-kidney pie, occasionally a steak (her favorite) she couldn't finish, not a bite of tripe. Dorothy and I had, you might say, a temperamental affinity; as I told her, "i am a lady but i am bohemian too" (217). None of those biographers who claim to know Dorothy ever gets it right, and neither do those few critics who have given her work more than trivializing commentary, for all of them to a person write me out of the story that is really ours together. They make a great hoo-ha over Dorothy and her canine companions du jour, but what they don't recognize is that she was always attended by a so-called dog that was really me in disguise. As Flush (another covert tabby) was to Elizabeth Barrett Browning was I to Dorothy Parker. Although my spirit was once "incarnated in the body of Cleopatra" (23), in recent centuries I have "transmigrated from body to body" (29) and seem fated forevermore to fast-forward through life on four feline feet, "one life up and the next life / down" (30). Dogs, if the truth be known, "don't have it any more they don't have it here," I say, putting front paw to breast like the old theater cat who "in a case of emergency played a bloodhound in a production of uncle tom's cabin" (110).

Dorothy Parker understood what it took to be a trouper, and sisters we were under the skin. Both of us knew very well the importance of disguise and putting on a brave front, and both of us were smarter and tougher than the women Dorothy wrote about. I flatter myself, perhaps, in thinking she learned resilience from me. Her poetry—she always called it "verse"—and stories told time after time the tales of women with fewer of the "aristocratic fixings and condiments" than their author (218). For Dorothy wrote of lasses too lovelorn for the flapper era in which they were born; or culturally and economically out of step with Rosie the Riveter during World War II; and in addition politically incorrect ever since the Women's Movement made mincemeat (why not, may I ask, the much tastier sushi?) of women's dependency on men that Betty Friedan labeled "The Feminine Mystique."

Indeed, *Enough Rope, Sunset Gun, Death and Taxes,* and many of Dorothy's short stories are inhabited by the kind of women who would have benefited from my brand of alley-cat toughness. The major motifs (what a swell word) of Dorothy's poems are love, loneliness, and death. Loneliness and death, however, are usually variations on the theme of romantic love—exploited or exploitative, betrayed, feigned, unrequited, abandoned, lost. The relations between men and women are disagreeable and duplicitous: "Scratch a lover and find a foe."[2] Dorothy's women characters seem doomed to perpetual emotional dependence on men, whose indifferences, fickleness, and callousness drives them to the despair implied in the books' macabre titles. Love relationships, so fleeting and superficial, are based on appearance (eyes "slant and slow," hair "sweet to touch"—"Prophetic Soul"), "dust-bound trivia" ("The Searched Soul"), and aaaah—youth. If lovers swear their devotion is "infinite, undying," one or both is bound to be lying ("Unfortunate Coincidence"). The woman is more likely to be the victim on her passion, however, for "Woman lives but in her lord; / Count to ten, and man is bored" ("General Review of the Sex Situation"). Dalliance, not marriage, is the aim of the men—and, in a modern twist—of some of the women, as well, for lovers are numerous, faceless, and somewhat interchangeable: "I always get them all mixed up" ("Pictures in the Smoke").

Dorothy's narrative female persona (another swell phrase) plays one of two typical roles. In one guise she is an abandoned lover, "brief and frail and blue" ("Sweet Violets"), weighted down by "heavy freedom" ("Prisoner"), and despair "The sun's gone dim, and / The moon's turned black; / for I loved him, and / He didn't love back" ("Two-Volume Novel"). The other role is much more in keeping with her public persona (there's that great word again)—and mine—a wisecracking, savvy, jaded woman who knows "it's just my luck to get / one perfect rose" instead of "one perfect limousine" ("One Perfect Rose"). Worldly wise, she can also recognize the earmarks of the predatory male (whose wife "is the lodestar of his Life"—"Social Note"), her own inconstancy ("I loved them until they love me"—"Ballade at Thirty-Five"), and the inevitable denouement ("Scratch lover and find a foe"—"Ballade of a Great Weariness"). Like myself, Dorothy mocks virginity ("Parable for a Certain Virgin"), scorns sedate society ("Inseparable my nose and thumb"—"Neither Bloody nor Bowed"), and will eagerly engage "in fun and such" until 3 a.m.—for I shall stay the way I am / Because I do not give a damn" ("Observation"). The hallmarks of this persona are "laughter and hope and a sock in the eye" ("Inventory").

Had I possessed an opposable thumb instead of having to rely on Archy, "once a verse libre bard [whose] soul went into the body of a cockroach" (20), to serve as my amanuensis, I'd have written exactly as Dorothy did. I'd have used capital letters, too, as she did, but Archy wasn't strong enough to operate the typewriter's shift mechanism, though he hurled himself upon the keys, "one slow letter after another" (20). Like so many of Dorothy's ladies, I was forever being lured to romance by any cat that "came by with a come hither look in his eye and a song that soared to the sky." I would follow "a down the street the pad of his rhythmical feet" (25) only to find that he—whoever he was—would "betray the trust of an innocent female" (61). Time after time I was seduced, abandoned, sadder and wiser, as were many of Dorothy Parker's pulchritudinous pussycats. Nevertheless, ever resilient, I shared with my favorite creatrix rather than her characters "the zest of the alley cat" (31); we relished our repast of ham on wry and proffered if for others to share: "i will not eat tomorrow / and i did not eat today / but wotthehell i ask you / the word is toujours gai" (129). So "wotthehell wotthehell," we always said to one another, "cage me and i d go frantic / my life is so romantic / capricious and corybantic / and i m toujours gai toujours gai" (24).

"Always the life of the party," neither of us was in the least domestic, a configuration of values we shared with Dorothy's heroines. In between marriages and sometimes during them Dorothy lived in hotels and smuggled me in from the nearby back streets (a euphemism for "alleys," *n'est-ce pas?*) to provide perspective on her oeuvre du jour. More and more, as she sought solace in *la boutielle* she wrote less and less, overcome by massive writer's block ("I can't write five words but that I change seven"). Archy and I tried to cover for her, but as my locution was perforce oral and Archy was alas unable to shift for himself (if you dare to call us handicapped, "if i wasn t an / aristocrat id rip you / from gehenna to duodenum" [217]), we had to wait for Dorothy to supply the capital letters and the punctuation and of course to provide whatever verbal arabesques she wanted. Sometimes we had a very long wait. Thus our literary production, though it retained the impeccable judgment, witty insouciance, and joie de vivre of our Muse, also appeared according to an innocence of deadline that struck all but the most forgiving as erratic caprice. In short, we seemed as unreliable, though as talented, as Dorothy did, and although our trio continued to collaborate on book reviews for *Esquire* (1959–62), we never attained the notoriety there that we had achieved in our earlier reviews for the *New Yorker* (1927–33).

I actually wrote some of Dorothy's most memorable lines, but with characteristic modesty I allowed her to take the credit, wotthehell did pride of authorship matter. Yes, yes, Dorothy and her husband Alan Campbell, handsome devil, well worth marrying twice (of their second wedding Dorothy told her great friend Lillian Hellman, "Lilly, the room was filled with people who hadn't talked to each other in years, including the bride and bridegroom,"[3] did collaborate on some twenty screenplays, including *A Star is Born* (1938), and he got credit where credit was due. But I digress. Archy and I shared Dorothy's pain at the saccharine, anthropocentric point of view manifested in A. A. Milne's sanitary universe of stuffed animals who had never lived life as we cognoscenti understood if from the underside. Pooh and Piglet and Eeyore and Kanga didn't "have it here," or there or anywhere else, so it was with great glee that I penned (I speak, of course, in the figurative sense) the grand finale to our review of the nouveau Milne volume:

"Tiddledy what?" said Piglet. (He took, as you might say, the very words out of your correspondent's mouth.)

"Pom," said Pooh. "I put that in to make it more hummy."

And it is that word "hummy," my darlings, that marks the first place in *The House at Pooh Corner* at which Tonstant Weader Fwowed up (518).

We took our success in stride—on two, four, and six legs respectively. In our most productive days, nights actually (as Dorothy said, "As only New Yorkers know, if you can get through the twilight you'll live through the night"[4]), we were writing reviews that added luster to our already illustrious subjects. Of Hemingway we said, "[Sinclair] Lewis remains a reporter and Hemingway stands a genius because Hemingway has an unerring sense of selection. He discards details with magnificent lavishness; he keeps his words to their short path" ("A Book of Great Short Stories," 461). We were likewise right on the money with Shirley Jackson's *We Have Always Lived in the Castle*, a "leader in the field of beautifully written, quiet, cumulative shudders" that "brings back all [one's] faith in terror and death" (575).

Of nearly equal importance, through sheer wit we immortalized—as Alexander Pope had done before us in *The Dunciad*—authors and volumes that have long since disappeared into remainder hell. As a denizen of the Left Bank in a former life, my favorite review remains, *naturellement*, "The Grandmother of the Aunt of the Gardener," an unforgettable anatomization of the otherwise obscure *Ideal System for Acquiring a Practical Knowledge of French* by Mlle. V. D. Gaudel, subtitled *Just the French One Wants to Know.* Here Dorothy slipped, with a little help from her friends, into her characteristic persona of a femme d'un certain age, struggling to learn a language that forever escapes her, in hopes of capturing a romantic culture also beyond her grasp. Challenged by the subtitle to "search the tome only for concrete examples of just the French one will never need," our heroine becomes progressively more frustrated and enraged by the ridiculous sentences the book proposes as essential: "I admire the large black eyes of this orphan," "It was to punish your foster-brother." "It might occur that I must thunder: 'Obey, or I will not show you the beautiful gold chain.' But I will be damned if it is ever going to be of any good to me to have at hand Mlle. Gaudel's masterpiece: 'I am afraid he will not arrive in time to accompany me on the harp'" (*Portable*, 547). I myself have incorporated these sentences into my normative discourse; I use them early, I use them often—invariably wowing my pals with their sophistication and finesse.

From start to finish of her writing career, Dorothy's portrayal of women—and all of her central characters are women (where, I ask, are the cats?)—whose self-worth depends on a youthful appearance, a sprightly demeanor, and an attractiveness to men (however crude, rude, or loutish they may be) is according to feminist standards, politically incorrect. Dorothy would have been more attuned to the temper of the times had she collaborated with Archy and me instead of with Arnaud d'Usseau on her last long work, *The Ladies of the Corridor* (1953). This is a play about pathetic women, aging, idle, and widowed residents of an expensive Manhattan apartment hotel, who lead lives of trivial desperation—"It's not so much age as manlessness," explained Dorothy.[5] One surly biographer (Marion Meade) reads it as "a drama bout being Dorothy Parker at fifty-nine," whose characters represent various facets of Dorothy herself, "feeling terrified, living in a hotel without a man," an alcoholic, a "would-be-suicide," and "the crone she feared becoming"[6] in betrayal of her reputation as—in Benchley's words—"the everlasting ingénue."[7] But what, I ask, is political correctness? Dorothy, like myself, was a political humanitarian, a defender of the civil liberties of laborers and blacks; she willed her modest estate to Martin Luther King, Jr.[8] Her activities in the 1930s as a chief organizer of the Screen Writers Guild and founder of the Anti-Fascist League in 1936 led to her being branded a "a premature anti-Facist" and therefore subversive and unfit to write movie scripts in the paranoid postwar McCarthy era.[9] That Dorothy could be simultaneously satiric and subversive, sybaritical and radical political is epitomized in an accolade writ by one of mine own admirers, "do real ladies / smoke pipes / or drink cocktails / or other alcoholic / beverages . . . or do they instead . . . / take a great / interest in civic / affairs and local / politics and / go around doing good."[10] Friends we were to the end. To cheer Dorothy from her increasingly alcoholic perspective I would "prance and pirouette"; "there's life in the old world yet," I would remind her.[11] But the voice that reached her most deeply was Lillian Hellman's deep-throated growl; "Oh, Lilly, come in quick," Dorothy would say, "I want to laugh again."[12]

C'est Tout was the only being in attendance at her death. *C'est Tout c'etait moi, toujours gai. C'est fini.* Wotthehell.

NOTES

1. Courtesy of Archy the Cockroach, Don Marquis, and Lynn Z. Bloom. The references to Mehitabel's life are from Don Marquis, *The Lives and Times of Archy*

and Mehitabel (Garden City, NY: Doubleday, 1950), 30; subsequent references in the text are given by page number.

2. Dorothy Parker, *The Portable Dorothy Parker*, ed. Brendan Gill, rev. ed. (New York: Viking, 1973), subsequent references to Parker's work come from this edition.

3. Lillian Hellman, *An Unfinished Woman: A Memoir* (1969; repr., New York: Bantam, 1970), 192.

4. Leslie Frewin, *The Late Mrs. Parker* (New York: Macmillan, 1986), 294.

5. Arthur F. Kinney, *Dorothy Parker* (Boston: Twayne, 1978), 97.

6. Marion Meade, *Dorothy Parker: What Fresh Hell Is This?* (New York: Villard, 1988), 350–51.

7. Frewin, 321.

8. Hellman, 195.

9. Kinney, 67.

10. Marquis, 458.

11. Ibid., 452.

12. Hellman, 195.

Part II
Feminist Issues

Dorothy Parker, Erica Jong, and New Feminist Humor

Emily Toth

WHEN FRANCES BERRY WHITCHER WAS DRIVEN OUT OF TOWN IN 1850 because her neighbors discovered that she was "The Widow Bedott" who had satirized them unmercifully, she observed: "It is a very serious thing to be a funny woman."[1]

She was right, of course: even in the twentieth century a funny woman—and especially one who laughs about sex roles and sex—is apt to be considered dangerous, if not subversive. Unless she keeps herself in Salingeresque seclusion, she'll be both feared and criticized, in terms ranging from "bitch" to "mammoth pudenda." She'll be attacked by both women and men for real and imagined sins, perhaps because she's saying through humor what oft was thought but ne'er so well express'd.

Still, writers of new feminist humor—like Erica Jong, E. M. Broner, and Rita Mae Brown—have a large and growing audience. When we measure the distance between Dorothy Parker and Erica Jong, we can see that even advertising can be right: we *have* come a long way.

⁂

Dorothy Parker (1893–1967) was, officially, the wittiest woman of the 1920s, and the best example of what I would call the more traditional female humor. Her wit was a weapon: "A girl's best friend is her mutter," she said.[2] Noted for her quick comebacks, she never repeated a wisecrack because she knew other people would.[3] And she specialized in truths close to home: nearsighted herself and very vain about it, she wrote

> Men seldom make passes
> At girls who wear glasses.[4]

Told that Calvin Coolidge—the slow-moving, colorless ex-President who rarely opened his mouth to speak—was dead, Dorothy Parker wondered aloud, "How could they tell?"

Some of her witticisms came from her sympathies—especially with underdogs, human or canine. Once she and a friend rode to a dog show with the friend's boxer, who was not part of the performance but came as their guest. On arrival, Parker was enraged to learn that the boxer could not come in with them. And then, mindful of canine sensitivities, she told him solicitously, "We are going to a fish show."

She was especially expert at the game of embrace-and-denounce. As Lillian Hellman reports in *An Unfinished Woman,* when Dorothy Parker met acquaintances at parties, she would hug them, flatter them, and tell them how delighted she was to see them. Then, when their backs were turned, she would say in her soft but penetrating voice, "Did you ever meet such a shit?"[5] And her barbs were frequently directed at women, and women who lived the kind of independent, emancipated life she did: "You know, that woman speaks eighteen languages?" she once told friends. "And she can't say 'No' in any of them."

I call Dorothy Parker's humor traditional primarily because of its targets. As all satirists do, she attacked affectation and hypocrisy,[6] but like such traditional satirists as Juvenal and Swift she often attacked women—for such stereotyped traits as cattiness, backbiting, and competition. While her short stories do tend to be more sympathetic, her verbal barbs and her poems—most of them from the 1920s—were composed for a mostly male audience, the other members of the Algonquin Round Table.

The Round Table had begun in 1919 as a group of people who liked to lunch together at the Hotel Algonquin on West 44th Street in Manhattan.[7] The founding members, besides Dorothy Parker, included Robert Benchley, Robert Sherwood, "F.P.A." (Franklin P. Adams), Alexander Woollcott, and Harold Ross.[8] There were women who attended occasionally—Edna Ferber, the columnist Alice Duer Miller (and Harpo Marx, whose screen image at least is androgynous)—but the group was really male, and Dorothy Parker was male-identified.

She was, by all accounts, the cleverest woman in New York. When she published her first collection of poems, *Enough Rope,* in 1926, the book was an instant best seller—one of the few best-selling poetry books in American history. But people bought it because the author was a media celebrity, and they seemed to appreciate it more for the surface Dorothy Parker the wisecracker, rather than for the serious analyst of the female condition.

In "Unfortunate Coincidence," for instance, she wrote:

By the time you swear you're his,
Shivering and sighing,
And he vows his passion is
Infinite, undying—
Lady, make a note of this:
One of you is lying.

A quick reader may smile in recognition, and then turn the page, without realizing that Dorothy Parker is making acute statements about relations between the sexes: they're often based on deception and games and one-upping. Other poems in *Enough Rope* suggest that romantic love is a delusion and a source of woe, and thoroughly irrational: "I shudder at the thought of men . . . / I'm due to fall in love again" ("Symptom Recital"). And for an allegedly witty book, there's quite a lot of morbid black humor, as in one of her most popular poems, "Résumé":

Razors pain you;
Rivers are damp;
Acids stain you;
And drugs cause cramp.
Guns aren't lawful;
Nooses give;
Gas smells awful;
You might as well live.

The subject matter is feminist, a woman's social criticism, but the underlying seriousness was often lost. Though she was witty on the surface, even in the 1920s Dorothy Parker knew that all was not well: she made at least two suicide attempts, and was drinking far too much. Apart from her individual psyche, in which there were some destructive patterns—an attraction to unsuitable men, in particular—she suffered from another problem that was never resolved: the identification of the author with her writing.

Certainly Dorothy Parker wrote poetry—and later, more prose—that seemed confessional, that used an "I" persona, but she was more complex than her image suggested. Dorothy Parker the celebrity was clever, brilliant, and quick—but without the compassion, melancholy, and warmth of Dorothy Parker's writings.

To an extent she cultivated her image: in her *Constant Reader* reviews (1927–33), for instance, she claimed if she'd encountered a book called *The Technique of the Love Affair* some years earlier, she might have avoided a lot of grief. She might have learned how to play hard-to-get; how to be "a regular stuffed chemise." In fact, if she'd had it long ago, observing, "maybe I could have been successful, instead of just successive."[9] She posed as a woman of the world: New York men do not think of nothing but "business," she writes; if they did, "then wherever *did* I get these bruises on my neck?"[10]

However, *Constant Reader* also has warm praise for Isadora Duncan, Katherine Mansfield, and other women. *Constant Reader*, in fact, is transitional: from the wisecracking Dorothy Parker of the 1920s, to the more compassionate Dorothy Parker of the 1930s, whose most enduring works are her short stories.

Parker's short stories have the sort of two-edged humor-and-pathos that many of her poems do; they're also about "little" things (by no means little to women). Readers are apt to laugh first, then feel embarrassed for laughing at such naked displays of human frailty. The combination of comedy (thinking) with tragedy (feeling) seems to be a Parker invention—as are her monologues, or soliloquies.

"The Waltz," for instance, is a young woman's cynical thoughts while waltzing with a young man.[11] She's just told him she'd "adore to" waltz with him, and then we read how she really feels: "I don't want to dance with him . . . being struck dead would look like a day in the country, compared to struggling out a dance with this boy. . . ."

Grimly, she acknowledges there's no way to say no when a man asks her to dance, and after all, he kicks her only occasionally. Maybe it's too much to ask of an almost stranger "that he leave your shins as he found them." So she goes along with the social game, telling him his "little step" is a bit difficult to follow, though "perfectly lovely," and at the end telling him, yes, she'd adore to dance another waltz with him.

Only at the Algonquin Round Table—and even that had its limits—could a young woman say exactly what she thought, and be considered witty instead of monstrous. (And even there, guests were afraid to go to the bathroom, lest Dottie Parker do them in while they were gone.) Otherwise, the social rules for women were as Dorothy Parker depicts them in "The Waltz": women were expected to please men. Parker's satirical target, then, is neither the clumsy young man nor the bruised young woman, but the social roles they are locked into—in short, the affectations and hypocrisies of a patriarchal society.

She attacks similar affectations in "Big Blonde," her best-known short story. Though the story is not at all funny—it does not conform to the Parker image—it was her greatest literary success. Parker won the O. Henry Prize for the best short story of 1929 with "Big

Blonde," the story of Hazel Morse, a large New York woman, "the type that incites some men when they use the word 'blonde' to click their tongues and wag their heads roguishly."[12] Hazel devotes herself to being popular with men. She's a good sport, admires their jokes and neckties, goes to speakeasies, goes to bed. When she's cheerful, men adore her, but she grows older, and her life seems pointless and empty. She falls into alcoholic hazes, and her attempt to oppose her life by ending it fails.While Dorothy Parker was much more aware than Hazel Morse, she also suffered from thoughtless men, alcoholism, and a sense of emptiness. And her wit was the equivalent of Hazel's blondeness: both had an image to live up to, an image that was only part of what they wanted to be.

In "Big Blonde" and the poems of *Sunset Gun* (1928) Dorothy Parker was posing questions women writers frequently ask: What good is tradition, or art, or love if it just makes women unhappy? Should a person be engaged in life or standing apart? Why can't women and men communicate? She seemed to see little possibility for change: neither an androgynous shifting of roles nor strong friendships between women. Her view of the world is female, but not feminist. And yet her stories through the 1930s continue to be amusing in a somewhat bittersweet way. Her characters—clinging young women, thoughtless young men, selfish rich people, shopgirls and maids—rarely learn from their experiences, but Parker's satire has an old-fashioned but unspoken moral message directed at readers: if you behave like these characters, you'll end up like them.

"A Telephone Call," for instance, is a warning soliloquy.[13] It begins:

> Please God, let him telephone me now. Dear God, let him call me now. I won't ask anything else of you, truly I won't. It isn't very much to ask. It would be so little to you, God, such a little, little thing. Only let him telephone now. Please, God. Please, please, please.

The cringing, the repetitions ("Please," "God," "little") and the feeling of helplessness are all familiar to anyone who has ever waited for a phone call. So, too, are the games the anonymous heroine plays to get herself through waiting: if she doesn't think about it, maybe the phone will ring. Or maybe she should count to five hundred by fives, and if it rings when she's at three hundred, she won't answer until she gets to five hundred. Should she call him? No, "you shouldn't keep telephoning them—I know they don't like that. When you do that, they know you are thinking about them and wanting them, and that makes them hate you." Parker doesn't have to mention patriarchal power; her "them" is enough.

"A Telephone Call" is sympathy and satire, part funny and part sad. Everyone recognizes the anxious vulnerability of the person waiting.[14] Moreover, "A Telephone Call" shows Parker's keen ear for what recent writers have called "female language"[15]: the overuse of apologies, repetitions, and qualifying words to tone down what a woman's asking for so she'll appear to be pleasing rather than demanding. It's the language of weakness—weakness that Dorothy Parker, with all her quick wit, understood.

Parker said she had always been a feminist, and while her stories usually deal with an unmarried "girl" and a "man," she also looks at other women's subjects, usually with a jaundiced eye. Motherhood, for example, usually means unhappiness. Mothers cling to their children in private and fawn and fuss over them in public; the children are silly, ungrateful, or peculiar. Mrs. Matson in "Little Curtis" chooses her adopted child in an eminently practical way: "as she selected all her other belongings: a good one, one that would last."[16] But her selection is an odd child who mortifies her by laughing hysterically at an inopportune moment.

Nor is the nuclear family a happier subject—though it, too, provides opportunities for ironic laughter at human frailties. The world generally in Parker stories is inhabited by manipulators disguising themselves as Good Souls. Mr. Bain in "The Wonderful Old Gentleman" lives off his daughter and son-in-law, graciously contributing morbid and grotesque decorations to their living room: a print of a train about to shatter a hapless car; an oil painting of two huddled, hopeless sheep in a blizzard.[17] The Bains, poor though they are, sacrifice everything for the old gentleman's comfort—and he, of course, leaves everything to his other, wealthy daughter.

Stories like "The Wonderful Old Gentleman" and "Little Curtis" have a delicious black humor about them: the focus is on the peculiarities of the Good Souls, not on the victimization of the truly good. They are fundamentally satiric, sometimes with a few telling details. In "The Custard Heart," for instance, Parker describes a lady of great wealth, beauty, and wistfulness, whose portrait shows her gorgeous pearls, delicate curls, and "slender arched feet like elegant bananas."[18] The lady, it turns out, chooses to be wistful and self-pitying—and that makes her an appropriate target for satire.

Parker, like most satirists of note, did have rules. With the exception of some of her barbs—when she was the wild wicked woman of the 1920s—she reserved most of her criticism for people who *chose* to be ridiculous. In "A Telephone Call" or the "The Waltz," it is not the dependent young woman who is to be laughed at. The clumsy or thoughtless young man, perhaps, but clumsiness or thoughtlessness can be rectified. Being dependent in a patriarchal social system can't be.

My point is that in her humor, Parker drew the line at criticizing the poor, the defenseless, the vulnerable—but those who wrote about her generally failed to see this. Throughout the 1930s, when she was involved in political organizing and support work for the Spanish Civil War, the newspapers and magazines continued to call her a wit and a poetess and a funny girl (though by 1940, she was a forty-seven-year-old "girl"). By the late 1930s, Parker had a past she could never live down.

She wrote less and less through the 1940s and 1950s, though Lillian Hellman says she never lost her wit: "so wonderful that neither age nor illness ever dried up the spring from which it came fresh each day."[19] Parker's last story, "The Banquet of Crow," appeared in the *New Yorker* in 1957, and is perfect Parker.[20]

Guy Allen has suddenly left his wife, Maida, after eleven years of apparently happy marriage. She tries to wait him out, long-suffering, hoping he's simply going through "the change"—until he tells her he really means it, and he's leaving for San Francisco. Then Maida, having already played the traditional martyr, makes up a unique fantasy. He'll come back, sadder but wiser, with unbecoming gray hair. And she'll make him suffer: she'll make him eat crow. "She made a little picture of him, gray and shabby and broken down, gnawing at a leg of cold crow, which she saw with all its feathers left on it, black and shining and disgusting." As the story ends, she's relishing that delicious fantasy, word-made-flesh.

"The Banquet of Crow" is one of Parker's most subversive stories: unlike so many Parker heroines, Maida Allen has some spirit and imagination. Her carnivorous vision—the banquet of crow—is thoroughly original; it's also Parker's clearest picture of women's anger against men, a muted or disguised theme in nearly all her poems or stories. Mrs. Allen's anger is creative, cleansing, good for her soul.

Had Parker lived longer, she might have been able to do more with her anger: she might have been able to create a more feminist vision of what should be, rather than what is. But when she died in 1967—leaving all her money to Dr. Martin Luther King, Jr., or upon his death, to the National Association for the Advancement of Colored People (NAACP)—the second wave of the women's movement had barely begun. The *New York Times* quoted her on humor: it must include a "disciplined eye," "a wild mind," and criticism. For Dorothy Parker it was often—probably too often—a form of self-criticism, of anger turned inward.

Even at the end, things didn't quite go the way she'd planned. Though she didn't want a funeral, one was held anyway. Actor Zero Mostel, speaking at the service, expressed her point of view: "If she had her way, I suspect she would not be here at all."[21] Dorothy Parker was a prisoner of her image: she was seen as superficial when she was profound, and funny when she was serious. Still, she was a pathbreaker and an inspiration, a needed role model, for many later women writers, among them Nora Ephron (1941–) and Erica (Mann) Jong (1942–).

When Ephron first came to New York, she and her friends used to meet for drinks at the Algonquin, and pretend to be the famous Round Table. Ephron, of course, got to play Dorothy Parker. But she found, after awhile, that the role wasn't funny, but boring: maybe even the Round Table itself hadn't been all it was cracked up to be. Eventually Nora Ephron turned to New Journalism, still using a humorous but sympathetic approach to the female condition, as in her essay "A Few Words about Breasts."[22]

When Erica Mann was growing up, she had two idols: Edna St.-Vincent Millay and Dorothy Parker. Millay was "a sort of white goddess"; Parker represented "black humor."[23] Parker, it turned out, was more influential: on dates, Erica Mann would recite Parker's "bitter-sweet verses whenever I could find a baffled adolescent boy who'd listen."[24] Parker expressed, especially in her short stories, "the great adolescent theme: unrequited love"—the romance we all ached for.[25] And not only was Parker witty—like Oscar Wilde and George Bernard Shaw, Erica Mann's favorite playwrights—but she was also a woman, the kind of clever woman Erica might become.

As always, the aspiring woman writer faced obstacles. As a Barnard student in 1962, Erica Mann heard a Distinguished Critic tell her writing class, "Women can't be writers." After all, what could they write about? "They don't know blood and guts and puking in the streets and fucking whores and swaggering through Paris at 5 a.m." Thirteen years later, Erica Jong recalled that no one challenged the Distinguished Critic: "We listened meekly—while the male voice of authority told us what women could or couldn't write." Afterwards, she wondered: how could she be the tough guy/writer/hero? How could a woman be the unique, brutish hybrid a writer had to be: "Tarzan crossed with King Kong?"[26]

Later, of course, she realized that the Writer-as-Beast was a myth, one of many used to discourage women writers. Why would a serious writer *want* to puke in the streets? When she began to see through the myths, she gained a healthy irreverence toward authority and a respect for her own originality and wit. Once she developed her own voice, she became one of the most important writers of her generation—but like Parker, she was pigeonholed.

Because *Fear of Flying* handles sexual desires (but not performances) with the kind of joie de vivre usually reserved for men, Erica Jong has been made into a media symbol of the "Sexual Revolution." Sex is to Jong what wit was to Parker: it's only part of what she's up to—but too many people see the image instead of the real writer.

Even before *Fear of Flying*, Jong was redefining a writer's experience in female terms. In "The Commandments," first published in *Aphra* in 1970, she writes about overcoming fears. Each of the six stanzas begins, "If a woman wants to be a poet," followed by three "she should's." Most of what she "should" do is unusual, if not bizarre: "She should feel for the movement along her faults"; "she should suck on French poets to freshen her breath"; "she should not write her poems in menstrual blood." The poet needs, really, to listen to her own voice, and in her poems and essays, Jong consistently refers to the poet as *she*.

Her first book of poems, *Fruits & Vegetables* (1971), concerns the equipment of the kitchen, women's domain. Jong, like Sylvia Plath, is concerned with female culture, and with setting her imagination free on the everyday objects women cut, slice, mince, sauté, fry, lick, and devour. Eating is joy, pleasure, poetry: "The first poem in the world / is *I want to eat*" ("Where It Begins.") Cheeses are peaceful, and want to merge only with the Great Eater ("Cheese"). The onion is "not self-righteous like the proletarian potato, nor a siren like the apple," nor does it show off like the banana. Rather, it indulges in endless self-scrutiny, searching its soul and finding only its skins ("Fruits & Vegetables.")

Eating is also a metaphor for the student-teacher relationship. As the teacher stands before the class, the students aren't hungry for Chaucer. "They want to devour her . . ." They don't want words: "They want a real lesson!" ("The Teacher").

The sense of being surrounded by food and being devoured by others is not new in women's writing: it appears in the mad housewife novels; in the poems of Sylvia Plath; even in "Peter Peter Pumpkin Eater." What is new is the poetic distance—the ability to laugh at the situation. That sort of laughter takes courage, for in a patriarchal society women are not supposed to laugh at their oppression. Even more, we are not supposed to laugh at men, as Jong does in a number of poems.

"On the Air," in *Half-Lives* (1973) pokes fun at the way men objectify sex, their own as well as women's. The hero, who has gone entirely mad, has the delusion that his penis is a radio station. It plays rock 'n' roll, and specializes in golden oldies. The woman who loves him plays along with his lunacy, enjoying his mustache that tingles like a tuning fork. She signals him to take station breaks, tells him to stop censoring the news, and listens to his paranoid fantasies: that the Federal Communications Commission has his number, and J. Edgar Hoover sends him static. Finally he knows how to displace guilt onto others:

> & when he wilts,
> he blames the FBI.

But Jong's poems are more than simply witty sallies in the "war between the sexes." Her poems are satires on traditional or "normal" perceptions. "Eggplant Epithalamion," for instance, includes a "Byzantine Eggplant Fable" about a Turkish husband who wants to divorce his wife. She was supposed to know a hundred ways to cook eggplant, but could muster only ninety-nine (even though these included wonderfully exotic variations, such as rolling the seeds in banana-flavored cigarette papers and getting her husband high). However, the wife manages to avert disaster: she gives birth to an eggplant. Because it's premature, she has to sit on it for days before it hatches. "I hope you're satisfied!" she screams, and the narrator adds: "(Thank Allah that the eggplant was a boy)."

Like "On the Air," the Byzantine eggplant fable follows its own logic: if we can believe that a penis is a radio station, or that anything is acceptable as the hundredth eggplant recipe, the poems make perfect sense. Women have always learned what they're to expect from life through fairy tales: Prince Charming comes, gives the kiss (fights the dragon, puts on the slipper), and they live happily ever after. "On the Air" and the eggplant fable are as logical as Snow White's or Sleeping Beauty's stories—but we learn a real lesson: some men have rather silly delusions, but if we go along with them, we can have a good laugh.

Fear of Flying (1973) is full of good laughs at the expense of men, and men's perceptions of women. Isadora Wing seems to be seeking sex, and her sexual encounters are frequently bizarre, such as the fling with the conductor who "loved his baton but never wiped his behind." But sex in marriage has "turned as bland as Velveeta cheese." She longs for the equivalent of "an overripe Camembert, a rare goat cheese: luscious, creamy, clover-hoofed." And she wants the "zipless fuck".[27]—sex without guilt.[27]

Isadora enjoys sex, but she also enjoys eating, drinking, laughing, writing poetry, and being literary, activities that were totally lost on some reviewers. Women writers may not be permitted to puke in the streets, but some Distinguished Critics did. The novelist Paul Theroux, for instance, wrote in *The New Statesman*:

> With such continual and insistent reference to her cherished valve, Erica Jong's witless heroine looms like a mammoth pudenda, as roomy as the Carlsbad Caverns, luring amorous spelunkers to confusion in her plunging grottoes . . .

> This crappy novel, misusing vulgarity to the point where it becomes purely foolish, picturing woman as a hapless organ animated by the simplest ridicule, and devaluing imagination in every line . . . represents everything that is to be loathed in American fiction today.[28]

Theroux's is only the most vicious of many hostile reviews, all of which seem to be extremely angry: angry, apparently, that a woman could write a book with a character who has the same sexual urges that a man does; angry that a woman could use street words (like "fuck") instead of the more traditionally feminine words for sexual organs or making love.

Moreover, Theroux seems to confuse Erica Jong and Isadora Wing—one author, one character—with all women, when he claims the novel pictures "woman as a hapless organ . . ." He seems angry for the same reasons Kate Chopin's detractors were angry in her day: Erica Jong has allowed her heroine to think about herself and her own desires, above being a wife or a mother or a sweetheart. She's let Isadora sin against the most sacred article in the doctrine of the separate spheres: the double standard. Worst of all, she's allowed her heroine to laugh at men.

Anger distorts perceptions. Those who read *Fear of Flying* calmly see that there's not that much sex in it. Adrian Goodlove, the ironically named lover for whom Isadora leaves her husband, is impotent most of the time, and not very good when he can perform. Brian, the manic first husband, becomes thoroughly uninterested in sex. When Isadora finally meets her zipless fuck on a train, she's repelled.

What Isadora really seeks is not a man, but her own identity. Her story, a female picaresque, involves the classic steps for a hero's adventure: separation from his own world; trials, or a labyrinthine journey; initiation into another world; descent to the underworld; ritual rebirth. Isadora's descent, her dark night of the soul, comes when Adrian leaves her alone in Paris.

But during and after her descent, Isadora does something no male hero ever did: she has her period. Menstruation represents her identity as female, the strong self she's seeking. When she takes a bath in the last scene, Isadora looks down and sees the mighty artifact: "the Tampax string fishing the water like a Hemingway hero" (339). Her quest is complete.[29]

Fear of Flying represents a witty redefinition of the picaresque, and of heroism. Some critics recognized it as a new departure; others, like Theroux, damned it as a sex book; still others, especially women, felt Isadora was not "liberated enough"—although Jong is showing her heroine groping toward freedom. "I wanted it to be clear that she was survivor," Jong says; a "programmatic political ending," in which, say "Isadora marched off into the sunset to establish a woman's commune," wouldn't make sense.[30] In any case, she had to keep saying, the author and the heroine are not the same. As Dorothy Parker showed, the author always knows more.

Both *Loveroot* (1975) and Jong's second novel, *How to Save Your Own Life* (1977) are more serious, even grave. Both involve death and resurrection: the death of a marriage (Isadora's and Jong's); the suicide of the poet Jeannie Morton (who resembles Anne Sexton); and the author's meeting, and falling in love with, another man.

The world is peculiar, laying traps for a famous author. In *How to Save Your Own Life*, Isadora has published a notorious best-selling novel, *Candida Confesses*, and strangers reward her with their problems, fantasies, and propositions: a Mississippi proctologist, for instance, wants her to send him her soiled underthings in a plastic bag. A cabdriver, hearing she wrote *Candida Confesses*, thinks she's the Happy Hooker.

Still, *How to Save Your Own Life* is a much more radical, and more difficult, book than *Fear of Flying*. Isadora is surrounded by loving female friends, more supportive than any of the men in her life except Josh Ace, the new lover. With Josh she relearns to laugh—but the laughter comes from joy, not from cynicism. *How to Save Your Own Life* is a rare American book: a love story with a happy ending. As Jong notes in the book, "It is innocence and open-heartedness that requires the true courage—however often we hurt as a result of it."[31] She wants what Anne Sexton had: the courage to be a fool.

Courage has been perhaps Erica Jong's greatest contribution to women's humor: the willingness to use parts of her own life in her writings, taking the risk that people will (as they have) think she's her heroine, Isadora. She's satirized pretensions and hypocrisies, especially men's; she's dared to write about women's urges in a lusty language men usually try to keep for themselves. She's also discovered that many people are threatened by sex, exuberance, and wit in a woman—but she intends to keep writing, extending her range.

Her current book-in-progress, intended as a "literary spoof, a romp," is a historical novel set in eighteenth-century England. Her heroine, born in 1710, will have numerous adventures and live by her wits, and the novel will be historically accurate. But books change and grow, and what emerges may be very different.

What is certain is that the new book will be satirical—and probably misunderstood. It will undoubtedly be called "sexy," whether it is or not; it may even be called "confessional," despite its eighteenth-century setting. As Dorothy Parker knew, public images change far more slowly than writers do: when Jong wrote about the Distinguished Critic who's blighted her hopes in college, she called her article, "Blood and Guts: a Woman Writer Thirteen Years Later." But the magazine—aware, apparently, of what would sell— changed the title to "Writer Who 'Flew' to Sexy Fame Talks About Being a Woman."

She's overcome, Jong feels, the advice Mr. Distinguished Critic gave her Barnard class. She wouldn't *want* to know blood and guts (besides menstrual blood, which fuels the imagination), or swaggering, fucking whores, or puking. She does want to trust herself, and lack of trust in herself was one of Dorothy Parker's greatest problems.

Parker's wit was, in many cases, an effort to conceal her fears, and even her background (she was uncomfortable about being half-Jewish.) Erica Jong has written openly, and wittingly, about being Jewish, and being a woman with fears. Her subject matter includes topics Parker could not touch, in part because of taboos: lust, menstruation, female masturbation. But she also considers possibilities Parker did not envision, at least in literature: true love and close, abiding friendships between women. As a writer of humor, Erica Jong does not mock women; nor, like Parker, does she write about maids and shopgirls in a somewhat distant, patronizing way. Rather, she writes about women much like herself, and risks being condemned for her choice.

The story of new feminist humor must include Erica Jong because of her courage as a pathfinder treating taboo subjects, and as a writer who wants to share her laughter *with* rather than against, others. Feminist humor, as practiced by such writers as Lisa Alther, Esther Broner, Gail Parent, and Rita Mae Brown, involves a critique of society's peculiar rules or norms—rather than a critique of the individual who doesn't fit in.[32]

When Erica Jong described her own sense of humor in an interview, she gave one of the earliest descriptions of the new feminist humor of the 1970s.

> I see the world as a tremendous circus. I am very anti-elitist, anti-authoritarian. My real view of the world is a satirist's view, and more often than not, I find the games we play to gain status very foolish.[33]

What would she do with her insights? "I want to share that laughter with somebody; I mean, I can't get on with people who take all that bullshit seriously."

Dorothy Parker didn't take it all seriously, but she could not see her way out. Erica Jong and the others see humor not only as defense, but as escape. Laughter is not only a medicine for the wounds inflicted by a patriarchal society: it may also be a cure.

NOTES

1. Martha Bensley Bruère and Mary Ritter Beard, *Laughing Their Way: Women's Humor in America* (New York: Macmillan, 1934), 7.

2. John Keats, *You Might as Well Live: The Life and Times of Dorothy Parker* (New York: Simon & Schuster, 1970), 19. Anecdotes cited here are from Keats's work, unless otherwise noted. At this time, his is the only biography of Parker, and it tends to be superficial and unsympathetic. Parker did not want a biography written, and her close friend and executor, Lillian Hellman, refused to cooperate with Keats's work.

3. Lillian Hellman, *An Unfinished Woman* (New York: Bantam, 1969), 195–96.

4. "News Item," in *The Portable Dorothy Parker* (New York: Viking, 1944; revised and enlarged, 1973), 109. At this time, nearly all of Parker's published writings appear in this Viking *Portable*.

5. Hellman, 186–87.

6. See, for instance, Molière's preface to *Tartuffe*, or Fielding's preface to *Tom Jones*.

7. The Algonquin's anniversary is celebrated in Arnold W. Ehrlich, "The Algonquin at 75," *New York Times Magazine*, 16 October 1977, 126ff.

8. For further information about the Algonquin Round Table, see R. E. Drennan, *The Algonquin Wits* (New York: Citadel Press, 1968) and M. C. Harriman, *The Vicious Circle* (New York: Rinehart, 1951).

9. *The Portable Dorothy Parker*, 522.

10. Ibid., 528.

11. Ibid., 47–51; from *After Such Pleasures* (1933).

12. *The Portable Dorothy Parker*, 187–210.

13. Ibid., 119–24; from *Here Lies* (1939).

14. Male students have told me they identify with the story as well: they've often counted to five hundred by fives before lifting the phone to call.

15. See Robin Lakoff, *Language and Woman's Place* (New York: Harper and Row, 1975), 8ff. Lakoff's work has been sharply challenged by other critics, notably Julia P. Stanley.

16. *The Portable Dorothy Parker* 339–53; from *Here Lies.*

17. Ibid., 52–64.

18. Ibid., 319–27.

19. Hellman, 187.

20. Dorothy Parker, "The Banquet of Crow," *New Yorker*, 14 December, 1957, 39–43.

21. Alden Whitman, "Dorothy Parker, 73, Literary Wit, Dies," *New York Times*, 8 June 1967, 1; "Dorothy Parker Recalled as Wit," *New York Times*, 10 June 1967, 33.

22. Nora Ephron, "Dorothy Parker" and "A Few Words About Breasts," in *Crazy Salad* (New York: Knopf, 1975), 133–36, 1–11.

23. Letter received from Erica Jong, 22 December 1977.

24. Erica Jong, "The Artist as Housewife/The Housewife as Artist," *Here Comes and Other Poems* (New York: New American Library, 1975), 259. Reprinted from *Ms.*, December 1972, 64.

25. Interview with Erica Jong, 10 August 1977. Much of the material in this article comes from my interview with Jong.

26. Erica Jong, "Writer Who 'Flew' to Sexy Fame Talks About Being a Woman," *Vogue*, March 1977, 158; "The Artist as Housewife/The Housewife as Artist," 262.

27. Erica Jong, *Fear of Flying* (New York: Holt, Rinehart & Winston), 36. Other references to this edition will be indicated by page number in the text.

28. Paul Theroux, "Hapless Organ," *The New Statesman*, 19 April, 1974, 554.

29. *Fear of Flying* as a picaresque quest novel is discussed in Mary Pringle Spraggins, "The Woman Androgyne: Jung, Jong's Isadora, and the Androgyny Debate," presented at the Midwest Modern Language Association meeting, 1975; and Janice Delaney, Mary Jane Lupton, and Emily Toth, *The Curse: A Cultural History of Menstruation* (New York: Dutton, 1976), 172–174.

30. "About a Book Called *Fear of Flying,*" promotional leaflet from Holt, Rinehart & Winston.

31. Erica Jong, *How to Save Your Own Life* (New York: Holt, Rinehart & Winston, 1977), 97.

32. For my ideas on women's humor and its relation to norms, I am much indebted to Judy Little's "Satirizing the Norm: Comedy in Women's Fiction," in *Regionalism and the Female Imagination* 3 (1977): 78.

33. "*Playboy* Interview: Erica Jong," *Playboy*, September 1975, 61ff.

"I Am Outraged Womanhood": Dorothy Parker as Feminist and Social Critic

Suzanne L. Bunkers

DOROTHY PARKER, WHO ONCE CALLED HERSELF "A LITTLE JEWISH GIRL trying to be cute," is perhaps best remembered for remarking that "men seldom make passes at girls who wear glasses"or for reacting to the news that Coolidge had died with, "How can they tell?" Then, too, Parker's most famous poem, "Résumé," is often quoted to attest to her matter-of-fact view of life and death:

> Razors pain you;
> Rivers are damp;
> Acids stain you;
> And drugs cause cramp.
> Guns aren't lawful;
> Nooses give;
> Gas smells awful;
> You might as well live.[1]

Occasionally a modern fiction anthology will include a Parker story such as "The Waltz" to typify the witty sarcasm inherent in her work. For the most part, however, Dorothy Parker and her works have been forgotten by both readers and critics. Those who have heard of Parker associate her with the Algonquin Round Table and the *New Yorker*, but few can remember even the title of her most famous short story, "Big Blonde," which won the O. Henry Prize in 1929. So little attention has been paid to Dorothy Parker in recent years that, as Brendan Gill comments, most people are surprised to learn that she died as recently as 1967—a woman of seventy-three, alone in a New York hotel room.[2]

Why unearth Dorothy Parker now, more than ten years after her death and over thirty years since her collected poems and stories were first published? Because her work deserves reexamination. Dorothy Parker was not only a wit but also a chronicler and a harsh critic of 1920s–1930s social roles. Her poems and short stories are

152

not simply "cute" or "funny"; they embody Parker's use of stereotypical female characters to satirize, more bitterly than playfully, the
limited roles available to American women during the 1920s and
1930s, decades when the predominant image of the American
woman was that of the sexually free, even promiscuous, flapper.

In keeping with her purpose as satirist, Parker's poems and short
stories criticize the status quo rather than define new, three-dimen-
sional female roles. As a result, her women characters generally
evoke mixed reactions from the reader: they seem pitiable, yet they
grate on the reader's nerves. They appear to be victimized not only
by an oppressive society but also by their inability to fight back
against that society. It would be easy to conclude that Dorothy Parker is hostile toward the "simpering spinsters" or "rich bitches" she
portrays in her poems and stories, but to do so would fail to take into
account her satiric purpose and technique. Parker is not satirizing
women per se; rather, she uses her pitiable, ridiculous women characters to criticize the society that has created one-dimensional female roles and forced women to fit into them.

My first encounter with Dorothy Parker was in 1965. A high school
student competing in the state speech contest, I was assigned "The
Waltz" as my humorous declamation speech topic. I learned from
others who had previously used "The Waltz" that this perennial favorite was a sure bet for "superior" ratings from the judges. So I
began practicing, first reading aloud to perfect the two opposing
tones used by the persona, then memorizing the material, and, finally, learning the waltz step that would accompany the speech. The
judges, true to form, laughed themselves into near-exhaustion and
awarded me with superiors. Although happy about the ratings Parker and I had received, I began to wonder if "The Waltz" were really
as funny as everyone thought. The persona, a young woman, at first
seems to be the stereotypical chatterbox until one notices that the
bulk of her "chattering" consists of a serious discussion with herself.
Even though she speaks politely to the clumsy man with whom she
is dancing ("Why, I'm simply thrilled. I'd love to waltz with you"),
her thoughts reveal her distaste for the social roles she is expected
to fulfill:

Ah, now why did he have to come around me, with his low requests? Why
can't he let me lead my own life? I ask so little—just to be left alone in
my quiet corner of the table, to do my evening brooding over all my
sorrows. And he must come, with his bows and his scrapes and his may-
I-have-this-ones. And I had to go and tell him that I'd adore to dance
with him . . . But what could I do? Everyone else at the table had got up

to dance, except him and me. There was I, trapped. Trapped like a trap in a trap.[3]

As the pair dances, the speaker's comments to her partner are the usual amenities deemed appropriate to the social situation: "Yes, it's lovely, isn't it? It's simply lovely. It's the loveliest waltz. Isn't it? Oh, I think it's lovely, too." But her witty and sarcastic thoughts reveal her true inner rage:

> I wonder what I'd better do—kill him this instant, with my naked hands, or wait and let him drop in his traces. Maybe it's best not to make a scene. . . . I've led no cloistered life, I've known dancing partners who have spoiled my slippers and torn my dress; but when it comes to kicking, I am Outraged Womanhood. When you kick me in the shin, smile. (48–49)

The pattern of sharply conflicting overt and covert messages in "The Waltz" characterizes the ironic tone of Parker's fiction, a tone also evident in poems such as "Love Song." In this poem the persona seems to be the ingenue-in-love, extolling her lover's virtues; however, she ironically undercuts this glowing admiration in the eighth and final line of each stanza. The tone of this line, playfully sarcastic in the first two stanzas, becomes decidedly bitter in the last stanza:

> My love runs by like a day in June,
> And he makes no friends of sorrows.
> He'll tread his galloping rigadoon
> In the pathway of the morrows.
> He'll live his days where the sunbeams start,
> Nor could storm or wind uproot him.
> My own dear love, he is all my heart—
> And I wish somebody'd shoot him.[4]

Here, as in "The Waltz," a tension exists between the surface and subsurface of Parker's satire. The lyric quality of "Love Song" is stopped short by the surfacing of the speaker's suppressed rage. Thus, the eighth line of each stanza conveys the irony of the speaker's situation as well as her dissatisfaction with social conventions, conventions that Parker mocks by her choice of style and tone in the seven preceding lines.

This conflict between surface convention and the desire to break through it is even more evident in Parker's short interior monologue, "A Telephone Call." Here the speaker is torn between her desire to break with convention by phoning the man she loves and her fear of violating this social taboo. She addresses God throughout this sketch, alternately pleading with him to let the phone ring and threatening to step out of her passive role by making the call herself. She views the man's failure to call her as her own fault, the result of some "sin" she has committed without knowing it; and she begs for God's forgiveness, promising to atone in a socially acceptable way:

> You see, God, if You would just let him telephone me, I wouldn't have to ask You anything more. I would be sweet to him, I would be gay, I would be just the way I used to be, and then he would love me again. And then I would never have to ask You for anything more.[5]

But even as the speaker promises to "be better," her repressed rage begins to surface. First she threatens the telephone: "Damn you, I'll pull your filthy roots out of the wall. I'll smash your smug black face in little bits. Damn you to hell." Then she turns her anger on her lover: "I wish to God I could make him cry. I wish I could make him cry and tread the floor and feel his heart heavy and big and festering in him. I wish I could hurt him like hell." Yet every time she threatens someone or something, she relents and repents. "A Telephone Call" is a tug-of-war between the speaker's social self and her inner self, seemingly a lighthearted game but actually a deadly battle. The battle's tension remains unresolved, however. "A Telephone Call" ends with the speaker still determined to make the all-important call, but still unable to do so.

The tension between social role expectations and the desires of the inner self does seem to be resolved in Parker's' eight-line poem, "Observation." This poem's structure parallels that of "Love Song": the first six lines depict the role that the female persona is expected to fulfill, while the last two lines reveal her reaction to this role:

> If I don't drive around the park,
> I'm pretty sure to make my mark.
> If I'm in bed each night by ten,
> I may get back my looks again.
> If I abstain from fun and such,
> I'll probably amount to much;
> But I shall stay the way I am,
> Because I do not give a damn.[6]

Once again, the initially buoyant tone becomes more cynical at the poem's end, a characteristic of many of Parker's poems, notably "Men":

They hail you as their morning star
Because you are the way you are.
If you return the sentiment,
They'll try to make you different;
And once they have you, safe and sound,
They want to change you all around.
Your moods and ways they put a curse on;
They'd make of you another person.
They cannot let you go your gait;
They influence and educate.
They'd alter all that they admired.
They make me sick, they make me tired.[7]

In "Men," Parker uses clichés such as "safe and sound" and clever rhymes such as "curse on/person" to establish a jaunty tone, which she then destroys in the poem's final line. Despite the poem's generally lighthearted tone, its message is quite serious. Men put women in an impossible situation, first encouraging them to exhibit certain types of "appropriately feminine" behavior and then punishing them for that behavior by insisting they change.

Poems such as "Love Song" and "Men" belie the low estimation that critics such as Edmund Wilson have made of Parker's verse: "Her poems do seem a little dated. At their best, they are witty light verse, but when they try to be something more serious, they tend to become a kind of dilution of A. E. Housman and Edna Millay."[8] Dorothy Parker's poetry ranges from two-line witticisms to serious, technically excellent sonnets. A careful examination of her poems reveals that Parker did not take writing poetry any more lightly than she did writing fiction. In her hands, poetry, like fiction, becomes an effective tool for social criticism.

In addition to first-person monologues such as "The Waltz" and "A Telephone Call," Parker's fiction includes longer stories. Many of these are third-person narratives that allow the reader to glimpse several characters from the perspective of an omniscient, somewhat cynical narrator. In these stories, as in her monologues, Parker uses female stereotypes to criticize social norms. In "The Wonderful Old Gentleman," the long-suffering Griselda figure, Allie Bain, is contrasted with the domineering bitch, Hattie Wittaker. These sisters share a vigil at the deathbed of their father, the "wonderful old gentleman."[9]

The reader soon discovers from the sisters' dialogue that Hattie is a self-assured schemer, quite conscious of appearances: "Mrs. Whittaker always stopped things before they got to the stage where they didn't look right." She has arranged for their father to live with the poorer Bains rather than with her husband and herself, and she has persuaded her father to leave her his entire estate. Hattie Whittaker, the stereotypical bitch, dominates everything and everyone around her.

Allie Bain, by contrast, is timid and submissive. Her life has not been happy, but she never complains. In fact, she seems to revel in her sorrows. Her father and sister use her because she allows herself to be used. Although Allie's situation is wretched, the reader cannot completely pity her, because she is such a Griselda figure. Nor can the reader completely hate the cold and proud Hattie, whose life consists of manipulating others. Despite her bad qualities, Hattie remains a forceful, assertive woman who knows exactly what she wants and exactly how to get it. Both characters evoke mixed reactions from the reader, which indicates that Parker does not merely intend these figures to be ridiculed but that her criticism goes beyond mocking specific satiric types. By satirizing the Griselda and the Bitch, Parker criticizes the American society that has produced these stereotypes and forced women into them. "The Wonderful Old Gentleman" is a serious indictment of American society, not an amusing portrayal of a sadomasochistic relationship between sisters.

In another intriguing story, "Horsie," the stereotypes used are those of the Old Maid and the Galatea. Miss Wilmarth, an "old maid nurse," is described in terms of confinement and limitation:

> She was tall, pronounced of bone, and erect of carriage; it was somehow impossible to speculate upon her appearance undressed. Her long face was innocent, indeed ignorant, of cosmetics, and its color stayed steady. Confusion, heat, or haste caused her neck to flush crimson. Her mild hair was pinned with loops of nicked black wire into a narrow knot, practical to support her little cap, like a charlotte russe from a bakeshop.[10]

Parker focuses on the nurse's facial features in particular to reinforce the image of the unattractive, even grotesque, woman:

> . . . her face was truly complete with that look of friendly melancholy peculiar to the gentle horse. It was not, of course, Miss Wilmarth's fault that she looked like a horse. Indeed, there was nowhere to attach any blame. But the resemblance remained. (260)

Miss Wilmarth, "sure and calm and tireless," has been hired by the wealthy Crugers to care for their infant daughter. The gawky, unattractive nurse stands in sharp contrast to Mrs. Camilla Cruger, the epitome of the sweet, dainty, and mesmerizing American woman:

... she had always been pale as moonlight and had always worn a delicate disdain, as light as the lace that covered her breast. . . . Motherhood had not brought perfection to Camilla's loveliness. She had had that before. (265)

While Nurse Wilmarth idolizes the Crugers' seemingly perfect existence, they call her "Horsie" behind her back and joke about her ugliness. She is their workhorse, and they use and abuse her much as they would an animal. Her physical appearance might make Miss Wilmarth seem repulsive, but she is also pitiable because of her social position. Neither married nor independently wealthy, she must work to support herself, her mother, and her aunt. She must fit into society as best she can, in the role of the undesirable "old maid" who is grateful for any recognition of her humanity from the rich sophisticates she serves.

Ironically, Camilla Cruger, the beautiful little rich girl, is no happier with her state in life than is Miss Wilmarth. In fact, Camilla's attitude throughout the story is that of boredom: boredom with her husband Gerald, with her baby Diane, and with her life in general. To everyone around her, Camilla represents the Galatean ideal of beauty, grace, and elegance. Yet she is dissatisfied. Her role, although more socially acceptable than Miss Wilmarth's, is just as confining.

The story's climax reveals how trapped both women are in their roles. As the nurse prepares to leave the Cruger household, Gerald, exuberant at the thought of being alone with his Galatea at last, brings Camilla a bouquet of dainty yellow roses and, as an afterthought, gives Miss Wilmarth a small corsage of gardenias. To the nurse, this gift signifies that Crugers at last view her as a person rather than as an object that has outlived its usefulness. However, her reaction to the gift horrifies Mr. Cruger because it breaks down the formal barrier between them:

Her squeaks of thanks made red rise back of his ears. . . . Gerald was in sudden horror that she might bring her head down close to them (the flowers) and toss it back, crying "wuzza, wuzza, wuzza" at them the while. (272)

Gerald, embarrassed, quickly reestablishes the necessary social distance as he packs Miss Wilmarth, her face "like that of a weary mare," into a taxi. Then he rushes inside to "get back to the fragrant room and the little yellow roses and Camilla." The story's final focus is on the nurse sitting in the taxi—a small, pitiful figure cradling her gift:

Miss Wilmarth's strange resemblance was not apparent, as she looked at her flowers. They were her flowers. A man had given them to her. She had been given flowers. They might not fade for days. And she could keep the box. (275)

On the surface, "Horsie" seems to satirize the egocentric and un-feeling Galatea while holding the long-suffering Old Maid up for sympathy and even pity. Parker's satire, however, goes deeper. By using the Galatea and Old Maid stereotypes, the author criticizes the self-centeredness and callousness of the society that has created and sustained these two female roles.

Hazel Morse, the principal character in Parker's short story, "Big Blonde," differs from the stereotyped female characters already dis-cussed in that she incorporates several stereotypes. Parker describes Hazel as "a large, fair woman of the type that incites some men when they use the word 'blonde' to click their tongues and wag their heads roguishly." The only relatively small thing about Hazel is her feet, which she jams into "snub-toed, high-heeled slippers of the shortest bearable size." Since there is no hope for her as an aspiring Galatea, Hazel takes another route toward her hoped-for acceptance by the American male. She becomes a "good sport":

Men liked her, and she took it for granted that the liking of many men was a desirable thing. Popularity seemed to her to be worth all the work that had to be put into its achievement. Men liked you because you were fun, and when they liked you they took you out, and there you were. So, and successfully, she was fun. She was a good sport. Men liked a good sport.[11]

Terrified at the prospect of not being dainty and marriageable, and aware that the good sport role will ingratiate her with men, Hazel plays this role even though it is unnatural to her. She believes that others expect it of her, and she wants desperately to fulfill their expectations. She soon finds security in a circle of female friends, all of whom are "other substantially built blondes," thus assuring that she will not have to face competition from petite, fragile beauties. Yet Hazel longs for marriage, and her fear of being an "old maid" increases with the years:

She was delighted at the idea of being a bride; coquetted with it, played upon it. . . . She wanted to be married. She was nearing thirty now, and she did not take the years well. She spread and softened, and her darken-ing hair turned her to inexpert dabblings with peroxide. (188)

The "Big Blonde" is a grotesque version of the Galatea, blonde but bloated, simply too large for the sex goddess mold.

At last, Hazel marries Herbie Morse, "thin, attractive, with shifting lines about his shiny, brown eyes and a habit of fiercely biting at the skin around his fingernails." For the first time in years, she feels she can relax and stop worrying about being a social misfit. She drops the "good sport" role but adopts another stereotypical role, that of the tender and submissive wife:

> Wedded and relaxed, she poured her tears freely. To her who had laughed so much, crying was delicious. All sorrows became her sorrows; she was Tenderness. She would cry long and softly over newspaper accounts of kidnapped babies, deserted wives, unemployed men, strayed cats, heroic dogs. (189)

Herbie, however, does not like this change in his wife; he wants a "good sport," not a "crybaby." The marriage fails and Hazel, single again, reverts to the "good sport" role, the only role she knows. She joins a poker-playing group of drinkers, takes on a series of paunchy lovers, and frequents Jimmy's, a meeting place for others like her: aging women, wrinkled and fat, no longer able to affect the role of the youthful, buxom woman:

> They were all big women and stout, broad of shoulder and abundantly breasted, with faces thickly clothed in soft, high-colored flesh. They laughed loud and often, showing opaque and lusterless teeth like squares of crockery. There was about them the health of the big, yet a slight, unwholesome suggestion of stubborn preservation. (198)

Although Hazel's appearance brands her as somewhat ridiculous, the reader's sympathy remains with her even when she gives up and attempts suicide. Here, as in all else, Hazel is doomed to failure. Parker's description of the scene portrays the "Big Blonde" as grotesque yet quite pathetic:

> The bed covers were pushed down, exposing a deep square of soft neck and a pink nightgown, its fabric worn uneven by many launderings; her great breasts, freed from their tight confiner, sagged beneath her armpits. Now and then she made knotted, snoring sounds, and from the corner of her opened mouth to the blurred turn of her jaw ran a line of crusted spittle. (206)

The story of Hazel Morse is Dorothy Parker's most bitter indictment of 1920s and 1930s American society and the roles to which it expected women to conform. The "Big Blonde" is defeated before she has begun because there is no suitable role for her. Her attempts to fit into various stereotypical roles fail because each role is too limited and confining for a real human being. Hazel Morse is the victim of a society, which has not provided her a reasonable place within it.

What, then, has Dorothy Parker accomplished by using stereotypes of women in her poems and short stories? First, by satirizing certain types, Parker can draw what seems to be playful attention to them while actually making a serious statement about her disenchantment with the roles forced on American women during the 1920s and 1930s. Parker's satire obligates the reader to look beneath the surface of her sarcastic humor to the social criticism, criticism that should not be ignored.

Second, because Parker's work is decidedly more feminist in its orientation than that of many other writers of the 1920s and 1930s, Parker uses female stereotypes differently from many writers. For instance, her use of the Bitch and the Galatea stereotypes differs in an important way from Ernest Hemingway's Bitches, such as Lady Brett Ashley and Mrs. Francis Macomber, or F. Scott Fitzgerald's Galateas, such as Judy Jones and Daisy Buchanan. In Hemingway's and Fitzgerald's works, stereotypical women characters are not portrayed as women whose roles have been dictated by society but as women who have chosen their own roles. In contrast, Parker's women characters are clearly products of their society's limited visions of acceptable, "proper" female roles. Thus, Parker's stories are a valuable addition to an accurate historical perspective on women's roles and the effects of those roles during an important period in American literature.

Finally, Parker's use of female stereotypes establishes her skills both as a writer and as a social critic. That she was awarded the 1929 O. Henry Prize for "Big Blonde" suggests that her work was receiving some serious attention during the late 1920s and early 1930s. However, her residual fame has come to rest on her sarcastic quips rather than on her social criticism. A reexamination of Parker's poems and short stories is in order. Perhaps this study will serve as a part of that reexamination.[12]

NOTES

1. Dorothy Parker, "Résumé," in *The Portable Dorothy Parker* (New York: Viking, 1973), 99.

2. Brendan Gill, introduction to *The Portable Dorothy Parker*, vii–xxii.

3. Dorothy Parker, "The Waltz," in *The Portable Dorothy Parker,* 47–51. All references to "The Waltz" are to this edition.

4. Dorothy Parker, "Love Song," in *The Portable Dorothy Parker,* 106.

5. Dorothy Parker, "A Telephone Call," in *The Portable Dorothy Parker,* 119–24. All references to "A Telephone Call" are to this edition.

6. Dorothy Parker, "Observation," in *The Portable Dorothy Parker,* 112.

7. Dorothy Parker, "Men," in *The Portable Dorothy Parker,* 109.

8. Edmund Wilson, "A Toast and a Tear for Dorothy Parker," *New Yorker,* 20 May 1944, 75–76.

9. Dorothy Parker, "The Wonderful Old Gentleman," in *The Portable Dorothy Parker,* 52–64. All further references will be to this edition.

10. Dorothy Parker, "Horsie," in *The Portable Dorothy Parker,* 260–75. All further references will be to this edition.

11. Dorothy Parker, "Big Blonde," in *The Portable Dorothy Parker,* 187–210. All further references will be to this edition.

12. Besides this article, the only recent academic work on Parker is Emily Toth's "Dorothy Parker, Erica Jong, and New Feminist Humor," *Regionalism and the Female Imagination* 3 (1977–78): 70–85.

Coda: A Look Back

I first encountered the collected works of Dorothy Parker in 1973, when I was a young graduate student at Iowa State University. I had enrolled in a course on satire, taught by Professor Leonard Feinberg; as I recall, Dorothy Parker was the only woman whose works we studied in that course. Effusive in his praise of Parker's writing, Professor Feinberg encouraged me to write a short paper on satire in her works; and my interest in Parker's short stories, poetry, and reviews continued after the course had concluded.

The following year, I chose Dorothy Parker as the subject of my master's thesis, "The Tragic Grotesque: Dorothy Parker's Women." In my thesis, I drew on Norris Yates's analysis of Dorothy Parker in *The American Humorist;* Yates identifies Parker's general character type as "the self-absorbed female snob," a species that Parker knew best "in its middle-class manifestation."[1] Parker's purpose, as I identified it then, "becomes social satire of the hypocrisy and hauteur characterizing 'ladies' of the Twenties and Thirties."[2]

Drawing on Yates's and Feinberg's analyses, I set out to explore two varieties of the female snob evident in Parker's work: the ingenue and the sophisticate. Feinberg defines the ingenue as "a naive, well-meaning person who travels through the world without understanding the hypocrisy, duplicity, and exploitation which [she] observes" (239). Central to this definition of the ingenue is the satisfaction the reader achieves from feeling superior to this character and from "evading the censor by inferring what the satirist's critical intention is."[3]

Feinberg defines the second character type, the ironic sophisticate, as one who "shares with [the reader] the detached, disillusioned view of a ludicrous spectacle."[4] The reader laughs with the ironic sophisticate rather than at her; however, because the ironic sophisticate does not function as an ironic commentator on the action, the reader feels no sympathy for her. In adapting Feinberg's definition of this character type to my analysis of Parker's short stories, I noted, "Parker's sophisticate, like her ingenue, is a figure for the reader's derision, and Parker's satire relies upon the reader's feeling of superiority to both types. Although both the ingenue and the sophisticate may appear as 'aggressive' snobs, neither seems 'pathetic' because both are presented as selfish and hypocritical."[5]

The ingenue figures in such Parker stories as "The Standard of Living" (1941), in which the author satirizes the lifestyle and attitudes of the young working girl who fancies herself a glamorous beauty. Two rather vacuous young women, Annabel and Midge, are at the center of this story; they are perceived as ludicrous by the already established glamour set. By the story's conclusion, readers, too, are laughing—not only at the ingenues' vanity but also at the value system that encourages them to cultivate this vanity.

Parker's story, "The Custard Heart" (1939) portrays the sophisticated, unfeeling female snob, as embodied in the character of Mrs. Lanier, whose special sorrow is her inability to bear a child. Mrs. Lanier bears her sorrow through her manipulation of the young men who visit her drawing room and through her disdain for the plight of her pregnant and unmarried maid, Gwennie. I concluded my analysis by stating, "Just as Mrs. Lanier extends no sympathy to Gwennie, the reader lavishes no sympathy upon the sophisticate. Mrs. Lanier is mockable, despicable, but not pitiable. Parker's satiric glimpse of the self-centered society matron sketches for the reader an outline of the empty values of the society in which Mrs. Lanier lives, values in large part responsible for the indifference which the lady shows to everything not directly associated with herself."[6]

In the next section of my thesis, I turned my attention to an exploration of certain of Parker's short stories that appear to pity rather than mock women character types. Drawing on Mark Van Doren's characterization of the "tragic and grotesque" female in Dorothy Parker's works,[7] I focused on women characters who intrigued me far more than either the ingenue or the female snob. I referred to this more complex character type as the "tragic grotesque"—the "self-victimized and socially unacceptable woman."[8] By performing a detailed close reading of the text, combined with a feminist critical analysis, I explored Parker's portrayals of Hazel Morse in "Big Blonde," Nurse Wilmarth in "Horsie," Allie Bain in "The Wonderful Old Gentleman," and Mary Nicholl in "The Bolt Behind the Blue."

My thesis concluded with my observations on what I viewed as Dorothy Parker's contribution to American literature through her portrayal of the "tragic grotesque." Although Parker did not refer to herself as a feminist satirist, her portrayals of American women of the 1920s and 1930s foreshadowed those of Sylvia Plath in *The Bell Jar* (1963) and Alix Kates Shulman in *Memories of an Ex-Prom Queen* (1972). In both novels, the principal character is a young woman unable to play the "vacuous career-girl or the submissive wife-and-mother" (32). I outlined one essential difference between Dorothy Parker's "tragic grotesque" and the women portrayed in these two novels, written three to four decades later: "Plath's and Shulman's characters reach a point where they will no longer 'play the game' and where they openly rebel against American role expectations (or, perhaps, against a lack of what they see as meaningful role expectation) for females."[9]

Four years later, in 1978, while I was working on my doctorate at the University of Wisconsin-Madison, my interest in Dorothy Parker's works was revived when I was invited to participate in a Modern Language Association (MLA) session focusing on women's humor. Professor Emily Toth, who coordinated this MLA special session, was the only other scholar who I knew was studying Dorothy Parker's work. Dr. Toth encouraged my research on Parker, eventually including my essay (based on my MLA paper and now reprinted above) in an issue of her journal, *Regionalism and the Female Imagination*, which was printed in offset and distributed by the University of Pennsylvania's English Department. In 1994, my article on Dorothy Parker was reprinted in Linda A. Morris's edited collection, *American Women Humorists: Critical Essays*.[10]

Thirty years have passed since my initial foray into the work (and world) of Dorothy Parker. Now, as then, I am convinced that Parker's satiric commentary on the status of American women during the Twenties and Thirties not only establishes her skills as a short-story writer and as a social critic; it adds significantly to a historical perspective on middle-class, white women's roles during an era that offered few alternatives for women who did not (or who chose not to) fit into so-called "proper" female roles of the day. Interest in Dorothy Parker's work has burgeoned since the early 1970s, when Emily Toth and I were doing what was then referred to as "spadework" feminist criticism; i.e., "digging up" the work of Parker and bringing it to the attention of a contemporary readership. Since I completed my doctorate in 1980, my research has turned toward an exploration of forms of women's autobiography. I remain a Dorothy Parker fan and, whenever possible, I introduce her wry social commentary to my students. I am convinced that the critiques included in this collection will add much more nuance and complexity to our study of this fine American writer.

NOTES

1. Norris W. Yates, *The American Humorist* (New York: Citadel Press, 1965), 266.

2. Suzanne L. Bunkers, *"The Tragic Grotesque": Dorothy Parker's Women* (MA thesis, Iowa State University, 1974), 1.

3. Leonard Feinberg, *Introduction to Satire* (Ames: Iowa State University Press, 1967), 239.

4. Ibid., 239.

5. Bunkers, 2.

6. Ibid., 5.

7. Mark Van Doren, "Dorothy Parker," *The English Journal* 23.7 (September 1934): 535–43.

8. Bunkers, 7.

9. Ibid., 32.

10. Linda A. Morris, ed., *American Women Humorists: Critical Essays* (New York: Garland Publishing, 1994).

Verbal Subversions in Dorothy Parker: "Trapped Like a Trap in a Trap"

Paula A. Treichler

Dorothy Parker's short story "The Waltz" opens with an italicized line of dialogue, presumably spoken aloud: "*Why, thank you so much. I'd adore to.*" An interior monologue, not italicized, follows at once, and contradicts what has just been said:

> I don't want to dance with him. I don't want to dance with anybody. And even if I did it wouldn't be him. He'd be well down among the last ten. I've seen the way he dances; it looks like something you do on Saint Walpurgis Night.[1]

This juxtaposition of internal and external voice doubles as the story's chief structural device and as its chief source of humor. What the protagonist says aloud—and from the beginning we have no doubt that it is a woman speaking—is polite and conventionally "feminine." But what she says to herself is marked by comic savagery and relentless malice toward her dancing partner: "For God's sake, don't *kick*, you idiot"; "What do you think I am, anyway—a gangplank?"

The formal contrast between inner and outer voice suggests how carefully the story's language has been manipulated. In fact, this structure of alternating and seemingly differentiated voices not only introduces and sustains the narrative, it also complicates and undermines many of the easy conclusions to which the narrative alone might lead us. The relationship between dialogue and monologue illuminates other crucial features of the story's style: the verbal play on notions of how women talk, the multiple meanings that emerge from vocabulary and metaphor, and the verbal density created by repetition, exaggeration, and irony. In a very real sense, the story is "about" these verbal interactions. Any meaning we attribute to it must grow out of and be tested against the intricacies of its style. Indeed, for all the seeming obviousness of its formal organization,

"The Waltz" presents us with a highly complicated verbal structure whose ostensible commitments are continually disintegrating. The language cannot finally sustain the clear divisions it has created. The structural boundaries between inner and outer speech dissolve and the two voices, despite their formal and semantic differences, collapse to form a story that is, in the end, talking about itself. The phrase "trapped like a trap in a trap" is a metaphor at the center of this verbal density. Only a language-centered analysis that looks closely at linguistic features and verbal form can offer a satisfactory account of the story's problems and concerns: any other kind of analysis may actually end up misrepresenting what the story says about women, and about their relationship to men.

I offer my treatment of "The Waltz" as a model for the study of Parker's writing, on which nothing very substantive has been written.[2] Her fiction, in turn, offers an almost emblematic entrance to the study of women and language. It is a rich source, for Parker's sensibilities were closely attuned to colloquial, spoken language, and to the verbal deceptions we practice on others and on ourselves. Parker's characters, but especially her female characters, are divided beings. Repeatedly they attempt to present to the world a good face, a calm and attractive self-portrait. They seek secure modes of self-deception and self-disclosure. "I haven't got a visual mind," Parker said, "I hear things."[3] And so the quest for self-presentation is intimately tied to language. Yet language is the greatest source of risk. Parker's fictional women are torn between their desires for disguise and their impulses toward disclosure, and they never quite master their words; their language threatens continually to reveal starkly, and perhaps irrevocably, the terrors, doubts, and humiliations of their lot.

Thus in "Big Blonde," Hazel Morse's pert slogans ("I'm swell," "Mud in your eye") reinforce her role as a "good sport"; but this is her only language and when in crisis she cannot forsake it. Exhausted from spending the day rounding up enough sleeping pills to kill herself with, she unthinkingly remarks, "Gee, I'm nearly dead." But she has swallowed the pills, and so the colloquial phrase is also literally true; this vaguely amuses her. "That's a hot one!" she says, as she drifts into sleep. Devoid of verbal resources, her consciousness can find self-expression only by endowing its familiar slogans rather broadly with irony. The same verbal device brings to an end the drunken monologue of Mildred Tynan in *The Ladies of the Corridor,* Parker's play (with Arnaud d'Usseau) about women growing old in a New York hotel. "Why don't you go take a running jump for yourself?" asks the disgusted bellhop, after telling Mildred that the other guests have complained about her singing and general noise. "Funny," she replies, "I never thought of that," and leaps out the window to her death.[4]

Parker's concern is with the delicate line that women walk obsessively between what can be said and what is forbidden. The war wife in "The Lovely Leave" struggles to be loving and heroic toward her soldier husband: "There had been rules to be learned in that matter, and the first of these was the hardest: never say to him what you want him to say to you" (5). During his brief leave, she tries unsuccessfully, through spritely gallantry ("Nice to see you, Lieutenant. How's the war?"), to disguise her loneliness and resentment. When she finally tries to express these feelings, they are dismissed as nonsense by her rushed and irritated husband. She has tried to be candid, but candor has been punished, and in desperation she is driven to expression that is wholly nonverbal: she "kicked the base of the door so savagely that the whole frame shook" (15). The young woman in "Dusk Before Fireworks" tries to speak with cold, proud detachment to the man who is discarding her—"Her words fell like snow when there is no wind" (141). The manner is entirely foreign to her, yet her return to more honest, impulsive language guarantees his contempt. "From the Diary of a New York Lady" records the shallow daily activities of a socialite. Dense with slang and italics, the story is Parker's most thoroughgoing mockery of women's speech. The narrator's fears of humiliation and loneliness can barely break the faddish surface of the language. In "Too Bad," a wife resolves to break the tedious patter of her marriage and converse with her husband on interesting and important topics; but her resolutions dissolve in his presence. At the mercy of the wifely role to which she is so unsuited, she hears herself, with dismay, chattering of her "daffy-downlillies." "To anyone else, she would have referred to them as daffodils" (175).

II

First published in the *New Yorker* in 1933, "The Waltz" is essentially one of Parker's celebrated soliloquies—which Brendan Gill described as "star turns by an acrobat working up at the top of the tent without a net" (*The Portable Dorothy Parker*, xx–xxi). But its incorporation of spoken dialogue plays explicitly upon the commonplace distinction between what we say and what we think: the structure systematically contrasts the italicized spoken dialogue (the external language of the world) with the unitalicized speech of the monologues (the internal language of the self). This is a provocative structural representation of women as divided beings and the reflection of this division in language.[5] It seems further to arise from the animating core of Parker's fiction, and offer us a distilled and potent version of her central concern with deception, division, and the risks of self-disclosure.

To begin with what is obvious: the italics in "The Waltz" at once instruct the reader's eye to divide the telling of the story between two graphically differentiated voices. The story is short (two pages in the *New Yorker* version); it begins and ends in italicized speech, alternating in all seven italicized short passages of dialogue spoken to the male dancing partner with six unitalicized longer internal monologues. I restrict the term "italicized speech" to the italic typeface in which the spoken dialogue is rendered graphically and in which words and phrases in the monologues are formally marked to show emphasis (that is, the features of stress, loudness, and intonation that occur in spoken language), to set aside foreign phrases, and so on.

The opening line is a response to a question that has been asked before the story starts; it extends the story to include verbal material that isn't there. "*I'd adore to,*" responds the speaker. Adore to—what? In accordance with standard discourse agreement, the elliptical infinitive omits the main verb "dance," which has occurred only in the question we have not heard. The omission exemplifies Parker's ease with colloquial speech and points us simultaneously backward and forward: we must return to the story's title, "The Waltz," or read on into the monologue, to find out *what* the speaker would adore to do. By that time, of course—by the time we read "I don't want to dance with him"—we know that she would *not* adore to.[6]

The opening dialogue and monologue, taken together, identify the story's situational context rather unambiguously as a dance. The male dancing partner is probably of college age (old enough to dance, young enough to be called "this boy"); the speaker's age is less clear, but she is older than her partner. The story's action is simultaneous with its narration; the speaker offers an ongoing commentary as the dance progresses. The opening line establishes traditional sexual roles: the female speaker responds to the male's initiative. The whole story is in some sense structured as a female response to the demands of a particular (male-initiated) social context; the speaker's passivity and accommodation are the expected characteristics of her role. Yet contradictions are built in from the first. The affirmation of the spoken dialogue is at once undercut by the stream of negatives in the subsequent monologue. The passivity of the female role is undermined by the narrative structure: the responsibility for getting the story told is solely the female speaker's.

The language of the spoken dialogue is unbrokenly "sweet" and accommodating. In the monologues, the speaker rages inwardly: Why did she accept this dance? Doesn't he know this is a waltz and not a football scrimmage? Will the music never stop? and so on. To herself, she calls him names that characterize his clumsiness, manic athleticism, and bad breeding: "Cannonball," "Butch," "the Triple Threat"; "How do you do, Mr. Jukes? And how is that dear little brother of yours, with the two heads?" (47). His flawed sense of rhythm especially irks her, and she calls him "Double-time Charlie" and "Swifty." Sports metaphors and repeated images of violence and physical pain communicate her experience of the waltz as a harrowing scuffle: "*Ow*! For God's sake, don't *kick*, you idiot; this is only second down. Oh, my shin. My poor, poor shin, that I've had ever since I was a little girl!" (48). Aloud, she asserts the traditional long-suffering female role, denying pain and accepting blame: "*Goodness, no, it didn't hurt the least little bit. And anyway it was my fault*" (48). But violent images immediately challenge both the irony and the empty gallantry, and portray him, not her, as the victim: "I wonder what I'd better do—kill him this instant, with my naked hands, or wait and let him drop in his traces" (48). The speculation poses a semantic dilemma: does one (actively) kill him or (passively) let him die? But the syntactic form is active: *she* will decide, and neither possibility is pleasant for him. But as the waltz proceeds, she appears to soften in her judgment: perhaps he's not so bad, only young and high-spirited. Exaggeration gives way to language that, though protected by its own potential for being interpreted as sarcasm, is nevertheless overtly kinder to him: "I love him. I love him better than anybody in the world." Her tribute builds rhetorical energy—until he mashes her foot again: "He is youth and vigor and courage, he is strength and gaiety and—*Ow*! Get off my instep, you hulking peasant!" (49). The series of abstract nouns surrounds the male with a verbal frame of masculine ideals. Though the abstraction may be ironic, it nevertheless serves to distance the speaker from the realities of the waltz.[7] But his clumsiness foils her attempt: in physical pain, she disrupts her own portrait with an involuntary exclamation that seems on the edge of being spoken aloud. Her shift to an imperative verb form reinforces the image of a "hulking peasant" who exists to be imperiously ordered about. Now relentlessly unforgiving, the speaker tries to get through the rest of the dance as quickly as possible; references to pain and death sharpen and multiply: "I'm past all feeling now. The only way I can tell when he steps on me is that I can hear the splintering of bones"; "I didn't know what trouble was, before I got drawn into this *danse macabre*" (51).

This outline of "The Waltz" suggests the general differences between the italicized and unitalicized portions. We may now look a little more closely at their language. The dialogue spoken aloud is supremely and stereotypically feminine and manifests most of the characteristics that Robin Lakoff attributes to "women's speech" in *Language and Woman's Place*; in fact, it is almost a blueprint for "ladylike" language.[8] It is thick with "feminine" particles, usually attached to "oh": "*oh, yes,*" "*oh, no, no, no,*" "*oh, darn,*" "*oh, goody.*" It is full of what Lakoff describes as "trivializing" words like "adore" and "thrilled" and of intensifiers like "simply," "really," "truly," and especially "so"—"*thank you so much.*" Its tag questions and repetitive adverbs and adjectives mark accommodation and acquiescence to a point of nearly total redundancy. Changes rung on the word "love" are particularly pervasive: "*Yes, it's lovely, isn't it? It's simply lovely. It's the loveliest waltz. Isn't it? Oh, I think it's lovely, too*" (49). Though the italics of the dialogue's typeface neutralize any graphic representation of stress and pitch, we can hear them unmistakably in such comments as "*It didn't hurt the least little bit*" (48) and "*Tired? I should say I'm not tired*" (50).[9]

The spoken dialogue consists entirely of "women's language" of this sort. It is presented as a verbal repertoire specifically shaped to the presence of a male. One of the functions of such utterances, in Lakoff's view, is to mark the speaker's genuine distance from the male power structure (thus the title of her book, *Language and Woman's Place*). Barbara Bellow Watson's discussion of power in literary texts suggests that the language of women may also represent a kind of deliberate "protective accommodation" that conceals whatever real power the speaker may have.[10] When the speaker of "The Waltz" remarks, "*Why, I think it's more of a waltz, really. Isn't it?*" (48), she appears to be seeking information: in fact she is giving it. She couches her knowledge (and knowledge is power) in deferential form. She must defer because she lacks real power and cannot afford to alienate members of the group that do not lack it. In any case, it is certainly fair to say that the spoken dialogues, in their unalleviated passivity and chirping monotony, rather cruelly caricature the way women are supposed to talk. But that phrase "supposed to talk" is important, for Parker's joke is double-edged. Though she satirizes women's speech and makes the spoken dialogue sound silly and shallow, how much sillier she makes the male dancing partner appear who silently—silently, that is, within the structure the story forces upon him—accepts such language as the way women really do talk. The exaggerated language of the speaker in "The Waltz" is socially impeccable and irreproachably "feminine"; but it is totally false.

Or so we must assume from what she says to herself. Each utterance she makes in "women's language" is immediately subverted; none of it is allowed to stand. The internal monologues mock not only the sentiments that she expresses aloud but also the language in which she has expressed them. Her recognition that she speaks in two voices wins us to her, for she seems to offer us the private, genuine feelings behind the regrettably necessary public code. "*Mind?*" she trills aloud. "*Why, I'm simply thrilled. I'd love to waltz with you.*" But at once the internal voice spitefully subverts the bubbly social formula: "I'd love to waltz with you. I'd love to waltz with you. I'd love to have my tonsils out. I'd love to be in a midnight fire at sea" (48). The repetition of the same linguistic structure equates the waltz with surgery and fire at sea. The equation transforms the meaning of "love" into "hate," a reversal that exposes the hypocrisy of the public voice. The active, participatory connotations of "I'd love to waltz" are undone by the link to almost archetypally passive experiences.

The internal monologues seem to offer the speaker a space where she may assert and preserve her private self. They allow her to exert some control over a situation in which she is powerless, and to distance herself from it in a variety of ways. That they partly parody the female language the dance setting demands is one of these. The feminine particle "oh" is, in the monologues, more commonly the irreverent, unladylike "*Ow!*" Or the language is mocked in other ways, through repetition, for example: "*Oh.* Oh, dear. Oh, dear, dear, dear." Or the form of the sentence is at odds with the meaning: "oh, yes, *do* let's dance together—it's so nice to meet a man who isn't a scaredy-cat about catching my beri-beri." This reference occurs as the speaker thinks over how she might have evaded this waltz: "I most certainly will *not* dance with you," she imagines herself saying, "I'll see you in hell first," and "Why, thank you, I'd like to awfully, but I'm having labor pains." These mock excuses form another of the semantic equations that are absent from the spoken dialogue: hell equals disease equals labor pains. The invocation of labor pains is particularly rich in irony: the classically acceptable feminine excuse for avoiding physical activity hints at the full scenario that underlies a single dance and includes courtship, marriage, children. The hypothetical reason for not dancing is identified with the hypothetical consequences of doing so.

The monologues serve also as face-saving manifestos on behalf of the inner self, offering emotional annotation to observable reality: though I am dancing with you, they say, I do not have to like you. Their language serves to encompass and distance individual sources of pain. Thus the speaker muses, "My poor, poor shin, that I've had ever since I was a little girl!" The comment singles out the shin and presents it isolated from the rest of the body, as an object for scrutiny and reflection. The speaker domesticates her trial of flesh and distances herself from the scene of it.

Whereas the spoken dialogue represses our sense of the speaker as an individual, the monologues seem rich in idiosyncratic personal history. Clever and sophisticated, they represent the milieu of an intelligent, literate woman, and draw from a wide rhetorical universe. Whereas the dialogue is relatively unchanging and predictable and represents a fairly cohesive verbal repertoire, the monologues are continually shifting in both form and function. In the dialogues, to cite one example, formal tense marking takes place for the most part in the present indicative ("*it's lovely*"); though there are also instances of marking for perfect, progressive, and conditional, they chiefly refer to temporal events within about a ten-minute time span. The monologues contain more diverse marking of tenses and range in reference far into the past and future.[11] The monologues incorporate disparate kinds of language and use these verbal elements in complex ways. Their range of features includes topical allusion (Jukes, George Jean Nathan); cliché ("small world"); literary reference ("I must look like something out of 'The Fall of the House of Usher'"); literary quotation ("When you kick me in the shin, *smile*"); swearing ("For God's sake"); reference to personal experience ("the time I was in a hurricane in the West Indies"); sports metaphors; images and metaphors of movement, violence, disease, and death; body images ("my hair is hanging along my cheeks"); snatches of theatrical allusion ("No, a thousand times no"); slang (and often dated slang, as in "a true little corker"); sophisticated "tough talk" ("I'll see you in hell first"); dialect ("he grew up in hill country, and never had no larnin',"); slogans ("nor heat nor pain nor broken heart"); and foreign phrases ("*danse macabre*").

This catalogue only begins to indicate the density of the monologues. They are also dense with verbal complication. One cluster of epithets, for example, characterizes the dancing partner as a genetic deviant: Jukes (the reference is to the descendants of a family of New York sisters who formed the basis, around the turn of the century, for a study of hereditary criminality), "you idiot," "hulking peasant," "degenerate cunning," "Saint Walpurgis Night." But the speaker jestingly imagines herself with beriberi and refers to herself as something out of the House of Usher, and the imagery becomes self-implicating as well. At the end of the third monologue, another example occurs. After being kicked, the speaker offers a series of excuses for the male dancing partner—"Maybe he didn't do it maliciously," and so on. But every sentence of the passage begins with a signal of doubt: "Maybe," "I suppose," "Probably," "I bet." The hedging clouds any real sense of affirmation; yet that excuses are offered at all effectively shifts the story's tone.

In contrast to the dialogues, certain aspects of the monologues reverse sex stereotypes. Sports metaphors, for example, seem to belong fairly undisputedly to masculine verbal turf. The speaker's easy references, then, to scrimmage, second down, and so forth, represent a deliberate encroachment onto this territory. Yet she clearly uses these terms ironically to mock the collegiate vocabulary and ideals of the male dancing partner. The metaphors function to signal, simultaneously, familiarity and contempt.[12] The monologues also add to our portrait of the speaker (as the dialogue does not), a portrait at odds with the ladylike language of the dialogue. The monologues also undermine the view, in the dialogues, of the dancing partner as a traditional strong, perfect, graceful, and inventive male. "What could you say to a thing like that?" wonders the speaker, her lexical choice characterizing him literally as an object. She imagines making social conversation: "Did you go to the circus this year, what's your favorite kind of ice cream, how do you spell cat?" (51). The parody of social patter portrays the dancing partner as a dimwitted child. This is no warmly maternal portrait of men as little boys; rather it suggests someone who lacks even basic social skills.

III

These ostensible contrasts between the spoken dialogue and the internal monologue create a number of general impressions about what is going on in the story. The spoken dialogue, the public voice that is addressed exclusively to the male dancing partner, purports to be humble, self-effacing, utterly accommodating. It is an irreproachable performance that perfectly conforms, without flaw or stumble, to the dimensions of its situational context. In contrast with this feminine public self is the mocking, ironically distanced, and subversive voice of the monologues. While the public self chatters incessantly and hypocritically, the inner self stands back, uncompromised. Only the italicized language is in the public domain and open, so to speak, to public inspection. The inner monologues can range freely from anger to mockery to sarcasm from a position of impregnable narrative detachment. The wit and malice of the monologues accordingly redeem the fawning coquetry of the public language. We, as readers, find the story funny because we can fully experience the resonances of contradiction: we are privileged within its carefully constructed frame (as the male dancing partner is not privileged) to cross and recross the dangerous boundaries between what is spoken aloud and what is felt and thought within.

But as I have been suggesting, a continual subversion of these effects has been taking place throughout the story, and as it draws to a close, they are dramatically undermined. The passage that most unequivocally thwarts the redeeming wittiness and irony of the monologues is this sudden outburst, embedded within a monologue about four-fifths of the way through the story:

> I hate this creature I'm chained to. I hated him the moment I saw his leering, bestial face. And here I've been locked in his noxious embrace for the thirty-five years this waltz has lasted. Is that orchestra never going to stop playing? Or must this obscene travesty of a dance go on until hell burns out? (50)

This passage clarifies and brings explicitly to the surface the venom and bitterness that have been clothed until now in cleverness, exaggeration, and other diverse kinds of verbal play. But here the speaker's wisecracking impudence falls away to reveal stark hatred. Sarcasm and irony have permitted the speaker to say things without committing herself to them, but here there is no hedging. There is rather a sense that the charade has lasted long enough. No mere humorous sketch about a woman at a dance can account for the meaning of this passage. Whatever restraints the story's comic function may have imposed upon its language, they are broken by these harsh and violent images. The statement "I hate this creature I'm chained to" is so blank and unadorned that nothing in the story's fevered exaggerations can have prepared us for its literal simplicity. It is far more than a verbal antidote to the reckless abundance of the word "love" in the preceding monologues. It reinforces and magnifies all the potential meanings that have accrued in the course of the speaker's earlier tirades: I meant every word seriously, it announces. Image and metaphor have concocted a portrait of the waltz that is dense with connotative possibilities and shadowy with other meanings. This passage assures us that we must look beyond the immediate situation to those other meanings, for more than a dance is clearly at stake. It is shocking, for example, that the male dancing partner has become "this creature"; the word makes him at once less human and more sinister than the manic, clumsy athlete he has seemed, until now, to be. He becomes anonymous: this depersonalized creature could be anyone, or everyone. The succession of proper names she has given him ("Jukes," "Butch") suggests that he is made up of replaceable identities, all contained within the word "creature." This parallels the names the speaker earlier gave herself: "Despair, Bewilderment, Futility, Degradation and Premeditated Murder" (47)—also names that threaten the boundaries of the story by bestowing archetypal, almost figural, qualities upon legions of anonymous women at dances.

"I hated him the moment I saw his leering, bestial face," she goes on. Her language falls outside whatever range of diction we associate with social dances. Rather it is unmistakably sexual, and reveals the waltz as a metaphor for sexual intercourse, with its familiar contrasts between elegant ideals and clumsy, painful realities. The interpretation invests with great comedy much of the imagery and verbal play of the preceding passages: "It's this constant rush, rush, rush, that's the curse of American life"; "And he worked up his little step himself, he with his degenerate cunning" (50). "Chained" becomes an image of sexual coupling, "Jukes" a suggestion of dangerous and unwholesome breeding, "gangplank" an echo of "gang-bang." The equation of labor pains with hell and with disease echoes the theme of degeneracy. The reference to Freud helps transform the dancing partner's physical transgressions (against the speaker's shin and instep) into violent sexual assaults. "I've led no cloistered life," the speaker says, "I've known dancing partners who have spoiled my slippers and torn my dress; but when it comes to kicking, I am Outraged Womanhood" (49). By invoking this note of feminine gentility (which the initial caps make self-conscious), the waltz becomes a rape. Her theatrical "Die he must, and die he shall, for what he did to me" becomes a special kind of theater: the raped woman's demand for vengeance. The self-effacing comments in the spoken dialogue seem then a parody of classic female self-accusation: "*No, of course it didn't hurt. Why it didn't a bit. Honestly. And it was all my fault*" (49). "Ah, what an easy, peaceful time was mine," she muses, and she gives him a name notorious from dirty jokes, "until I fell in with Swifty, here."

The waltz is a metaphor not only for sexual combat. The next sentence—"And here I've been locked in his noxious embrace for the thirty-five years this waltz has lasted"—seems at first, in the main clause, to signal a return to the old, easy humor; but the phrase "thirty-five years" catches us just as we are beginning to smile. "Eight hours" or "a thousand years" might be amusing figures in this context, but "thirty-five years" is too literal. It invokes not a comically exaggerated time frame but a realistic one. This radical shift in temporal context revises our notions of who the "creature" she's chained to is: thirty-five years is a long time. In this verbal context, he must be seen as a husband, or at any rate some kind of permanent male figure—or many figures, perhaps, who blend anonymously into each other. "Chain" and "lock" become descriptive of more permanent connections: of the bond of matrimony, for example. The speaker's repeated assertions that she "loves" her partner suggest the standard self-deceptions of women attempting to rationalize the dissatisfactions of conventional roles.

What this suggests is that the stakes are high. Every move, word, image is invaded by time and space to create a multiple series of possibilities, each of which risks failure, exposure, tedium, and despair. "The Waltz" is a comic story, but at its core is Parker's animating vision of death. "Is that orchestra never going to stop playing?" she asks. "Or must this obscene travesty of a dance go on until hell burns out?" We now know her age: it is the thirty-five years she has spent chained to her own body. The story's diverse particulars—waltz, courtship, sex, marriage, children—are manifestations of a vision of living death. And so is the language itself, for by now we cannot escape the self-conscious and claustrophobic resonances of the story's verbal structure. The speaker races through her soliloquies, as though speed and wit could animate with life a series of dead words. The story itself is the real *danse macabre*, and when the speaker says, "I hate this creature I'm chained to," there is a sense of suffocating in language, and in life.

The phrase *danse macabre* is characteristic, and central to Parker's obsession with death—an obsession that filled her work and her life and which, in both, seems to have been inescapably both comic and tragic. That is a commonplace enough characterization of a writer's approach, but rarely is it so profoundly embedded in the mechanics of style as in Parker's work. The anecdotes are often about death: when she worked for *Vanity Fair* she subscribed to two undertaking trade magazines, *The Casket* and *Sunnyside*. Her books have "funereal titles": *Sunset Gun, Enough Rope, Laments for the Living, Death and Taxes, Not so Deep as a Well, Here Lies*. She claimed to have named her characters from telephone books and obituary columns. Her verses draw heavily from the lexicon of death and dying: bones, shrouds, weeds, graves, linen, ghosts, and worms. "People ought to be one of

two things," she wrote, "young or old. No; what's the good of fooling? People ought to be one of two things, young or dead" (596).
She attempted suicide: Keats lists twenty-eight points of correspondence between Parker and Hazel Moore in "Big Blonde"—the failure of the attempt was one of them. Death is a crucial element in
"The Waltz," a "humorous" story. Likewise humor was, for Parker,
a not unthinkable element of death. (See Lillian Hellman's report
in *An Unfinished Woman*, 198–99, of Parker at her husband's funeral—an accidental overdose—when a woman who didn't much
like her came up and asked if there were anything she could do.
"Get me a new husband," said Parker. After a stunned silence, the
woman retorted: "I think that is the most callous and disgusting remark I ever heard in my life." "Dottie turned to look at her," goes
Hellman's version, "sighed, and said gently, 'So sorry. Then run
down to the corner and get me a ham and cheese on rye and tell
them to hold the mayo.'")

A single metaphor in "The Waltz," which occurs in the first
monologue, embodies this vision of death: "But what could I do?"
the speaker asks. "Everyone else at the table had got up to dance,
except him and me. There was I, trapped. Trapped like a trap in a
trap" (47). In the original 1933 *New Yorker* version and in the collection of stories *After Such Pleasures* that same year, "There was I" reads
"There I was." The change (or correction) to "There was I" in the
later versions strengthens the argument that the phrase is highly
self-conscious. The inversion in "There was I" embeds the "I"
within the complex repetitive locution: the nominative "I" as subject is compromised by the structure, trapped within it, and this
transformation sustains the portrait of a woman physically and verbally trapped: trapped at the table, she is trapped also by cultural
pressures and verbal imperatives of stifling density. When a man asks
you to dance, you must respond that you'd adore to. "Trapped like
a trap in a trap": the simile mirrors the meaningless repetition built
into ritualized interaction. It is also self-referential. Like the word
"waltz," the word "trap" has a rich connotative history. What does
it mean that the word recurs four times in two short sentences, and
forms a wholly unexpected and unusual collocation? The phonetic
features of the phrase resonate in our ears (like "snug as a bug in a
rug," perhaps) and act out "trap," its only concrete component. At
the same time it draws together other images of entrapment and enclosure in the story: "cloistered life," "plaster cast." But it also plays
on "man-trap," death trap," perhaps even "shut your trap," drawing them out of the common verbal reservoir of English to challenge
the speaker's own version of her helpless passivity. In a metaphor of

infinite regress, the vision of traps within traps undoes the innocence of her self-presentation. Women, so that they may be trapped, must themselves be traps.

The metaphor also undoes the story's own narrative presentation. It offers a version of mutuality, of complicity, that in turn dissolves any clear distinction between inner and outer speech. The notion of a trap trapped in a trap encapsulates the story's duplicities; it is the essence of subversion. Just as it subverts the speaker's self-portrait, it subverts the story's self-portrait: too strange for humor, just as "thirty-five years" was too literal, the phrase undercuts the story's pose. "The Waltz" does not really offer a contrast between the external language of the world and the internal language of the self. Instead it offers a series of verbal redundancies that play upon each other—a trap. It is a study in self-subversion.

Thus we should not be surprised to find that the story draws to a close characteristically. In the last monologue, metaphors of death and heaven culminate, and the speaker sees herself dead, dancing throughout eternity. By the time the orchestra finally begins to wind down, her life is passing before her eyes. At last there falls "a silence like the sound of angel voices," a promise of both bodiless peace and cessation of speech, and we, as readers, anticipate her release from the physical, psychological, and verbal bondage in which the story has placed her. But we find our way through images of death to a punch line that betrays us, this passage of dialogue, spoken aloud:

> Oh, they've stopped, the mean things. They're not going to play any more. Oh, darn. Oh, do you think they would? Do you really think so if you gave them twenty dollars? Oh, that would be lovely. And look, do tell them to play this same thing. I'd simply adore to go on waltzing. (51)

Thus the story returns us to its beginning (" Why, thank you so much. I'd adore to.") and encloses the speaker in a circle of her own words. The waltz is without end, and, in these last lines, without the accompanying internal monologue that subverts her acquiescence. Her words display her customary passive compliance, but, further, energetically assert her willingness to go on waltzing. She participates in perpetuating the situation, which called for what we were made to believe was intolerable hypocrisy. Her compliance demands that we reevaluate our perceptions of that hypocrisy.

The ending of the story reveals that the speaker has been lying to us as much as to her partner. It denies our sense that we have had access to her true feelings. Trapped in the trap of the story, we have read it in good faith, unaware that its language is utterly treacher-

ous. Literature written by women, Watson warns us, cannot be expected "to tell us much about so sensitive a topic [as power] in the
form of declarations, manifestos, plot summaries, or even the broad
outlines of characterization. We begin instead to look at such techniques as ambiguity, equivocation, and expressive symbolic structure" ("Power and the Literary Text," 113). In "The Waltz," we
encounter a symbolic structure with its ambiguities and equivocation intact. One structural device, the alternation of italicized with
unitalicized language, offers us two voices, separated from each
other. But the structure does not hold. The story's conclusion confirms its complications, as another device—the echo of the first line
in the last line—sends us back to the beginning of the story and
gives Parker's vision of a trap within a trap a formal equivalent.

IV

What are we to make of this complicity? In exercising her narrative authority, Parker abandons her protagonist to the story's language. As we return to the beginning of the story, we see that our
interpretation of " *Why, thank you so much. I'd adore to*" as shallow and
duplicitous is not accurate: what seemed to be duplicity is in fact
complicity. The language does not mock social realities but affirms
them. The points of interaction between the end and the beginning
of the story suggest some of this. The last dialogue gives the story a
kind of inevitability: the speaker is bound to dance again and again.
It also hints why this must be so, for the figure of "twenty dollars"
invokes the speaker's economic dependency on her partner, and
thus the economic inequalities that color many male-female relationships. The concrete figure of twenty dollars, the price of a one-
night stand, creates a sense of universal cheapening that specifically
suggests the dependence of a prostitute on her clientele. (In the
original 1933 version, the figure is fifty dollars, certainly a fee more
appropriate for a call girl than for a casual dance partner. In revising, Parker may have lowered the figure as the depression took
hold.) Yet the initial monologue is also tainted in other ways we had
not originally perceived: "I don't want to dance with him. I don't
want to dance with him. I don't want to dance with anybody. And
even if I did, it wouldn't be him." Her sentiments shift with each
sentence, and "even if I did" is a traditional signal that a firm stance
is weakening. We could reverse the ostensible meaning and be as
close to the truth: I do want to dance with him; I do want to dance
with somebody. And sure enough: "He'd be well down among the

last ten," she continues; her classification purports to sustain the assault, but negates the overall meaning of her speech by lengthening, dramatically, the list of men she *would* dance with—for virtually the whole world will do.

Meanwhile, the assumed humility of the dialogues has dropped away; their women's language has triumphed over the cheeky cleverness of the monologues. Seemingly unassertive, passive, the feminine public voice of the dialogues emerges as invulnerable: banal, certainly, but very strong. Parker's satiric treatment has not affected it, and it continues to exist in solipsistic impenetrability, circling the story with a smooth, unbroken surface. Its exaggerations clarify its function: what it will get you in the end is a dancing partner, a man, a livelihood. If there is self-mockery built somewhere into its delivery, it poses no threat: jazz musicians, it has been observed, hired to play "corny" music, will slightly exaggerate those qualities of the music they most despise; but their audience, also corny, will not recognize this affirmation of artistic integrity. Women's language has room enough for mockery without risk, for it is virtually content free. It functions essentially as phatic communication, affirming the speaker's status as an available female. Its content is irrelevant. It is as though the italics of the typeface have come to life and blanked out everything else: the women's language follows a single intonation curve whose continuous rising and falling voice repels all meaning. "I'd adore to" *needs* no additional verb, for it functions best as it is, literally as an open-ended statement of acquiescence.

We cannot view the spoken dialogue as an outer voice, external to the self. With its high predictability, redundancies, and low excitement, it might be better described as a kind of professional pidgin. It is a purely functional commercial language that takes no risks and gives nothing away. It adapts itself easily to fluctuating circumstances: a waltz, a marriage—the scenario can be rewritten without difficulty. It deflects inquiry: everything's fine, it announces to men, don't trouble yourself. And to other women it signals: save yourself, for *I* won't save you. Its value as a language of business lies in its vapidity: it offers only the information that is needed to sustain the encounter. In doing so, it very much represents a language of female survival.[13]

One is tempted, in this light, to view the monologues in contrast as the verbal account of both a privileged inner life and a series of secure judgments about external events. While the public woman looks after business, the gender-free consciousness of the monologues can confront itself and the world. Certainly the language of the monologues is rich in reference and allusion, in historical and

personal knowledge. Yet this very richness of allusion is their undo-
ing, for they cannot wholly control or personalize the range of verbal styles they contain. They are compromised by the world's all-too-
public language. That is all there is, the story says: there can be no
privileged refuge, no silence. "Why can't he let me lead my own
life?" the speaker wonders. "I ask so little—just to be left alone in
my quiet corner of the table, to do my evening brooding over all
my sorrows" (47). But each element in this supposedly private and
personal communication of disposition is in fact a cliché that ar-
rives, impersonally, at the speaker's disposal, with all its ironies and
compromises built in. The fluent speaker, so different ostensibly
from Hazel Moore in "Big Blonde," differs only in the selection of
her material and in its quantity, not in kind.

The supposedly public language of the dialogues absorbs nothing; it is impervious to influence or change. But the monologues are
in constant flux, absorbing everything, disintegrating into a uniform
verbal clutter. The private voice talks faster and faster, striving to encompass clichés, quotations, allusions, metaphors, this month's
slang. These verbal elements offer only temporary refuge to the
speaking, thinking self. However wittily and satirically they may be
used, they are in the end mere versions of Hazel Moore's "I'm
nearly dead." These essentially *borrowed* verbal forms can be pitted
against one another to record a search for liberation, but they cannot serve to construct an uncompromised and unique female self-
hood.[14]

This unresolvable problem runs through all of Parker's fiction
and extends as well to her sense of her own career. When the
speaker in "The Waltz" says "I hate this creature I'm chained to,"
it could also stand for Parker's attitude toward her own talent.
"Dammit," she told the *Paris Review*, "it *was* the twenties and we had
to be smarty. I *wanted* to be cute. That's the terrible thing. I should
have had more sense." In Parker's monologues, the first-person pronoun seems to act as a magnet for dense clusters of parody and wisecracking; hence, I believe, her desire later to move away from the
soliloquies and satiric conversations that had made her reputation
as a writer of fiction. "I want to do the story that can only be told in
the narrative form, " she said, "and though they're going to scream
about the rent, I'm going to do it."[15] She may have felt that aban-
doning dialogue and monologue would have freed her from the
need to undermine and satirize her own commitment to the search
for a uniquely female literary language. Yet that is very doubtful, for
her ambivalence in this respect characterizes much of women's
writing.

Women's literature records the working out of a series of personal, political, and artistic motives in *verbal* terms. Each move toward rhetorical change is compromised by the prior commitments of the language and by the pressure literary history exerts on the individual use of literary forms. The vision of what might be must struggle with what has been. Thus "The Waltz" simultaneously satirizes ritualized social interaction and embodies it. It is essential that studies of women's style acknowledge and document this paradox. To ignore it, to claim too much freedom for women writers and for women's language, is to reduce their real achievement—their struggle to remake a language dense with preexisting associations and values. Women's writing is a search for an authentic female voice, and, in many ways, its true subject is language.

NOTES

1. *The Portable Dorothy Parker* (New York: Viking, 1973), 47. Subsequent references in text. ("The Waltz" first appeared in the *New Yorker,* 2 September, 1933.)

2. Most writing on Parker consists of magazine articles and reviews by her contemporaries, and tends to be anecdotal or metaphorical—for example, Alexander Woollcott's often-quoted comment that her writings "are so potent a distillation of nectar and wormwood, of ambrosia and deadly nightshade, as might suggest to the rest of us that we all write far too much" (*The Portable Woollcott* [New York: Viking, 1946], 181). See John Keats's biography, *You Might as Well Live* (New York: Simon and Schuster, 1970); Anita Loos's autobiography, *A Girl Like I* (New York: Viking, 1966); Lillian Hellman's *An Unfinished Woman* (New York: Bantam, 1970); and Wyatt Cooper's "Remembering Dorothy Parker," *Esquire* 70, no. 1 (1968). Two attempts to treat Parker's writing seriously are Ann Douglas, "Feminist Criticism and Cultural History: Dorothy Parker and the 1930s," presented at the Modern Language Association, New York, December 1976; and William Shanahan, "Robert Benchley and Dorothy Parker: Punch and Judy in Formal Dress," *Rendezvous* 3, no. 1 (1968): 26. Shanahan does comment on Parker's style, but erroneously: unlike James, he writes, "[s]he did not mask her message with mandarin politeness and verbal duplicity" (26).

3. Dorothy Parker, interview by Marion Capron, in *Writers at Work: The "Paris Review" Interviews*, ed. Malcolm Cowley (New York: Viking, 1969), 80.

4. *The Ladies of the Corridor* (New York: Viking, 1954), 115.

5. The presentation of women as divided beings has been (and continues to be) an important theme in women's writing. Kate Chopin, in *The Awakening*, published first in 1899, writes of her heroine that "at a very early period she had apprehended instinctively the dual life—that outward existence which conforms, the inward life which questions" (New York: Capricorn, 1964, 35). "Confronting man," writes Simone de Beauvoir, "woman is always play-acting; she lies when she makes believe that she accepts her status as the inessential other; she lies when she presents to him an imaginary personage through mimicry, costumery, studied phrases. These histrionics require a constant tension: when with her husband, or with her lover, every woman is more or less conscious of the thought: 'I am not being my-

self'" (*The Second Sex*, trans. and ed. H. M. Parshley [New York: Knopf, 1953], 605).
See also Mary Ellmann, *Thinking About Women* (New York: Harcourt, 1968); Betty
Friedan, *The Feminine Mystique* (New York: Norton, 1963); Erving Goffman, *Presenta-
tion of Self in Everyday* (New York: Anchor, 1959) and *Strategic Interaction* (Philadel-
phia: University of Pennsylvania Press, 1969); Mirra Komarovsky, "Cultural
Contradiction and Sex Roles," *American Journal of Sociology* 52 (November 1946);
Cheris Kramer [Kramarae], "Women's Speech: Separate but Unequal," *Quarterly
Journal of Speech* 60 (February 1974): 14–24; Barbara Bellow Watson, "On Power and
the Literary Text," *Journal of Women in Culture and Society* 1, no. 1 (1975): 111–18.

   6. For an extended discussion of such pointing functions in language, see
M. A. K. Halliday, "Descriptive Linguistics in Literary Studies," in *English Studies
Today*, ed. A. Duthie (Edinburgh: Edinburgh University Press, 1964).

   7. Ian Watt notes that "the application of abstract diction to particular persons
always tends towards irony, because it imposes a dual way of looking at them: few
of us can survive being presented as general representatives of humanity" ("The
First Paragraph of *The Ambassadors*: An Explication," in Glen A. Love and Michael
Payne, eds., *Contemporary Essays on Style* [Glenview, Ill.: Scott Foresman, 1969], 277).
G. W. Turner's discussion of the protective functions of sarcasm and irony (and
their potential risks) is relevant to this passage of "The Waltz." *Stylistics* (Middlesex:
Penguin, 1973).

   8. Robin Lakoff, *Language and Woman's Place* (New York: Harper, 1975), 53–57.
I do not intend to address the empirical validity of Lakoff's impressions (but see
Sally McConnell-Ginet, "Our Father Tongue: Essays in Linguistic Politics," *Diacritics*
[Winter 1975]: 44–50, and Barrie Thorne, review of Lakoff, *Signs* 1, no. 3, pt. 1
[Spring 1976]: 744–46). I might only observe that Lakoff's comments are conceivably more descriptive of women's language in fiction than women's language in
"real life." The suspiciously close conformity between her hypotheses and Parker's
fiction suggests to me that Parker's dialogue, so pervasive and influential, has
helped shape a fictional tradition and in turn our notions of women's speech. Such
language may exist primarily in fiction (or on television, etc.), where its independent existence may be what creates our intuitive sense that Lakoff's impressions are
accurate.

   9. Though I am speaking here of the fact that italicization literally neutralizes
the familiar representation, through italics, of stress and pitch, italics are also
thought to neutralize the importance they purport to mark. Thus in *The Haunted
House at Latchford*, first published in 1873, Mrs. J. H. Riddell refers to letters full of
"feminine italics," and, in particular, to a long letter "in which italics vainly endeav-
ored to express her ladyship's astonishment at the phenomenon" (*Three Supernatu-
ral Novels of the Victorian Period* [New York: Dover, 1975], 216–17). Italics are, in fact,
a subject in the study of women's language about which there is a great deal to be
said.

   10. Lakoff, *Language and Woman's Place*, 16–17; Watson, "Power and the Literary
Text, " 113.

   11. See Robin Lakoff, "Tense and its Relation to Participants," *Language* 46, no.
4 (1970): 838–49; and David Crystal and Derek Davy, *Investigating English Style*
(Bloomington: Indiana University Press, 1969), 125–46.

   12. "It is of interest," writes Lakoff, "to note that men's language is increasingly
being used by women, but women's language is not being adopted by men, apart
from those who reject the American masculine image [for example, homosexuals]
. . . The language of the favored group, the group that holds the power, along with
its nonlinguistic behavior, is generally adopted by the other group, not vice versa

(*Language and Woman's Place*, 10). See also Sally McConnell-Ginet, "Intonation in a Man's World," *Signs* 3, no. 3 (1978): 541–59. Parker satirizes "men's language" as well as women's. In "Too Bad," for example, she describes a dull husband: "Mr. Weldon turned a page, and yawned aloud. 'Wah-huh-huh-huh-huh,' he went, on a descending scale. He yawned again, and this time climbed the scale" (180). Elsewhere she explicitly documents the alienating aspects of male speech, as in this exchange between the soldier husband and his wife from "The Lovely Leave": "Hell," says the husband, searching for something to polish his belt buckle with. "I don't suppose you've got a Blitz Cloth, have you? Or a Shine-O?" His wife coldly replies, "If I had the faintest idea what you were talking about, I might be better company for you" (15).

13. Turner, *Stylistics*, 209–13, discusses phatic communication and its functions. Language considered deviant in some settings may in fact represent adaptive behavior for survival. For examples, this is a therapist's characterization of speech in hysteric patients: "The vocabulary may on first acquaintance seem novel and unique, but repeated interviews reveal the narrowness of its range, as expressions reappear and detract from the flexibility of language. The initial impressions of vividness decreases as one discovers the extent to which the hysteric makes use of the conventions and clichés of the language community in which he operates . . . a static quality eventually arises from the cumulative effect . . ." (Maria Lorenz, "Expressive Behavior and Language Patterns," in *The Study of Abnormal Behavior*, ed. Melvin Zax and George Stricker (New York: Macmillan, 1964), 140–41. This is not to say that Parker's speaker is pathological, but that the speech described here may also represent language without risk, hence language with considerable survival value.

14. Compare Geoffrey H. Hartman's remarks: "the more you load language with quotations or allusive matter, the more it subverts meaning. Puns, in which this load becomes an overload, are a special case of this subversion: however witty and explosive, however energetic their yield of meaning, they evoke in us a sense of leprous insubstantiality, of contagion that might spread over language as a whole" ("Forum," *PMLA* 92 [1977]: 308).

15. Dorothy Parker, interview by Marion Capron, in *Writers at Work: The "Paris Review" Interviews*, ed. Malcolm Cowley (New York: Viking, 1958), 75, 80.

CODA

"Verbal Subversions in Dorothy Parker: 'Trapped Like a Trap in a Trap'" was only my second scholarly publication. It was first presented as a paper at a conference on language and style at City University of New York in 1976, one of those conferences where you can't find the schedule, the elevator, or the room. The other speaker in my session was Alice Jardine; at that point I had never heard of her, French feminism, or deconstruction. I thought I had fallen into an alternate universe and was only glad that Dorothy Parker was there too. The "publication history" of my essay was fraught and lengthy, and by the time it saw life in print I knew a lot more about French feminism, deconstruction, and Alice Jardine.

(Somewhere I still have my copy of Alice's paper generously explicated for me by Nelly Furman one sentence at a time.)

In 1976, almost nothing of scholarly value had been written on Parker. Although several of the ideas are now familiar—textual subversion, for example, or the complex identity of the authorial "I"—I'm fond of the essay and have not revised or updated it for the present volume. I am delighted that Rhonda Pettit has undertaken this project and that Parker will increasingly receive the serious scholarly attention she deserves.

Black on Blonde: The Africanist Presence in Dorothy Parker's "Big Blonde"

Amelia Simpson

THE STORY "BIG BLONDE" (1929) ARTICULATES SOME OF THE AMBIVA-lence with which Dorothy Parker's work approaches feminist inquiry.[1] There is a vicious style to Parker's compassionate portrait of a woman hopelessly trapped in social codes of femininity. Just as intriguing, however, is the way race is inscribed in a text so overtly marked as a reflection on gender.[2] Foregrounding the Africanist presence in the text discloses the real source of the story's power to disturb. Blackness surfaces in Parker's story in a way that provides an unusually clear example of the use of racial difference in white America's contemplation of itself.[3] In concert with the critical project Toni Morrison pursues in *Playing in the Dark: Whiteness and the Literary Imagination* (1992), the present observations represent an effort to "avert the critical gaze from the racial object to the racial subject; from the described and imagined to the describers and imaginers; from the serving to the served."[4] By shifting our sights to consider the function of three seemingly minor black characters in Parker's "Big Blonde," we are given a penetrating view of the divides of American identity, and of one white author's attempt to write that identity. Parker's story compellingly exposes the way gender and race are mutually constitutive, and how blackness constructs and contests the privilege of whiteness.

"Big Blonde" won Parker the national O. Henry Prize for the best short story published that year. Arguably her strongest work, it is generally viewed as an unusually affecting tale about feminine vulnerability. The story is frequently read as a kind of "autobiographical fiction," and it contains many echoes of the author's own failed relationships with men, her drinking problems, and her loneliness and suicide attempts. But the connection is probably more subtle. Parker's writing and her life reveal a drama of negotiation with the urge to challenge on the one hand, and to surrender on the other. As Nina Miller points out, Parker's public persona was "desirable to the extent that she was . . . modern and reassuring to the extent that she left certain basic femininities intact."[5] Marion Meade, one of Parker's biographers, suggests she was both liberated and constrained, exploited and self-exploiting.[6] The nasty tongue she cultivated earned her a name as one of the founders of the male-dominated Algonquin Round Table, yet the record shows little room at that table for moods not witty or cynical. Parker's trademark mouth gave her entry to a masculine domain she evidently aspired to join, but much of her work is devoted to complaining relentlessly about the terms by which women are forced to operate in a male-dominated world. Her telephone stories, for example, find women always on the short end of the conversation. Parker invented herself as a bad girl, and she was original in her badness, but often sorry in her girlness. She successfully wisecracked her way to a seat at the table with the boys, but she is frequently remembered more for that status than for her writing.

The 1994 film *Mrs. Parker and the Vicious Circle* does little to disturb the conventional view of Dorothy Parker as a clever but self-aggrandizing and troubled personality. The "vicious circle" seems to refer as much to Parker's drinking habits and penchant for sleeping around as to the sharp-tongued crowd she joined regularly for banter at the Algonquin. Not much is made of her literary talent. The film is sprinkled with poems, but they are delivered in a slurred and mumbled undertone that is difficult to decipher and hints at manic depression and drunkenness more than the idea of serious literary endeavor. An editor of Parker's once complained that her work didn't amount to much more than a series of "asides."[7] But Parker was a gifted writer who struggled seriously alongside others engaged in mapping the social and moral contours of American culture. She is more than a camp follower, as John Updike implies when he writes: "[Her] life brushed against most of the strands of American literary life from 1920 to 1950."[8] Parker survives in the push and shove of contradiction that gives a story like "Big Blonde" a hold on us still. In that text, the author produces a narrative about the subjugation of white women in America, using the scaffolding of blacks in America. Three Africanist figures, who at first glance appear to serve only the interests of narrative expediency, are in fact the key to Parker's architectural paradox. Their presence problematizes the text beyond its interrogation of the cultural construction of the "big blonde" as an ideal of femininity. The question of gender resonates in another, more suggestive way in the presence of Africanist figures who reveal that such a construction is also informed by views of race. The proximity of the historically bought black body to the kept white one contaminates and opens the narrative to a wider contemplation of the institutions and practices of slavery.

I

"Big Blonde" is the tale of Hazel Morse. The story's title gives a familiar formula for femininity, a code tapped out by the appropriately named Morse. Her surname reminds us that the dumb blonde, like any stereotype, is human identity reduced to uninflected code. Her given name records the haziness of the view from inside such a construction. The author uses blondeness to eroticize the character and give her a badge of shallowness.[9] Morse is the blonde built for amusement and display, a woman "of the type that incites some men when they use the word 'blonde' to click their tongues and wag their heads roguishly" (275). Morse and her women friends, "other substantially built blondes," are supported by such men who call up when they are in town on business (276).

Morse is a woman whose identity is something others bestow on her. When the story begins, she is a dress model in her twenties. By the end, she is a tired party girl in her midthirties, surviving in an alcoholic haze, self-destructing before ever building a self. She is dumb blondeness reduced to a blur, to "flabby, white" flesh made slow by age and alcohol (275). Morse's body is Parker's subject. The author details its decline in increments of degradation, from the "inexpert dabblings with peroxide," to the feet squeezed each night into undersized "champagne-colored slippers" (277, 292). Morse, like the other blondes in the story, is passed around from man to man, yet, "in her haze, she never recalled how men entered her life and left it" (292).

Parker's protagonist is distinguished from the others by a more radical emptiness. The author has her materialize out of nowhere. Her only relative, a "hazy widowed mother," dies when the story begins (275). Morse surfaces intact, a big blonde in her midtwenties, in New York City, in the 1920s, a woman with no history, no future, and only a vague sense of the present. She is no different a decade later: "At her middle thirties, her old days were a blurred and flickering sequence, an imperfect film, dealing with the actions of strangers" (275). Morse is a permanent stranger with a familiar face.

Parker insistently presses her protagonist into the corsetted role of the party girl. A brief marriage is an experiment with emotional liberty: "To her who had laughed so much, crying was delicious" (278). But the experiment fails; Morse is unreadable except as the party girl, the "good sport." She is permitted only one mood, that of gaiety, and her role is rigidly enforced:

> She was instantly undesirable when she was low in spirits. Once, at Jimmy's, when she could not make herself lively, Ed had walked out and left her. "Why the hell don't you stay home and not go spoiling everybody's evening?" he had roared. (290)

Morse is quickly and brutally punished for the least deviation. Apart from her role as party girl, she hardly exists, and indeed tries not to: "She slept, aided by whisky, till deep into the afternoons, then lay abed, a bottle and glass at her hand, until it was time to dress and go out for dinner" (293). Eventually Morse longs only for escape: "She dreamed by day of never again putting on tight shoes, of never having to laugh and listen and admire, of never more being a good sport. Never" (293). She buys a quantity of sleeping pills and sinks into unconsciousness.

At this juncture, Parker introduces a set of three new characters. It is no coincidence that they are black. These figures bear the heavy body of the sleeping Morse across the narrative bridge back to speech. They rescue her, and they do more. They illuminate Morse's condition, and they complicate the narrative. They engage the story of the blonde in a deeper dialogue with her keepers. Morse's "colored maid" Nettie, the "Negro" elevator attendant George, and a "dark girl," constitute the Africanist presence in "Big Blonde." Nettie keeps house and, after Morse's suicide attempt, carries out the "ugly, incessant tasks in the nursing of the unconscious" (302). It is Nettie, too, who discovers Morse in a coma and goes to George for help. Together, they find a doctor in the building, interrupting him while he is entertaining a "dark girl," evidently a prostitute, in his apartment. Although the "dark girl" is not explicitly identified as black, the adjective and her working status contrast conspicuously with the blondeness and nonprofessional status of Morse and her women friends.

The white figures (Morse, the doctor) and the black figures (Nettie, George, the prostitute) emerge in sharp contrast to each other. Morse herself has become a blank, drooling slab of a body:

> Mrs. Morse lay on her back, one flabby, white arm flung up, the wrist against her forehead. Her stiff hair hung untenderly along her face. The bed covers were pushed down, exposing a deep square of soft neck and a pink nightgown, its fabric worn uneven by many launderings; her great breasts, freed from their tight confiner, sagged beneath her arm-pits. Now and then she made knotted, snoring sounds, and from the corner

of her opened mouth to the blurred turn of her jaw ran a lane of crusted spittle. (299)

The doctor's approach to the medical emergency is professional, impersonal, and remote. He barely speaks, and regards Morse as nothing but a "nuisance" (301). The black figures, on the other hand, negotiate a range of emotions, from fear, wonder, and excitement, to compassion, irritation, and scorn. Their manner is impulsive, intimate, and indiscreet. The black figures are set apart by their expressiveness, and by other markers as well. They are portrayed as childlike, their speech is different, and they have no names or first names only.[10] Although they are adults, the black characters are referred to as "boy" and "girl," where the whites are "men" and "women." The black figures are even shunted off to the end of the narrative, positioned away from the body of the text.

From the start, then, the text formally establishes a disjuncture between black and white. That structural and figurative separation exposes white as central, commanding, and controlled, while black is shown as peripheral, subordinate, and undisciplined. Parker is clearly implicated in the conventions of representation that place blackness in a sphere inhabited by primitive or childlike Others. From that position, the black figures serve to highlight white stature and authority. The segregating structure, however, also allows blackness to inform whiteness in other, unintended ways. As Morrison observes in another context, "there are unmanageable slips."[11] If blackness shows white in control, it is also seen as detached and lifeless. The inhumanity blackness ascribes to whiteness shapes and sharpens the author's vision of femininity, while yielding unanticipated significance as well.

Nettie is the most important of the three black figures in "Big Blonde." One wonders why the other two are there at all. The answer lies in their function as surrogates, stand-ins for missing registers of experience. In this case, and in keeping with the well-documented history of blackness as a sexualizing trope in Western discourse, the two characters foreground the theme that is implicit throughout the story, starting with the title itself—that of illicit sexuality.[12] The conspicuous fashion in which two minor black figures raise the subject of sexual commerce and desire contrasts to its muted treatment elsewhere. Morse and her crowd represent a marketplace where men pay and women are kept, but the commercial nature of the transaction is masked by a logic of social alliances. Racial difference undercuts that logic to expose a politics behind

Morse's abandonment of her own body. She is depicted as sexually indifferent, neutral to the advances, for example, of boyfriend Ed:

> It became his custom to kiss her on the mouth when he came in, as well as for farewell, and he gave her little quick kisses of approval all through the evening. She liked this rather more than she disliked it. She never thought of his kisses when she was not with him. (284)

The expression of sexual awareness, desire, and agency is displaced onto the Africanist figures of the elevator attendant and the prostitute. Called to the bedside of the comatose Morse, George prods her "so lustily that he left marks in the soft flesh [of] the unconscious woman" (299). The prostitute, in turn, cries after the doctor as he reluctantly departs to tend to the emergency: "Snap it up there, big boy. . . . Don't be all night" (300).

Along with their usefulness to the narrative design, these two, apparently marginal, black characters function discursively to underline the theme of illicit sexuality. The dark girl makes transparent the nature of the transaction that commodifies the big blonde in America. She articulates and links the codes of commerce and sex. By introducing race to the gendered field of sexual commerce, her meaning also spills over into another trade in bodies to connect Morse to the historical text of the black body. George, too, functions through his blackness. The contact between his blackness and Morse's whiteness makes his poking at an unconscious body more than just sexual taboo.

Only a page after the episode in which Parker has George prod Morse's soft flesh, the author describes the doctor's treatment of the same body:

> With one quick movement [the doctor] swept the covers down to the foot of the bed. With another he flung her nightgown back and lifted the thick, white legs, cross-hatched with blocks of tiny, iris-colored veins. He pinched them repeatedly, with long, cruel nips, back of the knees. (301)

The infliction of a series of pinches, which Parker pointedly labels as "long" and "cruel," indicates an impulse to punish. Since the doctor's duty is to police the border Morse has attempted to cross, his reaction to her is necessarily punitive as well as professional. But it is possible to imagine another border here as well—one that is challenged by the sexualized contact between the black male (George) and the white female (Morse), and between the black female (the "dark girl") and the white male (the doctor). It is worth noting, in this regard, that the author calls attention in the passages depicting these episodes to the whiteness of Morse's body. The intervention of the Africanist figures, whose presence serves but also threatens to disrupt racial hierarchy, elaborates on the meaning of Morse's "punishment" by placing her in the context of a disintegrating self that is explicitly white.

Although their roles are brief, George and the prostitute draw attention to the function of the racial Other to serve and also to complicate and disturb. The third of Parker's Africanist figures—Nettie, the "colored maid"—has a larger role in "Big Blonde." Nettie is central to the narrative play of accommodation and disruption that the Africanist presence represents. On the one hand she is a serviceable figure. She cooks, cleans, and runs errands for Morse. Yet for all her serviceability and subaltern status, Nettie is pivotal. She is particularly important to the narrative denouement. Nettie foregrounds and inflates the white woman's unfolding drama of isolation, and she can do so because her blackness guarantees her separateness. Parker reminds us explicitly each time Nettie appears that she is the "colored maid," as if to give special emphasis to her difference. Nettie becomes the final enforcer of the social code that imprisons the big blonde. It is Nettie who delivers the last blow. Parker makes the black figure the embodiment of the bonds of slavery.

The maid makes three appearances in "Big Blonde," each linked to a stage of Morse's descent into increasingly bewildering confinement and dependence. Nettie first surfaces when Morse's short-lived marriage fizzles and Ed, the first boyfriend, takes possession. He persuades Morse to move to an apartment more convenient to him, near the train station:

> She took a little flat in the Forties. A colored maid came in every day to clean and to make coffee for her—she was "through with that housekeeping stuff," she said, and Ed, twenty years married to a passionately domestic woman, admired this romantic uselessness and felt doubly a man of the world in abetting it. (288)

The maid facilitates an arrangement that deepens Morse's isolation and renders increasingly conditional her apparent freedom. Nettie gives coherence to a domain explicitly framed to serve male interests. The maid's function is to keep the narrative house in order. Yet, while Nettie allows the author at this point in the text to foreground a paradigm of gender oppression, the regular reminders of racial difference introduce another element to the developing theme of freedom and enslavement.

When Nettie next appears, she is buying liquor for the suicidal alcoholic. Morse has managed to purchase a quantity of Veronal tablets, and she addresses the tablets with religious fervor. Nettie hovers helpfully nearby, an "angel" of deliverance:

> She put the little vials in the drawer of her dressing-table and stood looking at them with a dreamy tenderness.
> "There they are, God bless them," she said, and she kissed her fingertip and touched each bottle.
> The colored maid was busy in the living-room.
> "Hey, Nettie," Mrs. Morse called. "Be an angel, will you? Run around to Jimmy's and get me a quart of Scotch."
> She hummed while she awaited the girl's return. (295–96)

When Morse takes the final step and swallows her pills, the maid will be the net that catches her in her fall. She is Parker's solution to the problem of how to end the story. Without Nettie, Morse dies in a haze, pleasantly knocked out, herself cheated, and cheating us, of the full spectacle of her misery. A rescued Morse, on the other hand, is a woman without the blinds, finally and fully alive and aware. The character who saves Morse assumes the ungenerous, dismissive, inhuman qualities of all of the blonde's keepers. Nettie becomes, in effect, the punishing voice of the social body that creates and destroys Morse. Rather than embrace across the racial divide, the two women mark it. Nettie is the net that catches, but also traps. Although she nurses Morse back to life, no understanding grows between them. The gender identity that Parker explores through the figure of Morse is inscribed in a hegemonic discourse of racial difference.

Nettie's role after Morse regains consciousness is an example of the ironic reversal that Michele A. Bimbaum notes in her analysis of the literary function of the racialized Other in Kate Chopin's *The Awakening* (1899). In "Big Blonde," as in Chopin's text, the racialized Other can serve as a marker of the status quo of social hierarchy. In this context, "the oppressed become the oppressors."[13] When Morse finally comes out of a coma, able to do little more than weep at the "saturating wretchedness" that slowly returns with consciousness, Nettie only looks "coldly at the big, blown woman in the bed." "You can thank you' stars you heah at all," the maid scolds (302). Nettie irritably prompts Morse to express gratitude for the care: "Here I ain' had no sleep at all for two nights, an' had to give up goin' out to my other ladies!" (302). Parker brings in Nettie to witness but not treat, to rescue but not save. When Morse asks

"Didn't you ever feel like doing it? When everything looks just lousy to you," Nettie's response is a cool rebuke: "I wouldn' think o' no such thing" (302).

Immediately following this exchange is another which Nettie initiates and which effects a fundamental transformation in Morse. Her voice will split open for the first time and become knowing. She will shed her speechlessness, the vacuum of cliché, and speak for the first time with irony. The shift occurs after Nettie's scolding when she continues, using the same words Morse has heard many times before from her various escorts: "You got to cheer up. Tha's what you got to do. Everybody's got their troubles." Lying in what she had hoped would be her deathbed, Morse's response, "Yeah, I know," is her first declaration of self, of knowledge of her place in the world (303). This is the first ironic Morse we have seen.

Parker ends her story by repeating the epiphany. Morse has persuaded Nettie to pour them both a drink and she proposes a toast:

> "Thanks, Nettie," she said. "Here's mud in your eye."
> The maid giggled. "Tha's the way, Mis' Morse," she said. "You cheer up, now."
> "Yeah," said Mrs. Morse. "Sure." (304)

Morse's "Yeah . . . sure" is, again, a signal of recognition. She has emerged finally from a verbal world of formula—where small talk is all the talk there is—into the grip of powerful, disabused utterance. Enforcement of the code of the party girl has fallen to Nettie, its brutal tyranny displaced onto the black figure, whose giggle marks her difference and her indifference.

It is Nettie who is assigned the racial identity that erects a barrier between the two women. When the maid does not stay to share a drink with Morse, but instead, "deferentially [leaves] hers in the bathroom to be taken in solitude," the social code that is played out is structured by a racialized paradigm. The mistress/servant dichotomy casts the relationship as one of domination and subordination (303). The white woman's status, gradually eroded in the course of a narrative of gendered subjugation, is nevertheless still marked as a position of privilege in relation to the black servant. Thus if the rhetoric of racial oppression emerges suggestively in relation to Parker's theme of gender oppression, the text continues to operate on another level to reinforce, not interrogate, racial difference. When Morse hits bottom, for example, and survives to feel misery "crush her as if she were between great smooth stones," she compares herself to "weary horses and shivering beggars and all beaten, driven, stumbling things"—but not to Nettie (303).

The doctor is the one white figure who participates in Morse's "rescue." He saves her, but without piercing her isolation. Parker's ambivalence about assigning that role to a white character is reflected in the way she taints him, making him not quite white. Through his contact with the "dark" prostitute, the doctor is distinguished from the other white men in the story who prefer blondes. He is linked to blackness through George as well. There is a similar element of violence in the way the two men pinch and poke as they handle Morse's unconscious body. The two men meet across her body, as well as across the racial boundary where each seeks sexual contact. Blackness releases the doctor from the exacting codes of whiteness. His grayness makes possible his indifference to Morse's fate, an attitude that American slang tells us is not "white."[14]

II

Parker's black figures divulge a departure from personal to social pathology, from the solitary, pitiable drift Morse embodies to the menacing current in which she is caught. At the heart of "Big Blonde" is the commerce of human bodies. The Africanist presence alludes to that commerce, but also conceals it. Parker uses the subordinate, othered, inconsequential Nettie to outline the dilemma of captivity. She and the other Africanist figures in "Big Blonde" both serve and shield the author. They make it possible for her "to say and not say, to inscribe and erase."[15] Parker's narrative is thus rhetorically implicated in the perpetuation of racial difference and inequality.

It may be useful to imagine the consequences if Africanism were not available as a discursive device for Parker to employ, if there were no black figures in "Big Blonde," if the maid, the elevator attendant, and the prostitute were white. Certainly, the distance between that group of characters and Morse would be reduced. She would be familiarized, rather than estranged, by the surrounding figures. She would be more like them, one among them. In the absence of blackness, Morse would be less white, less innocent, less alone. She would be less effective in dramatizing her story of estrangement and alienation, and less able to contain and isolate the germ of another idea: that all American freedom is broadly and historically conditional.

Parker's narrative burrows into the vagueness of Morse's flesh in order to express a hard bone of truth about femininity. The racial implications of the big blonde are remarked only indirectly. She is regarded above all as an icon of male desire. But blondeness is liminal, not democratic. Blonde hair on nonwhite skin is a marker of difference, appropriation, or deviation. Gender displaces race in the consumption of the image of the blonde, yet the ideology that fuels that elision still binds the two together. In the context of Parker's story, blonde is connected to black through the vulnerability of the body. The leaks that allow race to surface in "Big Blonde" are a consequence of the author's willingness to expose fully the vulnerability of the female body. Parker's work suggests she regarded women as crucially expressive of the American identity. Her fiction and poetry are all about them. Most of Parker's women are closely attached to the American landscape. They evoke the stylish abandon and "modern love" of the twenties, the slippery pleasure and curse of American money, the rise and fall of one's place on the social ladder. Parker's women are caught up in the space and movement of loosening times. They are not introspective, not grounded or protected. They are placed in a gendered narrative with the view that ease of circulation is attached to a condition that menaces, entraps, and often dooms. Parker's women are not free. The authority they wield is contingent, and so they are rendered vulnerable, easily disabled, replaced. To the degree that Parker compares the status of women like Morse to that of slaves, "Big Blonde" represents a radical confrontation with American identity.

But if Parker places women in the same arena of vulnerability and oppression as blacks, at the same time she makes use of the codes of racial separation to create her narrative. That apparent contradiction, or sympathetic break, introduces to Parker's tale a breach that exposes the convergence of race and gender. Through that gap we see that the privilege of the big blonde is granted by racially constituted desire. Concerning the intersections of the oppressions of gender and race expressed in antebellum feminist abolitionist texts, Karen Sanchez-Eppler observes that "although the identifications of woman and slave . . . occasionally prove mutually empowering, such pairings generally tend toward asymmetry and exploitation."[16] Many decades later, Parker's story reflects the same struggle. The association of the condition of women with that of slaves in "Big Blonde" unfolds virtually exclusively through the story of a white woman.

Parker's use of racial difference is not the same as racism. The author was sensitive to racial prejudice, and denounced it explicitly in two stories from her major collections—"Arrangement in Black and White" (1927) and "Clothe the Naked" (1938). Unlike in those tales, however, the Africanism in "Big Blonde" is not studied. Indeed, it is likely inadvertent. As such, it is revealing of a different register, of blackness not as a theme but as a mechanism of and for the imagination. The blackness in "Big Blonde" brings race into the story of gender oppression, but the oblique approach leaves unexamined their interdependence and the consequent possibilities for negotiating positions of otherness.

Morrison shows how black characters in American literature by white authors do not have to be mere background detail, simple props for setting up action, but rather that they "ignite critical moments of discovery or change or emphasis." She explores Africanism in literary expression as a device that develops from the need to write a social identity that rests in a fundamental sense on a shudder of recognition. American literature tells again and again the compelling story of "a nation of people who *decided* that their world view would combine agendas for individual freedom *and* mechanisms for devastating racial oppression" (original emphasis). Literature is one site where the unfree body is put to work to guarantee the free one. Reading the Africanist presence in Parker's story not only illustrates how crucial blackness is to American literary expression, but also helps to explain an elusive author. To ignore the way American Africanism shapes the visions and structure of works by writers like Dorothy Parker depletes us. Morrison warns that "all of us, readers and writers, are bereft when criticism remains too polite or too fearful to notice a disrupting darkness before its eyes."[17] If Hazel Morse is more than a forgettable floozy, it is because Parker's story charts a passage of cultural conception and deception through the channels of gender and race in America.[18]

NOTES

1. Dorothy Parker, *The Portable Dorothy Parker* (New York: Viking, 1944). All further references in the text will be to this edition. This article is dedicated to my father, who kept a little salmon-pink Dorothy Parker book around the house for me to read young and remember years later.

2. The words "race" and "gender" are used throughout to indicate the "commonsense" meaning deployed within Western hegemonic discourse.

3. I use the word "America" here in the narrow sense to mean only the United States.

4. Toni Morrison, *Playing in the Dark: Whiteness and the Literary Imagination* (New York: Vintage, 1993), 90.

5. Nina Miller, "Making Love Modern: Dorothy Parker and Her Public," *American Literature* 64:4 (1992): 767.

6. Marion Meade, *Dorothy Parker: What Fresh Hell Is This?* (New York: Villard, 1988).

7. Joan Acocella, "After the Laughs," *New Yorker*, 16 August 1993, 78.

8. John Updike, "Witty Dotty," *New Yorker*, 25 April 1988, 112.

9. A number of examples from Parker's stories and letters record her use of blondeness in women to designate the superficial and the foolish. In "The Standard of Living," two shopgirls strolling along Fifth Avenue and fantasizing they are rich are blonde fluff. The "assisted gold" hair of the protagonist of "Arrangement in Black and White" underlines her ignorance. Blondeness is used similarly in Parker's letters from Meade 37, 38, 90, and 121.

10. Karen Sanchez-Eppler, in *Touching Liberty: Abolition, Feminism, and the Politics of the Body* (Berkeley: University of California Press, 1993), points out that one of the comparisons early feminist activists drew between the woman and the slave was the loss of her name. The author cites Elizabeth Cady Stanton in 1856: "A woman . . . has no name! . . . like the Southern slave, she takes the name of her owner" (19). In "Big Blonde," Parker underlines the acquisition of a male name as a ritual of female identity. Before her marriage to Herbie Morse, Hazel Morse is just a "big blonde." Her female friends adopt the surnames of "dimmed spouses" from whom they are divorced or separated (289). But Nettie, the one female black figure with a name, has no surname at all. She is "owned" in a different way.

11. Morrison, 58.

12. The association of blackness and eroticism in Western discourse is explored by a number of authors. See Mary Ann Doane, "Dark Continents: Epistemologies of Racial and Sexual Difference in Psychoanalysis and the Cinema," in *Femmes Fatales: Feminism, Film Theory, Psychoanalysis* (New York: Routledge, 1991), 209–48; Richard Dyer, "White," in *The Matter of Images: Essays on Representations* (London: Routledge, 1993), 141–63; Sander L. Gilman, "Black Bodies, White Bodies: Toward an Iconography of Female Sexuality in Late Nineteenth-Century Art, Medicine, and Literature," in *Race, Writing and Difference*, ed. by Henry Louis Gates, Jr. (Chicago: University of Chicago Press, 1985), 223–61; Jill Matus, "Blonde, Black and Hottentot Venus: Context and Critique in Angela Carter's 'Black Venus,'" *Studies in Short Fiction* 28:4 (1991): 467–76; and Ella Shohat and Robert Stam, *Unthinking Eurocentrism: Multiculturalism and the Media* (New York: Routledge, 1994).

13. Michelle A. Birnbaum, "'Alien Hands': Kate Chopin and the Colonization of Race," *American Literature* 66:2 (1994): 301–23.

14. The use of "white" as an adverb to mean "in a fair upright manner" as in "treated us white" is listed in *Webster's Third New International Dictionary of the English Language*, unabridged (Springfield, MA: Merriam-Webster, 1981). "White" as a slang usage synonymous with "upright," and "honest" is listed in *Roget's International Thesaurus* (New York: Thomas Y. Crowell, 1950).

15. Morrison, 7.

16. Sanchez-Eppler, 15.

17. Morrison, viii, xiii, 91.

18. I would like to thank the editors and readers at *College Literature* for their valuable help in preparing this article.

Premium Swift: Dorothy Parker's Iron Mask of Femininity

Ellen Pollak

> To be happy one must be (a) well fed, unhounded by sordid cares, at ease in Zion, (b) full of a comfortable feeling of superiority to the masses of one's fellow men, and (c) delicately and unceasingly amused according to one's taste.
>
> —H. L. Mencken

> If artists and poets are unhappy, it is after all because happiness does not interest them.
>
> —George Santayana

> It is true that Mrs. Parker's epigrams sound like the Hotel Algonquin and not like the drawing-rooms and coffee-houses of the eighteenth century. But I believe that, if we admire, as it is fashionable to do, the light verse of Prior and Gay, we should admire Mrs. Parker also. She writes well: her wit is the wit of her time and place; but it is often as cleanly economic at the same time that it is as flatly brutal as the wit of the age of Pope; and, within its small scope, it is a criticism of life. It has its roots in contemporary reality.
>
> —Edmund Wilson

IN NOVEMBER 1927 DOROTHY PARKER, ONE OF THE MOST TRENCHANT SATIrists of modern times, published a short review in the *New Yorker* entitled "The Professor Goes in for Sweetness and Light." Her subject was a book called *Happiness* by William Lyon Phelps, a Yale professor of English well known as a women's club lecturer and a molder of public opinion. Affectionately known in Yale circles as "Billy the booster" because of the inimitable capacity of his endorsements to create best sellers overnight, Phelps would become popular in the 1930s as "tastemaker of the airwaves" through his weekly radio appearances on the "Swift Hour" variety program; hence his recent dubbing by author Joan Shelley Rubin as "Swift's Premium Ham."[1]

The purpose of this essay, whose title playfully adapts Rubin's already playful epithet, is to suggest an intertextual relationship between Parker's review of Phelps and the writings of Jonathan Swift, especially his two early prose works *The Battle of the Books* (1704) and *A Tale of a Tub* (1704). Such a relationship cannot be established with empirical certainty, since Parker makes no direct reference to Swift either in her review or elsewhere in her work. She left no library in which to forage for editions of Swift's writings, no letters, no memorabilia, nor any complete, firsthand inventory of her clearly voluminous reading. Emily Toth records her impression of a general, though not necessarily direct, Swiftian influence in Parker's satire and biographer Leslie Frewin testifies to Parker's delight in and admiration for Swift, whom he claims that "she adored" and whose work "she loved reading."[2] But more compelling as evidence of Parker's deployment of Swift as an operative point of reference in "The Professor Goes in for Sweetness and Light" is a careful reading of the text itself within both its immediate and extended cultural and political contexts. Such a reading strongly suggests that Parker not only knew Swift but meant to invoke him—at least in the minds of some educated readers.

Parker's attack on Phelps is scathing enough without the added force of blows delivered through her sly intertextual triggering of Swift's texts; it does not require an educated reader. Reading Swift in her satire, nevertheless, helps one to apprehend "The Professor" with a richer, more plural sense of its layered ironies. For despite its slight length, barely over a thousand words, "The Professor Goes in for Sweetness and Light" is more than a local critique of a current best seller; it is also a devastating analysis of the gender, class, and ethnic biases inherent in the social and intellectual values of the Ivy League. Parker uses Swift both to level an attack on Phelps as a modern "hack" and to articulate her own problematic status as a woman writer positioned simultaneously inside and outside the historically male-dominated traditions of literary criticism and satire.

"The Professor" takes the form of a mock-defense, one of Swift's favorite satiric strategies. Assuming the voice of a female speaker at a women's club luncheon—perhaps addressing the sort of audience Phelps himself often addressed—Parker begins by enlarging upon the magnificent simplicity of Phelps's diminutive work:

Professor William Lyon Phelps, presumably for God, for Country and for Yale, has composed a work on happiness. He calls it, in a word, *Happiness*, and he covers the subject in a volume about six inches tall, perhaps four inches across, and something less than half an inch thick. There is something rather magnificent in disposing, in an opus the size of a Christmas card, of this thing that men since time started have been seeking, pondering, struggling for, and guessing at.[3]

While one might assume that Parker here merely indulges in satiric hyperbole to belittle Phelps's book, the material object itself testifies both to her narrator's literal-mindedness and to the accuracy of her own physical account. A gift item on the scale of, say, Charles Schulz's 1960s best seller, *Happiness Is a Warm Puppy*, Phelps's *Happiness* in fact neatly fits the dimensions given in Parker's text.

Parker's narrator is deferential and a bit inept. She digresses, but is unable to explain the logic of her own peregrinations. Her mode of argument appears less rational than impressionistic and heavily anecdotal. Phelps's book, she remarks with self-effacing dismissiveness, reminds her

> though the sequence may seem a bit hazy, of a time that I was lunching at the Cap d'Antibes (oh, I get around). I remarked, for I have never set up any claim to being a snappy luncheon companion, that somewhere ahead of us in the Mediterranean lay the island where the Man in the Iron Mask had been imprisoned.
>
> "And who," asked my neighbor at the table, "was the Man in the Iron Mask?"
>
> My only answer was a prettily crossed right to the jaw. How expect one who had had a nasty time of it getting through grammar school to explain to him, while he finished the rest of his filet, an identity that the big boys had never succeeded in satisfactorily working out, though they gave their years to the puzzle?
>
> Somewhere, there, is an analogy, in a small way, if you have the patience for it. But I guess it isn't a very good anecdote. I'm better at animal stories. (461–62)

What is the analogy that the reader is being asked—under the guise of the narrator's self-deprecating evasion—to have the patience for? What is the point, if there is one, of Parker's anecdote? Why does she say she is better at animal stories? Unlike Phelps, this narrator does not presume to compete with the "big boys." The definition of happiness is a puzzle for greater minds than hers, a historical enigma as inscrutable as the Man in the Iron Mask, that mysterious prisoner whose identity remained concealed behind a mask of black velvet throughout his life and who eventually died unnamed in the Bastille in 1703. This "little woman" is in no position to take on such a daunting task; she will stick to bedtime stories.[4]

At another level, though, the narrator's reference to animal stories is misleading. For beneath her display of humility and authorial incompetence lurks both an erudite allusion and an intellectual savvy glimpsed only in that worldly aside where she cynically assures the reader that she "gets around." Wasn't it a fictionalized version of that renowned animal fabler Aesop, after all, who coined the phrase "Sweetness *and* Light" in his long descant upon an argument between a spider and a bee in Swift's mock-epic history of *The Battle of the Books*?[5]

Phelps is a professor, a learned man; Parker's narrator is merely an uneducated woman, an American tourist in France with enough of a smattering of European popular culture to make dinner-table conversation but with an utter lack of intellectual authority. When her male luncheon companion asks a stupid question, disclosing his lack of knowledge of the "identity" of the Man in the Iron Mask ("Who *was* the man in the Iron Mask?"), it is her inability to respond rather than the ignorance prompting his question that becomes the object of self-deprecating humor. This is quintessential Parker. The narrator's self-mockery is, of course, disingenuous—an exposé of the social hypocrisy of gender relations masquerading as an attack on female vacuity. Regardless of the facts, the mask of male superiority remains intact—as unyielding as iron or as the narrator's seemingly inescapable mask of velveteen femininity.

But the full force of Swift's ghostly presence is not felt until somewhat later in Parker's text, when readers learn that the magnitude of Professor Phelps's arrogance, like that of the narrator's male luncheon companion, is directly proportionate to his ignorance. In his lack of indebtedness to his literary and philosophical forbears, he is more like Swift's self-generating and self-sufficient modern spider, who "*scorns to own any Obligation or Assistance from without*," than like the diligent, ancient bee whose "*infinite Labor*" and far-ranging pursuit of beauty and truth bring home "Sweetness *and* Light" (*Battle*, in Swift, *Tale*, 234–35):

> The professor starts right off with "No matter what may be one's nationality, sex, age, philosophy, or religion, everyone wishes either to become or to remain happy." Well, there's no arguing that one. . . .
>
> "Hence," goes on the professor, "definitions of happiness are interesting." I suppose the best thing to do with that is to let it pass. Me, I never saw a definition of happiness that could detain me after traintime, but that may be a matter of lack of opportunity, of inattention, or of congenital rough luck. If definitions of happiness can keep Professor Phelps on his toes, that is little short of dandy.
>
> We might just as well get on along to the next statement, which goes like this: "One of the best" (we are still on definitions of happiness) "was given in my Senior year at college by Professor Timothy Dwight:

'The happiest person is the person who thinks the most interesting thoughts.'" Promptly one starts recalling such Happiness Boys as Nietzsche, Socrates, de Maupassant, Jean-Jacques Rousseau, William Blake, and Poe. One wonders, with hungry curiosity, what were some of the other definitions that Professor Phelps chucked aside in order to give preference to this one. (462–63)

Promptly the well-informed reader of Swift starts recalling one definition Professor Phelps has either dismissed or overlooked. "What is generally understood by *Happiness*," observes Swift's narrator in *A Tale of a Tub*, ". . . will herd under this short Definition: That, *it is a perpetual Possession of being well Deceived* . . . The Serene Peaceful State of being a Fool among Knaves" (Swift, *Tale*, 171–74). Parker may indeed be a victim of lack of opportunity and congenital rough luck, but inattention seems to be a trait more peculiar to "Billy" Phelps, that privileged son of Yale. We begin to understand what Parker means when she implies that her professor does not always "go in" for sweetness and light; like the peripatetic bee, she is indeed the one who "gets around."

Does Parker considerately prime the reader for an allusion to Swift by including her own tale of a tub? "[T]here is this to be said for a volume such as Professor Phelps's Happiness," she remarks offhandedly,

It is second only to a rubber duck as the ideal bathtub comparison. It may be held in the hand without causing muscular fatigue or nerve strain, it may be neatly balanced back of the faucets, and it may be read through before the water has cooled. And if it slips down the drain pipe, all right, it slips down the drain pipe. (462)

Admirers of her work may well object that since Dorothy Parker did not attend college—according to one biographer, her formal education ended when she was only fourteen[6]—she would be unlikely to have read Swift, especially not such rarified works as *The Battle of the Books* and *A Tale of a Tub*. Although first used by Swift in *The Battle of the Books*, the phrase "sweetness and light" became familiar only later, when Matthew Arnold appropriated it in his 1869 treatise *Culture and Anarchy*, a work Parker was more likely to have known. As Rubin has documented in her recent study, *The Making of Middlebrow Culture*, Arnold's program of diffusing "sweetness and light" through the dissemination of "the best that has been thought and said in the world" sustained currency and ongoing cultural significance in the efforts of early twentieth-century culture makers to define literary standards and sensibility within a distinctly American and increasingly consumer-oriented context. Living in New York as a staff writer for *Vanity Fair* between 1915 and 1920, Parker may well have known—or known of—Stuart Pratt Sherman's 1917 *Matthew Arnold: How to Know Him*, a work celebrating Arnold's lifelong effort to make "aristocratic taste prevail in a world which was becoming rapidly democratic."[7] And she may have been familiar with the climate of heated criticism and debate surrounding Sherman's subsequent celebration of the Anglo-Saxon Puritan tradition in his 1923 book, *The Genius of America*, which because of its disdain for unassimilated immigrant populations was roundly condemned in *The Nation* by one of her Algonquin set associates, Ernest Boyd, as a brand of "Ku Klux Kriticism."[8]

While neither Swift nor Arnold is mentioned explicitly in "The Professor Goes in for Sweetness and Light," Arnold's express concerns (as well as those of his American followers) do dovetail ironically with those of Parker, whose review provides an indirect commentary on the murder conviction and subsequent execution of the famous anarchist radicals Nicola Sacco and Bartolomeo Vanzetti. The title of Arnold's treatise, *Culture and Anarchy*, neatly epitomizes the sinister connection that Parker's review seeks to expose between what she views as Phelps's disturbing cultural elitism and the political scapegoating and persecution of two working-class Italian immigrants who had been tried and found guilty of the murders of a factory paymaster and guard in South Braintree, Massachusetts, on 5 April 1920. In Boston on 10 August 1927 (when, after almost seven years of legal maneuvering, Sacco and Vanzetti were scheduled to die), Parker had been arrested, jailed overnight, and fined five dollars for participating in a demonstration advocating a stay of execution. Late in her review, moreover, she expressly invokes Sacco and Vanzetti's cause through a reference to Harvard University President Abbott Lawrence Lowell and his role on the Fuller Committee, which had investigated the fairness of their trial but ultimately found in favor of the court. Sacco and Vanzetti died in the electric chair on 22 August 1927—on Dorothy Parker's thirty-fourth birthday. Matthew Arnold's concern with the relationship between culture and anarchy, though with an ironic twist, was Parker's too.

It would appear, then, that in criticizing Phelps, Parker was using Arnold's idea of "culture" ironically to debunk the inherent hypocrisy of an educated American elite who, under the guise of democratizing learning, sought to homogenize and purify American intellectual life by reconciling genteel, Arnoldian values with the demands of an increasingly commercialized publishing industry. In doing so she participated in an already well-established intellectual tradition of criticizing the politics of American middlebrow culture makers, the so-called merchants of light.[9]

Still, while Arnold may have held more influence in Parker's day, there is no reason to assume her ignorance of Swift. As Parker once remarked for a newspaper interview during her tenure in the early 1960s as Distinguished Visiting Professor of English at California State College in Los Angeles, "Because of circumstances, I didn't finish high school. But, by God, I read."[10] Indeed, while there remains disagreement among biographers as to how many years Parker actually spent at Miss Dana's finishing and college preparatory school in Morristown, New Jersey, where she followed a standard course of study including Latin, English, the Bible, and history, all seem to agree that the young woman who would later become known to *New Yorker* readers as "The Constant Reader" did in fact read constantly. According to Frewin, Parker had already sampled an impressive array of British authors before she arrived at Miss Dana's, largely in spite of the curriculum at Blessed Sacrament Academy, where she attended elementary and secondary school. Included, in addition to Swift, were works by Pope, Dickens, Hardy, Carlyle, Shakespeare, and Thackerary (whom she claimed to have first discovered at age eleven).[11] At Miss Dana's she also became acquainted with Horace, Virgil, Catullus, Aristotle, Socrates, Goethe, Montaigne, Martial, and La Rochefoucauld; in addition, scholars have commented on the subsequent influence of classical poetry on her work.[12]

By 1927, moreover, Parker had maintained close, longtime working friendships with Harvard graduates Robert Benchley and Robert Sherwood, whom she had first met in May 1919 and with whom she regularly lunched in the early 1920s at the famous Algonquin Round Table with such other notable literary types as Heywood Broun and Edna Ferber. In such an atmosphere of sophistication and educated wit, itself resembling the ambiance of the Scriblerians, it would hardly be frivolous to speculate that Swift might have come up. According to his son Nathaniel, Robert Benchley had resolved at one point to write a history of the humorists in the age of Queen Anne and by 1927 had "a growing collection of books about the Queen Anne period, of which he finally gathered about a hundred."[13] Parker, who had intimate knowledge of Benchley's intellectual pursuits, would have had access not only to his thoughts during this period but also to his library. Nor would there have been any paucity of editions of Swift's work generally available to her. A volume of *Selections from the Prose Writings of Jonathan Swift*, edited with notes and an introduction by Cornell University Professor F. C. Prescott, was published in New York in 1908, and another New York edition of *A Tale of a Tub, The Battle of the Books and Other Satires* was brought out by E. P. Dutton & Co. in 1909, with three subsequent reprintings (in 1911, 1916, and 1920). In addition to Humphrey Milford's 1919 Oxford edition of *Gulliver's Travels, A Tale of a Tub, and The Battle of the Books,* two editions of *Gulliver's Travels* with introductions and notes followed in 1925 and 1926.[14]

The conspicuous absence of direct reference to Swift in Parker's review, moreover, would perfectly suit her satiric purposes. Since Parker undertakes to lodge her critique of the professor through the medium of a distinctly "feminine" (and thus not well-educated) persona, it makes eminent sense for her to mask her debt to Swift, even as her allusive context enables Swift's own words to deliver the crowning blow to Phelps. That she slyly omits explicit mention of Swift in her ironic inventory of representative "Happiness Boys" seems less a sign of his irrelevance than a way of pointing through parody to the dismissiveness and incompleteness of that version of intellectual history represented by Phelps's own privileging of the "modern" genius of Timothy Dwight (a Yale professor like himself, no less) over the wisdom of diverse continents and ages. In a gesture of ironic narration that might be characterized as Swiftian in its complex handling of masks, Parker manages simultaneously to perform a masquerade of "femininity" and, through an indirect display of erudition, to demolish Phelps's claims to cultural superiority. In the process she blasts Phelps's false presumption that intelligence correlates with cultural privilege, producing a withering political commentary on the disturbing dogma that emanates from the elite American academy. *Happiness,* she demonstrates, is not just a silly book, a diversionary piece of harmless sentimental poppycock: its underlying assumptions are dangerous.

Phelps begins *Happiness,* as Parker's narrator notes, with a number of self-evident and irrefutable assertions. He invokes the universal human desire for happiness regardless of nationality, sex, age, philosophy, or religion, and later he seems to understand that "Happiness is not altogether a matter of luck" but "is dependent on certain conditions" (463). The narrator responds to the first of these pronouncements with characteristically submissive reverence:

> The author has us there. There is the place for getting out the pencil, underscoring the lines, and setting "how true," followed by several carefully executed exclamation points, in the margin. It is regrettable that the book did not come out during the season when white violets were in bloom, for there is the very spot to press one. (462)

Beside Phelps's indelibly printed words the narrator's responses remain tentative and marginal; she uses a pencil and yearns to mark his text by pressing only white violets, whose petals leave no stain. But Parker's moral outrage is never very far from the surface, manifesting itself not only in deadpan assertions like "The author has us there" (which suggest that, to her, Phelps's platitudes have a certain coercive edge), but also in the incongruities created by her narrator's indiscriminate admiration for Phelps, despite his frequent and inadvertent self-contradictions. Parker evidently wants readers to see that even as Phelps expresses truths that seem to recognize the social bases of happiness, he indulges in a blithe obliviousness to the realities of social inequality:

> "Money is not the chief factor in happiness." . . . "I am certain that with the correct philosophy it is possible to have within one's possession sources of happiness that cannot permanently be destroyed." . . . "Many go to destruction by the alcoholic route because they cannot endure themselves." (463)

Against the backdrop of the Sacco and Vanzetti execution, Phelps's assertion that "correct philosophy" can provide "sources" of happiness that "cannot permanently be destroyed" assumes some rather sinister implications. Phelps at one point makes a statement so inanely optimistic that Parker (who by 1927 had weathered a broken marriage, a failed love affair, an abortion, two suicide attempts, and several bouts with alcoholism) cannot refrain from directly addressing it in an aside:

> "Life, with all its sorrows, perplexities, and heartbreaks, is more interesting than bovine placidity, hence more desirable. The more interesting it is, the happier it is." (Oh, professor, I should like to contest that.) "And the happiest person is the person who thinks the most interesting thoughts." (463–64)

Parker establishes her assessment of Phelps's sentimental whitewashing of social reality when she has her narrator extol his book's utter inoffensiveness. By now her use of the term "happily" has acquired a complex layering of ironic resonance:

> Here is a book happily free from iconoclasm. There is not a sentence that you couldn't read to your most conservative relatives and still be reasonably sure of that legacy . . . I give you my word, in the entire book there is nothing that cannot be said aloud in mixed company. (463)

Here, if only momentarily, Parker cannot resist trading her mask of timid propriety for one of cynical irreverence. There may be nothing in Phelps's book that cannot be said aloud in mixed company, but

> there is, also, nothing that makes you a bit the wiser. I wonder—oh, what will you think of me—if those two statements do not verge upon the synonymous. (463)

A swipe at women? Or at a culture that justifies its own complacence on the grounds that women need protection from the seamy side of life? Wisdom, Parker seems to be saying, resides in exploding lies, in telling the truth about life, even if that means indecorously betraying that men are sometimes self-serving and corrupt or that women have voices, bodies, eyes, and minds.

To Parker, Phelps's offensiveness depends upon his community of readers. When one's greatest catastrophe in life is losing one's rubber duck down the bathtub drain, it may be easy to be happy. But when one is unhappy about the conditions under which one lives, Phelps's denial of human evil and misery, his linking of intelligence and happiness—with its implication that those who are unhappy with their lot in life are neither interesting nor smart, and its unimaginative assumption that people drown their sorrows in alcohol only because they cannot endure themselves—may seem offensive. Such readers might be happier with Parkeresque irreverence.

It becomes increasingly apparent as Parker proceeds that what initially may have seemed a relatively lighthearted attempt to ridicule one foolish Brahmin of higher education is actually a serious critique with wide-ranging social significance. Parker's swipes at Phelps may look like prettily crossed rights to the jaw, playful blows delivered just in fun, but in fact they constitute serious indictments of a male WASP power elite—indictments leveled by Parker not just on her own behalf (as excluded woman and half-Jew), but also on behalf of other politically, culturally, and economically disenfranchised groups (like political anarchists, Italian immigrants, or factory workers). Although Parker's penchant for irony and masks makes it impossible ever to construe her personal gestures as entirely transparent signs, the fact that she left the bulk of her estate, some twenty thousand dollars at her death in 1967, to the Reverend Martin Luther King, Jr. (whom she admired but had never met), with her bequest to King to pass it on to the NAACP at his death seems consistent with the spirit of her review in its material expression both of commitment to the promotion of social justice and of respect for the realities of American cultural heterogeneity.

The final paragraph of "The Professor" registers Parker's bitterness and establishes its political context unmistakably:

> These are the views, this is the dogma, of Professor William Lyon Phelps, the pride of New Haven. And, of course, at Harvard there is now—and it looks as if there might be always—President Lowell, of the Fuller Committee. I trust that my son will elect to attend one of the smaller institutions of higher education. (464)

Parker is disturbed not just by Phelps's inveterate superficiality but also by the brutal complacency of his willful blindness to social injustice. Such blind complacency, she suggests, has become institutionalized in bastions of higher education and has devastating human implications. "The Professor Goes in for Sweetness and Light" is her expression of disgust at the massive immorality of this circumstance, an immorality underscored by the magical immunity that certain individuals, here represented by President Lowell, seem to acquire. Unlike Sacco and Vanzetti who, like white violets, easily (and apparently bloodlessly) bloom and die, leaving no trace behind, Lowell—son of the wealthy and influential Lowell family of Massachusetts—has cultural force and something like institutional permanence: "there is now—and it looks as if there might be always—President Lowell" (464). The intellectual folly of providing facile solutions to difficult problems, whether definitions of happiness or identities for the Man in the Iron Mask, may have political ramifications that take their toll in human terms. Was this the case in identifying the Braintree murderers? In a famous article in the *Atlantic Monthly* published in March of 1927, Felix Frankfurter asserted that the "only issue" at the trial of Sacco and Vanzetti "was the identity of the murderers":

> the killing of Parmenter and Berardelli [paymaster and guard] was undisputed. . . . Were Sacco and Vanzetti two of the assailants of Paramenter and Berardelli, or were they not?
> On this issue, there was at the trial a mass of conflicting evidence.[15]

Would it be possible to say that, given what Frankfurter called the "elements of uncertainty" at their trial, the conviction of Sacco and Vanzetti was, like Phelp's magnificently efficient explication of happiness, based on a mix of arrogance and ignorance?[16] While at the literal level Parker's narrator modestly takes for granted that no son of hers could ever possibly aspire to so much greatness as that embodied by Phelps and Lowell, the irony of her message is quite clear: as a woman with no direct power to prevent the values of such cultural icons from being reproduced, she can only "trust" that her college-bound son will wisely exercise his dubious privilege of choosing whether to pay homage to the "big boys."[17]

But no matter how ugly Parker's prettily crossed rights to the jaw become, they are never as distasteful to her readers as is Phelps's "pretty tribute to what he calls the American cow" to her. This is the "animal story" with which the eminent professor concludes his little book:

> The cow, he points out, does not have to brush her teeth, bob her hair, select garments, light her fire and cook her food. She is not passionate about the income tax or the League of Nations; she has none of the thoughts that inflict distress and torture. "I have observed many cows," says the professor, in an interesting glimpse of autobiography, "and there is in their beautiful eyes no perplexity; they are never even bored." He paints a picture of so sweet, so placid, so carefree an existence, that you could curse your parents for not being Holsteins. And then what does he do? Breaks up the whole lovely thing by saying, "Very few people would be willing to change into cows . . . Life, with all its sorrows, perplexities, and heartbreaks, is more interesting than bovine placidity." (463–64)

Does "the American cow" represent Professor Phelps's ideal of woman as a vacuous reproductive vessel? One is somehow reminded, though the sequence may seem a bit hazy, of that filet on the plate of the narrator's male companion at Cap d'Antibes, or of those "dams" whose children Swift's modest proposer so relishes the thought of cooking up.[18] Cannibalism notwithstanding, even animal life is not always as happy as it seems.[19] In any event, there is something profoundly disturbing to Parker—something chillingly like Gulliver upon his return from Houyhnhnmland—about a mentality that sentimentalizes cows, femininity, purity, and life (with all its miseries) while tacitly sanctioning the execution of human beings. Swift's definition of happiness thus once more comes to mind. Phelps is not simply a fool, but something much more troubling: a fool among knaves. Parker has produced a portrait of a world turned upside down. But it is not just the categories of wisdom and folly that are reversed in her review, or even those of culture and anarchy. In typical Swiftian fashion, she probes the very order of civilization and savagery and finds that order skewed. A woman needs not only irony but a mask of iron—some self-protective shield against facile knowledge of who and what she "really" is—when she registers so much savage indignation.

"Men seldom make passes / At girls who wear glasses," quipped Dorothy Parker, apparently innocently, in a short poem called "News Item" written in the summer of 1926.[20] Now, more than sixty years later, the aphoristic fame of these lines has superseded popular knowledge of their authorial provenance. Indeed, their anonymous appropriation by recent feminist theory, most notably by film critic Mary Ann Doane, who, in her landmark essay on the female gaze, uses them as the verbal corollary of an important cinematic commonplace, is itself moot testimony that Parker had tapped into a powerful cultural cliché. The image of the woman who wears glasses, argues Doane, "is a heavily marked condensation of motifs concerned with repressed sexuality, knowledge, visibility and vision, intellectuality and desire."[21] When Dorothy Parker, as female critic, scrutinizes the willful blindness of Professor William Lyon Phelps, she assumes a spectatorial stance that paradoxically "womanizes" and desexualizes her. (According to Parker's epigrammatic logic, the girl who wears glasses becomes an intellectual woman but thereby loses her girlish sex appeal.) To protect herself against rejection for her usurpation of the masculine-coded subject position of intellectual womanhood, therefore, Parker must deploy precisely the strategy identified in 1929 by Joan Riviere in her now-classic essay "Womanliness as a Masquerade"; she must produce herself as an excess of girlish femininity, masquerade as a blissfully myopic "little lady" who needs glasses but, like Gulliver, either does not know it or will not wear them, so girlishly smitten is she by seeing only what Swift elsewhere once called "the *Superficies* of Things" (Swift, *Tale*, 174), by being placidly and complicitously well deceived.[22]

Why would Dorothy Parker be thus inclined to align herself with Swift? One might point to similarities in the way both writers were positioned, or positioned themselves, in relation to major sites of cultural power. Parker shared with Swift an attraction to wealth and power laced with a sense of personal injury at not properly belonging to their ranks, and for both writers, this sense of personal injustice translated into championship of the downtrodden and oppressed. Swift's entire career was defined by a series of social, ethnic, and professional self-divisions. A writer who made his living by the Church, a clergyman who satirized religion, the son of English Protestants living in Ireland, first seeking refuge in England and then in Ireland, at one time hungry for advancement in English political life and for a deanery in England, at another champion of the Irish against the English, choosing finally "to be a freeman among slaves, rather than a slave among freemen," Swift was the living site of multiple and often conflicting loyalties.[23]

Like Swift, Parker moved in circles of wealth and influence where she never felt fully like either an insider or an outsider. Frequenting such offices and homes as those of Condé Nast and Herbert Bayard Swope, she was part of the upper class but not quite of them.[24] In 1917, as the half-Jewish Dorothy Rothschild, she had married the Hartford-born Edwin Pond Parker II, "a descendent in the ninth generation of William Parker, who had arrived in Hartford from England in 1636."[25] Estranged from her father, Dorothy had long rejected her Jewish roots. But as biographer Marion Meade notes, when Eddie's grandfather, the Reverend Edwin Pond Parker— Connecticut's "leading Protestant clergyman and one of Hartford's most distinguished citizens"—referred to her upon their first meeting as "a stranger within our gates," she experienced a heightened sense of her own ethnic identity:

> Stupefied at his mean spirit, she was harshly reminded of the chasm separating New England Congregational pulpits and the Lower East Side sweatshops. If she had felt no harmony with the Jews, it was now clear that she had even less in common with these Hartford Brahmins, "toadying, in sing-song, to a crabbèd god."[26]

Thus, when Parker later lambasted the New Haven- and Hartford-bred Professor William Lyon Phelps, son of a Baptist minister and descendent of that William Phelps who settled at Windsor, Connecticut, in 1638, she was attacking not only a particular instance of academic folly but also those strongholds of cultural privilege for whose comforts she longed but from whose inner circles she somehow felt constitutionally excluded.[27] Yale, Harvard, and the Massachusetts Lowells were simply institutionalized displacements of her (by that time all-but-former) New England in-laws, bastions of corrupted power that protected private interests in the false name of the larger community.

Parker mounts her critique of Phelps by creating for herself endlessly displaced identities. In poses akin to Swift's alternating masks of the cynic and the naïf, she by turns impersonates the "little lady" and the slightly sluttish "woman of the world." In addition, she mercilessly subverts her readers' ability to distinguish fact from fiction by sprinkling her narrative with various "interesting glimpses of autobiography." (She had, for example, actually spent part of the summer of 1926 at Cap D'Antibes at the villa of her new acquaintance,

Yale graduate Gerald Murphy, heir of the New York leather goods store Mark Cross.) Historically, critics have all too often mistaken Swift's masks for the man himself but Swift never goes out of his way as mercilessly as Parker does misleadingly to tantalize his readers with incidental autobiographical details. Situating herself half-in-the-real-and-half-not, Parker heightens our sense of the illusory or invented nature of even her "real" identity, itself always already mediated by culturally constructed versions of womanhood. If femininity is a fiction—a pose or mask behind which this author hides—so too, we are led to understand, is the "real" woman it professes to conceal.

Thus while Parker's use of Swift may illuminate her affinities with him, it also reveals some telling differences. Parker the reviewer and ravenous reader seems in the end to have identified as much with Swift's monstrous female embodiment of literary criticism in *The Battle of the Books*—that malignant deity of the Moderns, Criticism—as she did with Swift himself. A voracious, rotting, self-consuming, maternal presence who lies "extended in her Den, upon the Spoils of numberless Volumes half devoured" as at her "Teats . . . a Crew of ugly Monsters . . . greedily [suck]" (Swift, *Tale*, 240), Criticism is roused from her epic lethargy only by the necessity of preventing the destruction of her worshipers, the Moderns—especially that of Wotton, her favored son. To assist him without dazzling or overwhelming him with her divine repulsiveness, Swift's hungry goddess undergoes a miraculously dematerializing metamorphosis in which she is transformed corporeally from a physically sprawling maternal body into the neatly delimited compass of a male-authored text:

> She . . . gathered up her Person into an *Octavo* Compass: Her Body grew white and arid, and split in pieces with Driness; the thick turned into Pastboard, and the thin into Paper, upon which, her Parents and Children, artfully strowed a Black Juice. . . . In which Guise she march'd on towards the *Moderns*, undistinguishable in Shape and Dress from the *Divine B-ntl-y, W-tt-n's* dearest Friend. (Swift, *Tale*, 242–43)

Having thus disguised herself, Criticism takes "the ugliest of her Monsters" (243), flings it invisibly into Wotton's mouth, and vanishes in a mist.

Parker, one might argue, manages an analogous transformation of active rage into apparently demure textuality when—by means of a narrator also concerned for the well-being of her son—she decorously, though no less cannibalistically, "makes mincemeat" of Professor Phelps. Vaguely anorexic (despite her "hungry curiosity" about definitions of happiness, it is in fact only the narrator's male luncheon companion whom we actually see eat), this narrator's criticism is more admiring than analytic; it has the timidity of pencil marks and the arid innocuousness of pressed white (not purple) violets. Through it, Parker deftly dodges the stigma Swift himself attaches to female rage. (For surely Swift is never quite so repulsed by Gulliver, even in the latter's angriest and most misanthropic moments, as he is by the splenetic Mother of all Gall). By surreptitiously mobilizing Swift's satiric tests, Parker's assaults—like Swift's own monstrous goddess's—are rendered indirect, flung, as it were, into another critic's mouth.

Ironically, nevertheless, it is through this very self-transformation that Parker most compellingly establishes herself as a locus of moral outrage. For it is precisely in her identification with Swift's angry goddess that she is able most pointedly to differentiate herself from Phelps. Parker recognizes Phelps as a fellow literary critic, one whose word—like hers—has the power to make or break a book. But just as there is for Swift a difference between the malicious and protectionist lies produced by Lilliputian or Walpolian hypocrisy and those produced by the elusive masquerading satirist, so too there is for Parker a difference between the sophisticated literary hoaxes she perpetrates in the interest of brutal veracity and the intellectual charlatanry (with its truly brutal consequences) of the "academic" Phelpses of the world. Phelps and Parker may both go in for artificial sweetness, but only Parker's counterfeit invites detection or produces light. Parker's review may be intellectually demanding, may even solicit the attention of a certain highly educated class, but ultimately, and with deliberate irony, it is more genuinely "populist" in spirit than Phelps's "popular" little tome of platitudes. Through its appeal to a common sense of human suffering and shared humanity—that of women and Italian immigrants not excepted—it is far more accessible to the general public, if we understand that public in the truest sense to be constituted not by but across lines of class, ethnic, gender, and educational privilege.

Notes

1. Joan Shelley Rubin, *The Making of Middlebrow Culture* (Chapel Hill: University of North Carolina Press, 1992), 281.

2. Emily Toth, "Dorothy Parker, Erica Jong, and the New Feminist Humor," in *Regionalism and the Female Imagination*, ed. Emily Toth (New York: Human Sciences

Press, 1985), 71; Leslie Frewin, *The Late Mrs. Dorothy Parker* (New York: Macmillan, 1986), 16 and 17. Frewin's claims remain undocumented.

3. "The Professor Goes in for Sweetness and Light," in *The Portable Dorothy Parker* (New York: Viking, 1973), 461. All subsequent references to "The Professor," cited parenthetically by page number in the text, will be to this edition.

4. On the Man in the Iron Mask, see Sidney Dark, introduction to *The Man in the Iron Mask* by Alexandre Dumas (New York: Norton, 1955), 11–14. On the topos of the "little woman" in Parker's work and in that of other American female humorists, see Nancy Walker, "Fragile and Dumb: The Little Woman in Women's Humor, 1900–1940," *Thalia* 5, no. 2 (Fall/Winter 1982–83): 24–29.

5. Jonathan Swift, *A Tale of a Tub . . . The Battle of the Books and the Mechanical Operation of the Spirit* 2nd ed., ed. A. C. Guthkelch and D. Nichol Smith (Oxford: Clarendon Press, 1958), 233–35. All future references to *The Battle of the Books* and *A Tale of a Tub*, cited parenthetically by page number in the text, will be to this edition, cited parenthetically as *Tale* in the text.

6. Marion Meade contends that Parker stopped attending classes at Miss Dana's school for girls in 1908 during the spring of her freshman year (*What Fresh Hell Is This?* [New York: Villard, 1988], 27–28). In contrast, Frewin claims that there is solid evidence that Parker remained at Miss Dana's until the fall of 1910 (*The Late Mrs. Dorothy Parker*, 13); John Keats notes that Parker entered Miss Dana's as a member of the class of 1911 and, although he never specifically asserts that she actually graduated, he seems to assume that she did (*You Might as Well Live: The Life and Times of Dorothy Parker* [New York: Simon and Schuster, 1970], 21–28); and Arthur F. Kinney claims that Parker graduated from Miss Dana's in 1911 (*Dorothy Parker* [Boston: Twayne, 1978], 27).

7. Stuart Pratt Sherman, *Matthew Arnold: How to Know Him* (Indianapolis: Bobbs-Merrill, 1917), 1–2.

8. Stuart Pratt Sherman, *The Genius of America* (New York: Scribner, 1923); Ernest Boyd, "Ku Klux Kriticism," *The Nation*, 20 June 1923, 723–24. Interestingly, Parker's implicit charges against Phelps in her review (charges I attempt to explicate below) echo many of Boyd's charges against Sherman. The following two passages from Boyd's text, which disdain Sherman's hankering after American ethnic purity, seem especially pertinent: "Sinister Jews and Irishmen, apparently in the mistaken belief that they have any rights of self-expression in this great Anglo-Saxon republic, are actively engaged in the damnable work of undermining the Puritan stamina of the American people. Be Anglo-Saxon or be forever silent is, I gather, the exhortation which Mr. Sherman and his colleagues extend to the articulate few in the welter of races, creeds, and traditions which make up the America of today" (723); and "Before Mr. Sherman appeals to the artist on behalf of the community, he will have to make up his mind that the community is something vastly more complicated and less homogenous than is dreamt of in his Ku Klux philosophy" (724). According to Clare Booth Luce, Boyd was one of Parker's "intimate friends and great admirers" and a member of the Algonquin set (Keats, *You Might as Well Live*, 49).

9. Rubin, *Middlebrow Culture*, chaps. 2 and 5. See also Daniel Aaron's "Merchants of Light," his review of Rubin's book in *The New Republic*, 6 July 1992, 34–36.

10. Meade, *What Fresh Hell Is This?* 28.

11. Frewin, *The Late Mrs. Dorothy Parker*, 12–14.

12. Kinney, *Dorothy Parker*, 103ff.

13. "He left a standing order at the Holliday Bookshop that any book about that period, or any book relating to it in any way, should be sent to him, and he read

them all as they came in . . . After he had done a monumental amount of reading, beginning with all the works of all the humorists, he came to the reluctant conclusion that not one of them was funny" (Nathaniel Benchley, *Robert Benchley, a Biography* [New York: McGraw-Hill, 1955], 190).

14. H. Teerink, *A Bibliography of the Writings in Prose and Verse of Jonathan Swift D.D.* (The Hague: Martinus Nijhoff, 1937), 146–48.

15. Felix Frankfurter, "The Case of Sacco and Vanzetti," *The Atlantic Monthly*, March 1927, 410.

16. Ibid., 415

17. Parker in fact did not have children.

18. Jonathan Swift, *A Modest Proposal* in *The Prose Works of Jonathan Swift*, 14 vols., ed. Herbert Davis, et al. (Oxford: Blackwell, 1939–74), 12:11. It is perhaps germane here to quote a passage from Phelps's book that Parker regrettably omits from her review. Phelps is in the process of ruminating on the American cow: "After eating for an hour or so . . . she begins to chew the cud. Her upper jaw remains stationary, while the lower revolves in a kind of solemn rapture; there is on her placid features no pale cast of thought; the cow chewing the cud has very much the expression of a healthy American girl chewing gum. I never see one without thinking of the other. The eyes of a cow are so beautiful that Homer gave them to the Queen of Heaven, because he could not think of any other eyes so large, so lustrous, so liquid, and so untroubled" (William Lyon Phelps, *Happiness* [New York: E. P. Dutton, 1927], 45–47).

19. Parker's love of animals was well known. "That inveterate dislike of her fellow creatures which characterizes so many of Mrs. Parker's utterances is confined to the human race," wrote Alexander Woollcott. "All other animals have her enthusiastic support. . . . [A]ny home of hers always has the aspect and aroma of a menagerie. Invariably there is a dog. There was Amy, an enchanting, wooly, fourlegged coquette whose potential charm only Dorothy Parker would have recognized at first meeting. For at that first meeting Amy was covered with dirt and a hulking truckman was kicking her out of his way. This swinish biped was somewhat taken aback to have a small and infuriated poetess rush at him from the sidewalk and kick him smartly in the shins" ("Our Mrs. Parker," in *While Rome Burns* [New York: Viking, 1934], 151).

20. *The Portable*, 109.

21. Mary Ann Doane, "Film and the Masquerade: Theorising the Female Spectator," *Screen* 23 (1982): 82.

22. Joan Riviere, "Womanliness as a Masquerade," in *Formations of Fantasy*, ed. Victor Burgin, James Donald, and Cora Kaplan (London: Methuen, 1986), 35–44. Riviere's article was originally published in *The International Journal of Psycho-Analysis* 10 (1929): 303–13. According to Frank Crowninshield, who as the editor of *Vanity Fair* had published a number of Parker's early works, Parker herself "wore horn-rimmed glasses, which she removed quickly if anyone spoke to her suddenly" (quoted in Frewin, *The Late Mrs. Dorothy Parker*, 29). "She wore glasses at work because she was badly nearsighted," writes biographer John Keats. "But she always took them off when anyone stopped at her desk, and she never wore them on social occasions" (*You Might as Well Live*, 86). Donald Ogden Stewart, Dorothy Parker's longtime friend and Algonquin Round Table compatriot, later reminisced about the Dorothy Parker of the 1920s. "Every girl has her technique," he observed, "and shy, demure helplessness was part of Dottie's—the innocent, bright-eyed little girl that needs a male to help her across the street" (Frewin, *The Late Mrs. Dorothy Parker*, 66).

23. Swift to Alexander Pope, Dublin, 8 July 1733, *The Correspondence of Jonathan Swift*, 5 vols., ed. Harold Williams (Oxford: Clarendon Press, 1965–72), 4:171.

24. Kinney, *Dorothy Parker*, 43–44. "I hate almost all rich people," Parker once remarked, "but I think I'd be darling at it" ("Dorothy Parker," interview by Marion Capron, in *Writers at Work: The "Paris Review" Interviews*, ed. Malcolm Cowley [New York: Viking, 1958], 80).

25. Meade, *What Fresh Hell Is This?* 38.

26. Ibid., 41.

27. *Current Biography* (1943): 582, s.v. "Phelps, William Lyon."

The Remarkably Constant Reader:
Dorothy Parker as Book Reviewer

Nancy A. Walker

IN HER REVIEW OF THE *JOURNAL OF KATHERINE MANSFIELD* IN 1927, Dorothy Parker made a statement that could equally well apply to herself: "Writing was the precious thing in life to her, but she was never truly pleased with anything she had written."[1] Much later, in 1962, in her last book review for *Esquire,* Parker wrote of Shirley Jackson's *We Have Always Lived in the Castle* in a similarly revealing way, "this novel brings back all my faith in terror and death. I can say no higher of it and her" (575). Of all the forms in which Parker wrote—poems, stories, sketches, epigrams—her published book reviews, written as "Constant Reader" for the *New Yorker* from 1927 to 1933 and for *Esquire* from 1957 to 1962, may seem the most ephemeral parts of her career. Yet in her responses to the work of other authors, both in the heady years of the Algonquin Round Table and the emergence of the *New Yorker,* and thirty years later, when her work was all but forgotten, emerge some of the clearest and most telling indications of her literary sensibility. Whether serious or comic, Parker's reviews ring with the utmost candor; although she creates distinctive personae in the presentation of her opinions, the medium of the book review allowed for an expression of personal tastes that can provide insight into a woman of integrity and high standards.

The tone and style of the early *New Yorker* encouraged the kind of book review that seemed to come naturally to Parker. *New Yorker* founder Harold Ross and the young writers he hired were deliberate in their attempt to appeal to the urban sophisticate or would-be sophisticate, and the magazine thus fostered a stance compounded of gaiety and world-weariness, in which little was considered sacred and decided tastes regarding the arts were not merely welcome, but cultivated. Few articles—including book reviews—were signed with the authors' actual names; *New Yorker* writers typically used their initials or such labels as Parker's "Constant Reader." Yet within this near-anonymity, the writers developed distinctive voices that marked their pieces as their own, and they often used the first-person pronoun as a means of both personalizing their remarks and seeming to speak directly to the individual reader. Thus, for example, Robert M. Coates, who signed his book reviews "R.M.C.," opens his review of A. S. M. Hutchison's novel *Big Business* in August of 1932 by throwing himself on the mercy of the reader: "What are you going to do—do you mind if I ask you a personal question?—if you're a book-reviewer and you find yourself face to face with an Important Book that you can't possibly read?" (*New Yorker,* 13 August 1932). Such admission and appeal to the reader's understanding were not to be found in the *New York Times* book review section, nor in the reviews in *Harper's* or *Atlantic,* where the *New Yorker*'s engaging "I" was replaced by the distancing pronoun "one." The *New Yorker* thus sought to establish a different kind of authority for its reviewers than did these more staid and venerable periodicals. Instead of being "experts" in the field of the book being reviewed—often with academic credentials and/or affiliations—the *New Yorker* reviewers during this early period were intended to replicate the ideal readers of the magazine: people with taste and intelligence, but without pretense to superior knowledge or insight. Whereas a reviewer for the *New York Times* would calmly assess the flaws of a book that he (occasionally she) found lacking in merit, the *New Yorker* reviewer could be imagined flinging down the book in disgust. Indeed, in the review cited above, "R.M.C." reports quitting *Big Business* on p. 74, and giving up on Kurt Heuser's *The Journey Inward* on p. 106.

Even in the context of the *New Yorker* ethos, however, Dorothy Parker developed—or revealed—a much more distinctive personality than did her peers. Moreover, as though her pseudonym "Constant Reader" were prophetic, her book reviews in *Esquire* three decades later are so clearly from the same pen as to suggest that the reviews were an important forum for Parker's views on life as well as the literary scene. If the *New Yorker* fostered the authority of the individual reader rather than that of specialized expertise, Parker took the process a step further: she derives her authority precisely from seeming not to be one at all, projecting personae composed of enthusiasms, prejudices, and personal quirks, and developing a distinctive style—a style in which to deliver her no-nonsense opinions. "R.M.C." might occasionally confess to not finishing a book, but the "Constant Reader" did so more colorfully. In a single *New Yorker* review in 1931, she reports giving up on two books because of the authors' egregious style; in both cases she quotes passages to illustrate her point, and concludes, respectively, with "So I thought I wouldn't play any more," and "So I got the hell out of that" (*New Yorker,* 4 April 1931). In a 1961 *Esquire* review of Irving Stone's *The Agony and the Ecstasy,* she reports her frustration with fictionalized biography: "I wish people would either write history, or write novels, or go out and sell nylons" (*Esquire,* June 1961). The juxtaposition of the lingerie salesman to the writer conveys her scorn more effectively than would a paragraph of explanation, and it suggests as well that she consciously writes as a woman.

The variety of female personae Parker creates are one of the major sources of humor in the reviews. One of the most common of these poses is the mock innocent figure who pretends surprise at or enlightenment by the book being reviewed. This innocent figure is a direct descendant of one of the most time-honored humorous devices in American literature: the untutored observer whose commonsense remarks unmasked pretension or hypocrisy. Parker's pose of innocence often greets a book written with great earnestness by an author intent on explaining something; she adopts the role of willing pupil with such hyperbole that both her pretense and the book's overbearing nature become clear. Preparing to skewer Elinor Glyn's novel *It,* for example, Parker claims to have led a life too sheltered to be acquainted with Glyn's steamy romances: "I have misspent my days. When I think of all those hours I flung away in reading William James and Santayana, when I might have been reading of life, throbbing, beating, perfumed life, I practically break down" (465). She pleads a similar ignorance at the beginning of her review of evangelist Aimee Semple McPherson's *In the Service of the King* when she posits that she *should* have been able to predict that this "Somewhat Different Entertainer" would write a book. Since she has not, she notes, "I really must make a note on my desk calendar to have my head examined one day next week. I am beginning to have more and more piercing doubts that my fontanel ever closed up properly" (497). Perhaps Parker's most sophisticated use of this wide-eyed innocent stance occurs in her 1927 review of Emily Post's *Etiquette,* in which she mingles bits of Mrs. Post's advice with the creation of her persona:

> I am going in for a course of study at the knee of Mrs. Post. Maybe, some time in the misty future, I shall be Asked Out, and I shall be ready. You won't catch me being intentionally haughty to subordinates or refusing to be a pallbearer for any reason except serious ill health. I shall live down the old days, and with the help of Mrs. Post and God (always mention a lady's name first) there will come a time when you will be perfectly safe in inviting me to your house, which should never be called a residence except in printing or engraving. (476)

Something of Parker's intent in employing her mock-naive pose can be surmised from a comment in another review. Having called a book both "naïve" and "annoying," she remarks, "those two adjectives must ever be synonymous to me" (457).

Even when employing the mock-innocent stance, however, Parker is in some ways far removed from this figures's eighteenth- and nineteenth-century ancestors. Whereas they tended to be rustic men who spoke in regional dialects, Parker, in contrast, creates herself as urban, urbane, and distinctively female. While a Jack Downing or a Sam Slick represented the earthy values of the country in sharp distinction to the city, Parker is the consummate urbanite, making frequent references to landlords, cocktails, dinner parties, doormen, and city streets. Returning from a trip to Switzerland, she writes, "God keep me from chauvinism, but New York is beautiful" (528). Her reviews are peppered with literary and other cultural allusions, and in one review she refers to "making whoopee with the intelligentsia" (508). Against Upton Sinclair's anger in *Money Writes!* about the economic privilege of many of America's authors, Parker defends an author's choice to write about "jade and satin and the shining surface of old furniture" (470); no hayseed, she knows and articulates the difference between imitation and real pearls: "The neat surfaces of the imitations shine prettily; the real glow from within" (480).

References to pearls and satin help to feminize the voice of Parker as reviewer, but we need no subtle clues to the fact that she writes as a woman; she makes her gender overt again and again—not to suggest that her literary taste is in any way formed by it, but instead to establish a rapport with her readers. As critic, Parker is not a remote, objective figure, but rather an individual with distinct characteristics: she is a mediocre bridge player, is subject to insomnia, hates spring, loves dogs and horses, and delights in wordplay. Her stance is often that of the coquette, especially in the *New Yorker* reviews. Preparing to deliver negative reviews of novels by Fannie Hurst and Booth Tarkington in 1928, Parker offers a mock apology by claiming to have a bad case of the "rams," brought on, she assures readers, by a stalk of bad celery, because surely her consumption of "two or three sidecars, some champagne, . . . and a procession of mixed Benedictines-and-brandies" would not have brought her face-to-face with "a Little Mean Man about eighteen inches tall, wearing a yellow slicker and roller-skates" (483). She employs a somewhat different strategy to deflect the negativism of her review of Sinclair Lewis's *The Man Who Knew Coolidge* in the same year. In her pretense that a friend "is trying to make a lady out of me" in part by refusing to let her use the word "rotten," she manages to use the word six times in the review, along with such words as "heavy-handed," "clumsy," and "dishonest."

In the later *Esquire* reviews, Parker also writes as a woman, sometimes defending the female sex against stereotypical assumptions. In her review of Errol Flynn's *My Wicked, Wicked Ways*, she notes that Flynn attempted to woo Olivia de Havilland by putting a dead snake in her underwear. "But do you know," Parker comments sarcastically, "not even this caused her heart to soften! Ah, women, women, where, where thy sense of humor?" (*Esquire*, March 1960). Two years later, reviewing Jeannette Bruce's *The Wallflower Season*, she rails against literature aimed at the female market:

> [Bruce] chose to make it what is called a woman's story, which is undoubtedly profitable. A woman's story, a woman's movie, a woman's book—these are so many slaps against the conglomerate face of the sex. Apparently it is believed that women's little heads cannot contain anything that is not cheerful and cozy, with a delightful, comfortable and permanent ending. (*Esquire*, April 1962)

Also in these reviews of the late 1950s and early 1960s, Parker sometimes refers to herself as "Mother" creating an admonitory persona that seems in keeping with her advancing age, though her tone is as sprightly as ever. Reviewing a novel set in Scotland, for example, she writes, "as one who has been through many such novels, Mother was somewhat nervous about bursts of quaintness" (*Esquire*, January 1962). Far more bored than shocked by *The Memoirs of Casanova*, Parker writes, "Mother gets awfully tired of the calisthenics. There is a certain lack of variety" (*Esquire*, March 1961).

Neither Parker's mock-innocent nor her "Mother" persona is used to soften her criticism or undercut her authority. On the contrary, her posture as the somewhat vulnerable, self-mocking woman who has difficulty with foreign languages and fears retribution for negative comments—on not having been able to read Lewis's *Elmer Gantry*: "I shall undoubtedly fry in hell for my failure" (509)—is undercut by its own hyperbole, which strengthens the authority of her observations. The "little old me" facade is a velvet glove covering an iron fist. In her review of Benito Mussolini's youthful novel *The Cardinal's Mistress* (released in English translation in 1928), Parker first reports that she begged to be allowed to review it—"Please teacher, may I have it to take home with me?" (515)—but that she was "absolutely unable to read my way through it" (515). Perhaps the best-known punch that Parker-as-reviewer delivered occurs in her review of A. A. Milne's *The House at Pooh Corner*, which ends with the line, "And it is that word 'hummy,' my darlings, that marks the first place in *The House at Pooh Corner* at which Tonstant Weader Frowed up" (518). But other swipes are equally pointed. Quoting from the overwrought rhetoric of Aimee Semple McPherson's autobiography, Parker comments, "You see? And she can go on like that for hours. Can, hell—does" (497). Of the nearly six hundred pages of Theodore Dreiser's autobiography *Dawn*, she comments, "God help us one and all if Mr. Dreiser ever elects to write anything called 'June Twenty-first'!" (541).

Indeed, Parker's mock-innocent stance is most often employed in her negative reviews; as a humorous device, it provides the ideal setup for what often amounts to ridicule of a book she dislikes. In reviews of books she admires, there is no need for the humorous frame, and her tone can be almost reverential. The *Journal of Katherine Mansfield* she describes as "exquisite," and so intensely personal that she reports murmuring "Please forgive me" to its author as she finished it (451–52). No such personal response colors the prose of Edwin Clark, who reviewed Mansfield's *Journal* for the *New York Times*. Clark found the book "introspective" and "beautifully told," and notes passages of "enchanting loveliness," but he ends on the impersonal note of "one can discern that her letters are to be eagerly awaited" (*New York Times Book Review*, 9 October 1927). For Parker, Ernest Hemingway's *Men Without Women* is "a truly magnificent work. . . . I do not know where a greater collection of stories can be found" (460). Reviewing Hemingway's collection of stories for the *New York Times*, Percy Hutchison uses such words as "arresting," "passionless genius," and "masterly," but Hutchison also feels the need to make cautionary statements, wondering whether Hemingway's "originalities" will "fail to stand the test of time," and warning that "Hemingway is without a philosophy of life; his fidelity is all to surface aspects" (*New York Times Book Review*, 16 October 1927). Parker finds the collected stories of Ring Lardner so good as to be difficult to review: "What more are you going to say of a great thing than that it is great?" (526). And Vladimir Nabakov's *Lolita* she describes as "a fine book, a distinguished book—all right, then—a great book" (566).

This is not to suggest that there is no humor in Parker's favorable reviews. Her style is frequently witty, and sometimes downright comic, but instead of creating a comic persona, the humor is used as a means of driving home a point in a memorable way, in much the same way as the final lines of her poems serve as the punch lines. Thus, of the murder mysteries of Dashiell Hammett she writes in

1931 that he is "so hard-boiled you could roll him on the White House lawn" (539). In 1958, defending *Lolita* against accusations of pornography, she notes wryly that it was banned in France: "As it was written in English, there does seem to have been a certain amount of oversolicitude that the French masses would have had their morals upended by the reading of it" (565). Reviewing Katherine Anne Porter's long-awaited novel *Ship of Fools* in 1962, Parker notes with awe that Porter worked on it for twenty years: "To those of us who, after filling a postcard, are obliged to lie down and have wet cloths applied to our brow, this is not a book. It's the Pyramid" (573).

Given such straightforward—even blunt—assessments, it is little wonder that taken together, Parker's reviews for the *New Yorker* and *Esquire* provide an index to her literary tastes. Much the same could be said of anyone who writes book reviews over a period of time, but Parker's insistent use of the first-person pronoun lends a particular vibrancy to her sensibilities. Like most book reviewers, Parker appreciated good writing; for her, this meant writing that was clear, forceful, and spare—as she says of Hemingway, whom she admired greatly, "prose stripped to its firm young bones" (460). Whereas Aimee Semple McPherson exhorts, and Theodore Dreiser is verbose, Hemingway "keeps his words to their short path" (461). For Parker, style is sufficiently important that she cannot get past the flaws she finds in Dreiser's writing. She is impatient with critics who downplay Dreiser's style: " 'Of course,' each one says airily, 'Dreiser writes badly,' and thus they dismiss that tiny fact, and go off into their waltz-dreams" (541). Indeed, her fellow *New Yorker* reviewer Robert M. Coates comes close to doing just this in his review of Dreiser's *Tragic America*. Although he does not claim for Dreiser "a mighty message," he remarks that "I'm not going to start complaining now about that much-mentioned style of his" (*New Yorker*, 30 January 1932). In her review of Dreiser's *Dawn*, she states clearly her impatience with such a critical stance:

> It is of not such small importance to me that Theodore Dreiser writes in so abominable a style. He is regarded, and I wish you could gainsay me, as one of our finest contemporary authors; it is the first job of a writer who demands rating among the great, or even among the good, to write well. If he fails that, as Mr. Dreiser, by any standard, so widely muffs it, he is, I think, unequipped to stand among the big. (542)

Parker's attacks on bad writing are often couched in a wit that lends them added force. Puzzling over the title of Fannie Hurst's

God Must Be Sad, which she finds "strangely offensive," Parker sur-
mises that "He must have been sad when he saw Miss Hurst's hanging participles" (*Esquire,* January 1962). She complains about one
author who "has taken to himself a trick of diction that causes me
to summon the men in the white coats to carry me away from it all.
That is the transformation of nouns into verbs—thus, if you go to a
lunch counter to buy a cup of coffee, you are not served with a cup
of coffee; you are coffeed; and when you have drunk the brew, you
dime the counter. . . . the book and I parted company when the
traveling brother saw a child who lilac'd a grave" (*Esquire,* April
1960). Occasionally, Parker pulls herself up short when her own
writing violates one of her own rules. Having commented that an
author has not created a "fun book," she continues parenthetically:

> (I'm fighting what experience tells me is a losing battle against the use
> of the word "fun" as an adjective: he's a fun person, it's a fun play, it's a
> fun book. I had to give up on "divine," "fabulous," and though I still
> take on about the use of "diction" when what is meant is "enunciation,"
> I have a terrible fear it will go into the language. But "fun" as an adjec-
> tive, no, a thousand times no.) (*Esquire,* June 1961)

Only rarely does Parker give good marks to a book that she concedes
is poorly written. One example is Isadora Duncan's *My Life,* the style
of which Parker also describes as "abominable," but whose passion
and struggle redeem the account, so that Parker can write, "somehow, the style of the book makes no matter" (480).
    Such an exception points to another of Parker's literary stan-
dards: a marked preference for candor, courage, that which is
deeply felt and rings true. Not for her the name-dropping and self-
importance of Margot Asquith's *Lay Sermons* (1927), which "has all
the depth and glitter of a worn dime" (456). Parker is particularly
put off by Asquith's self-centeredness: "The affair between Margot
Asquith and Margot Asquith will live as one of the prettiest love stories in all literature" (456). In her disdain for the book, Parker was
at odds with John Carter, who reviewed it for the *New York Times.*
While Carter concedes that "pietistic literature . . . cannot altogether escape the blight of the pulpit," he nonetheless finds Asquith's essays "packed with common sense" and "occasionally
brilliant" (*New York Times Book Review,* 23 October 1927). Writing
that suggested personal superiority acted as a red flag to Parker, and
some of her greatest praise goes to books that strike her as "honest"
rather than pretentious. Of Harlan Ellison's *Gentleman Junkie and
Other Stories of the Hung-Up Generation,* for example, she writes, "Mr.

Ellison is a good, honest, clean writer, putting down what he has seen and known, and no sensationalism about it" (*Esquire* January 1962). She finds a hubris similar to that of Asquith in William Lyon Phelps's small volume titled *Happiness*, which seems to her merely a collection of unenlightening platitudes, suitable, she notes, for reading in the bathtub, "and if it slips down the drain pipe, all right, it slips down the drain pipe" (462). Although she admires Sinclair Lewis's *Main Street* and *Babbit*, she finds his *The Man Who Knew Coolidge* "dishonest" (509); precisely the opposite is true of James Thurber's portrait of *New Yorker* founder Harold Ross in *The Years With Ross*, which "proves its protagonist to be a breathing man" (572).

As consistent as Parker's dislikes are her enthusiasms. She championed the short-story form against the greater popularity of the novel, noting in 1927 that "literature, it appears, is here measured by a yard-stick" (459). This comment appears in her review of Hemingway's short-story collection *Men Without Women*, in which she points out that despite the excellence of his first book of stories, *In Our Time*, Hemingway was not "discovered" until he published *The Sun Also Rises*. *In Our Time*, she says, "caused about as much stir in literary circles as an incompleted dogfight on upper Riverside Drive," whereas upon the publication of his novel, "eight hundred and forty-seven book reviewers formed themselves into the word 'welcome'" (458). She also admired the stories of Ring Lardner, Max Beerbohm, and Rudyard Kipling, but had little patience with the repetitive plots of stories in mass-circulation magazines, those that "separated the Ivory Soap advertisements from the pages devoted to Campbell's Soups" (473), and in her review of *The Best Short Stories of 1927* she includes wonderful parodies of the openings of half-a-dozen formulaic plots. Plot formulas did not trouble Parker, however, when it came to detective mysteries. In a review of Ellery Queen's *The New York Murders* in 1959 she confesses, "I am become a confirmed user of Whodunits" (567), but much earlier, in 1931, she raved about the work of Dashiell Hammett, wondering why there was "entirely too little screaming" about it from what she calls the "literary lads" (538).

The phrase "literary lads"—and "booksy folk" in the same review—is a key to Dorothy Parker's method in her book reviews, which is to separate herself from "real" reviewers and critics and speak to readers as one of them: not "literary" or "booksy," but simply an intelligent, discriminating reader, like thousands of readers of the *New Yorker* or *Esquire*. Such a method is closely related to Parker's faux-innocent persona, but it is far more specific in establishing her relationship to a reader who might feel cowed by the critique of an H. L. Mencken or a Malcolm Cowley. Parker's most explicit statements of her position occur in her 1928 review of Fannie Hurst's novel *A President is Born*. She begins by acknowledging her "deep admiration" for Hurst's other work, and then directly addresses the reader: "possibly in your company I must admit this with a coo of deprecating laughter, as one confesses a fondness for comic strips, motion-picture magazines, chocolate-almond bars, and like too-popular entertainments." Then, having made it known that she is no fan of *A President Is Born*, she continues: "This is, they say, her Big Novel. (If you were a real book reviewer, you would say, 'Miss Hurst has chosen a far larger canvas than is her wont.' I wish I could talk like that without getting all hot and red.)" (485). Another telling parenthetical address to the reader occurs in her commentary on a book titled *Appendicitis*, by a doctor named Thew Wright. Her setup for a hilarious account of the book (similar to her review of Emily Post's *Etiquette*) is a discussion of her insomnia, which *Appendicitis* has done a fine job of curing; at this point she remarks, "(Well, picture my surprise when this turned out to be a book review, after all! You could have knocked me over with a girder.)" (505). Reviewing Christopher Isherwood's *Down There On A Visit*, she reports delaying her remarks about it until late in her column "because I thought fitting words for it would be wafted to me. Well, they didn't waft—who are those cheats who get the right words told to them in their dreams?" (*Esquire,* May 1962).

Not only does Parker's method serve to distance her from "literary lads" and those she calls in one review "they of the cool, tall foreheads" (459); her humor also undercuts their authority. In a 1928 *New Yorker* piece that is more an essay than a review, she writes of the "Literary Rotarians" that swarm New York, and reports that she once went to a literary gathering filled with "people who looked as if they had been scraped out of drains," including one man who had won a prize from "*Inertia: a Magazine of Poesy* for the best poem on the occupation of the Ruhr district" (493). The piece ends with an indictment of intellectual snobbery:

> An enviable company, these joiners-up, with good cheer and appreciation for their daily portion. And about them always, like the scent of new violets, is the sweet and reassuring sense of superiority. For, being literary folk, they are licensed to be most awfully snooty about the Babbits. (494–95)

More subtly, Parker coyly questions the authority of major reviewers as she writes an early—and largely negative—review of Sinclair Lewis's *Dodsworth*: "And how am I to know, until I have read the Book Supplement of the New York Sunday *Times*, whether or not this is a truly important work? I cannot, with the slightest sureness, tell you if it will sweep the country, like *Main Street*, or bring forth yards of printed praise, as did *Elmer Gantry*. My guess would be that it will not" (523). Years later, Parker sounds a similar note when she says of a novel she likes, "I do not know if this is an important book—people lately talk so competently about importance, that it is hard to know whether they mean it for themselves or for the rest of us" (*Esquire*, March 1960).

It is through Parker's refusal to claim authority, then, that her book reviews achieve it. She presents readers with an unpretentious, sometimes self-mocking voice that, while it expresses strong opinions, pretends no Olympian knowledge or status. Her use of humor is evenhanded: she uses it to make fun of shallow, silly, or just plain bad published work, but she also turns it on herself in order to personalize her critiques. If at times this technique constitutes a conscious pose, it is not a mask behind which Parker hides, but instead a means of conveying what she values. And, as a bonus, the reviews contain some of her own best, most spirited writing, which is the reason, finally, that we continue to read them with such pleasure.

NOTES

1. Dorothy Parker, "The Private Papers of the Dead," in *The Portable Dorothy Parker* (New York: Viking, 1973), 451. All subsequent in-text references to numbered pages will be to this edition of Parker's work.

Being and Dying as a Woman in the Short Fiction of Dorothy Parker

Andrea Ivanov-Craig

I never see that prettiest thing—
A cherry bough gone white with Spring—
But what I think, "How gay 'twould be
To hang me from a flowering tree."
—"Cherry White," Dorothy Parker

MOST READERS FAMILIAR WITH DOROTHY PARKER'S FICTION AND POETRY encounter themes of death and dying thrown off or inimitably lanced by the woman humorist's famous sarcasm. In the same way, those who come to an understanding of Parker through the filter of biographical texts and discourse inevitably face interpretative reports of her attempted suicides. Readers are often led to assume that this talented and exceptionally witty woman expended herself in verbal wisecracking, party repartee, and heavy drinking, wasting resources otherwise better spent in "serious" work. For instance, Robert Altman's film production of Parker's life, *Mrs. Parker and the Vicious Circle* (1994), directed by Alan Rudolph, is largely informed by the mythos of the failed serious artist.[1] At two points in the film, at least, male figures tell Parker (Jennifer Jason Leigh) that she should think about how she is expending herself. As Charles MacArthur (Matthew Broderick) begins to seduce her he tells her he lied when he told her she was his favorite writer. He dismisses the "fluff" she has written, and then casually admonishes her, "If I were you, I'd worry." Later in the film, a young, bearded psychoanalyst advises her during a party with her Algonquin cronies. Remarking on the excessive time her friends spend in entertaining and being entertained, he comments that the "serious side of your nature is lost, and then you can't write. Life is something more than being able to breathe." Parker replies, "Do I have to believe that to feel better?"

Rudolph's interpretation was most likely influenced by Parker's biographies, among them *You Might as Well Live* by John Keats. In discussing the round of parties and late nights so attractive to the New York crowd, Keats compares Parker to Ernest Hemingway, stressing the "artistic" streak in both that was better nourished in solitude. Keats writes that Parker was "cozy" with the amusing and familiar faces, yet sharply critical of them, insecure and ultimately aloof.[2] At one point in her life, she confessed to Beatrice Ames, the wife of Donald Ogden Stewart and one of her few woman friends, that she was "wasting her talent," drinking not writing. Although Rudolph's (and Leigh's) Parker often lives up to her legendary vitriol, she too comes to doubt her achievements. In a rather pretentious but telling moment at the Round Table, Parker states, "I think far too wide of a stretch is made of the word, 'artist.' For I don't think that word is elastic. If I did, I'd be better company."

Reading Parker's life and work in such a light thus becomes the act of reading "Dorothy Parker," or what Dorothy Parker *could have been*. Her identity as a woman, for instance, was riddled with contradictions. As opposed to male humorist James Thurber's "anxiety of influence" in the wake of the achievements of senior *New Yorker* writer and wit, Robert Benchley, Parker experienced a pressure, not so much to exceed and overturn, as to "fit in." Later in her life she said, "It was the twenties, and we *had* to be smarty. I wanted to be cute. That's the terrible thing. I should have had more sense."[3] Parker sought out the company of men, amusing, charming, and emulating them with the sharpness of her wit. To a degree, she was considered "one of the guys"; in addition to keeping up an equal position in her banter with Benchley, Robert Sherwood, and the occasional company of Algonquin Round Tablers, being "cute" marked her off as a woman. However, biographers believe that her continual socializing and "life of the party" mentality succeeded in glossing over the severity of her troubles, even as her repeated suicide attempts called a kind of exaggerated attention to them. In the end, John Keats's comments on the unwanted pregnancy and abortion following her affair with Charles MacArthur are very revealing. Keats writes, "no one can know" if Parker suffered any trauma. "Perhaps Dorothy's friends were right to presume she had the mind of man imprisoned in a woman's body."[4] Keats's observation points to the prevalence of a certain kind of interpretative act: whether reading Parker's life or work, the issues of sexual identity, artistic or literary merit, and personal suffering and death become inevitably linked.

One wonders if Parker's later attempts to diminish the importance of her humor were also a kind of strategic interpretive act; a reading of herself that momentarily eclipsed the issues of sexual identity and the arena of personal suffering in order to "fit in," especially as a "serious" (modernist) artist. In a *Los Angeles Times* interview, she is quoted as saying, "Why, I'm not even an amateur humorist. I am very serious, and quite hurt when people laugh at some of my most earnest endeavors."[5] She begins denigrating her reputation as a humorist as early as 1934 and, in 1937, thinks of herself as once part of a "not especially brave little band" that "hid its nakedness of heart and mind under the out-of-date garment of a sense of humor"; she writes, "ridicule may be a shield, but it is not a weapon."[6] By 1939, her sentiments are unequivocal: "A humorist in this world is whistling by the loneliest graveyard and whistling the saddest song. There is nothing funny in the world any more."[7]

And yet, reading Dorothy Parker's "position" as woman humorist nevertheless continued, and her popular reputation began to rest primarily on a view of her verses and her association with the Algonquin Round Table. As I will argue, even among humor scholars such as Norris Yates, this popular reputation becomes a means of locating Parker's work as the doubly trivial; "trivial" because it is humor, and "trivial" because it concerns the lives and perspectives of women. A popular and contemporary evaluation of parody in Parker's work may have also yielded a similar verdict. For instance, in 1936 Max Eastman wrote that "the easiest way to make things laughable is to exaggerate to the point of absurdity their salient traits"; and for this reason, parody "ought to be judged more severely than other comic forms."[8] Much of Parker's work fails to be ranked with such texts as Joyce's *Ulysses*, or T. S. Eliot's *The Wasteland*, texts that began to complicate the use of the simple parody condemned by Eastman. Critics and reviewers who classify Parker's work as "light verse," or "prose squibs" also suggest that there is a categorical simplicity to her work. Parker, however, self-consciously adopts and deploys such critical opinion of parody and women's writing in poems such as "For a Lady Who Must Write Verse," in which she cautions "ladies" to "Show your quick, alarming skill in / Tidy mockeries of art" (238). Critics who emphasize Parker's acerbity and satire tend to see Parker's parodic strategies according to Eastman's views; however, when they conflate parody with the type of burlesque that emphasizes mockery or ridicule, rather than the production of comic effect, they are guilty of what Margaret Rose characterizes as the "modernist reduction." Modernist treatment of parody often splits off parody's critical aim (to attack an "original" or "authoritative" text) from its artistic function (to "transform it into something new" through "heightening" of imitation).[9] The parody in Parker's work does not exclusively mock or ridicule; rather, it may also be understood to "transform" our ways of thinking about gender.

For there is more at stake here than an attempt to overturn accepted, sometimes stodgy critical mandates. Parker's short fiction may be read in part as gender parody, enacted through masks and the strategies of literary satire and parody. Through influential investigations of masquerade, identity and such theorists as Jacques Lacan, Joan Riviere, Michel Foucault, and Nietzsche, Judith Butler develops the idea of gender parody, or the performative constitution of gender through various strategies of imitation and exaggeration. Based on a careful and complicated reading of the history and genealogy of the idea of gender, Butler writes:

> Hence, within the inherited discourse of the metaphysics of substance, gender proves to be performative—that is, constituting the identity it is purported to be. In this sense, gender is always a doing, though not a doing by a subject who might be said to preexist the deed. . . . In an application that Nietzsche himself would not have anticipated or condoned, we might state as a corollary: There is no gender identity behind the expression of gender; that identity is performatively constituted by the very "expressions" that are said to be its results.[10]

Although Butler takes poetic license with certain portions of Nietzsche's *On the Genealogy of Morals*, her formulation of gender parody is understandable as a rethinking of identity. In such parody, "female" characters and voices play women as they are culturally understood in any given social, historical, or political context. Such playing is fundamentally dramatic, in the sense that characters adopt different roles, or don different masks. The "little woman" figure noted by women's humor scholar Nancy Walker is one type of mask that we may see constructed (or we may construct) in Parker's texts. The " 'little woman' who finds herself absurd in a world which presumably makes sense to someone else"[11] may also be said to describe those female characters who mask a variety of fundamental uncertainties in an exaggerated "littleness" or "bigness." Female characters also mask themselves through their cynical and sometimes melancholy appropriation of themes of dying and death. Indeed, in Parker's fiction and poetry, there is a sense of claustrophobia in the either/or choice of living or dying that is directly linked to the either/or choice of being one's gender, as opposed to playing one's gender.

In fact, much of Parker's humor draws its strength from both whimsical and cynical fantasies of escape through death. The way out of the claustrophobia or trap of suffering is death; the way out of the seesaw of gender avowal and disavowal is nihilism. If Parker's characters are trapped in someone else's dictates of what the female "is," then their misery and isolation in what Butler refers to as the "heterosexual matrix of desire"[12] may be summarily stopped by going through the black door. On a biographical level, the idea of death does for Parker what the idea of life as a woman could not— she becomes one of the tormented but living dead, and therefore, possibly, one of the Romantic (and thus serious, literary) suffering artists. Joan Riviere argues that "women who wish for masculinity may put on a mask of womanliness to avert anxiety and the retribution feared from men";[13] or, as Butler explains it, the woman masquerades "knowingly in order to conceal her masculinity from the masculine audience she wants to castrate."[14] Similarly, the woman in masquerade may wish for masculinity "in order to engage in public discourse with men and as a man as part of a male homoerotic exchange."[15] However, if the masquerade of femininity fails in some way, or if the woman feels trapped by it, she may be tempted to annihilate both mask and wearer through death—or, what is more telling, through the masquerade of death. Suicide, or more precisely, dying, rather than living as a woman, allows her to engage in the "public discourse" of such mythos as that of the troubled artist. However, the paths through such a mythos are grounded in that same attempt to "be" what one is essentially only acting. I will thus trace the ways in which Parker effects this attempt in three of her most widely anthologized stories, as well as consider the types of parody by which she tries to undermine this attempt.

Published in January 1928, "A Telephone Call" is one of Parker's first critically acclaimed monologues, particularly interesting because it has been and still may be read as satirizing social norms (namely, showing the silliness of women's dependencies). Along with "Big Blonde," this was the only other prose piece by Parker to be published in the *Bookman*, a literary magazine reputed for its selection of only the most promising artistic works. Seward Collins, editor of the *Bookman* and "discriminating patron of the arts," was struck by Parker's growing reputation as a wit and conversationalist.[16]

The title of the story is misleading, for what occurs in the story is not a conversation by telephone, but a discourse on such a call. The text begins with a less than stately invocation: "Please, God, let him telephone me *now*" (119). The speaker of/in the text bargains with God throughout the piece, and one of her deals is to wait and to count. The monologue thus "ends" with the count, "Five, ten, fifteen, twenty, twenty-five, thirty, thirty-five . . ." (124). The speaker must wait for a call indefinitely, because, by the rules of (gendered) social etiquette, she cannot make the call herself. At one point, the speaker remarks:

> I know you shouldn't keep telephoning them—I know they don't like that. When you do that, they know you are thinking about them and wanting them, and that makes them hate you. But I hadn't talked to him in three days—not in three days. And all I did was ask him how he was; it was just the way anybody might have called him up. (119)

The ambivalence toward being a woman—when it means "performing" as a woman—comes in the statement of these rules. After the invocation and the decision to count comes the first "law" of social etiquette. You (as a woman) should not telephone men, for "When you do that, they know you are thinking about them and wanting them, and that makes them hate you" (119). In fact, the entire paragraph centers on the statement of this rule and of the speaker's attempt to justify her violation of that rule. Technically, there is no direct expression of her desire; her wish is to "let him telephone her," to be wanted, not to want. The frantic excuse, "but I hadn't talked to him in three days—not in three days," only emphasizes the fact that her desire has not diminished.

The statements of "rules" begin to splinter off into the speaker's own self-regulatory, imperative statements: "I must stop this. I mustn't be this way" (120). Soon enough, however, she returns to rule making:

> They don't like you to tell them they've made you cry. They don't like you to tell them you're unhappy because of them. If you do, they think you're possessive and exacting. And then they hate you. They hate you whenever you say anything you really think. You always have to keep playing little games. (122)

The speaker's words echo, foreshadow, and feed into the experiences of Hazel Morse in "Big Blonde." She spends her nights out with men, who "liked you because you were fun. . . . Men liked a good sport" (187). They are repeated in the thoughts of the wife of the soldier in "The Lovely Leave"; in writing letters to the husband, "there had been rules to be learned . . . and the first of them was the hardest: never say to him what you want him to say to you" (5).

In addition to the sin of being a "bad sport," there is thus the commandment to play "little games." Not only are true communion or expression denied the speaker through the absence of the phone call, but such expression is not permitted, not possible. The speaker thought that she could avoid the "game." "I thought this was so big I could say whatever I meant," she says, but then concludes, "I guess you can't, ever. I guess there isn't ever anything big enough for that" (122). The comic effect here results from the parody of the love story cliché: "This thing is bigger than the both of us." The speaker wryly implies that it is the man who is not "big enough." The "little games" indeed may be understood as the whole set of rules and expectations that comes with a woman's performance of her sex and gender. To cite them this way, and to wistfully pine for the thing that is "bigger," are both statements of desire, however comic or undermined by cliché. It is, in capsule, the expression of the ambivalence of being or acting the woman (whom you dislike and see as sham), of feeling/being the woman who desires (and who you wish could truly express this desire).

However, the "little games" and the failure of expression bring us back to the consideration of language and the third type of cue for laughter, which is also the third "clue" of gender. In her rhetorical and linguistic analysis of "The Waltz," Paula Treichler cites Robin Lakoff's notion of "women's speech"; "It is full of what Lakoff describes as 'trivializing' words like 'adore' and 'thrilled' and intensifiers like 'really,' 'truly,' and especially 'so'—'*thank you so much.*'"[17] "A Telephone Call" is a monologue of less than six pages, and the speaker uses the word "little" at least twenty-one times. Its usage varies, but as the single most repeated word in "A Telephone Call," it indicates that "little" games are indeed being played. Such exaggerated use of a trivializing word calls attention to the constructedness of this woman's discourse.

The realm of women's experience has traditionally fallen into the cultural category of the minor, the trivial, the "little." The speaker's use of the word "little" therefore becomes a linguistic mask of changing features; it is the essence of contradiction and ambivalence, and of conformity and solidarity (with other women). It is an ironic weapon used in anger against authority, and it is a satiric imitation of the facades women use to fool themselves. Mostly, however, it is part of a larger strategy that employs exaggerated imitation (including the parody of clichéd discourse) for comic effect to render in language the experience of being a woman.

Norris Yates calls Dorothy Parker's women "idle" and "middleclass" as the counterpart to Ring Lardner's "idle middle-class man." The comparison, besides being a part of the larger agenda to construct a legible history of American humor, illustrates a conception of the "trivial" common to modern criticism. Yates writes that

Parker's "frequent use of the diary form, the monologue, and trivial dialogue" is what "invites" comparison to Lardner's "idle" man. What exactly does such a "trivial dialogue" consist of, and why are the uses of these forms the mark of an "idle" woman? The assumption is that such women are free from the economic pressures of work, and thus may devote time to such "trivial" (read nonproductive, nonskilled, or nonprofessional) activities as personal autobiography and talking. Not that Yates is necessarily critical of such subjects; he writes, "Sometimes her idle, middle-class females are smug and aggressive; sometimes they are pathetic like Lardner's victims'; sometimes both. Occasionally, they are more amusing than anything else."[18]

"Amusing" is a telling word. It is precisely the "amusement" that such "idle" people seek; it may be, after all, the chief reason we read humorists. To be fair, Yates is simply representative of critical and popular reception of Dorothy Parker up to the late sixties and the first feminist reevaluation of her work. Yates's review is not wholly dismissive after all; he recognizes a "darker vein" in "The Waltz" and "The Little Hours," in which "the two main characters are self-victimized by their own giddiness and lack of perspective."[19] Yet again, to read "The Waltz" as a drama of self-victimization is perhaps even more disturbing than its lighthearted dismissal as "trivial." Clearly, it's time we look at Parker's most noted "dialogue" through other theoretical lenses.

Simply put, "The Waltz" continues the same situational, thematic, and linguistic concerns of "A Telephone Call," and, to a lesser extent, the other "monologues" in the Parker canon. However, "The Waltz" is unique because it is neither truly a "dialogue," such as that occurring in "Here We Are," "New York to Detroit," or "Too Bad," nor is it a "monologue" in the style or form of "The Little Hours," or even "Just a Little One," in which the main character addresses another (implied) character. Instead, "The Waltz" is a stylized representation of a dialogue; as such, its italicized (spoken) language is opposed to the plain text interior monologue of the speaker. The formal duality, of course, repeats the ambivalence of being a woman, donning a mask, or performing a gender. Paula Treichler writes that the monologues "seem to offer the speaker a space where she may assert and preserve her private self." The italicized language, such as "*Oh no, no, no. Goodness, no. It didn't hurt the least little bit*" is meant, by implication, to represent the public self, or as Treichler explains it, a "functional commercial language which takes no risks and gives nothing away." It "very much represents a language of female survival."[20] While, as may be predictable,

Treichler argues that this opposition is eventually undermined (and, as I shall maintain, unambiguously questioned from the first), it is the *idea* of a duality, a masquerade, and a well-marked linguistic separation that renders such terms as "trivial dialogue" grossly misleading. That this "dialogue" occurs on a dance floor (the site of middle-class, "idle" activities, the realm of middle-class women's glories and defeats) comes to imply that the performance is a battle and is fought on the first and only ground where it may be conducted and fought. As such, the speaker reinvests the space of "leisure" time engagements with political significance.

Treichler states that a "continual subversion" of what is spoken by what is felt is undermined "dramatically" by a sudden outburst four-fifths of the way through the story.[21] In this interior exclamation, the speaker says, "I hate this creature I'm chained to. I hated him the moment I saw his leering, bestial face. And here I've been locked in his noxious embrace for the thirty-five years this waltz has lasted" (50). Treichler claims that "whatever restraints the story's comic function may have imposed upon its language, they are broken by these harsh and violent images."[22] Yet, actually, the first "harsh" remark made in the story is an unequivocal, "I don't want to dance with him," followed by the "deathly" allusion to his dancing as "something you do on Saint Walpurgis Night" (47). Several paragraphs before we arrive at her confession of hate, he kicks her and she exclaims, "Ow!" and calls him an "idiot" (48), and a few paragraphs later, a "hulking peasant" (49). Treichler also notes that the expression, "thirty-five years" is "too literal," concluding that it is actually a reference to the "thirty-five years she has spent chained to her own body."[23] She claims that there is a "shift" from the "old, easy humor" of the monologue in which exaggerations are common. However, this "shift" is dubious, since, in the very same paragraph in which she declares her hatred, the speaker is still using loose hyperbole. Her dance partner does a step that requires "two stumbles, slip, and a twenty-yard dash" (50). And, in the very next monologue, she is complaining about her decision to go on waltzing "throughout eternity," and wondering if she won't notice "after the first hundred thousand years" (50). In short, Treichler may be constructing a specific climactic "point" where there is none; the violence, opposition, and "subversion" are necessarily more diffuse.

On the whole, however, Treichler's 1980 study of "The Waltz" contains some important feminist rhetorical and linguistic insights. She chooses to see it as satire rather than parody, arguing that the text "simultaneously satirizes ritualized social interaction and embodies it," when perhaps it is more accurate to see this as parody's incorporation of the original discourse of women's trivial speech. Treichler does, however, note specific instances of parody in the monologue ("Oh!" in the dialogue becomes "Ow!" in the monologue), and makes a valuable reference to Robin Lakoff's work in "women's speech."[24] But it is important to remember that "The Waltz" employs situational, thematic, and linguistic parody that leads to both the questioning of gender and the comic refunctioning of preformed languages. "The Waltz" does parody an excessive femininity, but even more to the point, it sets up, maintains, and deconstructs an illusion of duality. The idea of a monologue in which only "true" expression occurs (what the speaker "really thinks") is an outright, even if comforting, ruse.

Granted, the situational humor of "The Waltz" already implies that the woman's unique experience is hardly what is at issue; as in "A Telephone Call," readers laugh at least in part because all language—whether private or public, false or true—is *their* language. Treichler and other feminist rhetoricians and linguists have written about women's struggle with a "borrowed" language, but "A Waltz" foregrounds the possibility of a personal, if not unique language, while simultaneously denying it. Compared to the pedestrian, frilly "spoken" discourse of "Why, I think it's more of a waltz," and "*you're just being sweet, to say that*," the language or the monologue is solid, literate, and clever. It is also unadornedly expressive. "I wonder what I'd better do—kill him this instant, with my naked hands, or wait and let him drop in his traces," she says after receiving a kick in the shin (48). The anger is personal, unique, and yet the phrase, "with my naked hands" is borrowed, echoing a score of other graphic metaphors, such as "in cold blood," or "point blank." The monologue, then, repeats the other extreme of the hyperbolic range, parodying "masculine" language just as the dialogue does so with "feminine" language. With no purely monologic speech, but only the imitation of such speech, it becomes harder to identify the true and discrete, private self. On the one hand, we might conclude that a careful study of both "The Waltz" and "A Telephone Call" leads us to no "real" woman speaking, but only to a series of parodic comments and borrowed languages that masquerade as unique personal thought and feeling. On the other hand, we must surely admit that the illusion of duality is a successful one. When the speaker of "The Waltz" poses the rhetorical question, "What can you say, when a man asks you to dance with him?" she presumes both an already determined answer and the lack of one. Whatever she decides to say, she has already set up a formal duality between what she says to the reader (the illusion of pure being), and what she says to her dance partner (the illusion of pure performance). More radically, the choice between an answer dictated and no answer at all posits a subject who is already there to make the choice—not one who is constituted by the choosing itself.

Thematically, Dorothy Parker's "Big Blonde" (1929) is a sequel to "A Telephone Call" and "The Waltz." When critics and biographers turn to a discussion of "Big Blonde," they usually hail it as her most "serious" accomplishment in the short story, and go one step further to cite Parker's own pride at finally doing something artistic and lasting. By implication, "Big Blonde" represents the antithesis and the antidote to Parker's rash of "cuteness" and "smartness" that she believed plagued her early career and the decade of the twenties in general. By modern critical standards, "Big Blonde" undoubtedly raised Parker's reputation in the literary world, even overcoming the stigma of the more trivial of her verses and chatty prose pieces.

Yet, ironically, the very same themes or discourses of her most trivial pieces continue in this story. Paula Treichler writes that in Parker's monologues, "the first-person pronoun seems to act as magnet for dense clusters of parody and wisecracking; hence, I believe, her desire later to move away from soliloquies and satiric conversation that had made her reputation as a writer of fiction."[25] The parody and wisecracking nevertheless appear in "Big Blonde," although it is muted in keeping with the often muted actions and being of the story's female protagonist. Moreover, "Big Blonde" works as metafictional parody; it is a story about the story of gender, or rather, a discursive act about acting and "being."

The first signs of this parody are embedded in titular forms. The "Big Blonde" in this story is Hazel Morse, the "large, fair woman of the type that incites some men when they use the word 'blonde' to click their tongues and wag their heads roguishly" (187). From the very first, however, she tries to be or act the "little" part (187); and, once more, the "little games" of "A Telephone Call" continue. She takes pride in small feet, and "boxes" them in "snub-toed, high-heeled slippers of the shortest bearable size" (187). Her first name, "Hazel," neatly and poetically indicates the manner in which she lives. She remembers little, her "old days . . . a blurred and flickering sequence" (187), and once her alcoholism begins, she cannot "recall the definite day that she started drinking" (191). She "lived in a haze" of her drinking (193), or "in her mist" (197) of whisky-induced peace.

Yet even before Hazel finds her "haze," her life is divided into the familiar duality of "The Waltz" and "A Telephone Call." The activities of public life are as vapid as the words of the female dancer to her male partner. She models dresses and meets "numbers of men" with whom she spends "numbers of evenings . . . laughing at their jokes and telling them she loved their neckties" (18). Hazel thus learns the "rules" of being a woman: "men liked you because you were fun," and takes for granted that "the liking of many men was a desirable thing" (187). Unlike the speaker in "The Waltz," she lacks the sharp and literate parodies of quotations, or even the voicings of desperate desires in her time alone. She finds "no other form of diversion," and her "ideas, or, better, her acceptances, ran right along with those of the other substantially built blondes in whom she found her friends" (187). From the beginning, the narrative suggests that in place of a monologue, a private life, or some sort of marker of a "true" woman there is only a cipher, a blank space—perhaps just a "haze."

But because this is, after all, a narrative, things happen, time passes, and pressure is placed on the cipher of Hazel's private life. She begins to want things—to "be married" for instance, and to free herself from the "good sport" role. Yet even this desire seems less than genuine, and the "oh-such-a-pretty-picture" description of the couple's new apartment once again confirms that Hazel is engaged in a marriage game, rather than a love relationship. Instead, the emotions that seem to mark her being rather than her acting are the tears she expends for "kidnapped babies, deserted wives, unemployed men," and the like (189). The narrative weaves back for a moment and we learn that "even in her good sport days, she had been known to weep lavishly and disinterestedly" (189). This sophisticated turn from linear progression does two things: first, it confirms the illusion of duality between being and acting; and second, it complicates it, hinting that this crying is itself part of her act. To her friends in these "good sport" days, "her behavior at the theater was a standing joke" (189).

As the narrative progresses, the disparity between what is expected of her (husband, lovers, and friends tell her to "cheer up," be a "good sport" throughout the entire story) and what she feels becomes increasingly obvious. But no sooner do we recognize a "private" life or being than we find her plunged back into the fog: "She could not recall the definite day that she started drinking herself. There was nothing separate about her days. Like drops upon a window-pane, they ran together and trickled away" (191).

But while she is still in her comfortable haze of nonbeing, Hazel begins to think of death. She plays "voluptuously with the thought of cool, sleepy retreat," just as she had "coquetted" with the "idea" of being a bride (201). What begins to emerge is that her ideas are indeed chosen but misted over, and that her marriage, her drinking, and her attempted suicide are acts just as artificial as her much-deplored acting for men. She fails at all her acts, and her acts fail her. What is left, but the "hazy" decision to take up more acts? Her overdose of Veronal tablets merely angers a neighboring doctor at the necessity of having to pump her stomach. The maid's discovery of Hazel's overdose is far less exciting than is the thought that she can tell the doctor it's a "matter of life and death," which phrase she has plumbed from the shallow depths of her "thin store of reading" (207). The final moment of irony is almost anticlimactic; once Hazel has awakened from two days of unattractive stupor, her maid gives her a drink and tells her to "cheer up" (210).

The act of attempted suicide fails to free her from the duality of performance and being. The disturbing suggestion is that there is nothing to do, to "be" other than involved in acts, in this illusion of schism. The very pressure of the narrative upon Hazel (really to *be* someone) manifests itself at certain points in the cycle—when she "becomes" a bride, when she begins to cry, drink, act as a good sport, and, finally, when she tries to kill herself. The failure of these pressure points is actually the failure to fill up the blank space of her private life, to decipher the cipher. The doctor graphically illustrates the action of this cyclic pressure when he "plunged his thumbs into the lidded pits" above the comatose Hazel's eyeballs "and threw his weight upon them" (207). But Hazel gives "no sign under the pressure." She remains a cipher, or a selfless mound of flesh, with "thick, white legs" (207) and "flabby arms" (187) that will not die and will not wake up. In fact, at this moment in the narrative, the antics of those who try to revive her are bluntly comical. The doctor's plunging effort is met by a cry from the maid, but the elevator attendant watches the action and "chuckles"; "Look like he tryin' to push her right on th'ough the bed" (207). The doctor pinches the back of Hazel's legs with "long, cruel nips," but in answer to the maid's worried cry, "She won't die on me, will she?", the doctor states categorically, "God, no. You couldn't kill her with an ax" (208).

Dorothy Parker's turn to narrative form and the artistry of "Big Blonde" may be understood as the attempt to end her role as entertainer, or wit. Hazel Morse, and the speakers in "The Waltz" and "A Telephone Call," all seem ensnared in Fanny Brice's dilemma of "being":

Being a funny person does an awful lot of things to you. You feel that you mustn't get serious with people. They don't expect it from you, and they don't want to see it. You're not entitled to be serious, you're a clown, and they only want you to make them laugh.[26]

"Big Blonde" is not a "funny" story, but neither is it devoid of the type of gallows humor that appears throughout Parker's poetry. As if to emphasize that the comedy never ends (and, analogously, the performance of gender), Hazel lies down—to die laughing. "Guess I'll go to bed," she says, and then rhymes, "Gee, I'm nearly dead" (205). She quotes herself before slipping off into her coma, and comments, "That's a hot one!" (205).

Death in the Parker canon is, at its simplest, an escape from the act. In "Big Blonde," death is parodied, and literally "poked" fun at in the somnolent, drugged body of Hazel Morse. Biographers of Parker usually mention her penchant for collecting undertakers' magazines, and critics just as often point out that she derived her characters' names from obituary columns.[27] As she considers the idea of suicide, Hazel feels a "cozy solidarity with the big company of the voluntary dead" (201). Her final wisecrack to herself undermines the seriousness of death, paving the way to that "company" in comfort. Hazel's rhyme of "bed" and "dead" is reminiscent of many of Parker's verses, but it is also typical of the "gallows humor" discussed by Freud in his *Jokes and Their Relation to the Unconscious.* The man who jokes about catching cold from a bare neck as he walks to his execution exhibits a kind of "magnanimity" in his "*blague,*" and in his "tenacious hold upon his customary self and his disregard of what might overthrow that self and drive it to despair."[28] Hazel's recognition of the comic in the moments preceding what she thinks will be her death does reveal a kind of strength, perhaps even a glimmer of that "tenacious hold" on her "customary self." She finally is able to voluntarily amuse herself (albeit with her "voluntary" death), rather than be forced to amuse others.

And yet, as it is suggested in the story, even death is unreliable and no sure escape from the endless performance of gender. The deaths of women remain problematic. Once dead, they still cannot escape their gender, and, worse yet, they become symbols of "feminine" tragedy. Hazel's "decision" to face death gives us a sense—or perhaps illusion—of a true self as long as we index this self by her agency or ability to act on her own desires. But as Sandra Gilbert and Susan Gubar have discussed in regard to classical paragons of female power and aggression, the "female will-to-battle" is "historically rooted in male ideas about female sexuality, specially in the male notion that dead women are desirable and live women should not desire."[29] The idea that women should not desire (should not

tell "what they really think") is a familiar refrain in Parker dialogues, monologues, and narratives. In "Big Blonde," there are also
subtle suggestions of male necrophilia, as when the elevator boy encounters Hazel and prods her body "so lustily that he left marks in
the soft flesh" (206). But for the most part, the picture of the
"dead" woman is far from desirable:

> Mrs. Morse lay on her back, one flabby arm flung up, the wrist against
> her forehead. Her stiff hair hung untenderly along her face. The bed
> covers were pushed down, exposing a deep square of soft neck and a
> pink nightgown, its fabric worn uneven by many launderings; her great
> breasts, freed from their tight confines, sagged beneath her arm-pits.
> Now and then she made knotted, snoring sounds, and from the corner
> of her opened mouth to the blurred turn of her jaw ran a lane of crusted
> spittle. (206)

Women's sarcasm, cynicism, and parody in Parker seem to suggest
one thing: the desire for death goes hand in hand with the type of
debilitating desire for men that leaves women vulnerable to the ridiculous, or, in the case of Hazel Morse, the outright grotesque. In
service to this desire, Parker's women play by the rules, play "real"
women. However, as long as women define these acts as types of
being, then the only way out is through acts of "nonbeing." The
comic failure of the acts of being and dying is not an occasion for
self-mockery or ridicule, but for self-assessment.

Notes

1. Alan Rudolph, director, *Mrs. Parker and the Vicious Circle.* Screenplay by Alan
Rudolph and Randy Sue Coburn. New Line (Fine Line Features), 1994.

2. John Keats, *You Might as Well Live: The Life and Times of Dorothy Parker* (1970;
repr., New York: Paragon House, 1986), 126.

3. Ibid., 58.

4. Ibid., 90–91.

5. Randall Calhoun, *Dorothy Parker: A Bio-Bibliography* (Westport, CT: Greenwood, 1993), 13.

6. Dorothy Parker, "The Siege of Madrid," in *The Portable Dorothy Parker* (New
York: Viking, 1973), 589. Further references to Parker's work will be to this edition
by page number in the text.

7. Calhoun, 13.

8. Max Eastman, *The Enjoyment of Laughter* (New York: Simon, 1936), 156.

9. Margaret A. Rose, *Parody: Ancient, Modern, and Post-Modern* (Cambridge: Cambridge University Press, 1993), 172–73.

10. Judith Butler, *Gender Trouble: Feminism and the Subversion of Identity* (New York:
Routledge, 1990), 24–25.

11. Nancy Walker, "'Fragile and Dumb': The 'Little Woman' in Woman's Humor, 1900–1940," *Thalia* 5.2 (1982–83): 24–29.

12. Butler, 53.

13. Joan Riviere, "Womanliness as Masquerade," in Victor Burgin, James Donald, and Cora Kaplan, eds., *Formations of Fantasy* (London: Methuen, 1986), 35.

14. Butler, 52.

15. Ibid., 52.

16. Keats, 105. A few years later, Collins was also "struck" by Parker herself and traveled to Europe with her.

17. Paula A. Treichler, "Verbal Subversions in Dorothy Parker: 'Trapped Like a Trap in a Trap,'" *Language and Style* 13.4 (Fall 1980): 50.

18. Norris W. Yates, *The American Humorist: Conscience of the Twentieth Century* (Ames: Iowa State University Press, 1964), 266.

19. Yates, 269.

20. Treichler, 51, 58.

21. Ibid., 53.

22. Ibid., 53.

23. Ibid., 55.

24. Ibid., 59, 50–51.

25. Ibid., 59.

26. Regina Barreca, *They Used to Call Me Snow White . . . But I Drifted* (New York: Viking, 1991), 29–30.

27. Treichler, 55.

28. Sigmund Freud, *Jokes and Their Relation to the Unconscious*, ed. and trans. by James Strachey (New York: Norton, 1963), 229.

29. Sandra M. Gilbert and Susan Gubar, *No Man's Land: The Place of the Woman Writer in the Twentieth Century, vol. 1, The War of the Words* (New Haven: Yale University Press, 1987), 6.

Female Trouble: Dorothy Parker, Katherine Anne Porter, and Alcoholism

Ellen Lansky

> Oh, I should like to ride the seas,
> A roaring buccaneer;
> A cutlass banging at my knees,
> A dirk behind my ear. . . .
>
> My slaves I'd like to bind with thongs
> That cut and burn and chill. . . .
> But I am writing little songs,
> As little ladies will.
> —Dorothy Parker, from "Song of Perfect Propriety"

Aلthough they had many mutual friends and they both enjoyed the high regard of the U.S. literati, Dorothy Parker and Katherine Anne Porter were never friends nor even cordial acquaintances. They both preferred the company of men, even though this company often left them in a solitary and precarious social position. Despite their mutual disregard, it is worth considering their work together not simply because they shared a social circle but because they wrote about a shared social problem. An intertextual reading of Dorothy Parker's "Big Blonde" and Katherine Anne Porter's *Ship of Fools* brings together the authors and their fiction over a common complex: alcoholism and the "female troubles" that they encounter as they try to negotiate a life for themselves in a culture that asks them, as heterosexual women, to subordinate their bodies, desires, and aspirations to their male partners.

"Big Blonde," *Ship of Fools,* and the authors are linked through three key themes. First, though they subscribed to heterosexual norms—such as marriage—neither Porter nor Parker nor their alcoholic women characters were able to find long-term husbands or even reliable male partners.[1] The derision and disapprobation that the two characters endure as alcoholics and as improperly married women compounds their female troubles. Second, both Parker and

Porter establish a relationship among the alcoholic female protagonist, the disapproving narrator, and the reader. Michel Foucault's "Panopticism" chapter of *Discipline and Punish* provides a paradigm for investigating this relationship: the male partner and the reader are the inspectors in the Panopticon; the woman alcoholic is the watched inmate in the cell. Third, both texts link the woman alcoholic's experiences with drinking, powerlessness, and surveillance to a familiar feminist figure: the Madwoman in the Attic. The alcoholic woman's madness is exacerbated by the panoptic gaze, a gaze that seeks to control and punish her. In both stories, the alcoholic heterosexual women characters respond to the panoptic gaze through self-destructive or violent acts. The lives of the authors suggest at least one alternative to divert the panoptic gaze and avoid these violent or self-destructive responses.

FEMALE TROUBLE NO. 1: GENDER ROLES AND ALCOHOLISM

The alcoholic woman is a subversive figure in modern fiction and culture. She is subversive for many reasons. One reason is that she disrupts a paradigm in the culture of alcohol. In this model, the husband/man is the alcoholic, and the wife/woman is the accomplice. The alcoholic's role is to try to drink to excess with no negative consequences, and the accomplice's job is to invent and circulate stories and behaviors that repress, explain, excuse, and/or deny the alcoholic's drinking and the havoc it creates in the relationship. The criminal connotations of the word *accomplice* are inevitable. Nevertheless, this word emphasizes the aiding and abetting nature of the relationship between alcoholics and their partners. *Webster's Unabridged Dictionary*'s second definition of *accomplice* is "an associate in any undertaking." This meaning of accomplice also permits one to avoid the unstable term *codependency*.[2]

The alcoholic woman thus finds herself in a confused and sometimes dangerous position as she transgresses her traditional role as accomplice—a position marked female—and occupies the male-marked alcoholic position. Moreover, as heterosexual alcoholic woman *writers*, Parker and Porter were pulled by several strong opposing cultural imperatives for modern women. One imperative directed them to conform to certain traditional female roles: that they would find husbands and be wives. A second, contradictory imperative directed both women to take power positions as professional writers who commanded a salary and an audience. In both instances a woman has to subvert gender expectations to take this position.

Since being subversive was not considered an appropriate female action, Parker and Porter frequently earned the disapproval of at least one person—usually a husband or lover. Their relationships with the men in their lives were a bewildering mix of writing talent, alcohol, and power struggles.

Katherine Anne Porter's relationship with Eugene Dove Pressly was volatile from the beginning. She was reluctant to marry him because she knew that becoming Mrs. Pressly, the wife, would leave her with less time and space to develop her identity and career as Katherine Anne Porter, the professional writer. Pressly was keen to marry her and become the husband of the relationship, the man of the house. They spent some time together in Germany in 1931, drinking and fighting. Porter later told Enrique Hank Lopez, "I guess I was drinking more than was good for me . . . so I had to get away from there."[3] Pressly left for a job in Madrid. Joan Givner reports that "although Pressly's departure made it easier for her to work, she felt acute dismay at seeing him go, and remained during the whole of her time in Berlin ambivalent both about him and about the idea of marriage."[4] Despite her misgivings, she finally married Pressly, but marriage did not stabilize their relationship; rather, it magnified their gender and power conflicts. Givner reports that Pressly "admired her work but resented her absorption in it and eventually formed the habit of drinking while she wrote. He did, however, look after her devotedly."[5] Givner's description constructs Pressly as a drinking, petulant mate—a bad housewife who recalls certain depictions of Zelda Fitzgerald. Evidently, it was not a role that Eugene Dove Pressly, a handsome young man, wanted to play. By 1936, Givner claims that "the marriage was slowly but surely disintegrating," and on 1 April 1937 Pressly left for a job in Venezuela.[6] This job promised him a position as a man of affairs, a (powerful) white, middle-class male ambassador from the United States in a developing country, rather than a fishwife/housewife. Pressly's move was, in effect, the end of their marriage.

As partners, Pressly and Porter were similar to Alan Campbell and Dorothy Parker. Parker was eleven years older than the handsome Campbell. Campbell was as devoted to Parker as Eugene Pressly initially was to Porter. When she married Alan Campbell, most aspects of Dorothy Parker's life were in chaos. She seemed utterly incapable of taking care of herself. By contrast, Alan Campbell, as Parker's biographer Marion Meade reports, was utterly capable: "Having grown up with drinking parents, he instinctively understood that in these situations, somebody had to be responsible and usually it was himself. He knew what Dorothy badly needed was somebody to take care of her, and Alan took great pleasure in being a manager."[7]

Campbell's role as Dorothy Parker's manager/wife expanded when they moved to Hollywood. He became Dorothy Parker's screenwriting partner. He also became her drinking partner. Campbell's increasing drinking may have been a response to Dorothy Parker's insinuations that Campbell was gay, which, as Meade notes, was "the worst insult for Alan" that Dorothy Parker could concoct.[8] Perhaps he felt that drinking heavily proved that he was a John Barleycorn, rough-drinking heterosexual sort of man.[9] It is likely that Parker's drinking and pestering plus Campbell's increasing drinking and then his enlistment in the army hastened their divorce in 1947. Campbell then claimed to have fallen in love with a woman in England, which would have extricated him from his confused relationship with Parker and also demonstrated his heterosexuality.[10] Three years later, Parker and Campbell remarried. They resumed their roles as drinking partners, screenwriting collaborators, and domestic partners. Dorothy Parker was still the alcoholic/famous professional writer/husband and Alan Campbell was the drinking accomplice/wife—dependent on his husband's talent, celebrity, and connections. In his article "Whatever You Think Dorothy Parker Was Like, She Wasn't," Wyatt Cooper describes the confusing nature of their relationship: "It was an extraordinary one, incredibly close, each strongly identifying with the other, but also mutually antagonistic and somehow fearful and bitter toward the other."[11] It was neither productive nor safe for either partner. Alan Campbell's drinking concerned Dorothy Parker because it "made him aggressive, sloppy and sullen."[12] His drinking interfered with hers. They drank and fought and split up and got back together and drank and fought and wrote screenplays together. Finally, in a scene that anticipates *Valley of the Dolls*, Alan Campbell drank too much alcohol and ate too many Seconal pills and died on 14 June 1963.[13]

Both Parker and Porter found husbands, but neither one was willing to give up her writing career and devote herself entirely to her home and husband. In their relationships with husbands Eugene Pressly and Alan Campbell, Porter and Parker, respectively, upset the traditional alcoholic husband man/accomplice wife woman paradigm positions. Moreover, as professional writers able to command audiences and incomes, they also occupied the economic power position in the relationship, the one traditionally reserved for the husband. Both Campbell and Pressly were ultimately unhappy in their subordinate wife roles and both eventually took action to reverse these roles and resume their privileged positions as men in the culture. In these volatile relationships, each partner was unable to accommodate the other's needs, and apparently no one was willing to give up his or her desire to control and manipulate the other. All partners drank, which only worsened their problems. When marriage failed to make wives out of Parker and Porter, the relationships failed as well.

In their lives, Dorothy Parker and Katherine Anne Porter found themselves in a strange place on their culture's gender map: expected to look and act like women and write like men. Having internalized "writer" and "alcoholic" as masculine identities, they asserted their femininity in their outward appearance. They became female drag queens: women impersonating men in drag. Parker was attentive to her public ensembles and accessories: jewelry, furs, hats, a charming little dog, and even though she was myopic—no glasses. Givner notes that poets such as Dylan Thomas, Karl Shapiro, and Raymond Roseliep wrote poetic tributes to Porter's womanly beauty, but that Porter "sensed there was something demeaning in the worshipful adoration of a certain brand of sycophant."[14] Nevertheless, when Porter made public appearances, she dressed in high femme style: "she wore gorgeous dresses, added long evening gloves, large picture hats, and corsages as big as cabbages."[15] Both women perfected a sort of command performance of femininity for an audience of men while simultaneously performing masculinity in the arena of writing and drinking.

Further complicating these cultural imperatives and paradigms is that both women's literary status combined with their drinking abilities enabled them to have "homosocial" drinking relationships with other drinking men. As Hemingway's drinking buddy was Fitzgerald, Porter's was Hart Crane, and Parker's was Robert Benchley. Dorothy Parker's public drinking and her heterosexual preference placed her almost exclusively in the company of men, and in a way, she became one. The screenwriter Wyatt Cooper wrote in an *Esquire* article that he liked her because he felt he could talk to her "man to man."[16] Katherine Anne Porter apparently had a long history of getting drunk and making passes at young men. In her later years, when she was living in a duplex with Rhea Johnson as her neighbor, "she was invited to a party downstairs, drank too much, and made advances to the young man (Rhea Johnson), calling him Adam, the hero of 'Pale Horse, Pale Rider.'"[17] The Southern belle was also a dirty old man. But while they were respected as writers and drinkers—one of the guys—they were still expected to conform to modern notions of appropriate behavior for heterosexual women. Their male drinking buddies, lovers, editors, publishers, and acquaintances expected them to be capable of expressing appropriately both male and female behaviors. These expectations put immense pressure on both women—who were simultaneously trying to write, to drink, and to shore up failing marriages.

FEMALE TROUBLE NO. 2: THE PANOPTIC GAZE
AND THE WOMAN ALCOHOLIC

Even though some of their male partners seem sometimes sympathetic, there is a punitive edge to the kind of treatment these and other women alcoholics receive. Aiding and abetting an alcoholic is often an exercise in control and power. When the accomplice is a man, "keeping an eye" on the alcoholic woman is an exercise in discipline and punishment.

In the "Panopticism" chapter of *Discipline and Punish,* Michel Foucault explains that in order to discipline prison inmates by keeping them under constant surveillance, Jeremy Bentham conceived the Panopticon. The Panopticon is designed so that the cells are always visibly accessible to a central tower. The central tower is occupied by a supervisor who sees all the inmates all the time. The inmates, however, don't ever see the inspector. The situation of the inmate's visibility and the inspector's invisibility is not only a "guarantee of order" but also a guarantee of the inmate's subordination to the inspector's power. This inmate-inspector relationship, Foucault explains, is "the major effect of the Panopticon: to induce in the inmate a state of consciousness and permanent visibility that assures the automatic functioning of power."[18] Inmates learn to accept the discipline of the Panopticon. They become adjusted to being watched. Then they internalize the panoptic gaze, and they watch themselves. They learn first to accept correction or punishment, and then they learn to punish themselves. The inmates become their own inspectors.

Moreover, the panoptic power effect is not limited to prisons. Foucault contends that the Panopticon is "polyvalent in all its applications."[19] In fact, any institution can be structured panoptically. Foucault explains that "all that is needed . . . is to place a supervisor in a central tower and to shut up in each cell a madman, a patient, a condemned man, a worker, or a schoolboy."[20] Foucault's discussion of the Panopticon and panopticism can, and indeed must, be extended beyond all-male institutions and men. Panopticism also fixes its relentless gaze on women. Like Foucault's nineteenth-century criminals, schoolboys, and madmen, many nineteenth-century women lived in panoptic institutions. The Panopticon that women occupied was the house, a disciplinary space where they were supervised by male inspectors, particularly their husbands, fathers, clergymen, and physicians. A frequent visitor to the nineteenth-century panoptic house was the doctor who, with his morphine syringes, produced and supervised the "docile bodies" of drug-addicted women—sedate, sedated women who quietly stayed home under the gaze of their husbands and their doctors.[21]

The rise of the speakeasy as a heterosocial drinking venue enabled women to leave their domestic cells. Even out of the house, however, many of these women were still unable to evade the panoptic gaze. The New Woman ventured outside of the house and circulated in other cultural venues, under the watchful eye of male inspectors who occupied all the cultural power positions: husbands, clergymen, politicians, bankers, lawyers, physicians, and publishers. In Parker's and Porter's time, this disapproving man was often the alcoholic woman's drinking partner, as single women were unlikely to go to bars alone—unless they were prostitutes or willing to be seen as prostitutes. Porter, for example, proclaimed that "sitting alone at a bar . . . is something I've never done and never would"; she drank in the company of at least one man.[22]

The woman alcoholic receives this punitive gaze because, as Jean Paul Sournia notes in *A History of Alcoholism*, "female drunkenness has always been seen as more serious and degrading than the equivalent male excess."[23] Because an alcoholic woman—then and now—transgresses her culturally determined roles, she is a threat to a power structure invested in gender roles. Not wanting to forfeit his privileged position, the male partner encodes his power and control over his female alcoholic by fixing an intense "panoptic gaze" upon the alcoholic woman. His disapproving gaze permits him to control and manipulate the behavior of the woman he watches: counting her drinks and chastising her for any outward sign of drunkenness or untoward behavior. The alcoholic woman is scrutinized and punished for transgressing her culturally determined position. She is also scrutinized and punished for drunkenness.

"Big Blonde" and the Mrs. Treadwell sections in *Ship of Fools* each produce a female alcoholic character who is under inspection. These characters are aware of themselves being watched by men. Mrs. Treadwell and Mrs. Morse are targets for disapproving looks from inspectors because they do not measure up to the heterosexual culture's notions of female physical beauty, because they lack what Parker calls a "visible spouse," and because they drink.[24] They also watch themselves.

In the opening paragraph of "Big Blonde," the narrator inspects Hazel and sizes her up as follows: "Hazel Morse was a large, fair woman of the type that incites some men when they use the word 'blonde' to click their tongues and wag their heads roguishly" (271). Apparently, a "blonde" is pleasing to some male eyes, as she incites some men to make noises and gestures. However, tongue-clicking and roguish head-wagging are not gestures of gallantry. The clicking, wagging rogue compliments a blonde as he insults a blonde—perhaps he compliments her because he can insult her. The narrator's attitude toward Hazel is similarly roguish: approvingly disapproving.

Hazel does not repel the inspector's gaze or silence his noises and gestures. She lacks the power. Unlike a character such as Hemingway's Brett Ashley—who has the power to turn men into swine—Hazel Morse is no Circe. Rather, men look at Hazel and turn her into livestock. And Hazel has made a career of being watched by men. In her youth, Hazel "had been employed as a model in a wholesale dress establishment—it was still the day of the big woman, and she was then prettily colored and erect and high-breasted. Her job was not onerous"(275). Though in her younger days she presented to the inspectors a blonde figure at which they could click their cameras as well as their tongues, in the story's present, the "day of the big woman" is over. The narrator, then, positions the reader to gaze with approving disapproval at Hazel. From the outset, Parker presents Hazel's flaws and shortcomings as her most outstanding features, so readers have no compelling reason to like her. Indeed, Parker demonstrates (as will Porter as well) that readers also occupy an inspector's position, as she asks readers to see Hazel through the narrator's eyes. In the story's first two paragraphs, the narrator carefully notes Hazel's physical flaws and imperfections: her arms are "flabby"; her hands are "curious things" (275). Then the narrator likens the life story of Hazel Morse to a bad movie: "her old days were a blurred and flickering sequence, an imperfect film, dealing with the actions of strangers" (275). She's not beautiful or witty or mysterious. Her life, past and present, seems cheap and slightly sordid. Furthermore, though the narrator notes that "men liked her, and she took it for granted that the liking of many men was a desirable thing" (275), Hazel's popularity with men does not necessarily warm the eye of the inspector. In fact, the importance she places on "popularity with men" combined with her big blonde body make her more contemptible for the narrator and readers. Parker encourages this contempt. When the story was first published in 1929, the "smart set" New Yorkers and other clicksters who comprised Dorothy Parker's audience knew very well that the day of the big woman was over, and Parker knew it best of all. For them, the big woman had come to represent all the restrictions and prohibitions of the Victorian mother. The reader joins ranks with the skinny flappers and purveyors of diets and bathroom scales who scorn a big blonde.[25]

The reader is similarly situated in Porter's *Ship of Fools*. The novel's setting is a Panopticon. The narrator/inspector is always aware of the thoughts and activities of the passengers. The narrative point of view, shifting from cabin to cabin (cell to cell) is a panoptic gaze that gives the inspector/reader access to each character's thoughts and actions. There are literally dozens of characters in this novel, and all of them, as Porter's title signals, are fools. Furthermore, Porter's fools aren't charming jesters. Instead, they're dupes, suckers, and Porter's contemporaries knew never to give a sucker an even break.[26]

One such sucker is Mrs. Treadwell. Initially, the narrator notes that she is "an inconspicuous slender woman in early middle age, conventionally dressed in dark blue linen, with a wide blue hat shading her black hair and small, rather pretty face and intent dark blue eyes."[27] She seems not disagreeable nor even noteworthy until the narrator watches her raise "the short sleeve over her right arm, to glance again at the place where the beggar woman had pinched her" (26). In trying to avoid being "suckered" by a beggar, Mrs. Treadwell has been pinched—literally. One isn't sure whether one should or should not laugh at the thought of a middle-aged woman looking as if she's been in a physical fight. Mrs. Treadwell herself isn't sure how to respond. She tells herself "it had been like a bad dream. Naturally things like that can't happen . . . or at least, not to me" (26). Even worse, the bruise becomes a distinguishing feature. It catches the eye of other inspectors. Dr. Schumann, watching the passengers board, notes that "a middle-aged, prettyish woman in dark blue seemed very respectable, but a large irregular bruise on her arm below her short sleeve, most likely the result of an amorous pinch, gave her a slightly ribald look, most unbecoming" (29). Dr. Schumann's gaze is fierce. This is precisely the kind of look that Mrs. Treadwell seeks to evade.

With no visible spouses, Mrs. Treadwell and Hazel Morse are watched even more carefully. In public, they are expected to be charming and entertaining—good sports. Being a good sport means being upbeat, happy, and entirely interested in all of her male escort's concerns. It also means being seen. The good sport is a public figure, or rather she offers her figure for public inspections. Sometimes being a good sport means drinking with the inspector, but only if the inspector approves. In addition to Dr. Schumann, who eagle-eyes her bruise upon her embarkation, Wilhelm Freytag also keeps an eye on Mrs. Treadwell. When Mrs. Treadwell innocently approaches Freytag one day, he lashes out at her—as angrily and surprisingly as the beggar woman in Veracruz. He rages at Mrs. Treadwell for getting drunk and telling her cabinmate that Freytag's wife is Jewish. Apparently, Freytag disapproves of solitary drinking that results in drunken babbling, something Mrs. Treadwell presumably would not have done if she had been properly supervised. Pinched again, Mrs. Treadwell insists to Freytag, "I was not drunk, that is a slander" (249). But then, as soon as she denies her drunkeness, she deigns "to confess something. [She] had drunk a whole bottle of wine that evening. Out of boredom, out of stupor, out of indifference" (251–52). Freytag leaps on her again. He comes "so near she could feel his breath" (252). Freytag's proximity, his breath, and his rancor nearly overwhelm Mrs. Treadwell. She bursts into tears. Freytag relents. He approves of Mrs. Treadwell's appropriately feminine tears. He offers a handkerchief and a "good drink, a big cocktail" (253). Though he excoriates her for solitary drinking, he sanctions her drinking under his supervision.

Parker's Hazel Morse also finds herself under the eye of men who expect her to be charming and attentive, conforming to their notions of appropriate behavior for a woman. Hazel is in a particularly difficult spot because her husband, Herbie, and her male partners disparage her first for not drinking at all and then for not drinking in a suitably feminine manner. Initially, Hazel's notions about domesticity and wifeliness are completely confounded by alcohol. She has been instructed by the twentieth-century versions of conduct books she reads—"novels from the drug-store lending library, magazine stories, women's pages in the papers"—to desire "sweet, comforting evenings" (280). However, Herbie wants to drink, and because she becomes frightened that she will lose Herbie's love and her position as his wife, she decides to accompany Herbie on his drinking excursions. When Hazel exhibits the conduct book and Temperance tract-sanctioned "female role" of supervising and trying to control Herbie's drinking, he becomes enraged: "All right, crab; crab, crab, crab, crab, that was all she ever did. What a lousy sport *she* was" (280). He punishes her for what she considers to be appropriate female behavior, so she decides to be a "good sport" and drink with Herbie—which may not be the appropriately *feminine* thing to do according to the conduct books, but is the appropriately *wifely* thing to do according to her husband.

Both Mrs. Morse and Mrs. Treadwell find male drinking partners to authorize and supervise their drinking, but these men are willing to enable the drinking women only as long as the women conform to the men's notions of how women should drink. In "Big Blonde," Herbie is initially pleased that Hazel takes up drinking: "He was glad to see her drink" (281). But Herbie is not so approving when Hazel's drinking becomes regular. When Hazel asks him if he wants a drink before he leaves her and their life together, he shames her. Herbie "looked at her, and a corner of his mouth jerked up. 'Cock-eyed again for a change, aren't you,' he said. 'That's nice'" (285). She is not a good sport when she is constantly drunk or hungover, just as she was a lousy sport when she counted Herbie's drinks.

When Herbie leaves the marriage, his vacant position is quickly filled by a series of men who offer Hazel liquor and money in exchange for being a good sport. Hazel begins to note that "[e]ven her slightest acquaintances seemed irritated if she were not conspicuously light-hearted" (291). Her inspectors advise her to "have a little drink and snap out of it" (291), and Hazel complies. Her boyfriend/inspector, Ed, wants "her picture to look at, up in Utica" (287), as if he can keep an eye on her through the medium of a photograph. Ed and the string of inspectors who replace him in the watchtower observe Hazel—demanding levity and good humor at all times. Ed, for example, "would not listen to admissions of aches or weariness," and "[o]nce, at Jimmy's, when she could not make herself lively, Ed had walked out and left her" (290). Art shames her as well, commanding her to "pull [herself] together . . . and take that face off" (297). Hazel Morse must feel enraged about the fact that her marriage, with its promises of economic and emotional security, practically dissolves overnight, but a good sport does not show her rage. She is caught in a fierce, double panoptic gaze, one that disciplines alcoholism and one that disciplines women, sometimes sequentially, sometimes simultaneously. In this situation she cannot exhibit appropriate "female" behaviors, and she is punished by all of the inspectors.

In *Ship of Fools*, Mrs. Treadwell receives the same kind of treatment from a young officer who disapproves of her drinking style and her performance of femininity. First, he plies her with a nauseating array of cocktails, aiming for sexual favors in return. After too many drinks, the young officer wants to kiss Mrs. Treadwell—indeed, he expects it as a reward for his escort services. However, Mrs. Treadwell knows that drinking with and then kissing officers aboard one's ship are inappropriate feminine behaviors. Mrs. Treadwell suggests that they "wait until tomorrow and see then how they both [feel] about it" (439). This is a reasonable position for a woman to take, but evidently the officer feels because she is drinking, she is not the kind of woman who can say no to a man and mean it. He tells Mrs. Tread-well her reasoning is "simply terrible," and then he resorts to sham-ing. Officiously, he declares, "I do not believe you are sober" (440), indicating that her lack of sobriety encompasses numerous other vices and faults—all distinctly unfeminine. Then, after a few more rounds of banter that still does not produce the kiss he wants, he resorts to asserting his physical superiority. He "enveloped her wholly, waist, shoulders, arms, brought her instantly under control and kissed her violently on her mouth" (440). His kiss is her punish-ment for her "bad" performance of femininity.

Clearly, this incessant surveillance and disapprobation promises nothing but trouble for a woman alcoholic. Since the Panopticon's discipline for being appropriately feminine necessitates *not* being an alcoholic, a woman alcoholic is always already an entirely undisci-plined figure. Unfortunately, the inspectors view such an undisci-plined figure as a "madwoman."

FEMALE TROUBLE NO. 3: ALCOHOL AND THE MADWOMAN

The constant scrutiny, disapproval, and punishment that Mrs. Treadwell and Mrs. Morse experience affects them in the same way that panopticism affects Bertha Mason in Charlotte Brontë's *Jane Eyre* (1847), for example, or the female character in Charlotte Per-kins Gilman's "The Yellow Wallpaper" (1892): the watched woman becomes a Madwoman. The violent, rageful, destructive behavior that Mrs. Treadwell and Hazel Morse exhibit can be understood as a cultural construction, and one can look to Sandra Gilbert and Susan Gubar for an appropriate and useful interpretive tool, the Mad-woman. In their groundbreaking work, *The Madwoman in the Attic*, Gilbert and Gubar deploy Bertha Mason as the paradigmatic Mad-woman in *Jane Eyre*. Bertha Mason has a family history of mental ill-ness and alcoholism, and her marriage to the plundering Mr. Rochester only accelerates her predispositions through his disap-proval, forced confinement, and strict supervision. Under the con-stant scrutiny of Mr. Rochester and his deputy, Grace Poole, Bertha Mason's condition deteriorates. She makes several surreptitious midnight attacks on Mr. Rochester and Jane, and in a final violent and ultimately self-destructive gesture, she torches Thornfield Hall and leaps from its ramparts to her death. The Madwoman embodies the disempowerment, rage, and despair that women experience in a culture that sets them up for subordinate positions and punishes those who speak out, act out, resist.[28]

Madness is an unstable signifier that, like codependency, is often overused or used carelessly and therefore is best employed as a heuristic rather than a reified concept or clinical diagnosis. As such, the Madwoman is a useful feminist trope, especially in a discussion of women and alcoholism. Gilbert and Gubar have shown that the Madwoman is inscribed in the lives and work of nineteenth-century women authors such as the Brontë sisters and Charlotte Perkins Gilman. This figure appears well into the twentieth century in the lives and work of women such as Zelda Fitzgerald and Jane Bowles (both of whom died in mental institutions), in addition to Parker and Porter. As a trope, the Madwoman—confined and maligned—organizes an understanding of the "female trouble" that Dorothy Parker, Katherine Anne Porter, and their characters face.

Mrs. Treadwell's and Hazel's alcoholism and its consequences, including the incessant disapprobation of their male accomplices, induce thought disorders and psychotic behaviors that could merit a clinical diagnosis of psychosis, but are perhaps better understood as expressions of a Madwoman. Hazel seizes on the thought of death as a way out of the Panopticon. In the same way that she cannot pinpoint the beginning of her failing marriage or the beginning of her progressing alcoholism, "there was no settled, shocked moment when she first thought of killing herself; it seemed to her as if the idea had always been with her" (293). To her inspectors, her suicidal notions signal a thought disorder. To her, suicide is a logical consequence. It is an escape from a life that keeps her under constant, punitive surveillance. Like Hazel Morse, Mrs. Treadwell is heaped with abuse and alcohol until she attacks William Denny. However, in both tests, it is clear that violence is not the solution to the panoptic problem. The alcoholic woman remains under the disapproving surveillance of her associates, her narrator, her readers—and herself.

Hazel Morse is so inured to being watched that if no male inspector is around, she watches herself in the mirror. Clearly, she has internalized the method of the Panopticon, if not the desired results. In a telling gesture, she gazes into the bathroom mirror, toasts herself, then watches herself swallow twenty tablets of Veronal. She continues having a conversation with the mirror, berating her boyfriend Art "and the whole lot of them," and then making a little joke: "Gee, I'm nearly dead." The joke is pathetic, pitiable, even mad, but it "struck her as comic," and she gives an unforced laugh as she makes her way from the bathroom to the bedroom where she lies down to await death (298). Even when she is unconscious and near death, Hazel continues to be the object of "permanent observation," disapproval, derision, and shame. This is the hideous thing Nettie finds in Mrs. Morse's bedroom:

> Mrs. Morse lay on her back, one flabby, white arm flung up, the wrist against her forehead. Her stiff hair hung untenderly along her face. The bed covers were pushed down, exposing a deep square of soft neck and a pink nightgown, its fabric worn uneven by many launderings; her great breasts, freed from their tight confiner, sagged beneath her arm-pits. Now and then she made knotted, snoring sounds, and from the corner of her open mouth to the blurred turn of her jaw ran a lane of crusted spittle. (299)

Nettie brings in the elevator boy to look at Hazel, and then they fetch the male doctor-in-the-house so he can look at her as well.

Hazel's failed suicide attempt only intensifies her state of surveillance. She cannot get out of the Panopticon. When the house doctor is finished with his treatment/punishment, Nettie takes his place as inspector. When Hazel awakens, what Nettie sees is no longer a dishy big blonde but rather a "big, blown woman in the bed" (302). Nettie greets Hazel with the same kind of shaming questions she used to get from Herbie and the Boys: "What you been trying to do, Mis' Morse? . . . That's no way to ack, taking them pills" (302). Hazel's response to Nettie's questions and her own awful realization that she failed to kill herself is to ask for a drink. Her toast to Nettie is "Here's mud in your eye" (304)—a not-so-whimsical wish for a woman who wants people to stop looking at her.

A key scene in *Ship of Fools* links Hazel Morse's apartment to Mrs. Treadwell's cabin and to Bertha Mason's attic. Mrs. Treadwell, alone at last and drunk after spending an evening drinking with an officer, "leaned very close to the looking glass and studied her features thoughtfully, and began to amuse herself with painting a different face on her own, as she used to do for fancy dress balls" (442). As Mrs. Treadwell sits playing solitaire in front of the looking glass, which becomes a giant panoptic eye that watches her unblinkingly, her "strange assumed face . . . no longer amused her but seemed a revelation of something sinister in her character" (442). The panoptic mirror is disparaging, pointing out Mrs. Treadwell's shortcomings and faults. It's the same mirror that looks at Hazel Morse swallowing Veronal. Mrs. Treadwell's response to the mirror is to "[rummage] in her dressing case for her sleeping tablets" (442). The sleeping tablets and alcohol seem to catalyze her rage and violence. When William Denny knocks on the wrong door, Mrs. Tread-

well's response parallels a scene in *Jane Eyre* in which Mr. Rochester
and his would-be wedding party barge into Bertha's top-floor prison.
Enraged at the intrusion and the very sight of Rochester, Bertha
"sprang and grappled [Rochester's] throat viciously, and laid her
teeth to his cheek: they struggled."[29] In *Ship of Fools*, Denny barges
in on Mrs. Treadwell, blows "a pestiferous breath in her face" (444),
and grabs her breast. Mrs. Treadwell, as enraged as Bertha, pushes
him hard enough to knock him down. Then she pounds his face
with the heel of her spike-heel sandal.

In *Jane Eyre*, Bertha Mason is immediately "mastered," "pin-
ioned," "bound . . . to a chair" for her attack on Rochester, but in
Ship of Fools, Mrs. Treadwell seems to have vanquished her foe.[30]
However, Mrs. Treadwell's victory is short-lived. Although nobody
watches the beating, the steward (who finds the mate to Mrs. Treadwell's weapon-sandal) and Dr. Shumann (who treats the telltale
heel-shaped marks on Denny's face) are so alert to any aberrations
in Mrs. Treadwell's behavior that they are able to visualize her actions and condemn her accordingly. She spends the rest of her voyage in a sleeping pill–enhanced silent isolation. Her cabin becomes
a segregation unit, a Madwoman's attic.

FEMALE TROUBLE NO. 4: YOU MIGHT AS WELL LIVE

The final scenes for Mrs. Treadwell and Hazel depict a gloomy
prognosis for the heterosexual alcoholic woman. When Mrs. Treadwell leaves the *Vera*, she is full of malevolence, alcohol, and sedatives.
On the pilot boat for Boulogne, Mrs. Treadwell "seated herself with
her back to the ship she was leaving" (468). Although she does not
look at the ship, the ship continues to look at her. Neither the passengers, the crew, the narrator, nor the reader gaze with sympathy
or sadness upon the receding figure of Mary Treadwell. The parting
glance is a bitter one.

The reader has a similar bitter response at the end of "Big
Blonde." One can't help but feel sympathy toward Hazel when she
looks into her glass of whiskey and hopes that "[m]aybe whiskey
would be her friend again" (304). Drinking whiskey after a deliberate drug overdose suggests the logic of an alcoholic—to whom this
kind of reasoning makes perfect sense. One feels sorry for her when
she prays "without addressing a God, without knowing a God. Oh,
please, please, let her be able to get drunk, please keep her always
drunk" (304). To Nettie, she repeats the toast she gave herself in the
mirror, "Here's mud in your eye." Nettie, who is still watching, gig-

gles and gives Hazel one last reprimand—the same reprimand she gets from her inspector/boyfriends: "You cheer up now" (304). Hazel tries to give a "stiff upper lip" tough-guy response: "'Yeah,' said Mrs. Morse. 'Sure'" (304). It's the kind of rejoinder that Hemingway's Jake Barnes might give in a similar situation. "'Yeah' . . . 'Sure'" has the same tough tone as "isn't it pretty to think so" at the end of *The Sun Also Rises*.[31] The difference is that there is nothing hard or tough about big blonde Hazel, and so her attempt at brave irony is lame, pathetic, pitiable. The doctor's prognostic statement, "[y]ou couldn't kill her with an ax," becomes a bitter curse. Hazel Morse is doomed to a long, miserable life.

Parker and Porter both experienced the "female troubles" they represent in their alcoholic women characters. Both women finally sank into their alcoholism at the ends of their lives. In their declining years, Parker became pathologically neglectful, and Porter became almost uncontrollably rageful. John Keats reports a lingering image of Dorothy Parker: "[a] friend recalled that he and a motion picture actor . . . came to pay homage to a lady, only to find a crone sitting on the floor, surrounded by bottles, who looked up at them blearily from a rug strewn with dog feces."[32] The old crone lived this way until she had a heart attack and died in 1967 at age seventy-three. In her *New Yorker* article "After the Laughs," Joan Acocella reports that Parker said to a friend, "Don't feel badly when I die . . . I've been dead for a long time."[33] Porter had a series of strokes, and she aged as badly as Parker did. Givner reports that "as her father and sisters had done before they died, she was growing hostile, furious, and at times violent."[34] Porter's last assistant, Bill Wilkins, claimed that Porter seemed to have been stricken with a "sort of madness" because she was so difficult, so vituperative.[35] Porter's decline was not blissfully rapid, and her raging decrepitude did not seem to shorten her life. She died in 1980, a venomous ninety years old.

Finally, the problem that Mrs. Treadwell embodies at the end of *Ship of Fools* is the same problem Hazel Morse embodies at the end of "Big Blonde"—the same problem Parker and Porter knew in their lives. This common problem is that the panoptic gaze makes the heterosexual alcoholic woman a Madwoman, and the inspectors who watch her and drive her mad also doom her to live a miserable life. However, Parker and Porter found a way to deflect the panoptic gaze. As writers, they were able to construct a corpus, a body (of literature) that drew the gaze. The deployment of these bodies of writing, then, gave the women some respite. As a result, though they both suffered in their lives, neither woman exercised Bertha Mason's option and set the house afire. Instead, Dorothy Parker and Katherine Anne Porter both decided that, as Parker puts it, they "might as well live."[36]

NOTES

1. For an excellent discussion of trouble, see Judith Butler, *Gender Trouble: Feminism and the Subversion of Identity* (New York: Routledge, 1990). Also, I owe my title, at least in part, to John Waters's film *Female Trouble*. Recent work on Dorothy Parker is mostly biographical and popular rather than critical, and many current scholarly articles on Katherine Anne Porter have been biographical as well, focusing especially on her duplicity, nastiness, and decline. *Dorothy Parker and the Vicious Circle*, a feature film starring Jennifer Jason Leigh, premiered in 1994, and *The Ten Year Lunch*, a gossipy documentary featuring Heywood Broun, Jr., in 1987. Writing about Parker tends to be biographical. See also Joan Acocella, "After the Laughs," *New Yorker*, 16 August 1993, 76–81, which marked Parker's centennial; Nina Miller, "Making Love Modern: Dorothy Parker and Her Public," *American Literature* (1992): 763–84; and Marion Meade, *Dorothy Parker: What Fresh Hell Is This?* (New York: Penguin, 1988). For articles on Katherine Anne Porter, see Janis P. Stout, *Katherine Anne Porter: A Sense of the Times* (Charlottesville: University Press of Virginia, 1995), and "'Something of a Reputation as a Radical': Katherine Anne Porter's Shifting Politics," *South Central Review* 10, no. 1 (Spring 1993): 49–66; Robert Brinkmeyer, *Katherine Anne Porter's Artistic Development: Primitivism, Traditionalism, and Totalitarianism* (Baton Rouge: Louisiana State University Press, 1993); Enrique Hank Lopez, *Conversations with Katherine Anne Porter: Refugee from Indian Creek* (Boston, MA: Little, Brown, 1981); and Joan Givner, *Katherine Anne Porter: A Life* (New York: Simon and Schuster, 1982). Givner published a second edition of *Katherine Anne Porter: A Life* (Athens: University of Georgia Press, 1991) in which she includes some updated information about Porter's relationship with Josephine Herbst, whom Porter denounced to the FBI during the McCarthy era. Other articles focused on Porter's character include Janis P. Stout, "Katherine Anne Porter's 'Reflections on Willa Cather': A Duplicitous Homage," *American Literature* (1994): 719–35; Mary Gordon, "The Angel of Malignity—The Cold Beauty of Katherine Anne Porter," *New York Times Book Review*, 16 April 1995, 17; and J. Cory, "*Ship of Fools*: Katherine Anne Porter in Decline," *Four Quarters* 34, no. 3 (1985): 16–25.

2. Codependency is a concept with nebulous parameters, and one problem with this concept is that its own promulgators have failed to provide it with intellectual currency. For discussions about the definition of codependency see Amy Mashberg, "Codependency and Obsession in *Madame Bovary*," *Dionysos* 2, no. 1 (Spring 1990): 29; Melody Beattie, *Codependent No More* (San Francisco, CA: HarperSan Francisco, 1987), 31; and Ramon Asher, *Women with Alcoholic Husbands: Ambivalence and the Trap of Codependency* (Chapel Hill: University of North Carolina Press, 1992). Recently, the term *codependency* has been the subject of much debate, with many feminist health professionals and social scientists questioning its validity. See, for example, Gloria Cowan and Lynda Warren, "Codependency and Gender-Stereotyped Traits," *Sex Roles* 30 (May 1994): 634, and Louise Armstrong, introduction to *Challenging Codependency: Feminist Critiques*, ed. Marguerite Babcock and Christine McKay (Toronto: University of Toronto Press, 1995), x–xi. The prevailing arguments for and against the concept of codependency have gotten bogged down in

their own lack of parameters and their heterosexist assumptions: mainly, that in a relationship, the problem person (usually, but not necessarily, a drug addict or an alcoholic) is always a heterosexual man (probably white and middle class) and the codependent is always his wife (ditto). Additionally, neither the proponents nor opponents of the concept of codependency are addressing codependency as a condition related specifically to alcoholism and drug addiction, which are the sites of its initial promulgation (see Mashberg; and Catherine MacGregor, " 'Especially Pictures of Families': Alcoholism, Codependency, and *Crime and Punishment,*" *Dionysos* 3, no. 2 [Fall 1991]: 5).

3. Lopez, 209.

4. Givner, *Katherine Anne Porter* (1991, ed.), 11. Subsequent references are to this edition.

5. Ibid., 245.

6. Ibid., 303

7. Meade, 232.

8. Ibid., 300.

9. John Crowley, *The White Logic: Alcoholism and Gender in American Modernist Fiction* (Amherst: University of Massachusetts Press, 1994). See chapter 2 on Jack London's *John Barleycorn.*

10. Meade, 328, 327.

11. Wyatt Cooper, "Whatever You Think Dorothy Parker Was Like, She Wasn't," *Esquire,* July 1968, 111.

12. Ibid., 390.

13. Ibid., 392

14. Givner, 11.

15. Ibid., 12.

16. Cooper, 112.

17. Givner, 433.

18. Michel Foucault, *Discipline and Punish: The Birth of the Prison,* trans. Alan Sheridan (New York: Vintage, 1995), 200. Thanks to Professor Michael Selmon, who sent me a copy of his 1994 Modern Language Association paper, "Belasco Meets Foucault."

19. Ibid., 205

20. Ibid., 200.

21. One such inspector was the Temperance advocate Senator Henry William Blair. Blair writes that "although there is much intemperance among women . . . still, the gentler sex is comparatively free from the dreadful practice" (397). While Blair recognizes that women do drink, he implies that drinking women—especially what he calls the "fast and wealthy" ones—are inherently deplorable because they subvert his attempts to give gender assignments to behaviors: drinking is "male" or "masculine," certainly "common among men," while abstinence is "female" (397). For Blair, then, the drinking woman is unnatural: she is a monster (see Henry William Blair, *The Temperance Movement: or, The Conflict between Man and Alcohol* (Boston, MA: W. E. Smythe, 1888).

22. Darlene Unrue, *Truth and Vision in Katherine Anne Porter's Fiction* (Athens: University of Georgia Press, 1985), 94.

23. Jean-Charles Sournia, *A History of Alcoholism* (Cambridge, MA: B. Blackwell, 1990), 22.

24. Dorothy Parker, "Big Blonde," in *The Portable Dorothy Parker,* by Dorothy Parker (New York: Viking, 1973), 275–306. Subsequent references are to this edition and will be cited parenthetically in the text.

25. Ann Douglas, *Terrible Honesty: Mongrel Manhattan in the 1920s* (New York: Farrar, Straus and Giroux, 1995), 135.

26. Ibid.

27. Katherine Anne Porter, *Ship of Fools* (New York: Signet/NAL, 1963), 25. Subsequent references are to this edition and will be cited parenthetically in the text by page number.

28. Sandra Gilbert and Susan Gubar, *The Madwoman in the Attic: The Woman Writer and the Nineteenth-Century Literary Imagination* (New Haven: Yale University Press, 1979), xii. For a "panoptic reading" of "The Yellow Wallpaper," see John Bak, "Escaping the Jaundiced Eye: Foucauldian Panopticism in Charlotte Perkins Gilman's 'The Yellow Wallpaper,'" *Studies in Short Fiction* 31 (1994): 39–46.

29. Charlotte Brontë, *Jane Eyre* (1847; repr., New York: Penguin, 1984), 321.

30. Ibid., 321.

31. Ernest Hemingway, *The Sun Also Rises* (1926); repr., New York: Scribner, 1970), 247.

32. John Keats, *You Might as Well Live: The Life and Times of Dorothy Parker* (New York: Simon and Schuster, 1970), 302.

33. Acocella, 78. Djuna Barnes made a nearly identical statement to her biographer Andrew Field. Jane Bowles also experienced the end of her life as a living death. Millicent Dillon notes an incident in which Bowles asked her friend David Herbert for his copy of her *Collected Works.* Apparently, he thought she was going to write a friendly inscription in it. Instead, Herbert recalled that "[w]ith a trembling hand she picked up a pencil and added 'of Dead Jane Bowles'" (see Millicent Dillon, *A Little Original Sin: The Life and Work of Jane Bowles* [New York: Anchor Books, 1982], 342).

34. Givner, *Katherine Anne Porter,* (1982, ed.), 504.

35. Ibid.

36. Dorothy Parker, "Résumé," in *Portable,* 154.

Part III
Classroom Encounters

Reading, Responding, Composing:
A Revisionary Approach

Phillip Arrington

IN HIS ESSAY "RESEARCH STRATEGIES FOR THE STUDY OF REVISION PRO-cesses in Writing Poetry," Gabriel M. Della-Piana offers a five-phase "writing as revision model" to explain and to describe the revision practices of poets.[1] Beginning with a mental "preconception or set," that initial expectation of what a text will be, its affect on readers, or some fertile word, phrase, or image, the poet eventually learns to "discriminate" between that preconception and the actual draft he or she is producing. If these two components fail to match, and if the poet *sees* that they don't, dissonance follows and, if this state continues, it creates "tension," that need to close the gap between intention and text. This tension dissolves, if at all, only through the poet's "reconception" of the intention, the text, or both (106–7).

Della-Piana's model, besides being quite abstract and obviously dependent on the terminology of cognitive psychologists' accounts of perception, is tentative and provisional. Della-Piana does not insist, for example, that these strategies are always or necessarily "conscious" or "that the elements described *flow* in a *fixed* sequence." Nor does he believe—and this admission is crucial for teachers of composition, intermediate or advanced—"that one *will* see dissonance, feel tension, or try to resolve the tension by matching one's intentions with one's perception of what the work does." Moreover, he points out that his model "does not imply that there is only one process or set of processes shared by all writers." Whereas his is "a model of the process of writing-as-revision," it is a model content to outline the "commonalities" among the "diverse" revising schemes of writers and poets (107–8).

Bracketed with qualifications as Della-Piana's revisionist model of writing is, it finds analogous descriptions in the work of Donald Murray and Nancy I. Sommers, among others.[2] In fact, in one sense Della-Piana's model is more complex than, say, Murray's threefold process of "prevision, vision, and revision" in that Della-Piana is sensitive to the conflicts that writers see and experience over longer stretches of time. While it is true that Sommers and Murray want to explain the revision strategies of experienced or professional writers of prose, not poetry, the similarities in their various theoretical descriptions intimate broader but still provisional discoveries about the revising practices among poets and prose writers.

But there is another analogy I want to consider here: that of the relationship between writing-as-revision and responding and reading as revision. For some time now, cognitive psychologists and information theorists have been trying to articulate those perceptual and cognitive processes by and through which we interact with the world around us.[3] And although there remains more caution and controversy than certainty in what this research means, many experts agree that our mental "schema," our ways of seeing and knowing the world, depend as much on what we have seen and known as they do on what we expect to perceive and recognize in any given situation. The most salient feature of these schema is, in Ulric Neisser's phrase, "adaptive variation."[4] If incoming data from the environment fails to match those constructs we already possess for making sense, we quickly modify these constructs according to the exigencies of the moment. Thus, seeing and knowing take place in time and, like our responses, are subject to change—even deformation—as the situation requires.

The temporalizing of human response strategies can easily be seen in phenomenological descriptions of the reading of literary texts. For illustrations, we need only consult the reading act as described by Wolfgang Iser, Michael Riffaterre, Johnathan Culler, and Stanley Fish.[5] Fish, for example, substitutes the question "What does a text do?" for the earlier, more New Critical question, "What does a text mean?" (386–87). Once we've granted this substitution, reading "involves an *analysis of the developing responses of the reader in relation to the words as they succeed one another in time*" (387–88; emphasis added). For Fish, as for Iser, Riffaterre, and Louise Rosenblatt,[6] the meaning of a story or a poem is "an event" in which readers make, unmake, and remake the meaning of the words within "the temporal flow of the reading experience" (389). So defined, reading, like responding and writing, is fundamentally a "revisionary" act. We read within the shadow of our preconceptions—as these are determined by our culture, history, and individual temperament—and project forward from them, into the "not-yet-read." Along the way, we make "themes" of what we've read, of what we've experienced in what we've read, and construct "horizons" of what's to come, based on those themes. Neither Fish nor Iser, however, would have us think that this revising process in our reading is merely continuous and without problems. Literary texts, for instance, contain "gaps," "blanks," to use Iser's terminology, which on the one hand block a reader's search for easy closure and on the other invite a reader's capacity for inventing the connections between these gaps. And there is no guarantee, of course, that any reader will accept this invitation to participate and therefore to revise his or her preconceptions about what a text is supposed to do.

If these are features of literary texts, and if these texts by definition create occasions for revisionary comprehension, can the same be said of non-literary texts? In short, is any act of reading revisionary, or must the text be Joyce's *Ulysses* or one of Sir Thomas Browne's essays before we can make use of phenomenological descriptions of this process? Even while admitting the crucial differences between, say, making an interpretation of Joyce's novel as opposed to an interpretation of a newspaper article, we find Frank Smith defining reading comprehension as that "reduction of uncertainty" wherein "the term meaning identification . . . helps to emphasize that comprehension is an active process." For Smith, a psycholinguist, "meaning does not reside in surface structure [that is, the 'visual information' composed of letters, words, phrases, sentences, or even larger units]" but in the "deep" structure of what readers "already know" and "what they want to know."[7] Between a reader's memory and prior knowledge and a reader's desires and anticipations is the text, about which we make "global" and "focal" predictions, with the former continuously being modified by the latter and the latter, the former (Smith, 169). At the "global" level readers approach a novel or a chemistry textbook within the matrix of those preestablished conventions that constitute those types of texts. But these conventions, and the expectations that they arouse, are not static; they shift according to the "focal" predictions we make as we read and comprehend each unit of meaning, however large or small we make that textual unit. From its title and opening pages, for example, Swift's *Gulliver's Travels* appears to be a travel-book similar to others of its type written during the eighteenth century. Soon, however, even the least discriminating of readers will start to realize that the conventions of travel literature do not altogether explain Swift's distortions. And there are "global" expectations that escape the purely generic, for certain readers desire certain types of texts at particular times while others prefer quite different reading. One reader, we can imagine, may slam Swift's book to the floor, as not only a failed travel-book but a ridiculous farce. This reader does not choose to fill the Iserian gap between generic expectation and textual fact, and he or she has stopped reading at the first appearance of dissonance. Another reader, however, thinks, "Ah, this isn't a travel-book at all but some type of wild fantasy," and has therefore revised expectations and continues reading, and revising.

The unifying premise between Smith's psycholinguistic theory of reading, that of the phenomenologists, and the revising model Della-Piana, among others, proposes—that premise is this: reading, like responding and composing, is an event with a history, a history filled with pauses, hesitations, conflicts, resolutions, and renewed sources of tension. More precisely, these conflicts can, when readers and writers discover them, generate new meanings, ones in which previous ways of making sense are seen again, in a new light. However different the texts—and there is quite a difference between readers who want to reduce the "uncertainty" of a text and those who read texts whose aim is to increase, not reduce, uncertainty—readers do strive for coherence in what they read. A chemistry text, certainly, if the reader already has the "nonvisual information," permits more rapid closure than Swift's satire. Yet in either case, readers seek meaning and often, if this search is frustrated too much, resort to quick and easy resolutions.

Admittedly, Smith, Fish, Iser, and Della-Piana represent divergent methods and take for their object of attention different types of texts. But this divergence rests on the common recognition that seeing, reading, and writing are "processes," not "products," taking place in and through time. A full exploration of this antithesis awaits its historian. The more immediate problem for teachers of *both* reading and writing is how to translate this revisionist approach, predicated as it is on the behavior and habits of mature, experienced, and professional readers and writers, into workable classroom strategies for students, many of whom, even in advanced composition courses, are not and do not aim to become experienced or professional writers.

Intermediate composition courses these days do introduce students to various revision strategies, but these strategies need to be reemphasized in advanced composition courses as well. Perhaps they should constitute the focus of this frequently ill-defined writing course. I have in mind here a sequence of various types of writing, with each based on a single literary text but whose rhetorical constraints vary and become increasingly complex. This sequence is not meant to impose a "linear" grid upon Della-Piana's revisionist model. Rather, each writing assignment repeats many of the tasks of the previous ones, builds upon them, as the final paper emerges out of the revising cycles—cycles in which new questions are posed, new discoveries made, introducing dissonance that writers seek to explore and to resolve, if possible, through added information.

For this is precisely the problem as Della-Piana phrases it: how to approach writing as a way of uncovering the antitheses and conflicts inherent in texts in order that, through rewriting, our students may see again and revise their preconceptions. Although artificial in nature, the advanced composition classroom would try to approximate as far as possible the indefinite time scheme of revising. This can be done, I submit, by shifting and varying the rhetorical constraints for each assignment and by introducing perspectives that require students to find more information to resolve the questions involved. In this way we allow the dissonance to appear within the initial drafts and responses to them, with medial and terminal drafts functioning as ways of rethinking and revising the initial ones. Therefore, writing is always a rewriting, a rethinking of the problem implicit or explicit in the first drafts.

To experiment with the broad implications of Della-Piana's scheme, I recently taught Dorothy Parker's "But the One on the Right" (1929) as the single text upon which I based a number of different writing assignments, each requiring a new revisionary strategy while reinforcing previous ones. Again, by "revising" I do not mean simply what Donald Murray calls "external revision," although that also occurs; I mean a different way of seeing Parker's text, with revision as the principal heuristic.

My choice of Parker's interior monologue as a seminal text is far from innocent or arbitrary. Like many composition teachers, I still believe that the dissonance literature produces through its distortions and indirections serves as a valuable point of departure for students. Moreover, I contend that the long history of rhetoric upholds the "literary" basis of writing courses, even if what students are in fact doing is finding out the ways literature is rooted in a writer's life, times, and culture. Even before Plato, the ancient sophists taught their students how to read and to interpret the poets. This discipline enhanced the twin studies of grammar and disputation.[8] In fact, within this tradition literature was always a means to an end just as rhetoric was more a quartet of concerns rather than today's popular triad. Thinking and speaking joined reading and writing as the major foci, from Quintilian to Erasmus. Literature was seldom viewed in and for itself, as we sometimes have done. It constituted the culture's transmitted heritage. Themes were approached didactically, and style was even then seen as an index of a writer's mind and the times in which it grew. Yet Quintilian and Erasmus share a common belief that through continuous practice in thinking, reading, and writing, students eventually learn the method of learning itself.

In trying to make sense of the internal gymnastics of one of Parker's most cynically intelligent but needy heroines, my students do not follow the strategies of these earlier rhetorical mentors in any absolute sense. But in another sense they do: they discover themselves through learning about other values, other beliefs, represented in the literature to which they are exposed. In their initial writings, I want merely to see them think through their responses to "Mrs. Parker." In posing a "reader-response" type of assignment, I do not have in mind some ideal reaction to Parker's narrator. Instead, my goal with this paper is for my students to arrive at a question that will introduce dissonance into their initial understanding of the character, their "preconceptions," to use Della-Piana's term. In short, I want students to ask themselves, "What is this Mrs. Parker really like?"

In the beginning, students have only limited responses to Mrs. Parker. They misunderstand her wit as the cynicism of boredom and class arrogance. This result is not totally unexpected, and I set up the short writing tasks in order to invite free and relatively impressionistic reactions to her character. I ask students to read the story and then make a rough list of whatever the character reminded them of. Here they can make use of metaphor as a way of expressing their feelings about Mrs. Parker and as a way of discovering ideas within those feelings.[9] The inherent analogical structure of a metaphor allows them to explore the unknown (Mrs. Parker) through the known. One student compared her monologue to the random "slashings" of a psychopath; another, to the hypocritical posturing of Diane on the comedy series, *Cheers*.

Once students have written for about five or ten minutes, generating their associations, and so on, I ask them to pick *one* of their metaphors or associations and to write a brief essay, with themselves as intended audience, explaining what the connection means. In another brief writing, they select a comparison or association to explain to another student. In each case, of course, the amount of development the writer gives to the idea varies according to the intended reader. The second essay should be longer than the first, although it may conceivably be based on the same metaphor. Once the second essay is finished, students exchange papers and read each other's responses to Mrs. Parker. At the bottom of the essay, each reader writes a summary of what the writer said and consults with the writer to see if both are in agreement. If they are not, of course, students have probably discovered together a moment in the essay that needs revision: they have found a point of dissonance between what the writer wanted to say and what was written. And this discovery invites both writer and reader to work together to resolve their conflict.

Next, I break the class into small groups of three or four students each and ask them to share and discuss their responses to Mrs. Parker. During these workshops, I wander from one group to the next, listening to students discriminate between one and then another student's impressions of Mrs. Parker. Usually, I ask them to look for differences in their perspectives on the character and, as I visited each group, I found many deriding this character, viewing her as a cynical, if not "pessimistic," harpy, callous in her thoughts about the "man on the left," the dinner party, and life in general, and cruelly imaginative in expressing this callousness. Yet in nearly every group, I found one student who thought Mrs. Parker witty, amusing, and intelligent, but terribly lonely and overly conscious about being a woman in a "man's world," governed by constraining social conventions.

These divergent interpretations of "What Mrs. Parker is really like" tell much about the different preconceptions of individual readers, their cultural, social, and psychological expectations. Almost all of the male students, for example, condemned the harsh treatment of the dinner companion to Mrs. Parker's left, while several females judged the character based on her superficial attraction to the man "on the right." Several students also noted her arrogance, which these readers found offensive and unjustified, and her social snobbery. Given the working-class backgrounds of most of the students in my class, this last reaction is not surprising; for in fact my students sensed very quickly a fictional "voice" in contrast to those with which they were already familiar. And they reacted negatively to a darker view of life.

The divergent reactions to Mrs. Parker, however, set the stage for a second reading of the story. In rereading Mrs. Parker's monologue, students copied down any word, phrase, image, or passage which (a) shows the character's cynicism, snobbery, and cruelty or (b) shows her loneliness, honesty with herself, and the pressure of sexual and social restraints. With the direct evidence from the story for both responses to Mrs. Parker, the class sorts through it, evaluating and discussing the weight of each quotation or incident. By the end of this process, I ask the students to write another essay about their reactions to Mrs. Parker—this time aimed at their classmates as readers and this time drawing upon the best supporting evidence from the story to illustrate their interpretation of her character.

These papers are exchanged and evaluated as before, but with an additional task of checking to make sure the direct evidence from the story *relates* to the overall response to Mrs. Parker's character. By now I have reached a second point of inquiry: What can students find out about this character beyond their own preconceptions about her and the support the story gives to them? My students supplied a quick response to that question. They could find out something about Dorothy Parker's life, her personality, and her other writings. In fact, many students were already aroused about this connection by the shared last name of both author and character. To satisfy this need for more information about Parker the writer, students found and read Thomas Grant's biographical sketch in the *Dictionary of Literary Biography*.

This need for more information on Parker the author, I might add, emerges out the several different ways of viewing her creation, Mrs. Parker. An appeal to the direct evidence in the text to support a response does not, therefore, put an end to the antithetical views of Mrs. Parker. And the antithesis itself signifies another level of dissonance that the text cannot resolve. Hence the obvious curiosity about the author's relation to her characters. There, students may think, would lie the key to answering once and for all the enigma of Mrs. Parker.

This confidence in the value of biographical information, however naive and misplaced, introduces a fourth writing assignment: a report summarizing the basic facts about Dorothy Parker's life, personality, and her other writings. But this report must in the end be synthesized with the facts of the story itself. Even with this added information, dissonance remains for the writer; and we may frame this conflict in the form of another question: To what extent does Mrs. Parker the character resemble Dorothy Parker the author?

"To what extent" cues students to make careful comparisons between their reports and the story. Some connections will be quite obvious. For example, most of the students discovered that Mrs. Parker's barbed one-liners matched those made by Dorothy Parker in real life. But other connections required sophisticated inferential abilities. The educational background of the character, her classical allusions, French phrases, and knowledge of literature—this background had been laid during the time the author spent in Miss Dana's school, with its rigorous curriculum. And Mrs. Parker's attitude toward men, sex, and the social rules governing both—these facts, too, require students to look more closely at the subtler shades of resemblance between character and author. Hence, although the biographical information about Parker resolves and explains some facets of Mrs. Parker's inner speech, it raises other difficulties that the writers need to solve.

Finding those connections between story and creator is the objective of the next draft, but this process can be aided if students first try to imagine a potential reader for this draft. Unlike previous writings, this draft cannot be aimed at other class members because they all share the same information and the same task. At this point, however, students and instructor can work together to invent an audience for the paper.[10] Students quickly suggest "any reader of the story," but this suggestion will need more qualification. Students need to explain a condition of interest for such a reader. Here, too, a satisfactory solution was soon found. The reader for the drafts would be familiar with Parker's story and curious about the fact that both author and fictional persona share the same last name. Beyond that, however, this fictive reader would know nothing of Parker's life or her other writings. What does such a reader need to know, then? Precisely those connections that exist between the story's persona and the author. This "need to know" also shapes the purpose of the discourse: to inform. And with a purpose and a reader matching their information, students compose their drafts.

In reading and evaluating these papers, I play the role dictated by the reader profile and purpose statement. Yet as I read through these papers, I noted numerous students who remarked that Dorothy Parker was a unique woman, being the first and only member of her sex to enjoy the fraternity of the rather exclusively male-dominated Algonquin Round Table. Such generalizations as these provide the starting point for the next draft. After pointing out this generality to my classes, I posed another question: What was the status of women in America during the late twenties and early thirties? To answer it, students would need to do a bit of reading in the history of that period and write a report, as they had done following the reading of Grant's biosketch, explaining what they were able to find out about this subject.

This report, like the first one, is the informational hinge linking it to a larger paper and a more complex synthesis of information. Students take the historical information and combine it with the biographical material after which they bring both to bear on the character of Mrs. Parker in the story. Just as students had to find ways to connect fiction to biography, so now they need to discover connections between history, biography, and fiction. By introducing the historical background in which Dorothy Parker lived and wrote into the writing process, I wanted them to rethink their discoveries made in the previous draft. Students could use the same reader and purpose, of course, but now a new kind of "dissonance" had to be recognized and resolved, making necessary an even larger synthesis than before.

Students conclude this cycle of writings on Parker's story by returning to that text and, using the knowledge and discoveries made in their previous drafts, developing a comprehensive interpretation of Mrs. Parker. Here students make an argument rather than simply report or respond. And they also create another reader profile for this draft, a profile of a reader who knows what they know but needs to be convinced of the connections between Parker's character, Parker herself, and the historical circumstances surrounding both author and creation. This final paper passes through at least one revision workshop, in which the goal is for students to evaluate whether the writer achieves his or her purpose for the proposed reader, and one more editing workshop, in which polishing and refining the paper's mechanics are the objectives, before the instructor evaluates the finished product.

To summarize, then: I have tried to articulate what I see as a basic, unifying principle between Della-Piana's "writing-as-revision" model, and those other models it encompasses and resembles, and those general descriptions of perception and cognition formulated by cognitive psychologists, descriptions that current reading theorists assume or extend into their own analyses of what it means to "read" a text, literary or nonliterary. That principle is that reading, like writing and responding to the world around us, is revisionary, a process admitting change, conflict, confusion, and resolution into its fluid but still identifiable boundaries. Moreover, I have tried to suggest how we might make revision the basis of advanced composition courses by teaching our students that revising, in its larger, more creative sense, is a different way of seeing and knowing any experience or object, a way of turning a text, say, in order to examine it from various angles: that of an individual reader's perspective, or of a group of readers, or from the perspective of the author's life and times.

Obviously, this notion of revision is more "global" than "focal," to use Smith's term. Yet I have tried to show how those more "focal" problems requiring revision, at the level of word, sentence, or paragraph, can be addressed within the broader constraints of purpose, audience, and research. In shifting these different rhetorical constraints, I have found that my students keep from getting bored with such extended examination of and writing on a single text—which is always a danger to be devoutly avoided in the type of pedagogical translation I have made. Such an approach does not, of course, solve all of the many problems our students have, whether in advanced or intermediate composition courses. Some students simply revise more effectively than others; they are capable of withstanding dissonance and ambiguity over longer periods than their peers. And I would add that one of the most prevalent "blocks" to revising—at least in the students I have taught using this approach—is students' narrow view of what revising in fact entails, a view probably derived from past experiences with other composition teachers for whom revising is no different from editing or proofreading. Certainly more research needs to be done on students' "preconceptions" about writing, and my own approach needs to be studied and experimented with on an extended basis. No doubt any model for the revision process will find itself caught up in the very process it seeks to describe. This result need not surprise or dismay writing teachers in search of quick and easy explanations of a very complex phenomena. Rather, it reveals how much revising is part of the thinking process itself, a process whereby we see and resee what we think through the embodying capacity of language itself.

NOTES

1. Della-Piana's article is in Charles R. Cooper and Lee Odell, eds., *Research on Composing: Points of Departure* (Urbana, IL: NCTE, 1978). His revisionist model of composing appears on 107. Further references to Della-Piana's essay appear in the text by page number.

2. See Murray's "Internal Revision: A Process of Discovery," in *Research on Composing*, 85–103, and Sommer's "Revision Strategies of Student Writers and Experienced Adult Writers," *College Composition and Communication* (CCC) 31 (1981): 378–87. Recent studies of revision extend and refine Murray's and Sommer's observations. See Carol Berkenkotter, "Decisions and Revisions: The Planning Strategies of a Publishing Writer," *College Composition and Communication* 34 (1983): 156–69, and Donald Murray's response in that same issue, "Response of a Laboratory Rat—or, Being Protocoled," 169–72; Mimi Schwartz, "Revision Profiles: Patterns and Implications," *College English* 45 (1983): 549–58; see especially Roland K. Huff, "Teaching Revision: A Model of the Drafting Process," *College English* 45 (1983): 800–816.

3. The work in cognitive psychology and information theory is extensive, but the works I have found most useful are as follows: Ulric Neisser, *Cognitive Psychology* (Englewood Cliffs, NJ: Prentice-Hall, 1967); Karl H. Pibram, *Languages of the Brain: Experimental Paradoxes and Principles in Neuropsychology* (Englewood Cliffs, NJ: Prentice-Hall, 1971); D. E. Berlyne, *Structure and Direction in Thinking* (New York: John Wiley, 1965), especially pages 256–60; James Gibson, *The Senses Considered as Perceptual Systems* (New York: Houghton Mifflin, 1966); E. H. Gombrich, *Art and Illusion: A Study in the Psychology of Pictorial Representation* (Princeton: Princeton University

Press, 1969); John S. Antrobus, ed., *Cognition and Affect* (Boston: Little, Brown, 1970); and Michael I. Posner, *Cognition: An Introduction* (Glenview, IL: Scott Foresman, 1973).

4. Neisser, *Cognitive Psychology*, 262.

5. See Wolfgang Iser, *The Act of Reading: A Theory of Aesthetic Response* (Baltimore: Johns Hopkins University Press, 1978); Michael Riffaterre, *Semiotics of Poetry* (Bloomington: Indiana University Press, 1978); Johnathan Culler, *The Pursuit of Signs: Semiotics, Literature, Deconstruction* (Ithaca: Cornell University Press, 1981); Stanley E. Fish, *Self-Consuming Artifacts: The Experience of Seventeenth Century Literature* (Berkeley: University of California Press, 1972). Further references to Fish will appear in the text by page number.

6. Louise Rosenblatt, *The Reader the Text the Poem: The Transactional Theory of the Literary Work* (Carbondale: Southern Illinois University Press, 1978).

7. Frank Smith, *Understanding Reading: A Psycholinguistic Analysis of Reading and Learning to Read*, 2nd ed. (1971; repr., New York: Holt, Rinehart & Winston, 1978), 157–58. Further references will appear in the text.

8. See W. K. C. Guthrie, *The Sophists* (London: Cambridge University Press, 1971), 45.

9. Numerous writing theorists identify metaphor or one of its close cousins, analogy, simile, or similitude, as an invention strategy. See D. Gordon Rohman, "Pre-writing: The Stage of Discovery in the Writing Process," *College Composition and Communication* 16 (1965): 112–14; Peter Elbow, *Writing Without Teachers* (New York: Oxford University Press, 1973), 48–75; Linda S. Flower and John R. Hayes, "Problem-Solving Strategies and the Composing Process," *College English* 39 (1979): 455; and James Moffett, *Coming On Center: English Education in Evolution* (Montclair, NJ: Boynton/Cook, 1981), 147.

10. On this approach, see Lisa S. Ede, "On Audience and Composition," *College Composition and Communication* 30 (1979): 291–95. Ede outlines two ways of dealing with audience: instructor imposition or student invention, the last of which she favors because it permits students to become actively involved in considering purpose and context and mode of publication (294).

The Hall Monitor Who Broke the Rules: Teaching Dorothy Parker's *The Ladies of the Corridor* as Feminist Drama

Ann M. Fox

A FEW YEARS AGO, I TAUGHT A SENIOR SEMINAR ON "AMERICAN FEMINISM and Theater, 1900–1960" at Washington University in Saint Louis to a group of talented, insightful students, who had tackled the plays on our syllabus like Sophie Treadwell's *Machinal* (1928) and Gertrude Stein's *The Mother of Us All* (1945) with verve and gusto. I eagerly awaited their responses to a play that, while less stylistically experimental than those mentioned above, I still admired as a particularly fine example of feminist playwriting: Dorothy Parker and Arnaud d'Usseau's *The Ladies of the Corridor* (1953).[1]

Their initial responses left me a little stunned. They had expected a work of comedic wit from the famously sharp-tongued Parker; they believed *this* work "too depressing," finding it boring, disjointed, and irrelevant. They could see in it neither an artistic challenge to the status quo in the manner of Djuna Barnes or Alice Gerstenberg nor an overt political statement like those made by Treadwell and Stein. They re-echoed the disdain of *New York Times* critic Brooks Atkinson, who in 1953 had called the play's premise "loosely contrived" and its stories "hackneyed."[2] I wondered: would our study of this play be nothing more than its excavation as a curiosity, then, a footnote to Parker's more illustrious literary career?

But what held my interest, and what convinced me to move forward with this play, is that several issues of dramatic and social import find themselves crowding into that corridor of Parker's. My students' dismissal of the play as irrelevant reflected a larger dilemma still inherent in the construction of a canon of feminist theater, namely that prejudices against a pluralistic view of feminist playwriting will cause us (and by "us," I mean those of us in academia specifically committed to advancing feminist drama) to undervalue our history and assign hierarchies of merit. Explicitly or implicitly, we are reinforcing the notion that there is a "right" way

279

to do feminist theater, and that right way is, for the most part, contemporary and antirealist. In recognizing the feminism incipient in Dorothy Parker's play, we combat the elitism inherent in the assumption that plays written for mainstream audiences cannot be used for political ends, the contention that realism cannot be recovered and transformed in feminist interests, and the relative paucity of information on how American women playwrights before the 1960s not only anticipated, but provided the groundwork for aesthetic innovations in playwriting that would serve as the hallmark of what we know as contemporary feminist playwriting.

Scholars wishing to study American women's playwriting for the commercial theater before the 1960s have found themselves encouraged to do reclamatory work. Good examples of such work are to be found in studies such as Helen Krich Chinoy and Linda Walsh Jenkins's *Women in American Theatre,* Judith Olauson's *The American Woman Playwright: A View of Criticism and Characterization,* Yvonne Shafer's *American Women Playwrights, 1900–1950,* Sally Burke's *American Feminist Playwrights: A Critical History,* and Brenda Murphy's *The Cambridge Companion to American Women Playwrights.* However, figures like Susan Glaspell, Lillian Hellman, and Clare Boothe Luce aside, the nature of early American feminism in the theater remains somewhat amorphous. Because so many of the plays were written in the style of dramatic realism for commercial theater, it is assumed they contain at least an implicit, if not often overt, reaffirmation of the dominant ideologies about race, gender, ethnicity, and economics. Some of them do. However, theater historians like Tracy Davis have stressed the importance of placing these works within their own cultural context, the better to appreciate the answers to "gender trouble" these women shaped at the intersection of stage images of women, cultural debates on women's place, and audience expectations.[3] Likewise, scholars such as Patricia Schroeder and Patti Gillespie have asserted the importance of acknowledging the diverse forms feminist playwriting can take;[4] Schroeder has further shown that it is possible to discern in seemingly mainstream works interventions into realism that provide the glimmerings of the aesthetic we call feminist theater today.[5] It is an exciting time to study women writing for the stage before the contemporary women's movement; plays wait to be uncovered and reevaluated by those equipped with an awareness of cultural context and an understanding of the plurality of feminist dramaturgy.

Dorothy Parker is such a playwright. Although she has merited a brief entry in Shafer's catalog of *American Women Playwrights, 1900–1950,* she remains conspicuously absent from discussions of the feminism of American theater before 1950. Part of this is undoubtedly due to her greater reputation as a writer of poetry and fiction, and to the fact that her plays were in no way commercially successful at the time they were produced. But an argument for rereading and understanding *The Ladies of the Corridor* as feminist drama that combines social critique and aesthetic intervention can be made. It provides a model for seeing the plays of Parker and her contemporaries as part of a continuum stretching throughout the century dedicated to revealing the usually hidden experience of American women.

Dorothy Parker's relationship with drama was figured in a number of ways, all of which are suggestive of the political and aesthetically innovative stance *The Ladies of the Corridor* would take. She worked at various points in her career as the drama critic for *Vanity Fair, Ainslee's,* and the *New Yorker;* an open derision of popular entertainment got her fired from *Vanity Fair,* but still she continued to "develop the sophisticated voice outraged at the paucity of entertainment on Broadway."[6] Not only did she lambaste superficiality in performance, racism and injustice in stage imagery disturbed her from her earliest days as a critic. In a 1921 review of *The Emperor Jones,* Parker would complain of theater's limiting opportunities for black actors to "an offer to play one-fourth of a quartet in an uptown cabaret and a chance to don a white cotton wig and say 'God bress you, Marse Robert,' as an old family retainer in a heart interest drama."[7] While none of her plays would address race issues, race consciousness was part and parcel of Parker's social consciousness, one that allowed her, in *The Ladies of the Corridor,* to attack ableism, ageism, classism, sexism, and homophobia.[8] Despite her disdain for spectacles such as the Ziegfeld Follies, Parker wrote for a number of musical revues, and her thinly disguised personality was part of more than one Broadway show. As one acquaintance wrote,

> A number of playwrights who knew Dottie well used her as a model for a character—usually a wisecracking woman, with either good looks or their remnants; she drinks too much; if she isn't suffering through an unhappy romance at the moment, one is just behind her; and often the threat of suicide hangs in the air.[9]

Parker would leave New York for California in the late 1930s to become a screenwriter; her many credits include *A Star is Born, Pride of the Yankees,* and *The Little Foxes.*

Her revues and screenplays aside, Parker's career as a dramatist resulted in four plays, all produced in collaboration with men. Parker's first play, *Close Harmony* (1924), was coauthored with Elmer

Rice, and was based on one of Parker's short stories, "Such A Pretty
Little Picture." Despite a promising preview in Wilmington, Delaware, and favorable reviews, and despite the involvement of well-
known and successful director Arthur Hopkins, the play ran on
Broadway for only four weeks. Parker is reported, after one particularly empty performance, to have wired to a friend: "CLOSE HAR-
MONY DID A COOL NINETY DOLLARS AT THE MATINEE. ASK
THE BOYS IN THE BACK ROOM WHAT THEY WILL HAVE."[10] Although she coauthored a second play, *The Happiest Man,* with Alan
Campbell in 1939, revues and screenwriting would dominate her
dramatic output until 1949, the start of a six-year period in which
Parker cowrote three plays in succession: *The Coast of Illyria* (1949),
with Ross Evans; *The Ladies of the Corridor* (1953), with Arnaud d'Usseau; and *The Ice Age* (1955), also with d'Usseau. *The Coast of Illyria*
was produced by Margo Jones in Dallas in 1949; based on the lives
of Romantic writers and siblings Charles and Mary Lamb, the play
ran for three weeks and never made it to Broadway. *The Ice Age,* Parker's second collaboration with d'Usseau, remains unproduced and
unpublished in manuscript form at Columbia University. The daring nature of the story, dealing with a married man's homosexual
relationship with his employer, was more than likely responsible for
its neglect.[11]

  All of Parker's plays deal with the stifling nature of convention,
and with characters who attempt to negotiate through the expectations of others toward some semblance of happiness. *The Ladies of
the Corridor,* which Parker called "the only thing I have ever done in
which I had great pride,"[12] was her most successful play, even
though it, too, enjoyed a limited run on Broadway of some forty-
five performances after opening 21 October 1953. Based on Parker's
experiences as a longtime resident of New York's Volney Hotel, the
play uses the setting of a residential hotel for ladies to interweave
three main storylines. We see the decline of Mildred Tynan, who has
fled an abusive marriage, but whose husband refuses to give her a
divorce. Economically dependent on his sporadic checks and unequipped to do any work, she is spending her final days in an alcoholic haze; her despair culminates in a suicidal plunge from her
window. Another story follows Lulu Ames, whose move to New York
from Akron, Ohio, after being recently widowed, underscores her
continuing attempts throughout the play to also leave behind the
stultifying convention that marked her married life. She becomes
involved in an affair with Paul Osgood, a charming and kind book-
seller a good deal younger than she. Ultimately, however, Lulu cannot shake her view of herself as existing only if she is everything to a

man, and her possessiveness drives Paul away. Parker also tells the story of Mrs. Nichols and her son Charles; an invalid, Mrs. Nichols keeps her son Charles tightly bound to her as her caretaker. When he attempts to break free by seeking a teaching job, she threatens to take to any prospective employer an old scandal in which Charles was accused of making advances to a young male student. The experiences of all the hotel's residents collectively diagram a particular kind of female experience from early marriage to middle-aged housewifery to widowhood, with disappointment and disillusionment being the hallmark of every point in that journey. Although the women are from all corners of the country—from the South, the Midwest, California, and upstate New York—their experiences all dwindle to the same tragic end, either literal death or death-in-life, in the same locale. Lurking in the background, alternately evoking the fates and a Greek chorus, are Mrs. Gordon and Mrs. Lauterbach, faded ladies of the corridor who prefigure the fate of all women in the hotel, measuring out their days in hair appointments, movies, and endless rounds of shopping and eating out. "That's right, honey. Keep going as long as you can. But remember, here we are, waiting for you," they assure Lulu ominously when she attempts to evade their grasp (36). The one happy ending is that of Connie Mercer, a friend and fellow resident of Lulu's, who finds fulfillment in a sense of self largely accomplished through her career as an interior designer outside the hotel environs.

Then and now, the play has been subjected to readings of mixed enthusiasm that have not talked extensively about its political nature. The play opened to the approval of five of the eight major New York critics (indeed, George Jean Nathan would later vote it the best play of the year). But the criticism it did receive was stinging. For example, Brooks Atkinson seemed to consider the whole project redundant and uninteresting:

> In "The Ladies of the Corridor," which was acted at the Longacre last evening, Dorothy Parker and Arnaud d'Usseau insist on pointing out that unattached ladies of venerable years are pathetic and lonely creatures. Unfortunately, everybody knows that without having to go to the theatre. "The Ladies of the Corridor" goes to considerable trouble to reiterate the obvious. On the whole it is a loosely contrived play with more stock ideas in it than you would expect from Miss Parker and Mr. d'Usseau.[13]

Although noting several good performances in this "long and phlegmatic" drama, Atkinson is dismissive of the issues at the play's core. The actors, he believes, can have little to say about what he considers an uninteresting assemblage of characters who are "commonplace and without talent." Connie Mercer's success and Mildred Tynan's end are read with the same laconic disdain: the former is simply "a widow who has found a career," while the latter is "a lonely dipsomaniac who embraces defenestration." Aptly enough, he reserves his praise for the most patriarchally identified of the women; Mrs. Nichols is not read as manipulative or controlling, but as "an admirable human being with strength of mind." In a review ominously titled "Gloom Service," *Saturday Review* reviewer Henry Hewes actually comes closer to appreciating Parker's portrayal of waste, understanding, for example, that in the character of Connie Mercer, we gain a glimpse "of what the others might have been." Yet Hewes, too, blames these women's plight on themselves rather than on their circumstances:

> In *Ladies of the Corridor* we feel that these women are almost deliberately responsible for their own condition. They have committed the sin of devoting themselves blindly and completely to their husbands and to their children without attempting to find larger and more useful interests for themselves. Their husbands and their children do not want such all-exclusive devotion and resent the obligation it puts them under.[14]

In Hewes's eyes, the play becomes a cautionary tale, not to a society that stifles women in conventional roles, but rather, to women who "love too much." His words echo the arguments of sociologists and journalists who, in the late 1940s and early 1950s, believed that American mother-worship was allowing women to put a stranglehold on their children. According to them, the

> female sex had devolved into a race of parasites—"an idle class, a spending class, a candy-craving class"—devoted to consuming all the money, affection and virility which men could offer. Mother worship was ostensibly based on the endless self-sacrifice of "mom," but in reality it was rooted in her insatiable appetite for devouring her young and preventing them from developing into independent adults.[15]

Parker's play would join the counterarguments to this contention, supporting the idea that if "society crippled women psychologically by foreclosing their options, women would continue to cripple their children. Freedom and autonomy represented the answer for both."[16]

Interestingly, even recent assessments of the play have dealt only in a limited way with its feminism. Biographer Marion Meade openly acknowledged that

> [Parker thought] of it as a feminist play that warned women "to stop sitting around and saying 'it's a man's world.'" Although the wasted lives of her characters disturbed her, she was inclined to believe that their illness was rooted not so much in age as in manlessness "and they should be better trained, adjusted to live life without a man," a problem that she herself had yet to resolve.[17]

As the end of this passage suggests, Meade's assessment of the play veers finally toward its autobiographical reflection of Parker. Arthur Kinney, while complimentary to the play, categorizes Parker's drama, curiously enough, as part of her literary "apprenticeship"— despite the fact that it was written toward the end of her life and writing career. The play is less for Kinney about the ravages of gender expectations on a total life lived than it is about the terrors facing women left alone in old age. He accuses Mrs. Nichols of "monstrosity and viciousness" without considering what has led her to this point; like Hewes, he partly places blame on the characters rather than the society that has relegated them to a life of retiring despair.[18] Even forty-four years later, Shafer's estimation of Parker's play is lukewarm:

> The intent of the play is to demonstrate the loneliness of the women and therefore the play is a series of scenes of unrelated action. This is part of the problem in the play. Unlike similar plays such as *Grand Hotel* and the highly successful Ferber and Kaufman play *Dinner at Eight* there is no interaction between the characters which leads to dramatic tension and irony.[19]

She calls Parker's playwriting career "a major disappointment[;] with her wit, her imagination, and her sympathy for marginalized people in society, she should have been able to write some memorable plays."[20] She considers very little of the play, and what might have made it an important feminist work.

How might we, then, uncover feminist elements in the play? To begin with, Parker's work reads as an intervention into popular stage images of women at the time. The era when the triumvirate of Arthur Miller, Tennessee Williams, and Eugene O'Neill ruled the American stage was well underway. Plays like *The Iceman Cometh* (1946), *Death of A Salesman* (1949), and *The Glass Menagerie* (1945) had enjoyed tremendous popularity in the decade preceding Parker's work. In the process, they had provided stage audiences with some jarring images of womanhood, images that largely followed the standard division of women into angels (Linda Loman, Laura Wingfield) or whores (O'Neill's prostitutes, Willy Loman's lover). Women remained largely on the periphery, and even when they took center stage, it was often to perform some essential imbalance. Parker has ostensibly placed these women before an audience in an attempt to provide another glimpse into their position. Like the prostitutes in O'Neill's *The Iceman Cometh,* Mildred Tynan drinks too much, is promiscuous, and holds close to the life-lie of a tomorrow that will never come. But we see the roots of her behavior in her entrapment not just by her own self-delusions, but by the control of a husband who supports her intermittently with money that is "late every month . . . just another way to humiliate" her (13). Like Linda Loman, Lulu was widowed long before her husband's actual death by his slavish devotion to his business. But as an early conversation with her son and daughter-in-law suggests, she is less willing to see her part in this as a noble necessity:

> LULU. I loathe the idea of mourning, but it seems to be expected of you. No, Betsy, I don't think you ever did see me in black. Bob's father disliked it so. Oh, at first I used to wear it now and then, just so he'd take some notice of me—if only to ask me to change my dress.
> ROBERT. Mother, you make Father sound like a monster.
> LULU. Do I, dear?
> ROBERT. Father was a busy man. He had a great many things on his mind.
> LULU. Only one. From the very beginning he was unfaithful to me.
> BETSY. Mother Ames!
> LULU. Oh, yes, he was in love with his business. He even slept with it three or four times a week—you remember that bed he had in his inner office. (19)

Where Linda defends Willy's devotion to his work, Lulu recognizes it as a conscious choice by her husband to separate himself from his family. She also recognizes her own bow to convention in choosing to stay with such a man, since there had "never been a divorce in the history of the family" (19). We can also read a compelling rewrite of a Tennessee Williams heroine in Mrs. Nichols. Mrs. Nichols becomes an Amanda whose desire to control her own child has a basis in her inability to control her own fate for most of her life, a subject I will address further in a moment.

In answering the limitations of female characters in popular plays by male playwrights, Parker's portraits extend and deepen the critique already fomented by popular plays by her female contemporaries with feminist themes such as *The Women* (1936) and *The Little Foxes* (1939). Such plays had already enjoyed wide success, even as they presented sharp critiques of societal constraints on women, and their echoes can be found in the world of the Hotel Marlowe. As in both previous plays, the ladies of the corridor find themselves sharply restricted by the social constraints required for "ladylike" behavior. Parker layers image after image of enclosure in the play; the women are neatly parceled out to the rooms of the hotel, kept out of sight and tucked away in a cellblock of sorts once they have outlived their usefulness. As Mildred Tynan bitterly notes, "Vegetables they are, sitting there in their bins, waiting for the garbage collector to come and get them" (112). The bank of pigeonholes for mail that form part of the opening set suggests their parceling out, as do the many references to the zoo and caged animals made in the play. Like the creatures Charles Nichols visits at the zoo on a daily basis, these women have been domesticated; their wildness gone, all they can do is be tended (indeed, at times even "serviced") by their keepers, the kindly staff (who are mostly men). As in *The Women,* since these women are accorded little importance in the world, they create a universe of their own in which the smallest decisions carry the weightiest import and serve, in the end, only as a means of filling time, as a typical comment by Mrs. Gordon suggests:

> What a day! I'm just about wore out. Had my polish changed; had my hair done; took those shoes back that were killing me. That little old clerk, selling me shoes that were shoes a size too small! I told him my feet are small enough as they are; always had compliments on my little feet. How do you like my hair? (5)

In turn, they carefully monitor and scrutinize the behavior of everyone who enters their sphere. When Lulu makes her first entrance, for instance, the women are quick to pass judgment on the most insignificant things:

> MRS LAUTERBACH. It's a lady all by herself.
> MRS. NICHOLS. Look at all that baggage. Two hat boxes—and what's that square one? A shoebox?
> MRS. GORDON. Those kind of things are nothing but an expense. Just means another tip to the porter.
> MRS. LAUTERBACH. What's that coat? Broadtail?
> MRS. GORDON. Won't wear.
> MRS. NICHOLS. No warmth to it. (9)

Warmth is decidedly needed in an atmosphere as chilly as the Hotel Marlowe. Left behind by the rest of society, unequipped to move out into a society that has deemed them outmoded, the women are frustrated and resentful. Lulu describes their predicament:

> LULU. I don't know how to get myself fixed up. There's something lacking. I guess there's something lacking in a lot of women; nobody's ever one of a kind. We were told you grew up, you got married, and there you were. But our husbands, they were busy. We weren't part of their lives; and as we got older we weren't part of anybody's lives, and yet we never learned how to be alone. (97)

As in *The Women*, one central response for these women is that they turn their energies against one another. Mrs. Gordon spends her time stealing trifles from the hotel, from dime stores and from the other women; even though her mask is one of simpering pleasantry, she gossips mercilessly about her fellow residents. She critiques Mrs. Lauterbach's weight, harps on Mildred's drinking, disdains Connie for working, and disapproves of Lulu's liaison with Paul Osgood. As the women engage in countless character assassinations, it is revealing that Mrs. Lauterbach reads and re-reads a book called *Murder in a Gilded Cage*. Connie warns Lulu to steer clear of their example, since "those women are dead, and death is contagious" (58).

The story of Mrs. Nichols and her son Charles, however, is Parker's most striking response to the depiction of mother-control exerted by figures such as Regina Giddens and Amanda Wingfield. In the process of rewriting these two figures, Parker integrates disabled and queer identities into her critique of gender constraint. Arthritic and in a wheelchair, Mrs. Nichols keeps her son tightly bound to her as a caretaker. When he attempts to break free by seeking a teaching job, she threatens to take to any prospective employer an old scandal in which Charles was accused of making advances to a young male student. What's perhaps most interesting about Mrs. Nichols's disability from a contemporary perspective is that as Parker introduces it, she eschews the conventional markers that might label the condition tragic or limiting:

> Mrs. Nichols, an arthritic, is confined to a wheelchair—not an old-fashioned cumbersome one, but a low, lightweight aluminum model such as paraplegics use. Despite her ailment, Mrs. Nichols is all elegance. She is dressed softly and beautifully. From the perfect hat set so carefully on her perfect hair to the pretty little feet partly covered by a light afghan, she is all expense, taste, and femininity. Charles Nichols pushes the chair. He is tall, lean, finely drawn. Look carefully at him, and he is beautiful. But he should have been handsome at first sight. (6)

Mrs. Nichols's wheelchair takes on the role as an extension of her perfect taste and poise, and even sleekness. The other women in the hotel notice it; when they urge her to come to a movie with them, and she demurs, calling herself a "nuisance," and "so conspicuous in this awful thing," one declares: "I wish I could be that kind of conspicuous. Why, when you come rolling into the movie house with Charlie pushing you, that chair's like a queen's chariot. I declare, you're positively regal" (11). The queenly Mrs. Nichols's femininity seems to be fairly conventional, as the description of her feminine perfection I have just mentioned might seem to suggest. Her patterns of address seem to mimic her patterns of dress: in talking to Charles, she uses the passive voice and leading questions until Charles begs her in frustration to be more direct: "Please stop asking me, 'don't I want to?' Just ask me, 'will I?'" (39). But that semblance of passive femininity soon reveals itself to be a veneer.

The reference to the "regal" nature of Mrs. Nichols, as well as her situation, is evocative of the royally named Regina Giddens of Lillian Hellman's *The Little Foxes*. The link is an important one to stop and consider. Regina, who kills her disabled husband so that she can take control of her family, certainly seems monstrous. Yet it is also possible to read this as Hellman's representation of an ambitious woman driven to such actions because she has been given no other outlet for her talents and energy. Denied a voice for a good deal of her married life, she learns to turn the tables with a vengeance when her husband falls ill. In the same way, we see that Mrs. Nichols has learned the lesson of control all too well. Her husband, we learn, died a month to the day before son Charles was born; since that time, Mrs. Nichols has assumed all control of the household. She has a gift for finance (as the pun indicated by her name, "Mrs. Nickels," signifies) but one that she was never allowed to exercise by her husband:

> He used to say we had enough money. He couldn't understand that he ought to make money into more money. I was the one who had to take over and do that. Well, he was a dear man. Sweet—not strong, but awfully sweet. (38)

She describes her deceased husband in affectionate, almost effeminate or "wifely" terms. Her appropriation of the masculine from the men around her does not stop here, however. She is also pictured frequently in the play pursuing a hobby of collecting stamps— having taken on a hobby that once belonged to her son.

Charles now lives with his mother in the Hotel Marlowe, going out

every day to—at least as he tells his mother—visit the zoo. That
Charles flees from the cages of the Marlowe's individual rooms and
the solitary confinement each patron suffers there to the zoo casts
the two locales as reflections of one another from which Charles—
like many of the women in the hotel—can find no real escape. His
mother encourages Charles to recount tales of his visit to the zoo,
urging him to "tell them (the other ladies) about Chiang." He replies, "there's nothing much to tell, Grace. She's just a nice old lady
with a man's name" (7). Curiously, Mrs. Nichols is something like
this elephant. Like the elephant, she is the "nice old lady with a
man's name" and the potential to wield destructive force. Like
Regina Giddens, Mrs. Nichols ultimately—figuratively, if not literally—kills the man in her life, her son, destroying his hopes of re-
establishing his teaching career. She does this by blackmailing him
into staying with her, threatening to reveal to any and all possible
employers that Charles had been accused of a homosexual liaison
with a student in years past.

But like the elephant Charles visits, Mrs. Nichols, too, remains cir-
cumscribed and imprisoned; the almost throwaway image of Chiang
early in the appearance of Mrs. Nichols and her son begins to provide a clue to understanding how Parker figures the former. Disability, as employed as theatrical device by Parker, takes on a curious
ambiguity in this regard. Metaphorically, it seems impossible to fix
into place, becoming the most fluid marker of the dangers and results of gendered fixity. Is it a reference to her husband's illness and
death? A way to underscore Mrs. Nichols's own maternal suffering
as a result of her son's supposed homosexuality? A manifestation of
the cruelty that leads her to blackmail Charles into staying with her?
A metaphor for the passivity that she, as a woman, is supposed to
have in this society? Ultimately, all these meanings stem from the
marriage that Mrs. Nichols has made to an unwavering belief in the
rightness of gender complementarity. But finding the strictures of
femininity not to her liking, she exercises power in the only other
way she can understand—inverting the power relationships to
usurp, and thereby implicitly reaffirm, the strictures of patriarchy.
She is not a gender-bender to flout it, but to further fix it into place,
even as she affixes stamps within her collection, even as her body
rigidifies from arthritis.

It is important to note here that although disability and queerness
are not treated as lived identities to be portrayed in all their fullness,
they still function importantly together; they enhance the power of
each other to denaturalize the constructions of gendered, bodily,
and heterosexual normativity that drive Mrs. Nichols, that them-

selves are more potently destructive forces than the bodily or sexual deviances that seem to threaten them. For example, Mrs. Nichols is utterly dependent on the existence of Charles's implicit homosexuality, which allows her to reinscribe her own power in relationship to him, to define herself against him and appropriate the masculine power in a patriarchal household where there can be only one master. His mother's insistence on the two of them as a dyad, as a couple, is a reflection of her internalization of patriarchy. Her son cannot have his own career and she must be taken care of; he becomes, in a sense, her wife. Femininity has failed her, but because she cannot see beyond the system containing it, it is projected onto the body of her son. His potential queerness is not the end result, but rather, the means with which to bind him permanently to her. Similarly, although disabled but full well economically and emotionally to care for herself, she still insists that her own "precarious" health depends on Charles, alternately invoking her own fragility yet giving the lie to a moral model of disability that would cast her as helpless or innocent. And so by the end of the play, Charles is without speech—or only echoes the words of others (and indeed, the other women comment that he looks older than his mother). He is one of the silent litany of women that open the door, greet each other, and greet a hopeless new day, every day, the "other" against whom the patriarch depends to reinforce (in this case) her own identity. Like Regina, Mrs. Nichols is a devoted servant of capitalism, disregarding who might be hurt along the way. Even her relationship with her son becomes a business transaction; she will not release him because she has purchased his presence by paying off his accusers. Her monstrosity comes not from being an aberration, but from embracing the power predominant in this society in a way that echoes and reaffirms the predominance of its male, heterosexual, ablebodied members.

It is also possible to read in Parker's work a stinging repudiation of the idealized images of femininity offered to women. Parker warns that women who become "ladies," who become "properly" retiring as wives and mothers, will ultimately *be* retired when they are outmoded. On the way to making this point, she particularly ravages the sentimental ideals of romantic love, domesticity, and motherhood. This point is made most particularly and thoroughly in the respective journeys of Lulu and Mildred. Lulu has arrived at the hotel to make a grab at freedom, to break free from the conservatism symbolized by her hometown of Akron, Ohio. And for a while, defying the expectations of those around her, she is successful. She transcends the sentimental surroundings and widow's weeds, transforming her rooms and herself into something fine. Her poodle becomes a symbol of Lulu's movement between worlds; though a fragile and fluffy animal, she is aptly named "Sassy." So, too, is her owner, who gives up the needlework and visits to her husband's grave that formed the core of her daily activities in Akron. Lulu has been resurrected from her own death-in-life existence to shake off her mourning dress, live on her own, and eventually take up with a younger man. Even when confronted with a younger version of herself in the marriage of son Bob and daughter-in-law Betsy (for Betsy also shows an excessive child-fixation and deference to her husband's ambition) she retains her humor and spirit. She eschews the company of the ladies of the corridor, as does Mildred. But Mildred is at the end of her journey, rather than the beginning. She has also made a grab at freedom from her husband, fleeing a past that was a deception and a lie. She recalls her youthful self on her wedding day, "all white and innocent, and I was sort of shining because I was so happy" (46). Her innocence becomes a rude awakening to a life with "Holy John Tynan, the Blessed Martyr of Santa Barbara. Yes, and the call girls, two and three at a time, and the whip in the closet" (113).

Both Lulu and Mildred learn that the veneer of femininity is an act that holds very little real promise for self-fulfillment underneath. Mildred comes to realize much more quickly than Lulu the immense difficulty of any move toward independence in this world when she is unable to support herself and is unwanted in a world that values youth and beauty. When Mildred tries to find a job so that she can escape the economic tyranny of her husband, all she can find are advertisements for

> "College graduates—teletypers—electronics—study to be an airplane hostess—photographer's model—five feet, eight, thirty-six, twenty-four, thirty-six—accountants, experienced—stenographers, experienced—tearoom hostesses, experienced—beauticians, experienced—young women—young women—girls—girls—girls. . . ." (51)

This is a world, Mildred realizes, that has very little practical use for the traditional markers of female "accomplishment":

> MILDRED. Let's see. What are my talents? What do I think I'm going to do anyway? Think I could teach French? I used to speak very nice French, all in the present tense. Maybe I could give music lessons to backward children. There must be lots of backward children around. I took music lessons for years. I finally got so I could play the "Minute Waltz" in a minute and a half. No, no fooling, what can I do? Oh, I

do know. I can arrange flowers. I'm really a whiz at that. People would come to our house and see my arrangements and say I must have Japanese blood in me. That was before the war, of course. (49)

Mildred, without education, no longer in the first blush of youth, without economic resources of her own, wastes away. She becomes frozen in a fear of "Everything. The dark. Morning. Tonight. Tomorrow. Next week. Forever" (45).

Lulu is similarly imperiled, although she is entrapped in a different way. Her friendship with Connie has exposed her to someone unafraid to "go dutch" with life, someone whose drive to conquer loneliness has led her to personal and professional fulfillment. And yet, she cannot step completely outside of the language with which society has equipped her. Although she has made a break toward freedom, Lulu eventually reverts to old patterns, particularly trapped by the rhetoric of romantic love, one that would have her reattach herself to a new man, to make herself "useful" again. She cannot imagine life other than as part of a duo with Paul—to the exclusion of all others. She refuses to meet his friends, and becomes increasingly possessive as the play wears on. Despite Paul's warning that "two people, no matter what their feeling, musn't feed entirely on each other," Lulu fantasizes about a relationship that excludes all others (86). Paul recognizes the danger of such an attitude, cloaked as it is in a veil of sentimentality:

It was a good, simple thing we had, Lulu, but you had to make it into a fairy tale with swoons and vows and bleeding hearts. You can't help it, because you have to sentimentalize everything. (110)

By play's end, Sassy has died, and along with her, it seems, Lulu's resolve to transcend "ladyhood." In the end, we're left unsure of Lulu's fate. For although she dresses in the colors of autumn and isolates herself in the hotel for several weeks, still she eschews the company of the ladies of the corridor, who offer to draw her into their fold:

Thank you, ladies. You're very kind. But there is really no need to worry about me. I'm quite all right. I'm not even scared. You see, I've learned from looking around, there is something worse than loneliness—and that's the fear of it. (120)

Even though the experience of Parker's ladies is limited to that of white, middle-class women, her play also anticipates that central concern of materialist feminist critics today: the imposition of cultural worth based on other conditions of existence besides gender. Parker's play indicts homophobia, ableism, ageism, and the economic entrapment of women, making her play transcend a simple call for "equality." Parker's play also anticipates aesthetic and thematic innovations that would become more commonplace with the overtly feminist theatre of the 1960s. *The Ladies of the Corridor* undermines many of the realistic conventions that seemed to lend "normalcy" to plays already successfully produced. Instead of focusing on a central protagonist, she chose to represent a continuum of female experience, telling diverse stories; no one character assumes superiority in this ensemble piece. No longer were figures like Linda Loman banished to the periphery; these were women's stories, and the few male characters in Parker's play must themselves, in turn, remain at the edges of the action. The private and domestic is given a weight and an importance that a reviewer like Atkinson found tiresome. And while the play draws to an end, there is no real closure, no neat resolution of the ravages that patriarchy has wrought on the lives of these women. Indeed, Parker was persuaded to cut out some of her more overt moments depicting this damage.[21] Finally, Parker does provide a model for hope in the person of Connie Mercer, to instill in her audience members a sense of how breaking free of this cycle of destruction can be achieved.

In teaching *The Ladies of the Corridor* as a feminist play, we can come to understand Parker's justifiable pride in it. We can recognize Parker's commiseration with those who felt themselves limited by the status quo, and her desire to move their stories beyond those contained in the ladies' lending library books—so old, so stale, so trapping in their romance. The implications for seeing Parker's play in a new way as one instance of feminist drama are far flung. Not only does it help us as we attempt to reconstruct theater history, it also sets an important precedent for how we understand the theatrical canon today. The theater landscape is no less dominated by white male writers today than it was in Parker's time; the works of a Mamet or a Shepard, while containing their own particular intrinsic worth, still set the standard for whose stories are told—and by and large, those stories leave out the majority of those in our society. Understanding and appreciating theatrical difference radiates out toward the exciting innovations being fomented by women, multicultural authors, queer playwrights, and disabled dramatists. It embraces difference in approach, life experience, and aesthetic, making our own university corridors welcoming, boisterous, joyful places.

NOTES

1. Dorothy Parker and Arnaud D'Usseau, *The Ladies of the Corridor: A Drama in Two Acts* (New York: Viking, 1954). All subsequent references in the text will be indicated by page number.

2. Brooks Atkinson, "Edna Best and Betty Field Are Starred in 'The Ladies of the Corridor,'" *New York Times,* 22 October 1953, 33:5.

3. Tracy Davis, "Questions for a Feminist Methodology in Theatre History," in *Interpreting the Theatrical Past,* ed. Thomas Postlewait and Bruce McConachie (Iowa City: University of Iowa Press, 1989).

4. Both Schroeder and Gillespie address the issue of pluralism in feminist theatre scholarship in *Theatre and Feminist Aesthetics,* ed. Karen Laughlin and Catherine Schuler (Madison and Teaneck, NJ: Fairleigh Dickinson University Press, 1995).

5. See Schroeder's excellent book *The Feminist Possibilities of Dramatic Realism* (Madison and Teaneck, NJ: Fairleigh Dickinson University Press, 1996).

6. Randall Calhoun, *Dorothy Parker: A Bio-Bibliography* (Westport, CT: Greenwood Press, 1993), 7.

7. Ibid., 15–16.

8. Parker's final gesture was one to address racial inequality. Upon her death in 1967, Parker would bequeath her estate to Dr. Martin Luther King, Jr. Although she had never met him, she had great respect for his work. Upon his death, her estate passed to the NAACP; today, Parker's ashes are interred at its Baltimore headquarters in a memorial garden by way of tribute.

9. Calhoun, 152.

10. Marion Meade, *Dorothy Parker: What Fresh Hell Is This?* (New York: Villard Books, 1988), 138.

11. It is interesting to note that a number of women playwrights treated homosexuality with a sympathetic eye during the decade. Besides Parker's own *Ice Age* and *The Ladies of the Corridor,* plays like Rose Franken's *Outrageous Fortune* (1943) and Sophie Treadwell's *Garry* (1954) took on homophobia.

12. Leslie Frewin, *The Late Mrs. Dorothy Parker* (New York: Macmillan, 1986), 278.

13. Atkinson, 5.

14. Henry Hewes, "Gloom Service," *Saturday Review,* 7 November 1953, 32–33.

15. William Henry Chafe, *The American Woman: Her Changing Social, Economic, and Political Roles, 1920–1970* (New York: Oxford University Press, 1972), 201.

16. Ibid., 215.

17. Meade, 350.

18. Arthur F. Kinney, *Dorothy Parker* (Boston: Twayne Publishers, 1978), 99.

19. Yvonne Shafer, *American Women Playwrights, 1900–1950* (New York: Peter Lang, 1995), 425–26.

20. Ibid., 427.

21. Many of these cut scenes have been reprinted in the preface to Dorothy Parker and Ross Evans's *The Coast of Illyria* (Iowa City: University of Iowa Press, 1990).

Mrs. Parker and the History of Political Thought

Sophia Mihic

In "THE USES OF LITERATURE FOR THE STUDY OF POLITICS," JOHN SCHAAR notes the "abstract," "cool," and "distancing" tone and quality of commonly accepted terms of political discourse and calls them a "parched public language." "Such a language leaves out half of life," he writes, "and renders much of our real politics inaccessible to us."[1] A reading of Dorothy Parker's "Big Blonde" is by contrast hot, concrete, and immediate. It angers. But who will be angered by whom is always a surprise when I teach the text in my Modern Political Thought course. Who deserves our sympathy? Hazel Morse who spirals toward self-destruction? Or her husband Herbie Morse who leaves her? Is someone to blame? Or is the institution of marriage the problem? Probing these questions unravels the story in a way that can make terms of political discourse more accessible. Anger and sympathy are provoked by the underlying themes of domination and submission in "Big Blonde"—by how, that is, one interprets the relationships of power in the story—and reflection on these emotions can thus compel reflection on equality and inequality. Schaar cites several terms that make up the cool and distancing language of political discourse—for example, "contract," "right," and "law"—and "equality" and "inequality" could be listed among these. The problem is that these are also the terms of a parched pedagogy. When teaching modern political thought, one can find oneself confronted by a group of students who can manipulate and discuss assigned texts and pertinent concepts without a moment's pause and reflection on what they are actually talking about. Students can read the classics—by Machiavelli, Locke, Hobbes, Rousseau, Wollstonecraft, Hegel, Marx, and Mill—and walk away unscathed. Schaar's tactic for dealing with this disconnect is a turn to literature. He presents Herman Melville's *Benito Cereno* "as a meditation on authority and rebellion" and reads the text as an elaboration of Machiavelli.[2] Following Schaar in this essay, to an extent, I will present "Big Blonde" as an illustration of the dynamics of domination and inequality definitive of and within social conventions and read the text as an elaboration of Rousseau. I, however, want to quibble a bit with Schaar—or, more precisely, push his approach further. I will probe as well what the pairing of Parker and Rousseau teaches us about interdisciplinarity and the plural canons of Western thought.

Schaar's approach is a model of inclusion based upon theme. Since Melville writes about what the tradition of political thought writes about, Melville should be canonized. He should be part of the tradition because he meets the criteria of, let us say, "citizenship" in it. In "Big Blonde," one could argue that Dorothy Parker, too, meets these criteria. But, with Parker, I will proceed on the assumption that we do not have to be limited to a model of mere inclusion when considering relationships between literature and political thought. When we find her work on a modern political thought syllabus,[3] what we encounter is analogous to an act of civil disobedience: a breaking of the law that reinforces, clarifies, brings to life, and gives salience to the canon of political thought. My students are troubled by "Big Blonde." The story provokes a creative tension in their thinking much like Socrates provoked as invigorating gadfly in Athens.[4] Civil disobedience as a mode of political action brings the moral law to bear on the laws of the state. But by offering canonical disobedience as a strategy of interpretation, I do not want to suggest that literature is a superior canon that can adjudicate political thought. My aim is to instead respect its distinctiveness as well as the distinctiveness of the canon that defines my field. Schaar and I are each political theorists. Our subfield is a humanist enclave in the discipline of political science; and our home in a social science requires defense of our perspective's relevance and politicalness. Schaar's essay is a victory in this ongoing battle, because *Benito Cereno* is shown to be quite relevant to the study of politics. But our understanding of canonical encounter does not have to be limited to the question of what literature contributes to political theory. If the turn to literature gives life to and invigorates the canon of political thought, we should suspect that literature is also affected. How so?

I will first follow Schaar's strategy and read Rousseau with Parker's aid. Then the essay will consider the reverse tensions produced by their pairing, and ask what reading Parker with Rousseau's aid teaches us about "Big Blonde."

Rousseau argues that inequality and domination are definitive of all human sociality, of language and of consciousness itself. When we make distinctions, we define differences; neither thought nor speech can proceed without distinctions; and these differences establish hierarchies that create inequalities. There can be no convention without these distinctions in language and thought and thus there can be no human interaction without inequality. Rousseau's position is thought-provoking in its own right. Why supplement his *Discourse on the Origin of Inequality* and read inequality and domination through the relationship between Hazel and Herbie Morse? Parker's story hits home in a way that Rousseau does not. When one first explains to a class that Rousseau's state of nature is a heuristic device with which we can probe the relationships between nature and convention in human affairs, eyes glaze over. While the meanings and relevant dimensions of the term "convention" are often elusive, the same theme in "Big Blonde" is more difficult to avoid. Students immediately understand that Hazel's being a "good sport" for men by "laughing at their jokes and telling them she loved their neckties"[5] is fake. They can begin to understand that "nature versus nurture" is too simplistic for understanding the complexities of the distinction as Rousseau presents it. The problem, in his work, is that the divide is indeterminate, seemingly impossible to sustain, yet compelling. With Hazel's artifice as example, they can thus intuit the difference between appearance and reality. From there we can move back to the initially soporific heuristic device that helps us parse the two as convention and nature. When told that Rousseau understands gender as a conventional performance, students may scribble in their notebooks with little thought. But they will sense the foreboding with which Parker describes Hazel's and Herbie's apartment. The stage setting of their marriage, and of their marriage's failure, included:

> a Mission-furnished dining-room with a hanging central light globed in liver-colored glass; in the living room were an over-stuffed suite, a Boston fern, and a reproduction of the Henner "Magdalene" with the red hair and the blue draperies; the bedroom was in gray enamel and old rose, with Herbie's photograph on Hazel's dressing-table and Hazel's likeness on Herbie's chest of drawers.[6]

Gender as performance is not just about highly orchestrated spectacles: a wedding is a small act in the performance of a marriage. Gender as performance also matters when making lunch and dinner,[7] or when otherwise furnishing a home with assumptions and expectations of happiness. And the care with which Parker describes the Morse apartment suggests early on in the story that their stage is a set without substance.

Rousseau clearly signals that his invocation of a state of nature is a heuristic device rather than an actual history. My contention is that "Big Blonde" is a similar story. In the *Origin of Inequality*, Rousseau hypothesizes a historical narrative: "it is no light undertaking to separate what is original from what is artificial in the present nature of man, and to have a proper understanding of a state which no longer exists, which perhaps never existed, which probably never will exist, and yet about which it is necessary to have accurate notions in order to judge our present state."[8] In *Emile*, Rousseau posits a parallel biographical narrative. "I have hence chosen to give myself an imaginary pupil," he writes,

> to hypothesize that I have the age, health, kinds of knowledge, and all the talent suitable for working at his education, for conducting him from the moment of his birth up to the one when, become a grown man, he will no longer have any need of any guide other than himself.[9]

Rousseau thinks with fictions. Natural man emerges from either the figurative womb or the figurative state of nature and through contact with others begins his education and enters into the human artifice. If first human contact is the separation from nature, why must we have accurate notions of this never-existent condition? And, more to the point, how do we have any notion of the difference between nature and convention? Rousseau presumes that we can and do intuit this distinction. "He will soon sense," Rousseau writes of his pupil's teacher (and then of us), "or the reader will sense for him, whether he follows the progress of childhood and the movement natural to the human heart."[10] And Hazel has some sort of similar sense:

> She wanted to be married. She was nearing thirty now, and she did not take the years well. And she had had a couple of thousand evenings of being a good sport among her male acquaintances. She had come to be more conscientious than spontaneous about it.[11]

Hazel recognizes a distinction between the natural and the conventional as she finds herself slipping from spontaneity. Rousseau focuses on this distinction, which is the difference between appearance and reality, because he reads it as an origin of inequality and domination in human affairs.

"Such, in fact," Rousseau concludes in the essay on inequality, "is the true cause of all these differences; the savage lives in himself; the man accustomed to the ways of society is always outside of himself and knows how to live only in the opinion of others."[12] This is overwhelmingly where Hazel lives. But, perplexingly, all men and women live in society and thus we all live outside ourselves. Differences and distinctions are the basis of human sociality and coextensively for Rousseau are the basis of language.[13] And the positing of differences—beautiful and ugly, good and bad, like all modes of comparison creates relationships of inequality.[14] How do these create domination? In *Emile*, Rousseau notes the child's ability to dominate via manipulation of positive and negative responses. "The first tears of children are prayers. If one is not careful, they soon become orders. Children begin by getting themselves assisted; they end by getting themselves served."[15] If we live in the eyes of the child and struggle for his giggles rather than his cries, he will have power over us and come to realize it. After marriage, Hazel tried to give up being a good sport. "She had not realized how tired she was." She lost not only her spontaneity but her conscientiousness as well. "If her head ached, or her arches throbbed, she complained piteously, babyishly. If her mood was quiet, she did not talk. If tears came to her eyes, she let them fall."[16] For a time, Herbie played at the novelty of home life with her, and placated her tears. "But time slid by," Parker writes, "and he found that there was never anything *really, personally* the matter."[17] Hazel had become seduced by the pleasures of vicarious tears.

> "Honestly," she would say to Herbie, "all the sadness there is in the world when you stop to think about it!"
> "Yeah," Herbie would say.[18]

An absence of the real is again sensed. But what is the real? Hazel's approving comments on neckties when playing the good sport certainly were not. Or, were they at one point? Does one cross a threshold into corrupt contrivance? Parker suggests that Hazel now plays at an idea of marriage. "A terrific domesticity had come upon her," we are told, "and she would bite and scratch to guard it."[19] But by following this new script, she fails to live successfully in the eyes of the pertinent other. She no longer has Herbie's approval.

Throughout his accounts of the development of human sociality, Rousseau returns again and again to sexuality and the consequent development of gender differences among the many activities that prompt the development of language and convention.[20] This development, presented as a movement of both progress and decline,[21] demonstrates how behaviors once spontaneous could become corrupted by conscientious contrivance, and illustrates how a domesticity once sweet and secure could become fierce and hollow. "Young people of different sexes," Rousseau speculates on the early steps from a state of nature,

> live in neighboring huts; the passing intercourse demanded by nature soon leads to another, through frequent contact with one another, no less sweet and more permanent. People become accustomed to consider different objects and to make comparisons. Imperceptibly they acquire the ideas of merit and beauty which produce feelings of preference.

The competition to distinguish oneself in the *Discourse on the Origin of Inequality* involves a competition over love, and over the object of love:

> By dint of seeing one another, they can no longer get along without seeing one another again. A sweet and tender feeling insinuates itself into the soul and at the least opposition becomes an impetuous fury. Jealousy awakens with love; discord triumphs, and the sweetest passion receives sacrifices of human blood.[22]

As Hazel's marriage deteriorated: "The idea of intimacy with another man was terrible to her; the thought that Herbie might be seeking entertainment in another woman sent her frantic."[23] But as Herbie's rejection of her continues—"[s]he had no more vicarious tears; the hot drops she shed were for herself"[24]—she turns competitively to others for affirmation. "Drinking with them," Parker writes,

> Mrs. Morse became lively and good-natured and audacious. She was quickly popular. When she had drunk enough to cloud her most recent battle with Herbie, she was excited by their approbation. Crab, was she? Rotten sport, was she? Well, there were some that thought different.[25]

She finds solace by turning to a new audience, to new men, but this tactic will prove unsustainable as well. "Each one began to look at the others and wanted to be looked at himself," Rousseau tells us, "and public esteem had a value. The one who sang or danced the best, the handsomest, the strongest, the most adroit or the most eloquent became the most highly regarded. And this was the first step toward inequality and at the same time, toward vice."[26]

Parker's portrayal of Hazel's decline begins with failed attempts at keeping the Morse marriage together. Hazel begins to drink with Herbie, but their moods are elevated only momentarily and they dissolve into fighting. They spend less and less time with each other, and she comes home one afternoon to find him packed to leave:

"Only her photograph remained on his bureau, and the wide doors of his closet disclosed nothing but coat-hangers." Herbie finally announces that he's "through with the whole works."[27] She dazedly says good-bye, and then proceeds through a series of dazed relationships with men until she happens upon the idea of killing herself. That script, too, fails.

As Rousseau presents it, awareness of that something else in convention, which he figures as the natural, is always episodic and fleeting. And the revelation of the real that prompts Hazel's suicide attempt is one such moment. When she sees a horse being beaten to its knees, she becomes aware of her own similar situation. In contrast to the excessive self-regard of living in the opinion of others, Rousseau hypothesizes an appropriate self-regard and an alternative relationship to others. He argues that before his hypothetical human beings became corrupted by the positing of differences and inequality they had a natural capacity for pity. Natural pity does not make distinctions; it instead forces beings—animals as well as humans—to stop with concern when they see the suffering of a being like themselves.[28] "As she slowly crossed Sixth Avenue, consciously dragging one foot after the other," Hazel sees the beast, "a big, scarred horse pulling a rickety express-wagon crashed to his knees before her. The driver swore and screamed and lashed the beast insanely, bringing the whip back over his shoulder for every blow, while the horse struggled to get a footing on the slippery asphalt." They both struggled to stand. Hazel had "stood swaying on the pavement, unable to get her footing" before seeing this scene. And seeing her own suffering reflected in the horse's, an unshakable gloom came over her.[29] Rousseau gives us resources with which we could interpret this moment as liberatory: Hazel has a clear view of her situation and she can now work to change it. She chooses to change herself, to die, rather than change her world. Or, perhaps she is changed and refuses to continue in her world. This is an authentic moment, but it proves fleeting, and the precise contours of its authenticity are difficult to fix. Later that night, alone "[i]n her bedroom she undressed with a tense speed wholly unlike her usual slow uncertainty." She was not her usual self. "She put on her nightgown, took off her hair-net and passed the comb quickly through her dry vari-colored hair. Then she took the two little vials from the drawer and carried them into the bathroom. The splintering misery had gone from her. . . ."[30]

When I teach "Big Blonde" to elaborate Rousseau in my Modern Political Thought course, all readers recognize an inequality between Hazel and Herbie Morse. Some argue that the institution of marriage structures expectations that provide a framework for Hazel's oppression and decline. They fault the division between public and private life that secludes Hazel in the home and restricts her public encounters; and they argue that with a life of work she could have escaped a failing marriage as Herbie escaped theirs. With these readings, my students interpret gender along lines one might expect or even call standard: marriage structures feminine submission in contrast to masculine domination and in contrast to the possibility of autonomy for men. But on the question of domination per se, many of these readers have insisted on Hazel's power. They respond with anger to her weakness, but they argue that she is like the crying child in *Emile* who uses its weakness to dominate. With these readings, the class uses "Big Blonde" as Schaar would have political theorists use the turn to literature. They bring the gendered model of dominance and submission to a point of subject-object equivocation that unsettles the presumption of a facile male dominance. They are sophisticated students of Rousseau, because theirs is a complicated and troubling view of the pervasiveness of inequality.

Remember that Rousseau understands inequality as corrupt yet inevitable. Since inequality cannot be overcome, it must in his view be regulated. And thus Rousseau counsels the regulation of gender differences. "Wit alone," he maintains in *Emile*, "is the true resource of the fair sex—not that stupid wit which the social world values so highly and which is of no use for making women's lives happy, but the wit which suits their position and consists in an art of exploiting man's position and putting our peculiar advantages to their use."[31] Rousseau destabilizes gender by recognizing a capacity for feminine dominance, and then reinstates gender difference in a contrast between feminine and masculine power. Equality between men and women can be worked out by an orchestration of mutual tactics of dominance and submission (which puts man's "peculiar advantages" to woman's use). We have, then, a new set of questions to ask of "Big Blonde." How did Hazel fail on this less sunny view of marital union? Is it that she tried to dominate and failed? Was hers a failure of feminine power? Rousseau's response seems clear. "The world," he writes, "is the book of women. When they do a bad job of reading it, it is their fault, or else some passion blinds them."[32] Yet this definitive laying of blame raises as many questions as it answers. If all is conventional, as Rousseau arguably maintains, how can there be a perspective from which regulation can issue forth? Regulation in accordance with what and by whom? Are the revelations of "the real" enough of a remove? Or are these revelations simply the knowledge that all is conventional? My position, on Rousseau, is that the answer to this final question is yes: reference to the elusive natural signals awareness of the conventionality of human affairs.

This is a debated claim. Let us leave it and other questions regarding what we learn when we read Rousseau with Parker's aid to future students in Modern Political Thought classes not yet taught. Let us now ask, instead, what this essay's reading of Rousseau teaches us about Parker's "Big Blonde." Or, alternatively put: what does this particular encounter between literature and political thought teach us about interdisciplinary teaching and study?

We have seen in the pairing of Rousseau and Parker that "Big Blonde" drives toward a revelation of self for Hazel in the moment of identification with the beaten horse: a moment of identification between *two tired nags*. Is this a literal or figurative point? It is both. Parker, like Rousseau, presents the determination of the distinction between the real and the artificial as discernible yet fleeting and difficult to grasp. I want to suggest that "Big Blonde" can be read as an allegory—on Rousseau's model of fictive thinking, as a heuristic device—that compels reflection on the intricacies of the relationships between appearance and reality in human affairs. The text is in this way universal and hence literature as Monique Wittig defines literature in "The Point of View: Universal or Particular?" The argument of this essay is that there is no feminine writing: that writing cannot be literature if it is written from a gendered, and that would be a feminine and thus particular, point of view.[33] The encounter with Rousseau shows us the way in which "Big Blonde" is not feminine writing. But what is feminine writing if "Big Blonde" isn't? Does Wittig join those who would dismiss "lady writers" writing about women? No. The problem of particularities cannot be dispensed without a struggle, and Wittig addresses this point. "Djuna Barnes," we are told, "cancels out the genders by making them obsolete. I find it necessary to suppress them."[34] With Rousseau's aid, and Wittig's, I want to suggest that Parker in "Big Blonde" cancels gender by exhausting it.

Even in her period of transcendence, when she moves deliberately toward her suicide attempt, Hazel acts through a gendered script: she performs her trusted, if now worn, flirtatious good sport. But this is an act with a difference. She jokes and plays the good sport *with herself* after taking an overdose of pills.

> She felt in no way strange, save for a slight stirring of sickness from the effort of swallowing the tablets, nor did her reflected face look at all dif-

ferent. It would not be immediate, then; it might even take an hour or so.

She stretched her arms high and gave a vast yawn.

"Guess I'll go to bed," she said. "Gee, I'm nearly dead."

That struck her as comic, and she turned out the bathroom light and went in and laid herself down in her bed, chuckling softly all the time.

"Gee, I'm nearly dead," she quoted. "That's a hot one."[35]

To bed and to death she flirts *with herself*. But this flirtation with self is a deployment of gender that is too pervasive. Hazel coquetted with herself as she attempted death just as she had coquetted with the idea of being a bride when she attempted marriage. "Sophie ought to be a woman," Rousseau writes, "as Emile is a man—that is to say, she ought to have everything which suites the constitution of her species and her sex in order to fill her place in the physical and moral order."[36] The physical and the moral order, here, signal the natural and the conventional. "To be a woman means to be coquettish" Rousseau insists, "but her coquetry changes its form and its object according to her views."[37] Here Rousseau argues that the object upon which Sophie focuses must be controlled. When married, is Hazel's mistake that she coquetted with herself rather than with Herbie? "She was delighted," Parker writes, "*at the idea* of being a bride; coquetted with it, played upon it."[38] She may not have known, or been able to know her real self, but she relaxed into marriage by flirting with the idea that some other self was out there somewhere. But this, and everything always, was a flirtation for Hazel. Her femininity and the objects of her coquetry were unregulated. She was unaware of the conventionality of the conventions in which she floundered.

Feminine artifice supplements and consumes all relations in Hazel's life—even the fundamental relationship between self and self. The performance of gender in "Big Blonde" pervades all, turns in upon itself and distorts the reality of death. The interplay of sexual dominance and submission is the overt story of this text. But once we are lured in by these themes, we see that "Big Blonde" is a meditation on an inability to recognize and work within human convention. When I teach "Big Blonde," feminists in my class turn on Hazel and bemusingly celebrate Rousseau's orchestration of gender as a more appealing alternative. Wittig argues that a committed text, a text with a social theme, can never be literature because it cannot attain a universal point of view.[39] With Hazel's repeated failures—at marriage, at death, at life, at self—"Big Blonde" is certainly not a call to arms. It repulses, rather than inspires, gender identification in the response of readers. It did so, that is, in the response of my students. The text attains a universal point of view by compelling reflection on the indeterminate relations between nature and convention in human affairs—what exactly is it about Hazel that bothers you so much?—and by compelling reflection on how a refusal to engage convention can ultimately be an inability to engage one's own human agency.

Since Parker and Rousseau both write on these themes, should Parker be included in the canon of political thought? No. And political theory is better served in this case by recognizing the distinctiveness of her work. Parker does not, like Rousseau, go on to ponder the problems of political order produced by recognition of convention in human affairs. Yet when young women and men, who consider themselves feminists, turn with disgust from Hazel Morse and embrace what we can with warrant call Rousseau's sexism, it is clear how the study of literature invigorates the study of politics. This is precisely the sort of creative tension, an embrace of a position that one ostensibly opposes, that Socrates practiced pedagogically and even with his death as punishment for his act of civil disobedience. I find this tension invaluable when teaching and thinking. And the interdisciplinary encounter between Rousseau and Parker, as an act of canonical disobedience, reminds us that "Big Blonde," like all literature, is polysemic and ever potentially open. Rousseau's Parker teaches us that "Big Blonde" has new meanings when read by twenty-first-century readers.

NOTES

1. John Schaar, "The Uses of Literature for the Study of Politics: Melville's *Benito Cereno*, in *Legitimacy and the Modern State* (New Brunswick, NJ: Transaction Books, 1981), 53.

2. Ibid., 53, 68–71.

3. The syllabus is the institutional form of canon construction. See, Schaar, 56, and John Guillory, *Cultural Capital: The Problem of Literary Canon Formation* (Chicago: University of Chicago Press, 1993), 30.

4. Plato, *The Trial and Death of Socrates*, G. M. A. Grube, trans. (Indianapolis: Hackett Publishing, 1975), 33; and for overviews of the tradition of civil disobedience see Martin Luther King, Jr., "Letter from Birmingham Jail," in *Why We Can't Wait* (New York: Penguin, 1964), 79–80, 93–94, and Hannah Arendt, "Civil Disobedience," in *Crises of the Republic* (New York: Harcourt Brace Jovanovich, 1969), 49–102.

5. Dorothy Parker, "Big Blonde," in *The Portable Dorothy Parker* (1973; repr., New York: Penguin Books, 1976), 187.

6. Ibid., 188.

7. The "making lunch" example is Elizabeth Wingrove's precise wording in

personal communications. I am indebted throughout my teaching of Rousseau, and thus this essay, to her for many conversations on Rousseau and for *Rousseau's Republican Romance* (Princeton: Princeton University Press, 2000).

8. Jean-Jacques Rousseau, *Discourse on the Origin of Inequality*, in *Basic Political Writings*, Donald A. Cress, trans. (Cambridge, MA: Hackett Publishing, 1987), 35.

9. Jean-Jacques Rousseau, *Emile, or On Education*, Allan Bloom, trans. (New York: Basic Books, 1979), 50.

10. Ibid., 51.

11. Parker, 188.

12. Rousseau, *Discourse on the Origin of Inequality*, 80–81.

13. Ibid., 51.

14. Ibid., 56.

15. Rousseau, *Emile*, 66.

16. Parker, 198.

17. Ibid., 190; italics mine.

18. Ibid., 189.

19. Ibid., 190.

20. I will explicate Rousseau on this point, but see as well Jacques Derrida, ". . . That Dangerous Supplement . . ." in *Of Grammatology*, Gayatri Chakravorty Spivak, trans. (Baltimore: Johns Hopkins University Press, 1974), 141–64.

21. Rousseau, *Discourse on the Origin of Inequality*, 45; and see as well, Paul de Man, "The Rhetoric of Blindness: Jacques Derrida's Reading of Rousseau," in *Blindness and Insight: Essays in the Rhetoric of Contemporary Criticism*, 2nd ed. (Minneapolis: University of Minnesota Press, 1983), 121.

22. Rousseau, *Discourse on the Origin of Inequality*, 63–64.

23. Parker, 191.

24. Ibid., 193.

25. Ibid., 194.

26. Rousseau, *Discourse on the Origin of Inequality*, 64.

27. Parker, 194–95.

28. Rousseau, *Discourse on the Origin of Inequality*, 53–55.

29. Parker, 204.

30. Ibid., 204–5.

31. Rousseau, *Emile*, 371–72.

32. Ibid., 387.

33. Monique Wittig, "The Point of View: Universal or Particular?" in *The Straight Mind and Other Essays* (New York: Harvester/Wheatsheaf, 1992), 59–87.

34. Wittig, 60–61.

35. Parker, 205.

36. Rousseau, *Emile*, 357.

37. Ibid., 365.

38. Parker, 188, italics mine.

39. Wittig, 62.

"They Can See Me If I Cry": Feminine Language and Reader Identification in Dorothy Parker's "Sentiment"

Timothy P. McMackin

"I haven't got a visual mind. I hear things."
—Dorothy Parker

LITERARY CRITICS HAVE ANALYZED DOROTHY PARKER'S STORIES FROM feminist and linguistic standpoints, debating the extent to which Parker acts as a social critic by the way she humorously portrays people and their speech, especially women's speech. Many of these studies focus on what Sondra Melzer calls "Parker's unique exploration of female behavior, which inspires the contemporary critic to examine the forces in our society which drive that behavior."[1] Unquestionably, there is merit in this examination of her stories as social commentary, but I think that they also have meaning on a more personal level. Her characters, especially the nameless Everymen and Everywomen, are meant to be laughed at but also to serve as a mirror for the readers' behavior and speech habits. There is an intimately personal connection between the gendered dialogue in Parker's stories and the reader's reaction to that dialogue.

Linguist Robin Lakoff was one of the first to propose a definition of "women's language," and many linguists, most notably Elizabeth Aries, have followed her lead in basing their analysis of language on the hypothesis that "women's choice of speech style reflects their self-image." Put another way, women must learn both a "standard" and a "feminine" language, and deciding when to use one or the other "requires special awareness to the nuances of social situations, special alertness to possible disapproval."[2] It is this awareness of being under scrutiny that forms the basis of many psycholinguistic studies since Lakoff, but of course men are aware when they are being watched as well. The difference is that women make a "choice in speech style," a self-reflexive impulse to change themselves ac-

cording to the situation that the viewer places them into. This combination of self-awareness and self-adjustment clearly describes the
attitude attributed to women in John Berger's "Ways of Seeing": A
woman must "survey everything she is and everything she does"
and, implicitly, change to improve "how she appears to others."[3]
This self-reflexive nature, creating a connection of identification between art and audience, is the aspect of women's behavior that I will
examine in Parker's short stories.

Melzer observes the deep-seated role that speech plays in Parker's
stories, saying that they "make themselves stories by telling themselves through what people say."[4] Though part of the function of
speech in these stories is to satirize social systems and the people
affected by them, looking at the concept of "women's language"
from a psychological standpoint suggests an alternate function.
Since many of her stories are told entirely through speech, the characters' language is the only clue that the reader has to their identity.
Parker's stories mirror the psychological model of women's speech
in the way that they show women who manipulate their language to
present a particular image to the viewer inside and outside the story.
As a result, the reader functions as a character in the stories to better
understand the plot in stories like "The Last Tea" and "Lady with a
Lamp." In "Sentiment," however, identifying with the main character teaches the reader a pointed lesson about the damaging effect of
women's language.

On the surface, "The Last Tea" is a dialogue between two mirror-
image characters.[5] In the midst of their breakup, the former boyfriend and girlfriend try to retain what Arthur F. Kinney calls their
"self-respect" by citing the other social opportunities open to
them.[6] The boyfriend tells about his wild nights in speakeasies with
Carol McCall, the future movie star, and she recalls her dates with
Wally Dillon, the flattering dancer. The names drop a hint to the
reader, since "Wally Dillon" is an awkward-sounding name that does
not suggest the fun or mischief implied in "Carol McCall," with its
hint at a "call girl." Yet the descriptions of these dates have more
subtle linguistic differences that show who has the more lucrative
social opportunities and therefore controls the conversation and the
breakup. The female character's speech gives the reader the impression that she is not in a position of power in the conversation.

The only outside description of the unnamed woman character,
from the first sentence of the story, says that she is wearing an "artificial camellia" and has been waiting at her table for forty minutes
(49). Since she denies having been waiting two lines later, the fact
that she is described solely by her imitation flower corsage and not

any piece of clothing or physical characteristic immediately corrobo-
rates her artifice. On one level, her status as a liar casts some doubt
on her stories about her dates with Wally; they could be a complete
fiction, or at least exaggerated for her audience. On a deeper level,
however, her lying suggests that she is tailoring her language to take
control of the conversation:

> "Guess I must be late," he said. "Sorry you been waiting."
> "Oh, goodness!" she said. "I just got here myself, just about a second
> ago. I simply went ahead and ordered because I was dying for a cup of
> tea. I was late, myself. I haven't been here more than a minute."
> "That's good," he said. (49)

Knowing that her first line is a lie, the reader also makes the assumption that her feminine diction is an attempt to cover that lie. Here,
she repeats four times that she has only just arrived, and along with
the hyperbolic force of "dying for a cup of tea" and the mild oath
"Oh, goodness!" this feminine gushing is clearly designed to emphasize her point.

The reason that she is lying is not as important as the effect of her
deception in the story. Because her feminine language and her lie
are so closely linked in the first few lines, the reader naturally
matches similar feminine language later in the story to the same
face-saving lying. Like the syntactically unnecessary repetition of
"myself" in her first lines, her speech throughout the story makes it
clear to the reader that she is trying to maintain an appearance by
changing the focus of the conversation to herself. She describes her
social life by talking about herself, while he talks indirectly about his
dates by describing the things Carol does. Relatively more frequent
use of "self-referent" personal pronouns is generally a feminine
characteristic of speech,[7] and in this case, it makes the speaker
sound extremely self-centered, such as when she remembers staying
out late with Wally: "Goodness! I didn't get home till I don't know
what time. I must look simply a wreck. Don't I?" (50). The tag of
"Don't I?" rings out loud at the end of the passage, encouraging the
hearer as well as the reader to examine her and guess if she really
looks "simply a wreck." By contrast, the male character's dialogue is
based on the third-person description of Carol and her exploits,
such as "Can that girl hold her liquor!" (51). Stressing herself so
overtly and directly makes the female character's stories seem less
credible, but furthermore, it attracts the reader's attention to her
speech because her words are suspect. Her feminized speech is designed to attract the male character's attention, but it only succeeds
in attracting the reader's attention.

Most tellingly, her "me"-oriented language shows her self-reflexive attention to her place in the viewer's eye by bringing out the effect of his stories on her. She attacks his social standing not with her opinion of Carol's carousing antics but with the effect that such drunkenness has on her:

> "It's a funny thing about me," she said. "It just makes me feel sort of sick to see a girl drink. It's just something in me, I guess. I don't mind a man so much, but it makes me feel perfectly terrible to see a girl get intoxicated. It's just the way I am, I suppose." (51)

Again, as Kinney notes, the female character's intent is not to defend her reputation so much as her "self-respect."[8] Her reputation depends solely on how other people see her, but her self-respect includes how she sees herself reflected in their eyes. In this way, she is changing her appearance into something that may have more clout in the conversation, and she does this through her language and its representation of herself. The sentence-weakening elements of "I guess," "I suppose," and "just" work with her humble insistence that her statement is her own opinion, explaining it away twice as the way "it just makes me feel." She is asking the male character to validate the way the situation makes her feel, but this line of reasoning does not gain his attention; only the reader is coaxed into seeing her place in the conversation.

The language in "Lady with a Lamp" is among the most stylized in any of Parker's stories, even compared to her brutal satires of shallow gossips and city dwellers.[9] The unnamed narrator in "Lady with a Lamp" caresses her bedridden friend Mona with pages of baby talk, hyperbole, and hollow, meaningless speech. In fact, there is no solid evidence that the narrator is actually female, but the reader could not possibly come to any other conclusion after hearing her speech. This speech, heavily stylized in a casual situation that does not appear to call for it, must be designed for a certain effect. The process of discovering the intent behind that language makes the reader function as a character in the story, just as the language in "The Last Tea" targets the reader more precisely than the character that is its overt target.

One prominent speech construction in this story is the statement that is clearly not meant by the speaker and therefore conveys the opposite of its literal message. For example, the narrator mentions that Mona's sickness could be serious, but in response to Mona's implied objection, she agrees with "All right, Mona, then you're *not* sick. If that's what you want to say, even to me, why, all right, my dear" (144). Clearly, the narrator is not convinced. Similarly, her extreme understatement and hyperbole cast doubt on her words' meaning. She alternately babies Mona with "There, now, your pillows are all smooth and lovely, and you lie right down again, before you hurt yourself" and berates her with ambiguous insults like "You little idiot, you! Extravagant little fool!" (145–46). This baby talk denigrates both the speaker and the addressed,[10] but in this case, the reader's opinion of the speaker is being formed, since she is directly under inspection. Her speech, too highly stylized for its casual situation, brings up the main conflict of the story: is the narrator being overgentle and unintentionally demeaning toward Mona, or is she attacking a rival under the cover of innocuous speech?

The most common reading of "Lady with a Lamp" is that the narrator is a rival who enjoys reminding Mona of her painful abortion and breakup.[11] The main piece of evidence to this effect comes from the fact that she tactlessly brings up the subject of marriage and children repeatedly, expressing surprise when Mona begins to cry each time. The narrator certainly knows about the abortion, since she blames Mona's unfaithful ex-boyfriend for her sickness and blurts several times that "Yes, it is on account of him. Even if you didn't have an——" (149). It is difficult to believe that the narrator could be so unaware as to bring up these painful topics incessantly and still finish the story by blaming Mona for exacerbating her own condition: "*I'm afraid she's gotten herself a little bit upset.*"[12] Still, at this point in the story, there are no direct threats or insults to prove that she is malicious; rather, she is tactless in a muted, feminine manner of speaking.

For most readers, the narrator's tactlessness is too severe to ignore; by the end of the story, it should be clear that she is maliciously working Mona into an anxiety attack for some reason. However, from my point of view, the main theme of the story is not in the reader's end judgment but the path to this decision. Since there are no overt examples of maliciousness, the reader must pick up linguistic clues along the way, "reading into" the narrator's words to determine their meaning and purpose. The first few times that the narrator lightly refers to children or Mona's abortion could be accidental, but at some point the attentive reader will get suspicious at her repeated tactless comments and her apparent surprise at Mona's tearful reaction. In this way, the contrast between the well-mannered spoken language and the malicious intent directly redesigns the reader's portrait of the speaker, a move that Paula A. Treichler notes in Parker's story "The Waltz."[13] Since the monologue form of the story offers no information about the narrator but what she gives in her own speech, the only way to tell if the narrator is intentionally hurting Mona is to imagine the scene as Mona hears it. The reader must dissect the language of the monologue to look beyond the contradictions and hollow generalities to find the real meaning behind the speaker's voice: it is stylized to be used as a concealed weapon, and to use one's language in this way requires tremendous skill. As she lies to her conversation partner, she is also lying to the reader, as Treichler observes also happens in "The Waltz."[14] Mona's friend is aware that her audience is trying to uncover her motives and masks her language accordingly, a self-reflexive effect of her situation that targets the reader as well as Mona.

My purpose thus far has been to show how self-reflexive behavior in these stories, the tendency of Parker's female characters to constantly self-judge and adapt to an outsider's view, is expressed in the characters' language, encouraging the reader to examine and evaluate the characters' relationships from an insider's perspective. I think that the two stories covered so far show different facets of this theme, but the story that benefits most from its direct application is "Sentiment," first published in the May 1933 issue of *Harper's Bazaar*. While language and reader identification help explain the surface of Parker's other stories, such as why "The Last Tea" is not a parallel construction and how the reader decides that Mona's visitor in "Lady with a Lamp" is malicious, in "Sentiment" such an approach penetrates the inner workings of the story and demonstrates how language is directly involved in the implication of the reader into the story. There is no clear cue to analyze the purpose of the feminine language as in the beginning of "The Last Tea," but the narrator's speech contains self-reflexive elements that perform the same effect as in the other two stories. Her awareness of being watched and the reflection of that awareness in her speech combine to address the reader directly and implicate him or her in her situation.

Like most of Parker's other monologues, "Sentiment" is quick to set the scene and introduce the important themes. The first two sentences immediately raise the question of audience: "*Oh, anywhere, driver, anywhere—it doesn't matter. Just keep driving.*"[15] In a common form of Parker's, italics and a normal typeface separate speech directed to different audiences, in this case outward speech to the imaginary cabdriver and the internal monologue to the narrator. However, this distinction is superficial; instead of defining exactly what is said to whom, the italics create the illusion that the audiences can be clearly differentiated and that the internal speech is what the speaker "really thinks."[16] At one level, the different type tells what is said to the cabdriver and what is internal "speech," but strictly speaking, there is no cabdriver in the story, even less than there is any "Mona" in "Lady with a Lamp." The reader is hearing the direct and sudden command to the "driver," as well as the thought-speech that follows, placing the reader in two voyeuristic positions that are not often experienced at the same time.

Parker's use of quotation marks and offset excerpts from a sentimental poem—Edna St. Vincent Millay's "Sorrow" (1917)—are more examples of formal devices that link the narrator and reader on a level deeper than that commonly made in such stories. The quotation marks around the excerpts indicate that the narrator is quoting someone and, conventionally, speaking aloud, and the italics reinforce the idea of her speech act. As readers, we cannot help but "listen." Parker used other formal devices elsewhere in her work. The use of capital letters, for example, was one of Parker's common conventions as a book reviewer for the *New Yorker.* She once slipped in a "parenthetical address to the reader" to belittle an author: "This is, they say, her Big Novel."[17] This sentence is not actually contained within parentheses, but the capital letters, along with the "they say," serve the same function: they give a knowing wink to the reader, who presumably shares the wry inside joke about the author's reputation. Spoken out loud, the phrase "Big Novel" would likely have a sarcastic tone, and the capital letters convey that sound to the reader. In the same way, the formal constructions in "Sentiment" enhance communication between the reader and Rosalie, the narrator, by giving the reader an approximation of the spoken word, passing on information that would not ordinarily be available in textual form. More than simply referring to the impossibility of the reader hearing Rosalie's thoughts, the different typefaces, quotation marks, and the offset quoted poem suggest that she is shaping her speech for implied audiences.

This appearance of direct address is supplemented by Rosalie's poetic diction, which, in the context of this story, embodies "feminized language" in the same way that weakened constructions and baby talk signaled a hidden motive in speech in "The Last Tea" and "Lady with a Lamp." For this reason, Rosalie thinks that it was her speech that caused her boyfriend to break up with her, and she also wonders why an undefined "people" maintain that "it's wrong to be sentimental" (196). Treichler observes that in "The Waltz," Parker exaggerates diction in concert with "self-conscious" capital letters to make the character's speech seem like "a special kind of theatre."[18] In the same way, the formal elements of typeface and quotations work with Rosalie's theatrical speech in "Sentiment" to

demonstrate her awareness of an audience. Her poetic diction surfaces in her internal speech directed at the beggar woman on the
street: "Don't you wish you were I and could have a new hat whenever you pleased?" Imagining that the beggar is envying her hat, Rosalie lauds it as "a new hat, a beautiful hat, a hat that cost more than
ever you had" (195). These aggressive statements are tempered by
the formal, poetic syntax of "you were I" and "ever you had," as
well as the weakening tag of "Don't you wish" instead of the simple,
direct "You wish." Rosalie continues to imagine the effect looking
at her had on the beggar after the cab moves on: "I wonder did she
envy me, so sleek and safe and young" (195). Her diction rises until
she strikes a truly worthy phrase: "She is done with hoping and
burning, if ever she burned and she hoped" (195). This arrangement of verbs in chiasmus is appropriate in Latin and Greek poetry
but far too formal for casually spoken English. Rosalie self-
consciously admires the "lilt" in her phrase for a few lines, implicitly
encouraging the reader to do the same. The ornate, almost metered
quality of the language, stylized for an audience, attracts the reader's attention in a way that mirrors Rosalie's self-reflexive attention
to her speech.

Rosalie's self-evaluation leads her to look at her language from
her ex-boyfriend's point of view. Complete with quotation marks,
she imagines his speech chiding her for "that fool sentimentaliz-
ing," ending sharply with Rosalie's name (196). Parker rarely names
her main characters and narrators; the speakers in all of the other
pieces I've mentioned are unnamed. Only the characters discussed
and examined by the main characters are named. In this way,
Rosalie makes herself the topic of discussion, in the same way that
the female character in "The Last Tea" draws attention by adding
the tag of "Don't I?" to her physical self-description. Of course, the
speaker is not visible in that case, but in "Sentiment," the topic
under examination is Rosalie and her thoughts, which the reader
can see. Rosalie is aware enough of her situation and emotional state
to analyze them,[19] but she is also drawing other people to analyze
her by the way her dialogue is arranged.

Robin Lakoff argues that the "overall effect of 'women's language'" does not hide so much as "submerge" her identity.[20] It is
this "submerging" effect that occurs when Rosalie suddenly names
herself from an outsider's perspective, not making herself vanish but
turning herself inside out, into a simultaneous subject-object. Like
Suzanne L. Bunkers describes in "A Telephone Call," Rosalie experiences a "tug-of-war" linking her outside and inside self.[21] Looking
through her ex-boyfriend's eyes turns her own attention to herself,

fusing her identity as a subject with that of the topic of conversation. As she gets lost in her own thoughts, the fact that she has been encouraging the audience to participate draws them inside her self-evaluation as well. The result is the humorous yet painful relationship between narrator and reader that forces Rosalie's "cab driver" to make a deeper judgment about her than about any of the narrators in Parker's other stories.

The final stage in Rosalie's self-reflexive relationship with the reader comes out of this blurring of the distinction between speaker and subject. Previously, Rosalie admired her phrase of "She is done with burning and hoping" in its poetic construction, reflecting the intentionally stylized nature of her language that implicitly encouraged the reader to evaluate it. After her thorough discussion of sentiment and dramatizing oneself, she reflects on the impossibility of returning to happiness with the enigmatic phrase " 'Sorrow is tranquillity remembered in emotion' " (198). The fact that she marks the line formally with quotation marks and the British English spelling of "tranquillity" shows that it is stylized in the same way as before, but Rosalie responds to this quote with "Oh, I think that's quite good. . . . I wish I could say it to him" (198). Further, she corrects her thought-speech to conform to the first line of Millay's poem "Sorrow" that she has just recited, thinking that "steady" is not as accurate as "*ceaseless*" to describe her pain (197). This is an instance of feminine self-reflexive behavior in the extreme, since she, a fictional character, is rewriting her own thought and dialogue in the story with the reader in mind.

Of course, Rosalie is not saying this to her ex-boyfriend as she imagines; she is saying it to the reader. The reader, submerged along with her status as dual subject-object, is placed into the story as a surrogate for the judging ex-boyfriend. In "Lady with a Lamp," the reader must examine the narrator's motives, but in "Sentiment," the reader must examine his or her own motives. Hearing Rosalie wishing she could say her phrases to her ex-boyfriend is ironic, because he would clearly not approve of them. Furthermore, the climax of the story sends her on a sentimental rampage, creating overblown significance for a fictional event. This makes the story humorous, because the reader sees that Rosalie is still exhibiting the qualities that she is trying desperately to hide. However, it is also a painful element in the story because, functioning as a character, the reader acts as the ex-boyfriend and thus contributes to the pain of the breakup with a guiltily humorous attitude. The reader's role mirrors that of the character who caused Rosalie's pain. In this way, "Sentiment" symbolizes the powerful effect that self-consciousness can have on women and drives the point home with this twist of identification that gives the reader an example of how he or she could be personally guilty of this sort of oppression. Parker tricks the audience into becoming an accessory to Rosalie's pain and thus shows how a well-meaning person can unknowingly contribute to gender inequity through preconceptions about women's language.

NOTES

1. Sondra Melzer, *The Rhetoric of Rage: Women in Dorothy Parker* (New York: Peter Lang, 1997), 4.

2. Robin Lakoff, *Language and Woman's Place* (New York: Harper and Row, 1975), 7; Elizabeth Aries, *Men and Women in Interaction: Reconsidering the Difference* (New York: Oxford University Press, 1996), 104. Many psychologists have searched for a definite difference in men's and women's speech with mixed results; each researcher defines a different set of criteria to distinguish between the two, and what does indeed differentiate speech by one gender in one test fails to show a significant difference in another. For example, prefixing a declaration or something the speaker knows to be true with a qualifier like "I think" tends to weaken it and imply uncertainty, which is believed to be a characteristic of feminine speech (Lakoff, 54). However, Elizabeth Aries observes that in the example of a mother telling her child "*I think* it's time you cleaned up your room," the qualifier actually makes the sentence more of "an expression of certainty rather than uncertainty" (Aries, 104). It follows that a mere enumeration of linguistic structures in actual speech will not easily distinguish gender differences, since the same form can have different meanings in different contexts. Literary critics can explore "women's language" in a text with perhaps more success because, in contrast to the dynamics of actual human speech, literary speech takes place in a more controlled environment. A story's narrative provides a specific, more limited sense of context in which the fictional speech functions.

3. John Berger, "Ways of Seeing," in Melita Schaun and Connie Flanagan, eds., *Gender Images: Readings for Composition* (Boston: Houghton Mifflin, 1992), 387.

4. Melzer, 32

5. Dorothy Parker, "The Last Tea," in Colleen Breese, ed., *Complete Stories* (New York: Penguin, 1995), 49–52. Subsequent references will be to this edition parenthetically by page number.

6. Arthur F. Kinney, *Dorothy Parker* (Boston: Twayne, 1978), 135.

7. Aries, 126.

8. Kinney, 135.

9. Dorothy Parker, "Lady with a Lamp," in *Complete Stories*, 144–50. Subsequent references will be to this edition parenthetically by page number.

10. Rhonda S. Pettit, *A Gendered Collision: Sentimentalism and Modernism in Dorothy Parker's Poetry and Fiction* (Madison and Teaneck, NJ: Fairleigh Dickinson University Press, 2000), 169.

11. Kinney, 138.

12. Parker, 150. The italics are in the original; they denote outside speech similar to that in "The Waltz" and "Sentiment," even though "Lady with a Lamp" is, strictly speaking, an external rather than an internal monologue.

13. Treichler, 52, explores this effect in Parker's "The Waltz."

14. Ibid., 57.

15. Dorothy Parker, "Sentiment," in *Complete Stories*, 195–99. Subsequent references will be to this edition parenthetically by page number.

16. Andrea Ivanov Craig, "Being and Dying as a Woman in the Short Fiction of Dorothy Parker," in Shannon Hengen, ed., *Performing Gender and Comedy: Theories, Texts, and Contexts* (Amsterdam, Netherlands: Gordon and Breach, 1998), 104.

17. Nancy A. Walker, "The Remarkably Constant Reader: Dorothy Parker as Book Reviewer," *Studies in American Humor* 3:4 (1997): 12.

18. Treichler, 54.

19. Pettit, 150.

20. Lakoff, 7.

21. Suzanne L. Bunkers, "'I Am Outraged Womanhood': Dorothy Parker as Feminist and Social Critic," *Regionalism and the Female Imagination* 4:2 (1978): 27.

Behavior at Its Worst: Freudian Concepts in the Writing of Dorothy Parker

Donna Stamm

DOROTHY PARKER HAD A REMARKABLE PERCEPTION OF PERSONALITY AND its effects on behavior. Her stories do not reveal all the personality traits a character could possess, but she examines with excellent insight those peculiarities of personality upon which her stories revolve. For example, some of Parker's fiction deals with the failure of her characters to honestly communicate their feelings. The characters' external voices and outward actions are opposed to their inward feelings and private thoughts. They act out their worst behaviors, unaware that they are being anything but charming, fooling themselves but not the reader. We typically interpret this as Parker's use of dramatic irony, but if we read Parker's work with certain Freudian concepts in mind, it becomes clear that these are the kind of undesirable behaviors that originate in repressions, inhibitions, and conflicts. Put another way, Parker's short stories and poems reveal her knowledge of Sigmund Freud's psychoanalytic perspective of personality. To some extent, this is to be expected, given that his ideas were pervasive during her lifetime, and that Parker underwent a form of psychoanalysis more than once.

When Sigmund Freud introduced psychoanalysis through his books *The Interpretation of Dreams* (1899) and *Three Essays on the Theory of Sexuality* (1905), the impact was broad and significant. Scholars of human behavior now had a scientific basis for further study and experimentation, and as Frederick J. Hoffman has documented, writers in the 1920s had a new concept—the influence of the unconscious mind on everyday life and social interactions—with which to explore themselves and their characters. This deterministic approach was at the same time sexually liberating, explaining in part its appeal to a victorious postwar, post-Victorian society. Freud's ideas also became the object of ridicule and parody, so well were they known at all levels of culture in the second decade of the century and 1920s when Parker was launching her career as a theater

critic and writer of poetry and fiction. Hoffman cites several examples of literary and journalistic parody during the 1920s from *Vanity
Fair*, a magazine for sophisticates, and one for which Parker worked
until 1920.[1] Along with Freudian concepts came the treatment; people who could afford it underwent psychoanalysis to help them cope
with modern living.

Several members of the Algonquin Round Table—a group of writers and actors with whom Parker associated in the 1920s—were
among those who sought some form of psychotherapy, whether
strictly Freudian or not. Throughout her life, Parker suffered from
bouts of depression and alcoholism, and attempted suicide more
than once. In 1926, Parker underwent therapy sessions with Dr.
Alvan Barach, who tried unsuccessfully to persuade Parker to stop
drinking. Barach, who also had aspirations as a writer, associated
with the Round Table socially, and later treated two other members,
Heywood Broun and Alexander Woollcott. According to one biographer, Parker had little confidence in the psychoanalysis method, but
sought treatment again in the 1940s during the breakup of her marriage to writer Alan Campbell, then a soldier stationed in England.[2]
Some of her poems and stories, particularly those involving alcohol,
depression, or suicide, such as "Résumé" or "Big Blonde," are
sometimes read by critics as autobiographical accounts of her life.
Whether or not this is true, Parker's work demonstrates an awareness of Freudian ideas, in particular: a range of defense mechanisms, phallic personality, and the death wish. At times she reveals
her knowledge explicitly, while at other times it is implied through
character behavior.

An early, explicit approach to the subject comes in the form of a
poem and double-parody, "The Passionate Freudian to His Love,"
published in the 28 April 1921 issue of *Life*, then a magazine of
humor. The title alludes to Christopher Marlowe's "The Passionate
Shepherd to His Love," the well-known seventeenth-century pastoral lyric celebrating the kind of idealistic love that early-twentieth-
century writers often lampooned. Her verse structure differs from
Marlowe's—three twelve-line stanzas as opposed to six quatrains—as
she recreates the romantic escape she expects her readers to recognize as dated. The opening lines read:

> Only name the day, and we'll fly away
> In the face of old traditions,
> To a sheltered spot by the world forgot,
> Where we'll park our inhibitions.[3]

"Inhibitions" is the first of many Freudian terms, or terms charged with Freudian or Jungian meaning, the poem offers. Others include: "psychoanalyzes," "fantasies," "normal," "dreams," "interpretation," "symbolized," "subconscious," "desires," "repressions," "ego," "*ad libido*" (italics in context), "neuroses," and "psychoses." The poem's speaker, perhaps an analyst or merely anyone with a surface knowledge of modern psychology, uses a carpe diem argument laced with Freudian terms to seduce the beloved, and closes with two puns: "Where a Freud in need is a Freud indeed, / We'll be always Jung together." This incongruous combination of pastoral lyric with Freudian and Jungian terminology satirizes the notion that modern psychology answers all the issues raised in modern relationships. More importantly for this discussion, the ease with which Parker uses the terminology to parody both ideal love and psychology suggests a competent knowledge of Freud's ideas; a writer must understand a concept fairly well in order to parody it.

Although Parker mentions Freud by name in her story "The Waltz" ("Freud says there are no accidents"), most of her narrators, characters, and speakers (in poetry) who allude to Freudian ideas do so through their behavior and speech, rather than by overt naming. To orient ourselves toward this reading, a brief overview of Freud's components of personality—the id, the ego, and the superego—and their effect on behavior may be helpful. In Freud's view, the id represents the unconscious, instinctual, pleasure-seeking, unrestrained portion of the human personality. The hardworking ego is constantly mediating and compromising between reality and the urges of the id as it tries to produce a socially acceptable individual. The superego, or the conscience, then pressures the ego to be right, or moral in its decisions. This situation often produces anxiety. The ego, seeking to avoid anxiety, looks for a way of resolving the conflict imposed upon it by the wishes of the id and the morality of the superego through defense mechanisms. Freud's defense mechanisms, therefore, are unconscious methods through which the ego protects itself from anxiety and include repression, rationalization, displacement, sublimation, projection, reaction formation, and regression. Often these mechanisms work in combination. Several defense mechanisms can be found in Parker's work; I will examine those evident in the stories "The Bolt Behind the Blue" (1958), "The Waltz" (1933), "Big Blonde" (1929), and "Here We Are" (1931), and in her poems "Comment" (1926) and "Second Love" (1932).

The two main characters in "The Bolt Behind the Blue" have hidden motives. Mary Nicholl, a single, "poor and plain" woman who lives in a hotel room visits the rich and lovely Mrs. Alicia Hazelton in her spacious home. In the opening paragraph the narrator summarizes the relationship as mutually self-serving: Miss Nicholl visits and flatters Mrs. Hazelton in order to bask in material comfort she cannot afford herself, and Mrs. Hazelton indulges the visits to give her ego a boost.[4] Both characters are exhibiting the defense mechanism of reaction formation, which "involves expressing an id impulse that is the opposite of the one that is truly driving the person."[5] Early in their conversation, Miss Nicholl acts as if she adores Mrs. Hazelton: "'Oh, you're wise!' Miss Nicholl said. 'Wise *and* beautiful—you've got everything'" (338). Miss Nicholl's opposing inner feelings are revealed as she leaves Mrs. Hazelton's house: "What kind of a life is that, setting around in a tea gown counting her pearls? . . . I wouldn't change places with Alicia Hazelton for anything on earth" (349). Similarly, Mrs. Hazelton exhibits the conflicts that exist between the instincts, or id, and the desire to be socially correct. After Miss Nicholl leaves, Mrs. Hazelton thinks, "That was the trouble with such as Miss Nicholl—once they came, God, how they stayed" (349). Inwardly she dislikes Miss Nicholl and the fact that she is poor. Outwardly, Mrs. Hazelton tells her daughter, Ewie, "Oh, let me tell you, I'd be more than glad to change places with Mary Nicholl" (350). The id impulse of these women is being repressed and a socially acceptable reaction is being expressed, thus suggesting Freud's reaction formation.

The same combination of defense mechanisms also occurs in Parker's "The Waltz," a story with two voices: a nameless woman's external conversation with her dancing partner and her internal thoughts about him. When the story opens, the woman has been asked to dance, and she replies in a socially acceptable manner: "Why thank you so much, I'd adore to." Inwardly she is thinking, "I don't want to dance with anybody, especially not him."[6] Like Miss Nicholl and Mrs. Hazelton, she is repressing her feelings about the situation and saying the opposite, a dynamic she maintains throughout the whole story. Put another way, the stream-of-consciousness style of the internal voice is a clear example of the unrestrained id, while the polite external voice reveals the superego at work.

When the ego and superego are weak and the id controls the personality, a different behavior is observed, as we see in another character from "The Bolt Behind the Blue." Ewie, Mrs. Hazelton's eleven-year-old daughter, is a picture of Freud's unrestrained id. The id does not care about reality, what is the right thing to say, or the proper time to say it. The id is concerned only with instant gratification. While the two adults act in a socially acceptable manner, Ewie talks about blood, bile, and death. She refuses to kiss Miss Nicholl and yet kisses the dog, Bonne Bouche. She calls Miss Nicholl "Miss Nicker." She talks about the "dark blue baby" that Dellie, Mrs. Hazelton's maid, said was "doomed from the womb," and she makes up a song about it: " 'doomed from the womb, oh-h, doomed from the womb' " (340–41). Ewie is the antithesis of the pretentious, socially correct women in "The Bolt Behind the Blue." The id, acting alone without the intervention of the weakened ego, operates without restraints just as Ewie does.

This battle between the unrestrained id, the mediating ego, and the moral superego is humorously presented in some of Parker's poems as well. At times she captures the workings of the unrestrained cynical id. The speaker in the poem "Comment," published in *Enough Rope* (1926), struggles to be socially correct, though unrestrained cynicism wins out in the last line:

> Oh, life is a glorious cycle of song,
> A medley of extemporanea;
> And love is a thing that can never go wrong,
> And I am Marie of Roumania.[7]

As in "The Passionate Freudian to His Love," this poem contrasts the romantic ideal with modern cynicism about romance, but its Freudian connection is implied rather than explicit.

Another defense mechanism can be found in Parker's poem "Second Love," published in *Sunset Gun* (1932):

> How shall I count the midnights I have known
> When calm you turn to me, nor feel me start,
> To find my easy lips upon your own
> And know my breast beneath your rhythmic heart.
> Your god defer the day I tell you this:
> My lad, my lad, it is not you I kiss![8]

In this so-called love poem, the Freudian defense mechanism of sublimation is at work. Sublimation involves replacing id impulses that one wishes to be rid of with other more acceptable behaviors. The speaker in this poem represses her feelings for another while kissing her current partner. Her love for the person who is no longer there is being sublimated as she makes love to her new partner. Possibly the speaker thinks these feelings no longer exist because they are so deeply buried in the subconscious. However, as typical of many of Parker's poems, the restraining ego becomes weak while seemingly uncontrolled feelings come to the surface and the id must expose its true self in the last two lines of the poem.

Another defense mechanism, displacement, was a significant Freudian concept and Parker topic. Freudian displacement "involves shifting id impulses from a threatening or unavoidable object to a substitute object that is available."[9] The concept of displacement is expressed in Parker's short story "Here We Are," in which two unnamed newlyweds head for their honeymoon on a train.[10] Every spoken allusion to their upcoming sexual intercourse is abruptly cut off with the interjection, "I mean." The apparently virginal young lady is inwardly anxious about being alone with the young man, being away from her family, and about sexual intimacy, but she does not express it. Outwardly, she "displaces" this anxiety by arguing with her husband regarding his comments about Louise, her sister, and her hats. " 'It's too bad,' she said, 'You didn't marry somebody that would get the kind of hats you'd like. Why didn't you marry Louise? You always think she looks so beautiful' " (140). She doesn't want to say what is *really* bothering her, or maybe she does not consciously know what the source of her anxiety is. The young lady's ego takes charge and replaces the issues that are causing her anxiety with issues that are socially permissible to discuss with a new husband.

The young man in "Here We Are" exhibits the defense mechanism of repression as he hides his feelings about both Louise and his wife's hats he obviously does not like. Repression involves "unconscious denial of the existence of something that causes anxiety" and is the foundation of all the defense mechanisms developed by Freud.[11] The goal of all defense mechanisms is to repress unconscious impulses. Therefore, wherever defense mechanisms such as reaction formation, displacement, or sublimation occur there will also be repression. We see it again in the story with regard to sex. The young man, anxious and anticipating the imminent sexual experience, keeps on speaking about it: "We're not really married yet. I mean. I mean—well, things will be different afterwards" (141). The young man has sex on his mind and although he tries not to mention it, he repeatedly makes unconscious references to it.

The issue of sex is more directly addressed in Freud's concept of the phallic personality, one who is "brash, vain, and self-assured. Men with this type of personality try to assert or express their masculinity through activities such as repeated sexual conquests."[12] Those who have not resolved the conflicts of the phallic stage of development have difficulties in relating to the opposite sex in adulthood. These people have strong narcissistic traits and need constant admiration from members of the opposite sex. Men of this type may be womenhaters who appear on the surface to be charming and attractive but inwardly feel aggression and hate for the women they pursue. According to Freud, they are repressing their hate and aggression as they present an attractive and charming persona. This type of male appears in Parker's story "Mr. Durant."

The title character of "Mr. Durant" is a middle-class, married man who has an affair with Rose, a secretary in his office. The question of love, at least on Mr. Durant's part, is never an issue: "His interest in Rose did not blunt his appreciation of chance attractive legs or provocative glances." Having made his sexual conquest, he abandons Rose after she becomes pregnant, providing twenty-five dollars for an abortion but offering no other kind of support. Parker writes that Mr. Durant "felt surprise that Rose should ever have attracted him. . . . he looked back on himself as being just a big boy in the whole affair." His behavior and callousness—he "wished to God he had never seen Rose. He explained this desire to her"—exhibits the phallic personality. He continues to search for his next conquest, feeling "cozy assurance there would always be others."[13] Meanwhile at home, he contrives to dispose of a stray dog his children want to keep as a pet after he learns it is female, another example of his misogyny.

A more controversial Freudian concept found in Parker's writing is the "death wish," first published in Freud's book, *Beyond the Pleasure Principle* (1920). As Freud grew older and became ill, he theorized that along with his concept of the "life instinct" (the motivation to survive and experience the pleasures of the libido) there is an unconscious wish to die. Although largely rejected by scientists and society, the death wish attracted attention and offers an interesting angle on Parker's story "Big Blonde," first published in 1929. Hazel Morse is a "big blonde" who marries, divorces, takes a series of lovers, and falls into depression and alcoholism. Her thoughts about her impending suicide attempt are provocative: "There was no settled, shocked moment when she first thought of killing herself; it seemed to her as if the idea had always been with her." The fact that "the idea had always been with her" suggests a Freudian death wish that is buried within Hazel's subconscious. Hazel, as her life deteriorates, is no longer driven by the Freudian "life instinct"—the desire to survive and succumb to the pleasures of the libido. Alcohol, drugs, and death are a means of escape for Hazel from unpleasant life experiences. Feeling tired and yawning after taking her suicidal dose of pills, she says:

"Guess I'll go to bed. Gee I'm nearly dead."

That struck her as comic, and she turned out the bathroom light and went in and laid herself down in her bed, chuckling softly all the time.

"Gee, I'm nearly dead," she quoted. "That's a hot one!"[14]

Death seems pleasant and comic to Hazel. Her suicide attempt fails, but given that the idea of suicide "had always been with her," there is no reason to think she won't try it again.

In closing, I would like to return to an issue mentioned earlier, the autobiographical aspects of Parker's work. Marion Meade, one of Parker's biographers, claims that the character of Mr. Durant is based on Charles MacArthur, a lover of Parker's who left her after she became pregnant with their child; Parker then had an abortion.[15] Parker was also known to drink, become depressed, and attempt suicide more than once, and "Big Blonde" has been read as a reflection of that aspect of her life. To a certain extent, then, some of Parker's stories and poems might perform a Freudian analysis on their author's personality. Alternatively, Parker's work may reflect other people she knew or merely observed, besides herself and her lovers, personalities who exemplified Freudian concepts and thus became useful material for fiction and poetry. This possibility is all the more interesting if Meade's observation that Parker had doubts about psychoanalysis is true; Parker may have questioned other aspects of modern psychology as well. Regardless, Parker certainly knew enough about Freudian psychology to create remarkable studies of human behavior.

NOTES

1. Frederick J. Hoffman, *The Twenties: American Writing in the Postwar Decade* (1955; repr., New York: Free Press, 1965), 230–32. See especially note 56.

2. Marion Meade, *Dorothy Parker: What Fresh Hell Is This?* (New York: Villard, 1987), 158–62, 327, and James R. Gaines, *Wit's End: Days and Nights of the Algonquin Round Table* (New York: Harcourt Brace Jovanovich, 1977), 116–17.

3. Dorothy Parker, "The Passionate Freudian to His Love," in Stuart Y. Silverstein, ed., *Not Much Fun: The Lost Poems of Dorothy Parker,* ed. Stuart Y. Silverstein (New York: Scribner, 1996), 88–89. I would like to thank Professor Rhonda Pettit for her assistance with the analysis of this poem.

4. Dorothy Parker, "The Bolt Behind the Blue," in *Complete Stories* (New York: Penguin, 1995), 333. Subsequent references will be to this edition.

5. Duane P. Schultz and Sydney Ellen Schultz, *Theories of Personality* (Belmont: Wadsworth, 2001), 57.

6. Dorothy Parker, "The Waltz," in *Complete Stories*, 209.

7. Dorothy Parker, "Comment," in *Complete Poems* (New York: Penguin, 1999), 46.

8. Dorothy Parker, "Second Love," in *Complete Poems*, 132.

9. Schultz, 56.

10. Dorothy Parker, "Here We Are," in *Complete Stories*, 136–43. Subsequent references will be to this edition.

11. Schultz, 57.

12. Ibid., 64.

13. Dorothy Parker, "Mr. Durant," in *Complete Stories*, 26, 25, 26, 28.

14. Dorothy Parker, "Big Blonde," in *Complete Stories*, 117, 120.

15. Meade, 131.

Part IV
Conversations

Dorothy Parker's Letters to Alexander Woollcott

Arthur F. Kinney

DOROTHY ROTHSCHILD PARKER MET ALEXANDER WOOLLCOTT IN 1919 when his love of desserts took him into the Algonquin Hotel for Frank Case's lunchtime delicacies, and her coworker on *Vanity Fair*, Robert Benchley, introduced them. From the beginning, their friendship grew with a kind of instinctive, intimate solidarity: she found in his capacious energies, his love of parties, his incurable sociability, and his verbal dexterity much that had come to be herself. "He has," she wrote in a *Vanity Fair* portrait she called "A Valentine for Mr. Woollcott," "between seven and eight hundred intimate friends, with all of whom he converses only in terms of atrocious insult. It is not, it is true, a mark of his affection if he insults you once or twice; but if he addresses you outrageously all the time, then you know you're in. . . . He is at the same time the busiest man I know and the most leisured. He even has time for the dear lost arts—letter-writing and conversation. . . . Alexander Woollcott's enthusiasm is his trademark; you know that never he has written a piece strained through boredom." He was, in fact, the only one who dared—and dared successfully—to call the half-Jewish Parker "Sheeny." She would not have tolerated this from anyone else.

Yet it is not difficult to see what brought these two together, however improbable the friendship might first appear between the pretty, popular woman and the ostentatious, idiosyncratic man. For they were both, despite their gregariousness, essentially lonely: highly sensitive, vulnerable, defensive. Effectively orphaned by their families, both had been fighting to establish themselves through their natural talents at writing in the hard, brash days of personal journalism. They both had the knack for repartee, becoming two of the most publicized members of the Algonquin Round Table, the "vicious circle" of wits that F.P.A. (Franklin P. Adams) kept praising in his citations and quotations in the New York *World*. Fundamentally estranged from others and addicted to the theater, they both

331

watched life as a spectacle others played; and both made their livings at the time as drama critics—Parker for *Vanity Fair* (succeeding P. G. Wodehouse) and later the *New Yorker* (substituting for the vacationing Robert Benchley), and Woollcott for the *New York Times*. Both developed a flashy, capsule kind of criticism, a sort of fashionable journalism notable for its personal prejudices and friendships, and both revealed streaks of sentimentality even when they tried hardest to hide it. They both became self-conscious about themselves and their careers, and self-styled in their performances of wit. They were both given to fits of depression as well as manic moments of joy; still, they thought of themselves as sophisticated, and this seemed confirmed when Harold Ross asked both of them to become advisory editors when he founded the *New Yorker* as the journal of urban culture in the summer of 1925. What these previously unpublished letters from Parker introduce, then, is not so much a flippant set of observations that seem resonant of F. Scott Fitzgerald's flappers, but, more deeply, more tellingly, a language of shared insecurities only verbally buried in a vibrant slang.[1]

Parker's first extant letter to Woollcott, written sometime in 1926, captures the buoyancy of the times and the artificiality of their apparently careless but actually carefully groomed style. Parker was then in the midst of her affair with Seward Collins, heir to a national chain of tobacco stores and editor of the *Bookman*, and had sailed to Europe with him (and with Ernest Hemingway and Donald Ogden Stewart and his wife). When her relationship with Collins became strained, she left him to stay with Gerald and Sara Murphy on the Riviera, although the Stewarts had just introduced her to them.

✧

Villa America
Cap d'Antibes
A.M.

Dear Alec, so I thought you would like to know about the Murphy children's dog. It was a sort of joint dog, a present to all three of them. Naturally, there was a desparate [*sic*] time about finding a name that was truly worthy of him, on account of the width of the field. They finally narrowed that by deciding that they would call him after the thing they liked best in all the world. Days passed, because new yearnings and old memories kept coming up and causing argument. But eventually they reached an agreement. The dog's name is Asparagus.

Young Baoth Murphy, who has gone in for poultry, did me the greatest honor of my life; he named a chicken Dorothy, after me. The christening was done, so to say, blind, and Dorothy has since turned out to be rooster. But, as Baoth so well says, "What is that of difference?"

These opening sentences—both Parker and Woollcott are given to narrative as a form of communication—show how Parker could at once become a part of her day's jet set while standing deliberately outside, apart; the delicate balance is between an anxious involvement and a rueful sense of isolation.

It is entirely too lovely here now, and a person would be a fool to be any place else. All the younger sexual set has gone, and the weather is glorious—except the past few days, which have been given over to the equinox, making the water far too rough and full of currents for my purposes. Gerald Murphy, however, persists in his morning swim around the point of the Garoupe, so I think we can all look forward to a Smart Drowning any time now.

I am full of deferred health and twilit energy, and am working like a fool. Rotten it may be, and is, but it's an awful pile of work, just the same. And it's nothing, compared to what I tear up. Dear God, please make me stop writing like a woman. For Jesus Christ's sake, amen.

She had gone to the Antibes to write—a novel she said, for she wanted a career that was literary, not journalistic. But she found herself unable to start; the task was awesome, even threatening. Woollcott understood this, and her letter quickly becomes a series of avoidances.

My plans—let's have a nice chat about me, shall we?—are nebulous (surprise, surprise!) and I don't know what the hell. But every day is so nice, I don't think about the next one. And I really don't quite dare to come back to New York just yet. I am sure they would charge me duty on all my French subjunctives that haven't been used.

The spell of the tropics has me, and I haven't seen a New York paper or magazine for an egg's age. My daily reading is the Nice Eclaireur, which is almost entirely devoted to accounts of good, juicy murders. There has been a great vogue, lately, of doubling up old ladies, stuffing them into trunks, and sending them around the Continent until they become, shall we say, Noticeable. Ah, well, maybe all their lives they wanted to travel . . . There has also been a fascinating case of a specimen of well-grown Midi manhood, who took an attractive little girl of eight into a field, deflowered her, gouged out an eye, cut her mouth to her ears, twisted her arms around backward, set fire to her clothes, and then deserted her. The Eclaircur— and I think no more than rightly—referred to him throughout its story as "cet indelicat". . . .

I get awful hot flashes of homesickness—just like white people. I should so love to hear from you. If I had any news I would tell you, but there is nothing except the mild item that my hair is growing long and looks terrible. But anything you would say would be news to me. So you see. . . .

Dear Alec,—
Dorothy—

Parker's first marriage—to Edwin Pond Parker II, a young Wall Street broker descended from one of the old families of Hartford—ended in divorce in 1927; they were first separated during World War I when Parker served overseas and did not return immediately after the Armistice. Several relationships followed, but her marriage to Alan Campbell, an actor eleven years younger, seemed to bring Parker her first real joy in decades. She reveals this happiness to Woollcott in her letter to him from Denver where, shortly after the romance grew serious, they went by car, in 1934, for an acting job for Alan. She took her two dogs with them.

Dear Alec, did you know that the name "Denver" is composed of the words "golden" and "silver"? Well, it is. And the hell with it.

So the trip across the Continent, that I had dreamed of as a leisured progress toward the westering sun through grain bending to the wind, turned out to be more in the nature of a suicide compact, because the Colonel became inflamed with the feat of making Colorado in four days in that nineteen-twenty-nine sitz bath of his, and did it. But it was fun, and though I could not look you in the eye and say that the presence of the two Bedlington terriers went unnoticed, they really were awfully good. . . .

The reason I haven't written you, dearest Alec, is the hell we stepped right off into upon arrival. It seems that on our way out, we sent a telegram signed with both our names to Donald Stewart, whom I think you have met, and he showed it to a reporter on a Hollywood paper. [Stewart had gone to Hollywood to write scripts, one of many New York writers seeking more money in the early boom days there.] So we got out of the car into a swirl of reporters, camera men, sports writers, and members of the printers' union, which led to complete loss of head and employment by the Colonel of such phrases as "Westbury, Long Island" and "last October." So we were married, dearest Alec, at Raton, New Mexico, which will learn us not to send comic telegrams. Only it is lovelier than I ever knew anything could be, and we are in a sort of coma of happiness, interrupted only by finding a house, getting a servant, the Colonel's rehearsals, and the opening of "No More Ladies," in which the Colonel played the Rex O'Malley part and damn good, too. And I am sorry about all this secrecy, but we are telling only you and [Frank] Sullivan and Mr. A[dams] what really happened, because of the Power of the Press and the state of scare into which it threw us. And may God grant you never learn of the things I did by way of what is called keeping in with the reporters. I don't care who else sees those interviews I gave on What Marriage Means to Me and Should My Husband's Career Come Before My Own?, just so long as your pouncing eyes never leer along their lines.

We live in North Denver, which is like one of those places that you pass when the train starts slowing down, and you say to yourself, "Well, there's one thing, anyway,—I don't have to live in a dump like that." There are rows, stretching forever of horribly ornate little red brick bungalows, like small mortuary chapels, furnished almost entirely in colored beads and Congoleum. And all day long, sprinkling of the lawns goes on; it gets you finally, as did the rain, [W. Somerset Maugham's] play of that name. The ladies wear, when sprinkling, boudoir caps, about which I had forgotten, gingham wrappers and sneakers; the gentlemen wear shirts without collars but with collar-buttons, and straw hats like those affected by horsies. There comes over the human countenance, when its owner is holding a hose, an expression of vacuity so terrible that you walk down the streets with your hands over your eyes to escape it. We sprinkle, too; you have to, it's a city ordinance. Ordnance. Ordinance. Oh, the hell with it. But we have a really darling house, found by the grace of God and the Colonel's Southern charm, and we had three servants, one after one, the first week. Now we have a lady follower of Mrs. [Mary Baker] Eddy who calls me "honey" and nudges you when you don't immediately attend to the platter at your elbow. But she is good-humored and genteelly fond of her liquor. Drinking here is quite an interesting experiment, because of the altitude. Two cocktails, and you spin on your ass.

It is furiously hot, but that's all true about the nights being cold, so you don't mind it. Also the prices are delightful—fifty-five dollars a month for a furnished house, and five cents for a watermelon. Also we have met three or four nice people, which is big for a continent. I thought I was going to hate it, and I love it. I love it. I love being a juvenile's bride and living in a bungalow and pinching dead leaves off the rose bushes. I will be God damned.

But then her guard slips further; wisecracks falter.

I don't see much of the Colonel because he rehearses all day and plays all evening, including Sunday, but from what glimpses I have caught of him, he seems well and pleasant. This week they are doing "The Shining Hour" with Alan in the Derek Williams part, but I haven't yet seen it. I keep away from the theatre, because I once read in a movie magazine that Mrs. Clark Gable was held in high esteem in Hollywood because she stayed the hell out of her husband's business. The leading lady is Miss Lora Baxter, who looks like a two-dollar whore who once commanded five. Through some little misunderstanding on the press-agent's part, she is listed in the program as having played in New York in a drama called "Full Streams, Farewell," which gives that needed Milt Gross note. "The Shining Hour" is advertised as "A side-splitting comedy of family foibles and pleasures—clean as a whistle."

We miss you very badly, and love you something terrible.

Dearest Alec.

In 1934 Parker was forty, and Campbell, the son of a Scottish tobacco man from Richmond, a longtime landed cavalier, and a Jewish mother, daughter of a kosher butcher, was twenty-nine. He had gone to a military academy (hence Colonel), but he remained closely attached to his mother (who never approved of Parker). But Parker had had her own bad luck: her natural mother died shortly after she was born, and she blamed herself; it seems her Catholic stepmother blamed her, too. Campbell, in his way, gave Parker a home she never knew in childhood, as Woollcott was quick to recognize. In New York, Campbell had cooked and cleaned for Parker and helped her temper her drinking; he had been an important and calming influence. But now, in Denver, he seemed never to be around—and Woollcott consoled Parker by inviting her to return to his legendary houseparties on an island in Lake Bomoseen, Vermont. In a short time she was writing him again.

3783 Meade Street
Denver
Colorado

Listen, you dimensioned example of the insular, how do you think anybody is to get from Denver to Neshobe Island—by wishing? The carfare from here to New York is something over ninety dollars, without berth or food, and a plane ride, one way, is an even hundred and thirty. Do you think your father and I are MADE of money? No, dear. Once and for all, you may NOT have a car of your own until you have finished high school.

Dear Alec, I am afraid it is only too true about Hollywood. The Paramount contract, or Kiss of Death, has come. It is for ten weeks, and it seems the only way to get out from under that suffocating mass of debt which my doting husband calls Dottie's dowry. (By the way, how much do I owe you, Mr. W.?) Then there was that note I signed for my brother-in-law, during those days when I was known as Madcap Kitty, the Toast of the Troop. So you see. I feel pretty flat about it, when I consider all that elaborate shaking of dust from shoes that I did. Well. . . . But here are two things about it. Compared to Denver, Hollywood will seem like Athens. The other thing is that Alan will be there. He wears like brass, Alec.

The Colonel, if I understand his contract, which I most certainly do not, is to write dialogue and act, too, while I am to be purely a writer, as they already have Polly Moran signed up. I see by the papers that I am to work for Mr. Lee Tracy, the gentleman who micturated over Mexico. He does that, it appears, when he is not amused. I am planning to wear a shower-curtain to work.

My inclination is to file the whole thing under Horseshit, but the Colonel worries about finances—as, he points out, I should have been doing all these years. I guess it must be nice not to be in debt. . . . So, when the Elitch Gardens season closes September first—having hung up an untarnished record of not one respectable production—we pack up the Bedlingtons and take again to that god damned nineteen-twenty-nine model Rosinante of the Colonel's. The dogs look terrible. No one here knows how to shear them; no one here, in fact, has ever seen a Bedlington before, though the resemblance to sheep is frequently commented upon by the more sensitive. I am waiting for some really sweet photographs of them to be finished, before insisting on sending you one. Cora, you will see, turned out brave and proud and beautiful; but the Wolf has obviously just been voted the One Least Likely to Succeed. Poor Cora has had a horrible Summer, due to a peculiarly suburban circumstance. The parrot next door has learned to call "Cora!" and does it in a querulous, preremptory voice all day long. And poor, slavish Cora keeps jumping the fence, to find nothing but a fool green bird.

May I be the first to tell you that I have been sick, and in the most unattractive manner, all Summer long? The climate here is not for Baby; the Doctor—and the only fine things they have here are doctors, most of whom are forced to live here because of their own illness—says it often happens to those who come from what is contemptuously called the East. The ferocious dryness acts on your membranes and what results is a kind of hay fever, in the most aggravated form, or maybe it is I who am the most aggravated form. I have smiled my last tolerant smile at the mention of hay fever. It is God's own torment. At first, of course, I knew it was t.b. and took to reclining on couches in profile and addressing the Wolf as Flush [like Elizabeth Barrett Browning] (to which he answered affectionately, just as he does when you call Cora, Alan, or the ice-man) but it wasn't. End of profoundly unmoving bit of autobiography. . . .

Dear Alec, I should like to hear how you are and what you are doing and what you are going to do and where you will be and what became of those forty-seven pounds. Please.

I miss you something filthy.

Dear Alec.

Alan Campbell's marriage to Dorothy Parker largely ended gossip concerning her promiscuity, especially since his homosexuality was widely reported. She had hoped to change all that—to mother him in turn—but she failed nearly from the start; it did little to end her own self-abuse. So the lure of Hollywood was not, as with so many of her friends, just the lure of high salaries and little work; it was also the lure of a new lease on life with her husband. The Campbells signed with Paramount to begin work on an original story for Carole Lombard and Lee Tracy on 15 September 1934, and they did contribute to the dialogue for *Here Is My Heart* and *One Hour Late* although they were not credited. On their arrival, they stayed six months at a house owned by George Oppenheimer to help make ends meet; then, taking their own house in Beverly Hills, Parker did something not uncustomary: she threw an enormous party out of guilt and embarrassment and did not invite the Oppenheimers.

As Woollcott would sense, nothing much had really changed. There had not been—there never would be—a fresh start. Parker and Campbell bought a house that resembled the Southern mansion from which he had come; their close friend John O'Hara described it in a letter to F. Scott Fitzgerald in April 1936.

I stayed with Dottie and her husband when I first came out here. They have a large white house, Southern style, and live in luxury, including a brand new Picasso, a Packard convertible phaeton, a couple of Negroes, and dinner at the very best Beverly Hills homes. Dottie occasionally voices a great discontent, but I think her aversion to movie-writing is as much lazy as intellectual.[2]

The more private letter from Parker to Woollcott, however, written from that home at 520 North Cañon Drive in Beverly Hills in 1935, makes things, despite the surface attempts at wit, sound very different.

Well, Alec, here I am, just fresh from the Good Samaritan—or at least Pretty Good Samaritan—Hospital, where I have spent a week with intestinal hives. And that is the nearest I want to get to it, unless I do it myself. It seems I have had hives—why are all diseases with plural names considered comic?—ever since I got here, and last week it hit me in the gut, to use an Americanism. They have tried every test and they can't find out what give [sic] it to me. the doctor say [sic] something must be causing it; is it any wonder I have all the confidence in the world in him? As you read this, even allowing for the difference in time, I am sitting here shot so full of adrenalin I feel like Doctor Cornish's dog. I shall say no more about the physical side of my character than to tell you that I had two nurses. One day I was doing a cross-word puzzle and put it aside to sleep. When I woke up, the nurse cried gaily, "Look what I've done for you! I've finished your puzzle for you!" The other attendant never entered the room without cooing. "And how are our little hivies?" My state is now such that I not only hate all trained nurses, but all Canadians.

Alan and I are working on a little opera which was originally named "Twenty-two Hours by Air," but it has been kicking around the studio for a long time, during which aerial transportation has made such progress that it is now called "Eleven Hours by Air." By the time we are done, the title is to be, I believe, "Stay Where You Are." Before this, we were summoned to labor on a story of which we were told only, "Now, we don't know yet whether the male lead will be played by Tullio Carminati or Bing Crosby. So just sort of write it with both of them in mind." Before that, we were assigned the task of taking the sex out of "Sailor, Beware." They read our script, and went back to the original version. The catch for the movies, it seemed, was that hinge of the plot where the sailor bets he will make the girl. They said that was dirty. But would they accept our change, that triumph of ingenuity where the sailor just bets he will make another sailor? Oh, no. Sometimes I think they don't know *what* they want.

Aside from the work, which I hate like holy water, I love it here. There are any number of poops about, of course, but so are there in New York—or, as we call it, The Coast—and the weather's better here. I love having a house, I love its being pretty wherever you look, I love a big yard full of dogs. . . . Jeez, I miss you. The only time I am pulled apart by nostalgia is when I hear your voice on the radio. (I suppose you don't think that Kern birthday broadcast did us in, by the way.) [He had done a radio commentary on Kern's life and death.] I can't talk about it. I get to crying.

I am deeply ashamed of myself to say that it shocked me to read of Heywood's marriage [to Connie Madison, wife of John Dooley]. I make myself sick—why shouldn't he be happy, certainly he must love her, inquestionably [*sic*] she is fond of him, undeniably they have fun together, and so on, and so on. But there I am. I guess it's that I can't get over Ruth [Hale, his first wife]. I guess it's that I'm never going to get over Ruth.

There isn't a morning that I don't open the paper expecting to find a furious denial from her, scalding editors for their male gullibility. The account of her death in the Los Angeles Examiner was the last irony, the five-word record of the total failure of a life. The headline was: "Ex-wife of Heywood Broun Passes."

But she also confessed some compensations.

There are some nice people here—who would be anywhere, of course. I have always loved the Gleasons, and now I do it more. James Cagney is, I should say, the best person here, or, for that matter, just about anywhere. We saw a lot of Helen Hayes, whom I had never known before [now married to Charles MacArthur after his affair with Parker], and isn't she really a girl? Who is something swell is Bing Crosby. I will *really* be god-damned. . . .

Still,

Dear Alec. I should so love to hear from you. Dear Alec, I miss you very much. If I had had more time, I should have made this letter longer.
    Dear Alec.
    Dorothy

Parker soon learned that her literary reputation in New York was all that Hollywood really meant to purchase, but the one-line repartees which had become the mainstay of that reputation were out of place in the scripts, which her husband could craft well in a more traditional way. As a literary talent she was suddenly a misfit and—even worse—a misfit made to compete in a system where under the "backup" policy at Metro, writers were continually rewritten by other writers and most energy went to being last, for only the last won screen credits and pay raises. The jockeying for space in F.P.A.'s column in New York for the best bon mot of the day or the angling for the best witty comeback at the Algonquin was now more serious, and Parker's alcoholism, imported from New York along with her expectations for greater fame and more money, only worsened. "I'm as sane as you are!" Fitzgerald remembered her screaming from a window at the Metro writers building; someone else recalled a crying jag when she heard "I'll Get By." Quite unexpectedly, then, $5,200 a week—and a big house in Beverly Hills—was not enough.
    As usual, Parker's wit was her first and last defense against despair. In the correspondence, it becomes zany, even manic.

(Western Union, Beverly Hills, Calif. 2:47 p.m. October 13, 1934)
JUST HEARD THE LYRIC TO A SONG CALLED QUOTE THREE CHEERS FOR LOVE
UNQUOTE ONE LINE OF WHICH RUNS QUOTE SISS BOOM AH FOR FLOWERS
UNQUOTE STOP PLEASE COME AT ONCE=

DOROTHY

And again to Woollcott:

SELZNICK INTERNATIONAL PICTURES, INC.
9336 Washington Boulevard Culver City, Cal. [?1936]

Dear Gerald,

So last week, the board of directors of Selznick Pictures, Inc., had a conference. The four members of the Board sat around a costly table in an enormously furnished room, and each was supplied with a pad of scratch paper and a pencil. After the conference was over, a healthily curious young employe [*sic*] of the company went in to look at those scratch pads. He found:

Mr. David Selznick had drawn a seven-pointed star; below that, a six-pointed star; and below that again, a row of short vertical lines, like a little picket fence.

Mr. John Hay Whitney's pad had nothing whatever on it.

Dr. A. H. Giannini, the noted California banker, had written over, and over, in a long neat column, the word "tokas," which is Yiddish for "arse."

And Mr. Meryan Cooper, the American authority on Technicolor, had printed, in the middle of his page, "RIN-TIN-TIN."

The result of the conference was the announcement that hereafter the company would produce twelve pictures a year, instead of six.

I don't know. I just thought you might like to be reassured that Hollywood does not change.

With love and nostalgia,
(signed) DOROTHY

But "Wit has truth in it; wisecracking is simply calisthenics with words," Parker later told Marion Capron in an interview for the *Paris Review*; the distinction holds true in her recollection of the sums of money she made when her lines were not getting as far as the screen.[3] "It's like congealed snow; it melts in your hand." Regardless of this, Woollcott himself came to Hollywood in 1935; worked three days writing and acting in a short entitled *Mr. W.'s Little Game* about himself, a blonde, and a headwaiter thinking of words beginning with the letter L; earned himself $4,000—and went back to New York. He was popular enough with his newspaper writing, his features, his lectures—and, most of all, his radio broadcasts, from 1929 to 1940, earning him $500 each. "Woollcott speaking," they would begin and they gave him a great range for wit, for denunciation, and satire—and for sentimentality. On 22 June 1937, he went on the air with a memorable tribute to J. M. Barrie, and Parker wired him at once: I WOULD WRITE YOU A LONG TELEGRAM IF I COULD STOP CRYING OVER YOUR LOVELY BROADCAST. But for her, script assignments were few, her output meager. While Campbell worked steadily she had to be content admiring his stability and admonishing their moral corruption in Hollywood by turns; and she submerged her own failing energies to write the way Hollywood wanted her to write into an activity of a more political sort. In the later 1930s, Parker turned Marxist.

Political and social causes were not a new thing to her. On 11 August 1927, she was one of thirty-nine arrested in Boston for marching in defense of Sacco and Vanzetti; on 6 February 1934, while visiting New York, Woollcott enlisted her aid in staging a demonstration in the blue and gold Empire Room of the Waldorf-Astoria in support of waiters who were on strike; the same year, she and Campbell gave a huge benefit buffet in their Beverly Hills mansion to raise several thousand dollars for the Scottsboro Boys. She became a chief organizer of the Screen Writers Guild and in June 1936 she helped to found, with Frederic March and others, the Anti-Fascist League, dedicated to bringing fellow writers out of Germany while awakening Americans to the threat of Hitler's rise to power. Perhaps her lifelong compassion for the downtrodden, perhaps her aristocratic desire to be charitable to the less fortunate, perhaps her moral conscience over her decision to work in Hollywood for huge salaries, caused her to join Hemingway and Lillian Hellman in financing the film *The Spanish Earth* and in supporting the Spanish Civil War. She put up $500 for the film made by Hemingway with Joris Ivens and in time she was writing for the Communist-edited *New Masses* in New York her own firsthand accounts of war in Madrid. "Incredible, Fantastic . . . and True," printed there on 23 November 1937, was changed only slightly to become the story "Soldiers of the Republic" published by the *New Yorker* on 5 February 1938. It was a dramatic resurgence—truly a renaissance—for Parker, and Woollcott was elated. On 21 February 1938, he wrote Rebecca West, "I . . . enclosed a piece of Mrs. Parker's which I think it probable you have already seen but which I send along just the same on the chance that you haven't. It is the first thing she's printed in the *New Yorker* in several years and as good a piece as she ever wrote. Certainly it comes nearer to telling the reader exactly what she is like than anything else she ever wrote." Woollcott's papers include seven tearsheets of the story as well as long yellow galley-proofs of his own reprinting of it, at his expense, and with a prefatory note in which he calls it "better than Tolstoy or Stephen Crane." Parker might not have been so extravagant, but she was grateful for his interest and suggested in a telegram on 27 February 1938, that he might check the right to reprint with her publishers.

By 12 October 1940, however, Hemingway wrote his editor Maxwell Perkins from Sun Valley, Idaho, that he had to escape such visitors as Parker. "Dorothy Parker and her husband have come out here and Gary Cooper and his wife are here so there is plenty of company and so we are going to the primitive area of the middle fork of the Salmon river tomorrow although I like the people very much." Parker's account of that visit, concerned as it is in good measure with Hemingway's second wife (Pauline Pfeiffer) and his third (Martha Gelhorn, whom she had met, with Hellman, on a sea voyage to Europe), is considerably different. It appears in her only letter in longhand, written around December 1940 from her hospital bed where she was recovering from surgery.

Dear Alec, I think it is the dirtiest of all impositions to write to somebody in longhand, by means of a pencil. If I were you, I shouldn't even look at this. . . .

This has been a completely strange experience. I didn't know about pain before. Oh, well, hell—everybody has some pain; I didn't mean that. I mean I didn't know about a life in which there's nothing but pain—in which there isn't work or words or repute or money or anger or decency or filth or good or ill or even day or night—just nothing but pain. You find you keep thinking about it. It gives you a queer, puzzled feeling. . . .

Alan is out looking at houses now. I do not think this keeps him from sending love and nostalgia to you.

Dear Alec, I am so glad you know Martha Gelhorn. Alan and I have been doing a good deal of unison chanting about how she is for you—and for the Island. I think she is truly fine. Even leaving aside her looks and her spirit and her courage and her decency—though I can't imagine why they should be shoved aside—she is doing such a really good job. We were in Sun Valley with them a while ago, at a damned trying time for her. Pauline, whether on her own (I've never liked her) or by advice was still refusing divorce and at the same time demanding more money than there exists. Ernest has his two little boys—Pauline's kids—there with them. Well, Martha was perfect with them, as with the whole situation. And the kids gave her love and friendship and absolute trust. I have seen them come to her, with their paper and pencils, and ask her to tell them what to write to Mama. Well, just think what a cruel woman, or a vindictive woman, or even, God help us, an ordinary woman could have done with that one. And Martha was just perfect.

And I think she is doing a glorious job as to Ernest. I have known him, hard and well, for fifteen years. I love him and revere him. But baby, in his personal relationships, and particularly those with his women, he can only be called No Cinch. I've heard Martha, with complete good-humor and as one telling a funny story, report on some circumstance in her daily life with him that would drive any other woman white-haired—such as, say, the presence of rats in her sleeping-bag. And Ernest has answered, serious and frowning, "Well, look, Marty. You signed up to be tough, you know."

Well, I guess that's a statement of fact, at that. But she's being tough graciously and gaily. The others couldn't. I think this marriage will last, and keep fine.

My God, I'm tired. My God, you must be tireder.

I think I'd rather be where you are than any place in the world. I think being with Mrs. Roosevelt every day [Woollcott was occasionally staying at the White House] must be like getting to Heaven without going through the nuisance of dying. I am more grateful for her every time the clock ticks. And you know that's the way I should be.
Please remember everything.

Dear Alec _____

Dorothy.

Parker and Campbell began spending a great deal of time in a 1775 fieldstone farmhouse now, on 111 acres of land in Bucks County, Pennsylvania, built by a family named Fox. At first it provided ventilation from Hollywood; but in time it became a retreat used more and more after the death of Scott Fitzgerald—Parker was the first person Sheliah Graham told—and, the next day, of Nathanael and Eileen West. This was the place where Parker planned for her first child, until a putative miscarriage in the third month robbed her of any offspring. So then it was where (she would write in "Destructive Decoration" for *House and Garden*) she and Campbell spent time, energy, and money practicing interior design. "So our drawing-room is in pink, rose, scarlet, magenta, vermilion, crimson, maroon, russet, and raspberry." And, nearby, perpetually visiting her and criticizing her, was her husband's mother. Woollcott, meantime, was suffering from gallstones, following a slight cerebral hemorrage.

FOX HOUSE
PIPERSVILLE
PENNSYLVANIA

July twentieth. [1942]

Dear H. M. S. Indestructible,
    I have started some dozen letters to you, but the words "happy" and "glad" and "thankful" kept creeping into them, and they looked so little

for what I mean. So I shall refer to your recovery only obliquely. Dear Alec, will you promise to see to it that a seat is reserved for me at your hanging? For if ever a man was born to that end only!

I can write only about Alan and me, because I haven't seen anybody else. We have been down here without any servants, and life is housework and no other thing. Alan cooks and I clean, and who is then the gentleman? It isn't so much that I mind bed-making and sweeping and dish-washing as that I am undone by my incompetence. It takes me every minute of every day, and the results are such as would cause me to be fired without reference anywhere. This contributes generously to a low, brooding inferiority nagged along by the recurrent silent questions, "Well, for Christ's sake, what *are* you good for, anyway?"

The cloud is slightly stirred by the acquisition of a local matron, who comes to scrub floors. When I tried it, they looked like eccentrically placed frescos. She comes once a week and her price is above rubies. The only thing is she must bring along her little boy, because, I gather, no one in any right mind would keep him for her. His name is Horse—probing developes [*sic*] that it is spelled H-o-r-a-c-e, but it is rendered Horse. Horse has four years in time; in depravity he resembles a boulevardier of eighty. One of his minor projects is peering in at me, wherever I am, and making faces at me. I do not know what to do about this. I can't quite bring myself, at my age, to the point of going and telling his mother on him. Besides, Horse might say and believe that I started it—you know, the Grandma-wasn't-playing idea. He has other activities, such as trying with his naked hands to separate cats into pieces suitable for frying, and, his biggest success to date, the introduction of our hired man's three little children to their and his genitalia. I am unable to accustom myself to Horse.

Alan's mother—this train of thought does not stop at local stations—is so well, so active, so present! And her generosity with words! Now yesterday, in typical instance, she came in, looked at my newly-made bouquets, and said, "My, this room looks real pretty with all these flowers." But did she let it stop there, as a damyankee would? No, Alec. She went right on and said, "It certainly does look terrible without them."

It is all like that. Still, I do love this place, and Alan, so much as he can be in this time of the inescapable guilt and unease of waiting to hear about his application for army service, is happy here. He is in a whirlwind of small activities, which is perhaps the best way of filling the time until the big ones come. Anyway, it is his way, and he putters and rushes and is well . . .

Dear Alec, I am so damn glad you are well —————

Dorothy.

The antic wit and joking lines are still here; but they seem frayed now.

What such a letter assumes, moreover, is Woollcott's knowledge that Parker's war efforts had sobered her considerably. Her political activities had blacklisted both Campbell and her from getting jobs as scriptwriters; they were living on meager savings while Campbell attempted to become a colonel in fact rather than from an honorific title from school days. Parker busied herself raising money for causes in and around New York, and in spending what time she could with her husband. As usual, a very few others were close to her; Woollcott was in some ways still the closest. Surely her family was not. "Her loathing of kin was not confined to Alan's mother," Fred Lawrence Guiles remarks.

> She said her older sister, who was very beautiful and nine years her senior, attended Horace Mann High School in Manhattan where boy students predominated, but she was "very much interested in that" and later married "the most horrible, disgusting, outrageous German, the worst kind of German, you know." Her epithets, and they flew from her mouth with no apology, had a way of building into a kind of crescendo of revulsion. By the time of her death, she apparently had alienated or terrified nearly all of her own relatives so that only friends would call on her at her Manhattan hotel, never any family.[4]

She had always turned on those she admired (like Hemingway) or with whom she had pretended friendship; Lillian Hellman has written that "The game more probably came from a desire to charm, to be loved, to be admired, and such desires brought self-contempt that could only be consoled by the behind-the-back denunciations of almost comic violence."[5] It was also a matter of fear. Edwin Pond Parker II had enlisted in World War I and left shortly after their marriage and when the war ended, he remained overseas. There were rumors he was homosexual. When he returned, they had little in common: he provided wealth and pedigree but no humor and was outclassed by the wits of the Algonquin Club. Now, in 1942, out of work, Campbell was also enlisting. It could all happen again. Loneliness had always been her greatest terror, and betrayal was the worst loneliness of all.

She was most exposed when Campbell finally departed; it is an extraordinarily private moment she shared only with Woollcott. "I think," Woollcott wrote their mutual friend, Hollywood actor Charles Brackett, on 12 September 1942, from Bomoseen where he was recuperating, "I think I have never read any letter with greater interest than the one Dorothy Parker wrote me after she had seen Private Alan Campbell off to the wars."

FOX HOUSE
PIPERSVILLE, BUCKS COUNTY
PENNSYLVANIA

September second. [1942]

Dear Alec, Private Campbell has just gone, and I'm afraid I'm feeling a little like Dolly Gray. So I thought I would—Oh, hell, I wanted to talk to you. So here's this letter.

I am this minute back from Philadelphia, where I went with him to see him off. Seeings-off are usually to be regretted, but I am so glad that I went. Twice before he had had a card with a date and had appeared with his bag, all ready, but each time—that cutting off of that dog's tail by those inches—they had told him to go home and wait. Even to-day, the sergeant said to him, "Are you *sure* you want to do this?" Yes. He was sure he wanted to do this.

The enlistment office in Philadelphia (you know what I mean) is in the customs house—it is a great, bare room, used, I suppose, as a sort of warehouse before. Along one wall are a couple of benches, packed tight with men sitting down, and beyond them is a line of men, moving up, man by man, as a man vacates the bench to go to the enlistment sergeant, and the sitting men move up to give another place, and the standing men move along a place for their turn. They are the men coming that day to enlist in the army. All the while we were there, that line kept lengthening, and men were still coming in when we left. That goes on every day, all day. Jesus, Alec, I guess we're all right.

Most of them look poor—I mean by that, they haven't got coats on, they have soiled shirts and stained pants, their working clothes. The Lord God knows, those men who have made up their minds don't look poor in any other way and aren't poor! The majority of them are (is?) very young— "heartbreakingly young," I read in a piece by a lady who watched the troops go by and threw them roses, which were their immediate need. They are not in the least heart-breaking, and I think if you called them that they would turn out to be neck-breaking. They are young, certainly—several even had women standing beside them in line, their mommas, come to give consent to a minor's enlistment—but they're all right. There were many older men, too, carefully dressed, and obviously prosperous in their businesses—which they were willing to leave. There was nothing whatever pathetic about them, either. There were numerous Negroes. And nobody avoided them, as they stood in line with the whites nobody shied away from them or stood in silence. They all talked with one another, in the lowered voices you decently accord a big office full of busy men, but a man in line talked to the men on both sides of him. (Look, Alec, I'm not going to make any more pencil corrections. I know you will know what I mean.)

The greater part of the room is for the men who are going to camp that day. They all have their bags, and the only time I busted was at the sight of a tall, thin young Negro—"lanky" I belive [*sic*] is the word always employed—carrying a six-inch square of muslin in which were his personal effects. It looked so exactly like a bean-bag . . . And then I realized I was rotten to be tear-sprinkled. He wasn't sad. He felt fine. . . . I was ashamed of myself. And yet, dear Alec, I defy you to have looked at that bean-bag, and kept an arid eye. That, of course, has nothing to do with war. Except, also of course, that a man who had no more than that was going to fight for it . . .

Well, anyway, there were a few camp-stools—not enough, many were standing—for mothers and wives and friends and various interested parties. Many women had brought their kids, certainly because there were no nurses to leave them with, and the little ones pooped about and fought and whined and demanded drinks of water and in general conducted themselves like swine. But theirs was the only bad behavior. Not one woman but was fine. They were not quite of all classes. There wre [*sic*] no stinking rich nor fantastically poor. They were lower-to-middle and middle-to-upper. There wasn't one that didn't look proud and respecting, both of herself and of the man because of whom she was there. The men who were to go to camp—they didn't know where they were going, they are not told until they go, and that is, of course, quite right—stood in line, filed along to desks, filled out forms, and were finger-printed. They were not yet in the army. It was impressed upon them that they could get the hell out then, if they wanted to. No one went.

Then a sergeant called the roll of their names. I was astonished, Alec, at the preponderance of the short, quick English or Scottish or American names—Marsh, Kent, Brown, Downs, Leith. We think—due I am afraid to the newspapers—of factory workers, and most of these men were obviously those, a mess of consonants. God knows that is nothing against them, but it just happens that this especial day, those men who had volunteered were of plain, familiar names. There were only a couple of Gazzonottis and Schecovitxixzes. But, as I say, this is only this day. There was also, God help us, only one to represent my side—a lone Levy. I am delighted to say he was a fine looking young man.

They formed in two blocks of thirty men each—six men across, five men down. Then they took the oath of induction into the army of the United States. I had never heard it before, never seen men take it. It was a fine and solemn and stirring thing. It is flat simple and direct, as to what they pledge themselves to do, and it is in the form of a question—it begins "Do you—?" When the sergeant had finished reading it to them, those sixty men said "I do" as one man. I never heard a thing like that. There were no stragglers, no piping voices, no quavers. Precise and proud and strong it came, from sixty men—"I do." Jesus, Alec. I will not soon forget that sound. Then the sergeant talked to them, as decent a talk as I have evr [*sic*] heard. Then he said, "men on the right are to go to Fort Cumberland, men on the left to Fort Meade." Then he turned to the Fort Cumberland group and called "Private Campbell!" I had one horror-stricken moment when I thought he was going to say "stop biting your nails." But it turned out, when our private stepped forward looking pretty sheepish, that Private Campbell was to have charge of his detail, that the men were to report to him at the station, and obey his orders on the way to camp. I saw Private Campbell for a moment before they left for the station. Private Campbell said only, "I'm going to see they don't leave the car messy." Dear Alec, he will be a brigadier-general by Tuesday. Fort Cumberland, by the way, is where you go for a few days, to get your clothes and take your tests and be assigned to what they think is best for you. And I must say, I have the deepest respect for the way they seem to be trying to assign a man to his most useful job. From there, they are sent on some place else. I will let you know as soon as I know.

Then we went to the station. The Mothers and wives and friends all came too, and so did the kids, but the kids felt something and behaved superbly. The men were lined up in two rows, each man with his bag beside him— the varying kinds of bags. Alex! Ah, it really is a democratic war!—and Private Campbell, giving orders. I couldn't hear much—drat those acoustics in the Penn station at Philadelphia—but I did hear him say something and then add, "That is, if it's all right with you." I love Alan. Don't you Alec?

In the station, it was little bad. Oh, I don't mean everybody didn't go on being swell—but you know how it is, when a train's going out. The mothers and wives and girls all had tears in their eyes, and they all looked carefully away from one another, because you can be fine, yourself, but when you see tears, you're gone. Jesus, what fine people. Alec!

So while we were standing there, there came up to me a fat, ill-favored, dark little woman, who said to me, "Parn me, but aren't you Dorothy Parker? Well, I've no doubt you've heard of me, I'm Mrs. Sigg Greesbaum, Edith Gressbaum, you'd probably know me better as, I'm the head of our local chapter of the Better Living Club, and we'd like to have you come to talk to us, of course I'm still a little angry at you for writing that thing about men not making advances at girls who wear glasses, because I've worn glasses for years, and Sig, that's my husband, but I still call him my sweetheart, he says it doesn't matter a bit, well, he wears glasses himself, and I want you to talk to our club, of course we can't pay you any money, but it will do you a lot of good, we've had all sorts of wonderful people, Ethel Grimsby Loe that writes all the greeting cards and the editor of the Doylestown Intelligenser, and Mrs. Mercer, that told us all about Italy when she used to live there after the last war, and the photographs she showed us of her cypresses and all, and it would really be a wonderful thing for you to meet us, and now when can I put you down to come talk to us?"

So I said I was terribly sorry, but if she didn't mind, I was busy at the moment. So she looked around at the rows of men—she hadn't seen them before, apparently; all they did was take up half the station—and she giggled heartily and said, "Oh, what are those? More poor suckers caught in the draft?"

And an almighty wrath came upon me, and I said, "Those are American patriots who have volunteered to fight for your liberty, you Sheeny bitch!" And I walked away, already horrified—as I am now—at what I had said. Not, dear, the gist, which I will stick to and should, but the use of the word "sheeny," which I give you my word I have not heard for forty years [when Woollcott called her that] and have never used before. The horror lies in the ease with which it came to me—And worse horror lies in the knowledge that if she had been black, I would have said "You nigger bitch"—Dear God. The things I have fought against all my life. And that's what I did.

Well, so anyway, then they came down to the train, and then I left before the train pulled out, because flesh and blood is or are flesh and blood.

Alec, the private is a good man. He could have had a commission; he saw in Washington the men commissioned as majors and colonels and lietenat [sic] colonels,—cutters and directors and producers and assistants. He said—and that's all he ever said about it—"I don't think this is that kind of war." He enlisted without telling one soul. He had a job at which he was extremely good and at which he got a preposterous, in anybody's terms, salary. Just before he left, he had an offer of a six-months contract at Hollywood at twelve hundred and fifty dollars a week.

Of course it is right that he did what he has done—but no one told him what was right, except himself. He had had a bad time. When he was a kid, he liked his father; he has apparently always hated his mother. When he was fourteen, sensitive and cognizant, his mother divorced his father, took Alan, and never allowed him to see his father again. (His father died some three years after.) His resentment against his mother increased to the point where he cannot remain in the room with her —although she gives him some curious guilt, as only Southern mothers can, about his lack of filial duty. He went to New York after V. M. I.—because his father went there: he himself loathed a military college—did what he could and damn near starved. Hollywood was all assurance to him. He was good at what he did, he did it with all his conscience, he said whatever it was, it was honest work—not what came out of it, but what he put into it.

And I behaved like a shit to him, Alec. I screamed about Hollywood. I had much right on my side, but I used all the wrong things. I yipped about lowering of standards and debasing of principles. There was a lot in what I said. But there was nothing in what I thought I understood. Private Campbell's standards are not low.

He's given up a lot. His job, the house here he builded—no, I don't mean built, I mean builded—which, I think, means more to him than anything. Anything, of course, except what he must do. I know other men have done as much, but sometimes I see the other side. I hear men who say, "Gee, I'd certainly like to do something in the war—but there's my business I've got to look after, and everything." I hear women who say, "Well, let them take everybody but George. Goodness knows they don't need him—they've got enough men." They are not the natives or the workers around here, who are all we've seen, day by day. But when we've been in to New York, we've heard those things.

Now about Alan's mother. She always comes up to expectations, but this time she has outdone them and herself. When she heard Alan had enlisted, she made a scene that shook the oat fields. "Selfish", "heartless", "never thinks of me"—oh, it was great. Then when she found that did not induce him to desert the army, she found a happier—fpr [sic] her—role. She became a gold-star mother. Her heart was broken. She went all about the country side—she has a B card [for gas rationing], I guess for being Southern—telling all the neighbors of the sacrifice she was making for her country. In most cases the act flopped; their sons had gone before hers. But she got some of them. There was a little delegation that came up here and talked to Alan and me about that poor sick woman living all alone. Alan spoke to them. We ended friends.

Then she tried heart attacks. We brought out doctor, who pronounced her in perfect shape. She then, of course, hated him and us. I am not a vengeful woman, no matter what you have said—possibly for the perfectly working reason that if you just sit back and wait, the bastards will get theirs, without your doing anything about it, and it will be fancier than anything you could ever have thought up. But I would, for the sake of immediate action, give quite a large bit of my soul if something horrible would happen to that woman for poisoning Alan's last days here. . . .

And who am I to talk about people's families? On the way back from Philadelphia, I telephoned my brother and sister—whom I had negelected [sic] to inform that I was back in the East. I got my sister, and said Alan had enlisted and had gone. She said, "Oh, isn't that terrible? Well, it's been terrible here, too, all Summer. I never saw such a Summer. Why, they didn't even have dances Saturday nights at the club."

So then I tried my brother, who is not bad, but I got my sister-in-law. I told her about Alan. She said, "Oh, really? Well, of course, he's had a college education. That's what's holding Bertram back—he never had a college education." (She has a son named Bertram, approximately thirty-five.) "He'd just love to be an aviator, but of course he hasn't got a college education." I skipped over Bertram's advanced age for the aviation corps, and explained that the college-educated Alan has enlisted as a private. "Oh, really?" she said. "Oh, listen, Dot, we're going to take a new apartment, the first of October. It's got two rooms that the sun simply POURS in—and you know how I love sun!" I don't, Alec.

Honestly, if you were suddenly to point a finger at me and say, "Dorothy Parker, what is your sister-in-law's opinion of sun?" I should be dumb-founded.

Jesus Christ. People whose country is at war. People who live in a world on fire, in a time when there have never before been such dangers, such threats, such murders. . . .

Well. On the other hand, and so far outbalancing them, thank God, there are those boys in their sweat-stained shirts streaming in to enlist, there are those sixty men saying "I do" in one strong voice, there is Private Camp-bell, U.S.A. I think I'd like to write a story about that enlistment place. That isn't being phoney, is it?

I've got to write a lot of stories—if, of course, I can. I've got the farm to keep going, I've got myself, I've got Alan's mother. I've been feeling pretty guilty about not doing any war work. But if I can keep all this swinging, I'll be releasing a man for the front just as much as if I were welding in a fac-tory. I am proud to think that and to know it.

Dear Alec, I'll be here for a few days, and then I'm going in to the Ritz Tower. Alan knew the manager and got me a room, much less expensive than you think, though still too expensive. I will, though, as often as the hired man can spare gas to meet me at the station, come out here, because there are alterations going on, and I should say a few words. This address is always the one for me. Please, dear Alec, please.

I'll be embarrassed when this letter is sent. It's so long. I can only say, if I had had more time, it would have been longer. I think you know that my friendship could not be deeper and higher than writing you this, and know-ing you understand why and to whom I write it.

Dear Alec——

Dorothy.

The uncorrected misspellings—unusual for her—suggest a cer-tain lack of detachment, a certain haste. But she meant it when she thought she had a story for publication in the letter; a carbon copy of a carefully retyped portion of it—most of the letter from the beginning through the reply to Mrs. Greenbaum—is preserved in the Woollcott papers at Harvard. So is a second letter, on plainer stationery that reads across the top simply,

DOROTHY PARKER

Dear Alec, here is the other ending, and you know how scared I am of it. I don't, for heaven's sake, think you are urging anyone to spread anti-Semitism, but I can only hope to God I took off the curse, and you think it is all right. I tried various other means. There was one bit where I said "You big bitch," and then explained my horror at my choice of words, because she was really a small woman. But that, even to its mother, seemed to lack a certain force. It is true—and not, honestly, the lazy way out,—that the anecdote can be omitted, complete. Maybe it tends to break the mood—dear God, what kind of talk am I doing to you?

In any case, you must know how damn kind I think you are to take this trouble.

Dear Alec—

Dorothy

"That bird sings only when she's unhappy," Woollcott had said of Parker just after her marriage in 1934; and in a story a few years later, "The Lovely Leave," Parker described the estrangement between a soldier whose weekend leave has suddenly been shortened to a few hours (during which a bath is most important to him) and his lonely wife whose anxiety causes their whole reunion to go wrong. But of this letter nothing appeared. In January 1943, after pushing himself with journalistic ventures and wartime work, Woollcott agreed to appear for the Writers' War Board and the People's Platform as "The Town Crier" on CBS, discussing the subject, "Is Germany Incurable?" He took along his nitroglycerin tablets to combat his general arteriosclerosis, but he refused to have his doctor accompany him. His heart attack came while he was on the air, or so it was thought. Actually, it was a massive cerebral hemorrhage. The show went on while an ambulance took him to Roosevelt Hospital.

But by midnight the same radio network announced that Alexander Woollcott was dead.

NOTES

1. Woollcott's letters are housed at Harvard University.

2. John O'Hara, *Selected Letters of John O'Hara*, ed. Matthew J. Bruccoli (New York: Random House, 1978).

3. Dorothy Parker, interview with Marion Capron, ed. Malcolm Cowley, *Writers at Work: The "Paris Review" Interviews* (New York: Viking, 1958).

4. Fred Lawrence Guiles, *Hanging on in Paradise* (New York: McGraw-Hill, 1975).

5. Lillian Hellman, "Dorothy Parker," in *An Unfinished Woman* (Boston: Little, Brown, 1969), 212–28.

An Interview with Dorothy Parker

Marion Capron

Dorothy Parker lives in a midtown New York hotel. She shares her small apartment with a youthful poodle which has run of the place and has caused it to look, as Miss Parker says apologetically, somewhat "Hogarthian": newspapers spread about the floor, picked lamb chops here and there, and a rubber doll—its throat torn from ear to ear—which Mrs. Parker lobs left-handed from her chair into corners of the room for the poodle to retrieve—as it does, never tiring of the opportunity. The room is sparsely decorated, its one overpowering fixture being a large dog portrait, not of the poodle, but of a sheepdog owned by the author Philip Wylie and painted by his wife. The portrait indicates a dog of such size that in real life it must dwarf Mrs. Parker. She is a small woman, her voice gentle, her tone often apologetic, but occasionally, given the opportunity to comment on matters she feels strongly about, her voice rises almost harshly, and her sentences are punctuated with observations phrased with lethal force. Hers is still the wit which made her a legend as a member of the Round Table of the Algonquin—a humor whose particular quality seems a coupling of a brilliant social commentary with a mind of devastating inventiveness. She seems able to produce the well-turned phrase for any occasion. A friend remembers sitting next to her at the theater when the news was announced of the death of the stolid Calvin Coolidge. "How do they know?" whispered Mrs. Parker.

Readers of this interview, however, will find that Mrs. Parker has only contempt for the eager reception accorded her wit. "Why it got so bad," she has said bitterly, "that they began to laugh before I opened my mouth." And she has a similar attitude toward her value as a serious writer.

But Mrs. Parker is her own worst critic. Her three books of poetry may have established her reputation as a master of light verse, but her short stories are essentially serious in tone—serious in that they reflect her own life, which has been in many ways an unhappy one—and also serious in their intention. Franklin P. Adams has described them in an introduction to her work: "Nobody can write such ironic things unless he has a deep sense of injustice—injustice to those members of the race who are the victims of the stupid, the pretentious and the hypocritical."

Interviewer: Your first job was on *Vogue*, wasn't it? How did you go about getting hired, and why *Vogue*?

Parker: After my father died there wasn't any money. I had to work, you see, and Mr. Crowninshield, God rest his soul, paid twelve dollars for a small verse of mine and gave me a job at ten dollars a week. Well, I thought I was Edith Sitwell. I lived in a boarding house at 103rd and Broadway, paying eight dollars a week for my room and two meals, breakfast and dinner. Thorne Smith was there, and another man. We used to sit around in the evening and talk. There was no money, but Jesus we had fun.

Interviewer: What kind of work did you do at *Vogue*?

Parker: I wrote captions. "This little pink dress will win you a beau," that sort of thing. Funny, they were plain women working at *Vogue*, not chic. They were decent, nice women—the nicest women I ever met—but they had no business on such a magazine. They wore funny little bonnets and in the pages of their magazine they virginized the models from tough babes into exquisite little loves. Now the editors are what they should be: all chic and worldly; most of the models are out of the mind of a Bram Stoker, and as for the caption writers—my old job—they're recommending mink covers at seventy-five dollars apiece for the wooden ends of golf clubs "—for the friend who has everything." Civilization is coming to an end, you understand.

Interviewer: Why did you change to *Vanity Fair*?

Parker: Mr. Crowninshield wanted me to. Mr. Sherwood and Mr. Benchley—we always called each other by our last names—were there. Our office was across from the Hippodrome. The midgets would come out and frighten Mr. Sherwood. He was about seven feet tall and they were always sneaking up behind him and asking him how the weather was up there. "Walk down the street with me," he'd ask, and Mr. Benchley and I would leave our jobs and guide him down the street. I can't tell you, we had more fun. Both Mr. Benchley and I subscribed to two undertaking magazines: *The Casket* and *Sunnyside*. Steel yourself: *Sunnyside* had a joke column called "From Grave to Gay." I cut a picture out of one of them, in color, of how and where to inject embalming fluid, and had it hung over my desk until Mr. Crowninshield asked me if I could possibly take it down. Mr. Crowninshield was a lovely man, but puzzled. I must say we behaved extremely badly. Albert Lee, one of the editors, had a map over *his* desk with little flags on it to show where our troops were fighting during the First World War. Every day he would get the news and move the flags around. I was married, my husband was overseas, and since I didn't have anything better to do I'd get up half an hour early and go down and change his flags. Later on, Lee would come in, look at his map, and he'd get very serious about spies—shout, and spend his morning moving his little pins back into position.

Interviewer: How long did you stay at *Vanity Fair?*

Parker: Four years. I'd taken over the drama criticism from P. G. Wodehouse. Then I fixed three plays—one of them *Caesar's Wife,* with Billie Burke in it—and as a result I was fired.

Interviewer: You fixed three plays?

Parker: Well, *panned.* The plays closed and the producers, who were the big boys—Dillingham, Ziegfeld, and Belasco—didn't like it, you know. *Vanity Fair* was a magazine of no opinion, but *I* had opinions. So I was fired. And Mr. Sherwood and Mr. Benchley resigned their jobs. It was all right for Mr. Sherwood, but Mr. Benchley had a family—two children. It was the greatest act of friendship I'd known. Mr. Benchley did a sign, "Contribution for Miss Billie Burke," and on our way out we left it in the hall of *Vanity Fair.* We behaved very badly. We made ourselves discharge chevrons and wore them.

Interviewer: Where did you all go after *Vanity Fair?*

Parker: Mr. Sherwood became the motion-picture critic for the old *Life.* Mr. Benchley did the drama reviews. He and I had an office so tiny that an inch smaller and it would have been adultery. We had *Parkbench* for a cable address, but no one ever sent us one. It was so long ago—before you were a gleam in someone's eyes—that I doubt there *was* a cable.

Interviewer: It's a popular supposition that there was much more communication between writers in the twenties. The Round Table discussions in the Algonquin, for example.

Parker: I wasn't there very often—it cost too much. Others went. Kaufman was there. I guess he was sort of funny. Mr. Benchley and Mr. Sherwood went when they had a nickel. Franklin P. Adams, whose column was widely read by people who wanted to write, would sit in occasionally. And Harold Ross, the *New Yorker* editor. He was a professional lunatic, but I don't know if he was a great man. He had a profound ignorance. On one of Mr. Benchley's manuscripts he wrote in the margin opposite "Andromache," "Who he?" Mr. Benchley wrote back, "You keep out of this." The only one with stature who came to the Round Table was Heywood Broun.

Interviewer: What was it about the twenties that inspired people like yourself and Broun?

Parker: Gertrude Stein did us the most harm when she said, "Your're all a lost generation." That got around to certain people

and we all said, "Whee! We're lost." Perhaps it suddenly brought
to us the sense of change. Or irresponsibility. But don't forget that,
though the people in the twenties seemed like flops, they weren't.
Fitzgerald, the rest of them, reckless as they were, drinkers as they
were, they worked damn hard and all the time.

Interviewer: Did the "lost generation" attitude you speak of have
a detrimental effect on your own work?

Parker: Silly of me to blame it on dates, but so it happened to be.
Dammit, it *was* the twenties and we had to be smarty. I *wanted* to be
cute. That's the terrible thing. I should have had more sense.

Interviewer: And during this time you were writing poems?

Parker: My verses. I cannot say poems. Like everybody was then, I
was following in the exquisite footsteps of Miss Millay, unhappily in
my own horrible sneakers. My verses are no damn good. Let's face
it, honey, my verse is terribly dated—as anything once fashionable is
dreadful now. I gave it up, knowing it wasn't getting any better, but
nobody seemed to notice my magnificent gesture.

Interviewer: Do you think your verse writing has been of any benefit to your prose?

Parker: Franklin P. Adams once gave me a book of French verse
forms and told me to copy their design, that by copying them I
would get precision in prose. The men you imitate in verse influence
your prose, and what I got out of it was precision, all I realize I've
ever had in prose writing.

Interviewer: How did you get started in writing?

Parker: I fell into writing, I suppose, being one of those awful children who wrote verses. I went to a convent in New York—The
Blessed Sacrament. Convents do the same things progressive schools
do, only they don't know it. They don't teach you how to read; you
have to find out for yourself. At my convent we *did* have a textbook,
one that devoted a page and a half to Adelaide Ann Proctor; but we
couldn't read Dickens; he was vulgar, you know. But I read him and
Thackeray, and I'm the one woman you'll ever know who's read
every word of Charles Reade, the author of *The Cloister and the Hearth*.
But as for helping me in the outside world, the convent taught me
only that if you spit on a pencil eraser it will erase ink. And I remember the smell of oilcloth, the smell of nuns' garb. I was fired from
there, finally, for a lot of things, among them my insistence that the
Immaculate Conception was spontaneous combustion.

Interviewer: Have you ever drawn from those years for story material?

Parker: All those writers who write about their childhood! Gentle

God, if I wrote about mine you wouldn't sit in the same room with me.

Interviewer: What, then, would you say is the source of most of your work?

Parker: Need of money, dear.

Interviewer: And besides that?

Parker: It's easier to write about those you hate—just as it's easier to criticize a bad play or a bad book.

Interviewer: What about "Big Blonde"? Where did the idea for that come from?

Parker: I knew a lady—a friend of mine who went through holy hell. Just say I knew a woman once. The purpose of the writer is to say what he feels and sees. To those who write fantasies—the Misses Baldwin, Ferber, Norris—I am not at home.

Interviewer: That's not showing much respect for your fellow women, at least not the writers.

Parker: As artists they're rot, but as providers they're oil wells; they gush. Norris said she never wrote a story unless it was fun to do. I understand Ferber whistles at her typewriter. And there was that poor sucker Flaubert rolling around on his floor for three days looking for the right word. I'm a feminist, and God knows I'm loyal to my sex, and you must remember that from my very early days, when this city was scarcely safe from buffaloes, I was in the struggle for equal rights for women. But when we paraded through the catcalls of men and when we chained ourselves to lamp posts to try to get our equality—dear child, we didn't foresee *those* female writers. Or Clare Boothe Luce, or Perle Mesta, or Oveta Culp Hobby.

Interviewer: You have an extensive reputation as a wit. Has this interfered, do you think, with your acceptance as a serious writer?

Parker: I don't want to be classed as a humorist. It makes me feel guilty. I've never read a good tough quotable female humorist, and I never was one myself. I couldn't do it. A "smartcracker" they called me, and that makes me sick and unhappy. There's a hell of a distance between wisecracking and wit. Wit has truth in it; wisecracking is simply calisthenics with words. I didn't mind so much when they were good, but for a long time anything that was called a crack was attributed to me—and then they got the shaggy dogs.

Interviewer: How about satire?

Parker: Ah, satire. That's another matter. They're the big boys. If I'd been called a satirist there'd be no living with me. But by satirist I mean those boys in the other centuries. The people we call satirists now are those who make cracks at topical topics and consider themselves satirists—creatures like George S. Kaufman and such who don't even know what satire is. Lord knows, a writer should show his times, but not show them in wisecracks. Their stuff is not satire; it's as dull as yesterday's newspaper. Successful satire has got to be pretty good the day after tomorrow.

Interviewer: And how about contemporary humorists? Do you feel about them as you do about satirists?

Parker: You get to a certain age and only the tried writers are funny. I read my verses now and I ain't funny. I haven't been funny for twenty years. But anyway there aren't any humorists any more, except for Perelman. There's no need for them. Perelman must be very lonely.

Interviewer: Why is there no need for the humorist?

Parker: It's a question of supply and demand. If we needed them, we'd have them. The new crop of would-be humorists doesn't count. They're like the would-be satirists. They write about topical topics. Not like Thurber and Mr. Benchley. Those two were damn well read and, though I hate the word, they were cultured. What sets them apart is that they both had a point of view to express. That is important to all good writing. It's the difference between Paddy Chayefsky, who just puts down lines, and Clifford Odets, who in his early plays not only sees but has a point of view. The writer must be aware of life around him. Carson McCullers is good, or she used to be, but now she's withdrawn from life and writes about freaks. Her characters are grotesques.

Interviewer: Speaking of Chayefsky and McCullers, do you read much of your own, or the present generation of writers?

Parker: I will say of the writers of today that some of them, thank God, have the sense to adapt to their times. Mailer's *The Naked and the Dead is* a great book. And I thought William Styron's *Lie Down in Darkness* an extraordinary thing. The start of it took your heart and flung it over there. He writes like a god. But for most of my reading I go back to the old ones—for comfort. As you get older you go much farther back. I read *Vanity Fair* about a dozen times a year. I was a woman of eleven when I first read it—the thrill of that line "George Osborne lay dead with a bullet through his head." Sometimes I read, as an elegant friend of mine calls them, "who-did-its." I love Sherlock Holmes. My life is so untidy and he's so neat. But as for living novelists, I suppose E. M. Forster is the best, not knowing what that is, but at least he's a semi-finalist, wouldn't you think? Somerset Maugham once said to me, "We have a novelist over here, E. M. Forster, though I don't suppose he's familiar to you." Well, I could have kicked him. Did he think I carried a papoose on my back? Why, I'd go on my hands and knees to get to Forster. He once wrote something I've always remembered: "It has never happened to me that I've had to choose between betraying a friend and betraying my country, but if it ever does so happen I hope I have the guts to betray my country." Now doesn't that make the Fifth Amendment look like a bum?

Interviewer: Could I ask you some technical questions? How do you actually write out a story? Do you write out a draft and then go over it or what?

Parker: It takes me six months to do a story. I think it out and then write it sentence by sentence—no first draft. I can't write five words but that I change seven.

Interviewer: How do you name your characters?

Parker: The telephone book and from the obituary columns.

Interviewer: Do you keep a notebook?

Parker: I tried to keep one, but I never could remember where I put the damn thing. I always say I'm going to keep one tomorrow.

Interviewer: How do you get the story down on paper?

Parker: I wrote in longhand at first, but I've lost it. I use two fingers on the typewriter. I think it's unkind of you to ask. I know so little about the typewriter that once I bought a new one because I couldn't change the ribbon on the one I had.

Interviewer: You're working on a play now, aren't you?

Parker: Yes, collaborating with Arnaud d'Usseau. I'd like to do a play more than anything. First night is the most exciting thing in the world. It's wonderful to hear your words spoken. Unhappily, our first play, *The Ladies of the Corridor,* was not a success, but writing that play was the best time I ever had, both for the privilege and the stimulation of working with Mr. d'Usseau and because that play was the only thing I have ever done in which I had great pride.

Interviewer: How about the novel? Have you ever tried that form?

Parker: I wish to God I could do one, but I haven't got the nerve.

Interviewer: And short stories? Are you still doing them?

Parker: I'm trying now to do a story that's purely narrative. I think narrative stories are the best, though my past stories make themselves stories by telling themselves through what people say. I haven't got a visual mind. I hear things. But I'm not going to do those *he-said she-said* things any more, they're over, honey, they're over. I want to do the story that can only be told in the narrative form, and though they're going to scream about the rent, I'm going to do it.

Interviewer: Do you think economic security an advantage to the writer?

Parker: Yes. Being in a garret doesn't do you any good unless you're some sort of a Keats. The people who lived and wrote well in the twenties were comfortable and easy-living. They were able to find stories and novels, and good ones, in conflicts that came out of two million dollars a year, not a garret. As for me, I'd like to have money. And I'd like to be a good writer. These two can come together, and I hope they will, but if that's too adorable, I'd rather have money. I hate almost all rich people, but I think I'd be darling at it. At the moment, however, I like to think of Maurice Baring's remark: "If you would know what the Lord God thinks of money, you have only to look at those to whom he gives it." I realize that's not much help when the wolf comes scratching at the door, but it's a comfort.

Interviewer: What do you think about the artist being supported by the state?

Parker: Naturally, when penniless, I think it's superb. I think that the art of the country so immeasurably adds to its prestige that if you want the country to have writers and artists—persons who live precariously in our country—the state must help. I do not think that any kind of artist thrives under charity, by which I mean one person or organization giving him money. Here and there, this and that— that's no good. The difference between the state giving and the individual patron is that one is charity and the other isn't. Charity is murder and you know it. But I do think that if the government supports its artists, they need have no feeling of gratitude—the meanest and most sniveling attribute in the world—or baskets being brought to them, or apple-polishing. Working for the state—for Christ's sake, are you grateful to your employers? Let the state see what its artists are trying to do—like France with the Academie Française. The artists are a part of their country and their country should recognize this, so both it and the artists can take pride in their efforts. Now I mean that, my dear.

Interviewer: How about Hollywood as provider for the artist?

Parker: Hollywood money isn't money. It's congealed snow, melts in your hand and there you are. I can't talk about Hollywood. It was a horror to me when I was there and it's a horror to look back on. I can't imagine how I did it. When I got away from it I couldn't even refer to the place by name. "Out there," I called it. You want to know what "out there" means to me? Once I was coming down a street in Beverly Hills and I saw a Cadillac about a block long, and out of the side window was a wonderfully slinky mink, and an arm, and at the end of the arm a hand in a white suede glove wrinkled around the wrist, and in the hand was a bagel with a bite out of it.

Interviewer: Do you think Hollywood destroys the artist's talent?

Parker: No, no, no. I think nobody on earth writes down. Garbage though they turn out, Hollywood writers aren't writing down. That is their best. If you're going to write, don't pretend to write down. It's going to be the best you can do, and it's the fact that it's the best you can do that kills you. I want so much to write well, though I know I don't, and that I didn't make it. But during and at the end of life, I will adore those who have.

Interviewer: Then what is it that's the evil in Hollywood?

Parker: It's the people. Like the director who put his finger in Scott Fitzgerald's face and complained, "Pay *you*. Why, you ought to pay us." It was terrible about Scott; if you'd seen him you'd have been sick. When he died no one went to the funeral, not a single soul came, or even sent a flower. I said, "Poor son of a bitch," a quote right out of *The Great Gatsby*, and everyone thought it was another wisecrack. But it was said in dead seriousness. Sickening about Scott. And it wasn't only the people, but also the indignity to which your ability was put. There was a picture in which Mr. Benchley had a part. In it Monty Woolley had a scene in which he had to enter a room through a door on which was balanced a bucket of water. He came into the room covered with water and muttered to Mr. Benchley, who had a part in the scene, "Benchley? Benchley of *Harvard*?" "Yes," mumbled Mr. Benchley and he asked, "Woolley? Woolley of *Yale*?"

Interviewer: How about your political views? Have they made any difference to you professionally?

Parker: Oh, certainly. Though I don't think this "blacklist" business extends to the theater or certain of the magazines, in Hollywood it exists because several gentlemen felt it best to drop names like marbles which bounced back like rubber balls about people they'd seen in the company of what they charmingly called "commies." You can't go back thirty years to Sacco and Vanzetti. I don't do it. Well, well, well, that's the way it is. If all this means something to the good of the movies, I don't know what it is. Sam Goldwyn said, "How'm I gonna do decent pictures when all my good writers are in jail?" Then he added, the infallible Goldwyn, "Don't misunderstand me, they all ought to be hung." Mr. Goldwyn didn't know about "hanged." That's all there is to say. It's not the tragedies that kill us, it's the messes. I can't stand messes. I'm not being a smartcracker. You know I'm not when you meet me—don't you, honey?

Selected Bibliography

Although dated by now and missing some sources, Randal Calhoun's *Dorothy Parker: A Bio-Bibliography* (Westport, CT: Greenwood Press, 1993) remains the best single source for a listing of works, some of which are annotated, by and about Parker. Arthur F. Kinney's *Dorothy Parker, Revised* (New York: Twayne, 1998), also contains annotated primary and secondary sources, including useful background sources. Both include a list of screenplays. The selection below does not include original citations for previously published essays reprinted in *The Critical Waltz*, as they can be found in the acknowledgments section.

Primary Sources

Poetry

Enough Rope. New York: Boni & Liveright, 1926.
Sunset Gun. New York: Boni & Liveright, 1928.
Death and Taxes. New York: Viking, 1931.
Not So Deep as a Well. New York: Viking, 1936.
The Collected Poetry of Dorothy Parker. New York: Modern Library, 1944.
Not Much Fun: The Lost Poems of Dorothy Parker. Edited and with an introduction by Stuart Y. Silverstein. New York: Scribner, 1996.
Complete Poems. Edited by Colleen Breese. New York: Penguin, 1999.

Fiction

Laments for the Living. New York: Viking, 1930.
After Such Pleasures. New York: Viking, 1933.
Here Lies. New York: Viking, 1939.
The Collected Stories of Dorothy Parker. New York: Modern Library, 1942.
Complete Stories. Edited by Colleen Breese. New York: Penguin, 1995.
Laments for the Living. New York: BOMC Edition, 1995.
"Who Might Be Interested." In *Voices Against Tyranny: Writing of the Spanish Civil War,* edited John Miller, 192–97. New York: Scribner Signature Edition, 1986.

Drama

Close Harmony, with Elmer Rice. New York: Samuel French, 1929.

The Ladies of the Corridor, with Arnaud d'Usseau. New York: Viking, 1954.

The Coast of Illyria, with Ross Evans. Edited and with an introduction by Arthur F. Kinney. Iowa City: University of Iowa Press, 1990.

Reviews and Criticism

Constant Reader. New York: Viking, 1970.

Multigenre Collections

The Viking Portable Dorothy Parker. New York: Viking, 1944.

The Portable Dorothy Parker. New York: Viking, 1973.

The Poetry and Short Stories of Dorothy Parker. New York: Modern Library, 1994.

Editions Published Overseas

The Best of Dorothy Parker. London: Methuen, 1952.

The Collected Dorothy Parker. London: Gerald Duckworth & Co., Ltd., 1973.

The Penguin Dorothy Parker. Harmondsworth, England: Penguin, 1977.

The Sayings of Dorothy Parker. Edited by S. T. Brownlow. Introduction by Antony Rouse. London: Duckworth, 1993.

The Best of Dorothy Parker. London: Folio Society, 1995.

Recorded Readings by Parker

Dorothy Parker: Poems and "Horsie." Spoken Arts 726, n.d.

The World of Dorothy Parker. Verve V-15029, n.d.

SECONDARY SOURCES: THE WORK OF DOROTHY PARKER

Barreca, Regina. Introduction to *Dorothy Parker, Complete Stories*. Edited by Colleen Breese, vii–xix. New York: Penguin, 1995.

Bloom, Lynn Z. "Dorothy Parker." *Critical Survey of Poetry*. Edited by Frank N. Magill. 8 vols. Englewood Cliffs, NJ: Salem Press, 1981.

———. "Dorothy Parker." Vol. 5 of *Critical Survey of Short Fiction*. Edited by Frank N. Magill. 7 vols. Englewood Cliffs, NJ: Salem Press, 1981.

Bone, Martha Denham. "Dorothy Parker and *New Yorker* Satire." Diss., Middle Tennessee State University, 1985.

Breese, Colleen. Introduction to *Dorothy Parker Complete Poems*. Edited by Colleen Breese, xv–xxviii. New York: Penguin, 1999.

Fagan, Cathy E. "The Price of Power in Women's Literature: Edith Wharton and Dorothy Parker." In *Gender in Popular Culture: Images of Men and Women in Litera-*

ture, *Visual Media, and Material Culture,* edited by Peter C. Rollins and Susan W. Rollins. Cleveland, OK: Ridgemont Press, 1995.

Hollander, John. "Poetry in Review: Dorothy Parker and the Art of Light Verse." *Yale Review* 85:1 (January 1997): 156–64.

Hudson, Barbara Hill. "Sociolinguistic Analysis of Dialogues and First Person Narratives in Fiction." In *Language: Readings in Language and Culture,* edited by Virginia P. Clark, Paul A. Eschholz, and Alfred F. Rosa. Boston: Bedford/St. Martin's, 1998.

Kinney, Arthur F. *Dorothy Parker, Revised.* New York: Twayne, 1998.

Kline, Virginia. "Dorothy Parker." In *Encyclopedia of American Humorists,* edited by Steven H. Gale. New York: Garland Publishing, 1988.

Labrie, Ross. "Dorothy Parker Revisited." *Canadian Review of American Studies* 7.1 (Spring 1976): 48–56.

MacDermot, Kathy. "Light Humor and the Dark Underside of Wish Fulfillment: Conservative Anti-Realism." *Studies in Popular Culture* 10:2 (1987): 37–53.

McLuhan, Herbert Marshall. "The New York Wits." *Kenyon Review* 7 (1945): 12–28.

Melzer, Sondra. *The Rhetoric of Rage: Women in Dorothy Parker* (New York: Peter Lang, 1997).

Pettit, Rhonda. *A Gendered Collision: Sentimentalism and Modernism in Dorothy Parker's Poetry and Fiction.* Madison and Teaneck, NJ: Fairleigh Dickinson University Press, 2000.

———. "Here We Are," by Dorothy Parker. In *Beacham's Encyclopedia of Popular Fiction,* vols. 9–11, edited by Kirk H. Beetz. Davis, CA: Beacham Publishing, 1998.

———. "The Lovely Leave," by Dorothy Parker. In *Beacham's Encyclopedia of Popular Fiction,* vols. 9–11, edited by Kirk H. Beetz. Davis, CA: Beacham Publishing, 1998.

———. "The Waltz," by Dorothy Parker. In *Beacham's Encyclopedia of Popular Fiction,* vols. 9–11, edited by Kirk H. Beetz. Davis, CA: Beacham Publishing, 1998.

Puk, Francine Shapiro. "Dorothy Rothschild Parker." In *American Women Writers,* edited by Langdon Lynne Faust. 2 vols. New York: Frederick Unger, 1983.

Toth, Emily. "A Laughter of Their Own: Women's Humor in the United States." In *Critical Essays on American Humor,* edited by William Bedford Clark and W. Craig Turner, 199–215. Boston: Hall, 1984.

Van Doren, Mark. "Dorothy Parker." *English Journal* (September 1934): 535–43.

Walker, Nancy. "'Fragile and Dumb': The 'Little Woman' in Women's Humor, 1900–1940." *Thalia: Studies in Literary Humor* 5.2 (Fall and Winter 1982–83): 24–29.

Wallinger, Hanna. "Speech Patterns in Dorothy Parker." In *Style: Literary and Non-Literary,* edited by Wolfgang Grosser, James Hogg, and Karl Hubmayer. Salzburg University Studies Offprint. Lewiston, New York, and Salzburg, Austria: Edwin Mellen Press, 1995.

Yates, Norris. "Dorothy Parker's Idle Men and Women." In *The American Humorist: Conscience of the Twentieth Century,* 262–73. Ames: Iowa State University Press, 1964.

SECONDARY SOURCES: THE LIFE OF DOROTHY PARKER

Brown, John Mason. "High Spirits in the Twenties." *Horizon* 4.1 (July 1962): 33–40.

Bryan, Joseph. "Bittersweet." In *Merry Gentlemen (And One Lady),* 99–118. New York:

Antheneum, 1985. Reprinted in *Dorothy Parker: A Bio-Bibliography*, by Randall Calhoun. Westport, CT: Greenwood Press, 1993.

Calhoun, Randall. "A Biographical Sketch," 1–39. *Dorothy Parker: A Bio-Bibliography*, by Randall Calhoun. Westport, CT: Greenwood Press, 1993.

Cooper, Wyatt. "Whatever You Think Dorothy Parker Was Like, She Wasn't." *Esquire*, July 1968, 56–57, 110–14. (Reprinted in Calhoun.)

Crowninshield, Frank. "Crowninshield in the Cub's Den." *Vogue*, 15 September 1944, 162–63, 197–201.

Ephron, Nora. "Women." *Esquire*, November 1973, 58, 86.

Ford, Cory. *The Time of Laughter*. Boston: Little, Brown, 1967.

Freibert, Lucy M. "Dorothy Parker." In vol. 86 of the *Dictionary of Literary Biography*, 223–33. Detroit: Gale Research, 1989.

Frewin, Leslie. *The Late Mrs. Dorothy Parker*. New York: Macmillan, 1986.

Gaines, James R. *Wit's End: Days and Nights of the Algonquin Round Table*. New York: Harcourt Brace Jovanovich, 1977.

Harriman, Margaret Case. *The Vicious Circle: The Story of the Algonquin Round Table*. New York: Rinehart, 1951.

Hellman, Lillian. "Dorothy Parker." In *An Unfinished Woman*, 218–28. Boston: Little, Brown, 1969.

Hermann, Dorothy. "Dorothy Parker." In *With Malice Towards All*, 71–86. New York: G. P. Putnam's Sons, 1982.

Keats, John. *You Might as Well Live: The Life and Times of Dorothy Parker*. New York: Simon and Schuster, 1970; repr., New York: Paragon House, 1986.

Lauterbach, Richard E. "The Legend of Dorothy Parker." *Esquire*, October 1944, 93, 139–44. (Reprinted in Calhoun.)

Meade, Marion. *Dorothy Parker: What Fresh Hell Is This?* New York: Villard Books, 1987.

Miller, Linda Patterson. "Ernest Hemingway and Dorothy Parker: 'Nothing in her life became her like her almost leaving of it.'" *North Dakota Quarterly* 2:66 (1999): 101–12.

Pearl, Jane Helen. "Dorothy Parker Herself: A Psychobiography of the Literary Artist." Diss., Northwestern University, 1982.

Shanahan, William. "Robert Benchley and Dorothy Parker: Punch and Judy in Formal Dress." *Rendezvous* 3.1 (1968): 23–34.

Wilson, Edmund. *The Twenties*. New York: Farrar, Straus and Giroux, 1975.

Woollcott, Alexander. "Our Mrs. Parker." In *While Rome Burns*, 142–52. New York: Viking, 1934.

Film Versions of Parker's Life

Rudolph, Alan, director. *Mrs. Parker and the Vicious Circle*. Fine Line Features, 1994.

"Would You Kindly Direct Me to Hell": The Infamous Dorothy Parker. Arts and Entertainment *Stage*, 1994.

Slesin, Aviva, director. *The Ten-Year Lunch: The Wit and Legend of the Algonquin Round Table*. PBS American Masters, 1987.

DOROTHY PARKER WEB SITES: WORK AND LIFE

Academy of American Poets. "Dorothy Parker." *Academy of American Poets*, Poetry Exhibits. http://www.poets.org/poets/

Alexander, Rahne. Utica Drop Forge & Tool Co. http://www.xantippe.com/dorothy/

Dorothy Parker Society of New York. *Dot City: Dorothy Parker's New York.* http://www.dorothyparkernyc.com

Pettit, Rhonda S., compiler. "Dorothy Parker." Edited by Cary Nelson. *Modern American Poets* Web site, 2000. http://www.english.uiuc.edu/maps

———. "Dorothy 'Dot' Parker (1893–1967)." *Infography.* Fields of Knowledge. http://www.inforgraphy.com/content/100107089197.html

Reuben, Paul P., ed. "Dorothy Parker (1893–1967)." In *PAL: Perspectives in American Literature.* Chapter 7: Early Twentieth Century Literature. http://www.csustan.edu/english/reuben/pal/chap7/parker.html

Contributors

ROBERT D. ARNER is Professor of English at the University of Cincinnati and author of *Dobson's Encyclopaedia: The Publisher, Text, and Publication of America's First Britannica, 1789–1803*; *The Lost Colony in American Literature; James Thurber: An Introduction*; and numerous articles on American literature and popular culture.

PHILLIP K. ARRINGTON is Professor of English at Eastern Michigan University and the current Communications Coordinator for the Eastern Michigan University chapter of the American Association of University Professors. Professor Arrington teaches undergraduate courses in writing and literature and graduate courses in rhetorical theory and research in the theory and practice of writing. He has previously published in *College English, College Composition and Communication*, and the *Journal of Advanced Composition* and recently won best paper award at the Kenneth Burke Society Conference in May 2002. His research interests are in the relationship between reading and writing, rhetorical theory, and figurative language.

REGINA BARRECA is author of *They Used to Call Me Snow White, But I Drifted* (1991), *Perfect Husbands (and Other Fairy Tales)* (1993), *Sweet Revenge: The Wicked Delights of Getting Even* (1995), *Untamed and Unabashed: Essays on Women and Humor in British Literature* (1993) and *Too Much of a Good Thing is Wonderful* (2000). Barreca also edited the *Penguin Book of Women's Humor* (1996) and the *Signet Book of American Humor* (1999), as well as seven scholarly works, including *The Erotics of Instruction*. Professor of English Literature and Feminist Theory at the University of Connecticut, Barreca's Web site address is www.ginabarreca.com.

LYNN Z. BLOOM, Board of Trustees Distinguished Professor and Aetna Chair of Writing at the University of Connecticut, is completing *The Essay Canon* (2005), a canon whose research informs her recent textbooks including *The Arlington Reader* (2003) and *The Essay Connection*, 7th ed. (2004). Her creative nonfiction ranges from

"Teaching College English as a Woman" (1992) and "Living to Tell the Tale: The Complicated Ethics of Creative Nonfiction" (2003), both in *College English*, to "Writing and Cooking, Cooking" in *Pilaf, Pozole, and Pad Thai* and *Chronicle of Higher Education* (2001). Other research interests include autobiography (*Doctor Spock: Biography of a Conservative Radical* [1972], *Forbidden Diary* [1980, 2000]) and composition studies in such works as *Composition Studies as a Creative Art* (1998) and *Composition Studies in the New Millennium* (2003).

SUZANNE L. BUNKERS is Professor of English at Minnesota State University, Mankato, specializing in women's autobiography. Her books include *Diaries of Girls and Women: A Midwestern American Sampler* (2001), and *In Search of Susanna* (1996). She also is editor of two scholarly editions, *All Will Yet Be Well: The Diary of Sarah Gillespie, 1873–1952* (1993), and *The Diary of Caroline Seabury: 1854–1863* (1991), and of a collection of critical essays (with Cynthia Huff), *Inscribing the Daily: Critical Essays on Women's Diaries* (1996). Recently she served as consultant to Capstone Press's series on diaries, letters, and memoirs for elementary and middle school readers, editing *A Pioneer Farm Girl: The Diary of Sarah Gillespie, 1877–1878* (2000).

MARION CAPRON interviewed Dorothy Parker for the *Paris Review* in 1956.

ANN M. FOX is Assistant Professor of English and the Gender Studies Concentration Coordinator at Davidson College in Davidson, North Carolina, where she teaches courses about modern and contemporary drama, disability and literature, and feminist theatre. She received her Ph.D. from Indiana University, and her early scholarship traced the rise of feminist sensibilities in American commercial theater, with articles on this topic appearing in *Text and Presentation*. More recently, her scholarly work has centered on disability and theater; she has worked with the DisAbility Project, coauthoring articles in *Contemporary Theatre Review* and the *NWSA Journal* on the St. Louis–based political theater company. Her current study, *Scripting Disability on the American Stage: From Melodrama to the Millennium,* focuses on rereading representations of disability in twentieth-century popular American drama through the lens of disability studies.

ANDREA IVANOV-CRAIG is Assistant Professor of English at Azusa Pacific University in Azusa, California. Her enduring teaching and research interests include women's humor, literary theory, and American film and literature. Currently, she is working on eclectic gatherings and topics, such as motherhood, hope, and humor in writers such as Julia Kristeva, Harriet Beecher Stowe, and Ann Lamott.

KEN JOHNSON is Assistant Professor of English in the Humanities Department of Georgia Perimeter College in Atlanta, Georgia.

ARTHUR F. KINNEY is Thomas W. Copeland Professor of Literary History at the University of Massachusetts at Amherst. His book, *Dorothy Parker* (1978), was the first book-length study of Parker that addressed her work in detail, and was reissued in an updated version, *Dorothy Parker, Revised* (1998). His 1990 edition of her hitherto unpublished and forgotten play, *The Coast of Illyria*, shows how she used the Lamb circle (and contemporary research) as an analogy to the Algonquin Circle. He has also published the Woollcott-Parker letters in *The Massachusetts Review.* Primarily a Renaissance scholar, he has also published books on Flannery O'Connor and William Faulkner.

ELLEN LANSKY's essays on literature and addiction have appeared in *Dionysos, Literature and Medicine, The Language of Addiction,* and *Writing Addictions.* Her current research focus is Carson McCullers. She lives in Minneapolis and is an English instructor at Inver Hills Community College.

TIMOTHY MCMACKIN is a graduate student in professional and technical writing at Carnegie Mellon University, specializing in information design, software documentation, and writing for the Web. He earned a BA degree in English from Xavier University (Cincinnati), and has experience writing for marketing and advertising.

SOPHIA MIHIC is a graduate of the University of Florida and received her Ph.D. in political science from Johns Hopkins University in 1999. She teaches political theory and women's studies, writes on the philosophy of inquiry and the effects of interdisciplinary study in the social sciences, and is currently a fellow at the Illinois Program for Research in the Humanities at the University of Illinois, Urbana-Champaign.

NINA MILLER is the author of *Making Love Modern: The Intimate Public Worlds of New York's Literary Women* (1999). Formerly an associate professor at Iowa State University, she is currently working on a book about the lost history of anarchism in United States education, when not actively pursuing her new career in the nonprofit and arts sectors of metropolitan Denver. She may be reached at ninamiller21 @hotmail.com.

RUTHMARIE H. MITSCH is Managing Editor of *Research in African Literatures* at the Ohio State University. She received her Ph.D. in French (with a specialty in medieval French literature) from the University of Florida and has taught French as well as comparative literature at several universities and colleges. Her current scholarly interests are Arthurian literature (including Tristan) and francophone literature.

RHONDA S. PETTIT, author of *A Gendered Collision: Sentimentalism and Modernism in Dorothy Parker's Poetry and Fiction* (FDUP, 2000), has also compiled two Web pages devoted to Parker's work, located at these Web sites: *Modern American Poets* (edited by Cary Nelson; www.uiuc. english.edu/maps), and Fields of Knowledge *Infography* (www. infography.com). A member of the editorial board for both volumes of the forthcoming *Aunt Lute Anthology of Women Writing in the U.S.*, Pettit has published articles on poetry and poetics, as well as her own poetry. She is Associate Professor of English and Women's Studies at University of Cincinnati Raymond Walters College.

ELLEN POLLAK is a member of the English Department at Michigan State University, where she teaches feminist theory and eighteenth-century British literature and culture. The author of two books, *Incest and the English Novel, 1684–1814* (2003) and *The Poetics of Sexual Myth: Gender and Ideology in the Verse of Swift and Pope* (1985), she has also published a range of essays on topics related to women, gender, sexuality, and writing in early modernity.

AMELIA SIMPSON is a Mexico Country Specialist for Amnesty International, and Director of the Border Environmental Justice Campaign with the Environmental Health Coalition in San Diego, California, and Tijuana, Baja California, Mexico. She has published on the subjects of human rights, institutionalized violence, police training, popular culture, and race and gender in the Americas. Her books include *Latin American Detective Fiction* (1990) and *Xuxa: The Mega-Marketing of Race, Gender, and Modernity* (1993).

DONNA STAMM is a nontraditional fourth-year student at the University of Cincinnati majoring in Social Science with a minor in humanities, and is considering graduate school. Her interests lie in the integrative aspects of literature with history and the social sciences, especially in the area of women's literature and history.

EMILY TOTH, Robert Penn Warren Professor of English at Louisiana State University, teaches courses in women's lives and popular culture, food lore, and advice writing. Her ten books include *Ms. Mentor's Impeccable Advice for Women in Academia* (1997), five books on Kate Chopin, notably *Kate Chopin's Private Papers* (1998) and *Unveiling Kate Chopin* (1999), and *Inside Peyton Place: The Life of Grace Metalious* (2000). Her *Chronicle of Higher Education* advice column, "Ms. Mentor," may be found on the internet at http://www.careernetwork .com, click on "Ms. Mentor."

PAULA A. TREICHLER, in addition to being Director of the Institute of Communications Research at the University of Illinois at Urbana-Champaign, teaches social medicine, cultural studies, and feminist theory for the Institute, the College of Medicine, and the Women's Studies Program. She is the author of *How to Have Theory in an Epidemic: Cultural Chronicles of AIDS* (1999), and is writing *How to Use a Condom: The Trojan Story*, a cultural analysis of condoms in America since 1880. Among her other books are *The Visible Woman: Imaging Technologies, Gender, and Science*, with Lisa Cartwright and Constance Penley (1998), *Cultural Studies*, with Lawrence Grossberg and Cary Nelson (1992), *Language, Gender, and Professional Writing: Theoretical Approaches and Guidelines for Nonsexist Language*, with Francine Wattman Frank (1989), and *A Feminist Dictionary*, with Cheris Kramarae (1985). She has a Ph.D. in linguistics and psycholinguistics from the University of Rochester.

NANCY A. WALKER, formerly Director of the Women's Studies Program and Professor of English at Vanderbilt University, was a twentieth-century pioneer in the feminist analysis of women's humor. Her books on that topic include *What's So Funny! Essays on American Humor* (1998), *A Very Serious Thing: Women's Humor and American Culture* (1988) and, with Zita Dresner, *Redressing the Balance: American Women's Literary Humor from Colonial Times to the 1980s* (1988). She is also the author of *Kate Chopin: A Literary Life* (2000), *The Disobedient Writer: Women and the Narrative Tradition* (1995), *Fanny Fern* (1992), and *Feminist Alternatives: Irony and Fantasy in the Contemporary Novel by Women* (1990), and editor of *Women's Magazines 1940–1960: Gender Roles and the Popular Press* (1998) and a critical edition of *The Awakening*, by Kate Chopin (2000). She contributed articles to *International Journal of Women's Studies*, *Thalia*, *Southern Quarterly*, *Studies in American Fiction*, *Studies in American Humor*, *American Quarterly*, and *Denver Quarterly*, among others.

Index